FAYE DUNAWAY

with Betsy Sharkey

LOOKING
FOR GATSBY

MY LIFE

SIMON & SCHUSTER
New York / London / Toronto
Sydney / Tokyo / Singapore

 SIMON & SCHUSTER
Rockefeller Center
1230 Avenue of the Americas
New York, NY 10020

Copyright © 1995 by Faye Dunaway
All rights reserved,
including the right of reproduction
in whole or in part in any form.
SIMON & SCHUSTER *and colophon*
are registered trademarks of Simon & Schuster Inc.
Designed by Edith Fowler
Manufactured in the United States of America

10 9 8 7 6 5 4 3 2 1

Library of Congress Cataloging-in-Publication Data

Dunaway, Faye.
  Looking for Gatsby : my life / Faye Dunaway with
Betsy Sharkey.
      p.   cm.
  1. Dunaway, Faye.   2. Actors—United States—
Biography.
I. Sharkey, Betsy.   II. Title.
PN2287.D84A3   1995
791.43′028′092—dc20   95-34651 CIP
[B]
ISBN 0-684-80841-2

A leatherbound signed first edition of this book has
been published by Easton Press.

To my mother and my father,

to Bill, who showed me the way,

and to Liam—it all came to you.

Acknowledgments

I want to thank Warren Lieberfarb, whose idea this book was; Swifty Lazar, for his outrageous expertise; Chuck Adams and Michael Korda, for letting me write *my* book; Betsy Sharkey, my dearest friend; my very special friends Loretta Barrett, Hook Herrera, Gloria Scott, Cubby Selby, and Clare Seldon; my wonderful copy editors, Virginia Clark, Ted Landry, and Gypsy da Silva, and my tireless assistant, Mark Waldie.

And I want to thank Mac, my beloved brother, and all the characters in my life who created this story.

Gatsby believed in the green light, the or-gastic future that year by year recedes before us. It eluded us then, but that's no matter—tomorrow we will run faster, stretch out our arms farther. . . . And one fine morning—

So we beat on, boats against the current, borne back ceaselessly into the past.

ONE

YOU COULD STAND in the middle of the dirt road that ran in front of the house I was born in and look hard either way and see nothing but the long rows of peanuts snaking their way up to a stand of trees in the distance. The house stood on the edge of the Tipton farm, halfway between Two Egg and Bascom, in the flatlands of the Florida panhandle. Not much beyond peanuts and cotton will thrive in that loose, sandy soil. Tallahassee was the closest thing to civilization, and it was a hard day's drive by buggy, and not much faster in the Model A Ford my Olpa bought, but kept for special occasions.

It was January of 1940 when my father, John MacDowell Dunaway, not yet twenty and just five months married, got a job working for the Tiptons as a farmhand. For his labor, they paid him ten dollars a month, and gave him four acres to farm and the use of a one-room frame house put up years earlier to provide living quarters for the sharecroppers. The years had worn away most of the whitewash, and the sun had bleached the wood a soft gray. There was a tangle of wisteria vines and honeysuckle next to the house, and in the spring the air would be heavy with their perfume. Water came from an old iron pump behind the kitchen, and the outhouse was just beyond that.

There was little in the way of furnishings except an old iron bedstead and a horsehair mattress my mother had brought with her. But for my mother, Grace April Smith, and my father, who everyone called Dowell, the ramshackle old house was a godsend. In the face of Olpa's stringent opposition to the marriage, their first months together were tense ones, spent living at the Dunaway house. Though Ruby

11

Dunaway, my grandmother, was a kind of matriarch, who took my mother under her wing and taught her how to cook—a kindness my mother never forgot—the young couple was anxious to have a place of their own.

MY MOTHER was one of the last of seven children. She was the youngest daughter, a red-headed beauty, and my Olpa's favorite. She fell in love with my father on a Friday night at a peanut boiling at the Smith family farm a few miles outside of Bascom. It was September, harvest time, and a peanut boiling was one of the few social events that would draw courting-age couples from around Jackson County. She was fifteen, and though my father was only seventeen, he was considered a man. He had been working on his family's farm, or picking up odd jobs around the county, since dropping out of school in the eighth grade.

They barely spoke that night, but it was the beginning of a true southern courtship. There were buggy rides to Sunday services or Wednesday night prayer meetings, and the couple was always accompanied by one of Grace's five brothers, who teased her mercilessly. A huge fuss erupted one night when they were caught kissing by Olpa, who pulled my mother aside and issued a dictum that was later seared into my memory: "Better to marry than to burn." It was a powerful philosophical concoction born of his German heritage and infused with southern sensibilities of what was proper. Tension in the house eased when Dowell left for the Civilian Conservation Corps in Delta, Utah. But postcards made weekly cross-country journeys for the year he was there, and soon after he came home, they married. It was August 9, 1939, and World War II was breaking out in Europe.

Olpa had watched the courtship closely, deeply worried by the hot connection he sensed between this youngest daughter of his who had always been filled with intense feelings and the darkly handsome young man that he barely knew. Olpa accepted that she was in love with this boy; still it broke his heart when my mother dropped out of high school to marry. He didn't think Dowell would ever amount to much, and he made those feelings clear. But she was headstrong and haunted by dreams of a better life—a husband, a family, a house in town. When Dowell, her first serious boyfriend, presented the opportunity, she took it. My mother's passion for something more, to write a different destiny for a dirt-poor farmer's daughter, was to shape my entire life.

ON JANUARY 14, 1941, at 8:15 in the evening, I decided to make my entry, three months early. I've been told since that Capricorns are always a bit impatient with the pace of the rest of the world, and I can't say I disagree. Even now, I often start my days long before daylight, at four or five in the morning, and I end them late with a dozen things left that I still want to do. For years, I was never without a yellow legal pad and a yellow pencil for the lists I made each day to keep track of the ideas that raced through my head. I graduated to a Blackwing 602, which promised me "Half the pressure, twice the speed," when I read that Stephen Sondheim, whom I deeply admired, used them. Today the Blackwings are gone, replaced by mechanical pencils that require only a quick push and no break in the action. And the yellow pads, for the most part, have given way to small white notepads that I keep by my bed and my chaise longue.

Just four pounds, no hair, no eyelashes, my fingernails and toenails only half-formed, I was, to say the least, not much to look at. There was at least one casting agent who held with that early assessment. In the mid-sixties, when I first began auditioning for film roles, the casting director for *The Chase* suggested I concentrate on theater, that I wasn't pretty enough for the movies.

I walked the New York streets for hours and hours after that audition, shaken to the core, feeling sure that he must be right. Ultimately, Jane Fonda played the part, costarring with Marlon Brando. Thirty years later, I finally got my chance to act with Marlon.

THE FIRST DAYS and weeks of my tenuous existence were touch and go. I was so tiny my mother would cradle me on a pillow, lay her hand over my heart, and pray over and over again, "Lord, let it be beating." Though I was small, the labor had been hard, more than three days long, and in the final hours the midwife thought they might lose me.

My first childhood stories were spun out of my struggle to be born and to live. I was nursed on the notion that I began life against all odds and that it was a blend of God, my will, and my mother's sheer determination that kept me alive, though my mother always seemed to get top billing in this morality play. She even decided the moment she knew she was pregnant that I would be a girl—all the baby clothes she sewed by hand were pink. Since I fulfilled that first wish of hers, I grew up trying to fulfill all the others that would come over the years. Her disappointments sometimes seemed unrelenting, and I grew up not wanting to be one of them.

My name—Dorothy Faye—was given to me by one of the Tipton boys. Though I've often wondered why my mother had not chosen a name for this baby girl she had so longed for, it was to Ralph Tipton, a friend of my father's, that I owe my name. He had dropped by to see the new arrival just as the midwife pronounced me healthy. All that was left was deciding on a name so the birth certificate could be filed. Ralph suggested Dorothy Faye. My father thought it had a nice sound to it and my mother liked Faye, and so Dorothy Faye Dunaway I became.

Eighteen months later Dorothy Faye was reduced to Sister when my brother, Mac, entered the picture. By then my father had gone to work at the Panama City shipyard, a job which kept him from being drafted for a time and also kept him away from us.

My strongest memories of my father to this day are not of the times when he was there, but of waiting for him to come home. First from Panama City, later the war, and too often, from the other women in his life.

He moved us to a one-room house nearer Bascom, two if you counted the kitchen that was in a tiny lean-to in back. Though I was too young to notice, there was growing tension in my parents' relationship. My father stayed in Panama City most of the time, coming back on some weekends, staying away others. My mother concentrated on keeping up with two babies, and I set about learning to walk and talk—both of which, according to my mother's memory, I did months before I was supposed to.

If I try to trace back the roots of my ambition, they probably begin with my grandfather, Luther Simmion Smith. Olpa was a wiry string bean of a man with sharply drawn features, a ring of white hair around a shiny bald pate, and a voice that could whip through the house and bring everyone to attention. He was twenty years older than my grandmother, Maggie Lena Fears, nearing forty when they married and began raising a family.

He was a self-educated man who became a teacher and a preacher. But what Olpa knew best was farming, and he had his eye on more than four hundred acres just outside of Bascom that the bank had confiscated from someone who had fallen on hard times during the Depression. Olpa was able to buy it for the price of seven years of back taxes. No one had worked the land in years, but Olpa would walk it and imagine the long, neat rows of cotton and peanuts that he would plant, the homestead he would build for his young wife and growing family. He would rise every morning before daybreak, hitch up the mules, and, with his sons, make the five-mile trek to the farm. Acre by acre, they cleared the land, then planted it, working until sundown each day trying to cultivate a future out of the land. What little he made on the crops each year went to put food on the table and to pay for the house he and my uncles began building.

Many hours of my earliest childhood were spent in that house, my memories written in hazy sensations. One of my earliest memories remains my earning a penny a bushel picking cotton for my Olpa in the fields—hours in the hot sun trying to pull the cotton from the bolls without pricking my fingers. The war marched through those evenings through the crackle of static from the radio in the front room where everyone would gather after dinner for nightly reports from the front. With Olma's and Olpa's five sons, none drafted yet, there was keen interest. The squawking of the chickens in the afternoon meant Olpa had one in hand. Its neck wrung with a sharp twist, it would be delivered to my grandmother for plucking and cooking.

Almost any time of day there, I could take a breath and gulp in the sweet aroma of Olma's cooking, southern cooking—ham, grits, biscuits, gravy, greens—everything fried, baked, or boiled with a thick slice of bacon fat. Bits and pieces of conversations as Olma, my mother, and Aunt Josephine—Phine for short—cooked would drift out from the kitchen window. Their voices were seasoned by the South—one part Florida, one part Georgia, a dash of Alabama, and a dollop of thick, sweet honey. Listening to them taught me the sound of authenticity, a warm richness in the tones that can turn illusion into reality on the stage. It's the way a character expresses herself. What is she like? Where did she come from? What shaped her voice? When F. Scott Fitzgerald wrote in *The Great Gatsby* that Daisy had a voice "full of money," and later I found that Evelyn Mulwray in *Chinatown* would as well, what did that mean? For me, answering that is one very crucial step along the path that leads you to the truth of the character, and helps you bit by bit to build a framework for their life.

•

My GRANDMOTHER and mother were two very different creatures. There was always a sense that Olma never quite won the battle to bring order to her house, or her life. In my mother's house, everything, including me, had a place. Grace wanted to make a life that was not like her mother's. But then, maybe that is the legacy most mothers give to their daughters, because I was just as determined that my life would be my own.

My Olma's hair was salt-and-pepper streaked, long and woven into thick, German-style braids wound round her head. Love of snuff was the closest she came to having a vice. She never learned to read. And I remember her as finally losing all her teeth and never wearing false ones. But I adored her. While my mother expected everything of me, Olma asked for nothing. I was talking to a friend about my son a few years ago and said how much he loved his grandparents. "Well, of course he does," she said. "They have a common enemy—you." I knew what she meant. Mothers push their children, grandparents just love them.

Olma loved me without reservation and I treasured her in return. Though I never felt she played favorites, of all the grandchildren, deep down I believed she surely loved me best. Where my mother saw in me a companion and a confidante, as well as a daughter she intended to shape and mold into her image of success, my Olma just saw *me*, a mess of curly brown hair, gray-green eyes, and a smile.

One day when I was still small enough that I had to stand on a chair to reach the sink, I was helping Olma do the wash. I kept trying to squeeze the cloth dry, but water kept running through my fingers. Olma came over and took the cloth from my hand and said, "Here, let me show you how." She took one end of the cloth in one hand, the other end in the other, and wrung it dry. I had never seen two hands work together quite like that. Then she handed the cloth back to me and watched over me until I learned to do it. In that small way, Olma gave me a sense of how empowering knowledge can be. To learn how to do something, and to feel good about having done it well. And I loved her for it. As Clifford Odets said in *The Country Girl*, which I was later to play, "Then you've learned something . . . Ripeness is all."

When I was about five, she told me years later, I crawled up in her ample lap and whispered my grandest dream in her ear. "Olma,

I'm gonna be an actress. But don't tell Mother." I desperately wanted something in my life that would be exclusively mine, untouched and unexposed to the white hot glare of my mother's straight-A ambitions for me.

Now how I latched onto the idea of becoming an actress, I'll never know. It's something my family has debated for years. The movies had sifted into the fabric of the culture to be sure. I did, after all, have a cousin, Linda Darnell Cotton, who had been named after her mother's favorite movie star. But at that point in my life, I had never been inside a theater, much less seen a movie or a play. And I'm not at all certain that Olpa wouldn't have thought that the devil was likely to be lurking there in the darkness anyway.

Going to church with Olpa, which we sometimes did, meant passing by the only juke joint in Bascom. It was a rundown pool hall and when the doors would swing open, I could just barely glimpse shapes in the darkness and hear the raucous laughter. I'd look and though I'd shiver, I was drawn by the danger of it. This was the kind of place, dark and off-limits, where my daddy slipped away to at night. At the same time, I was fearful that it might truly be one of the gateways to damnation that Olpa envisioned, and I wouldn't resist as he'd pull me closer to him as we hurried by.

As much time as Olpa spent cultivating his land, he probably spent more cultivating his soul. By the time I was born, Olpa would spend his nights in a chair studying the Bible for hours. On Sundays Olpa was at the Baptist church in Bascom serving as a lay preacher, and his favorite sermons were based on the Bible's dramas of downfall and redemption. When he was angry, there would be a torrent of cussing that he felt somehow met with the Lord's approval. "Condemned," he'd say, "continental," "Constantinople," and "pusillanimous." The words, in various combinations, would be attached to the particular offense that had caught his attention.

For a time when my mother was still a child, Olpa managed to disrupt the entire rhythm of life for the family when his Bible studies led him to conclude that the seventh day, the true Sabbath, was actually Saturday. And since Olpa's authority was never questioned, the family moved into what we still call the Seventh-Day-Adventist period, and Saturday was set aside for religion. I'm not sure that anyone knew what made him change his mind, but one day the

Sabbath returned to Sunday and the family returned to church in town.

MY MEMORIES of my father's family, like those of my father himself, are much less distinct. While my mother's parents were Olma and Olpa, my father's were Grandmother Dunaway and Granddaddy Dunaway, a mouthful for a small child.

Granddaddy Dunaway was bedridden most of the time when I was young, and my grandmother, who was a graceful, elegant woman, spent her days caring for him. He was a World War I veteran who came back from the war with his lungs badly damaged and his farming days soon cut short by emphysema. There was a tank of oxygen always by his bed, and as I learned later, a bottle of liquor always under it.

We would go to their farm for Sunday dinners when I was younger, and I would steal away in the afternoons and snuggle down under the huge, homemade feather comforters that my grandmother had on each bed in the house. I will never forget the feeling of those feather quilts, and to this day I love down comforters because of that.

In the early years of their marriage, my mother was close to Grandmother Dunaway. But as my parents' relationship grew more strained over the years, and my father more distant, the ties to the Dunaways were weakened too. They were reserved by nature and laughter rarely penetrated the rooms, kept dark and quiet in deference to my grandfather's weak condition. Though my grandmother had a good heart and it was clear that she loved her grandchildren, hers was a silent, formal world in which I found little comfort.

WHEN I WAS two and a half my father left the shipyard to work in a packing plant in Tallahassee and moved us there with him. It had been eighteen months since we had lived together as a family, and the adjustment wasn't easy on anyone. My father didn't make much at the packing plant, and not all of what he did earn made it home. Rumors of other women ate away at my mother, though she rarely knew for certain in the early years.

I'm not sure which she hated more, the nights he wouldn't show up or the ones he would come in hours late, having had far too much to drink. In some of my earliest memories, my mother and I are standing on the porch, like sentries, awaiting my father's nightly returns. It was a lonely assignment that left me trying to ease my mother's pain and still win my father's affection. In the end, with my father, there was only pain.

But in those early years, Grace was still young and not about to give up on her dreams, or her marriage. Unable to make ends meet with the little money my daddy brought home, she dispatched a letter to the War Department and within weeks my father was drafted and the monthly allotment checks were sent home. Years later I thought, My heavens, she put my father in the army. But when I asked about it, I was told that it wasn't likely that the War Department would have paid that much attention to a single letter. Chances are he was on the list to be drafted anyway. She was a woman of guts and determination, though, my mother, and she did something about the problems.

With Dowell destined for the army, Olpa offered to help them buy a house in Bascom, and my mother jumped at the chance. My father, a new and unwilling recruit in 1944 with the U.S. involvement in the war escalating, had other things to worry about. It meant we would return, once again, to Bascom. So the house was bought with $600 down that Olpa gave them, and a $1,200 loan that my mother began to pay off with her monthly allotment—the bill was $22 a month. The day my father left for Japan, he brought me home a white waffle piqué dress that was covered with pink roses. When he walked out the door I was inconsolable, crying and crying before I finally crawled into bed where I lay facing the wall, refusing to move for hours. It would become like a low-grade infection in my life, my father's leaving, and my sense that he was never there. I never felt his love, though I believe it was there. My mother's love, for all its glare, I always felt and never questioned. There was a real strength to that love that walked hand in hand with all her hopes and dreams for me.

I REMEMBER as a child thinking our house in Bascom was the most wonderful house in the world. It had six rooms, high ceilings, and two porches that provided the stages where most of the family life took place. Not long after my father left, Olma and Olpa, who were growing older, turned the farm over to my uncles and moved in with us. Then the house became a gathering place. On Sunday afternoons, the men would sit out front and talk about the weather and whatever pestilence was threatening the cotton. And the women would spend the afternoon cooking, then retire to the back porch and visit, which seemed mainly comprised of relating the local gossip.

It was a lively, horse-playing southern family. My mother and my uncles all played the guitar, and the day rarely ended without someone strumming a tune. They were all wonderful storytellers, country raconteurs who knew how to send a shiver down your spine or make you fall down laughing. No one ever had to look far to find a ready-made audience in me and my cousins. We'd sit there punctuating the tall tales with our giggles and squeals.

It was also a very lean time. The farm wasn't producing enough to support the ever-growing extended family, and there were weeks in the winter when all we had for dinner was tomato gravy. Mother would put oil in a cast-iron skillet, then a handful of flour, and brown it, then add tomatoes that she and Olma had canned in late summer. She'd pour the steaming tomato gravy over fresh biscuits she'd make from flour, buttermilk, and lard, and call us in to dinner.

The house itself was simple—bare wood floors and unfinished walls. Out back, I made a restaurant playhouse, its outline drawn in the dirt with a switch from a tree. Old boxes were gathered up and those I used for chairs and tables. I ran it, taking orders, cooking the pretend food, and in general telling everyone what I thought they should be doing. At five I was already headstrong and used to being in charge, and my little brother, Mac, was chief bottle washer.

He was the sweetest boy, with this angel's face. At the time it seemed to me that he never did anything wrong. I, on the other hand, got a double dose of my mother's will and intensity, that need to achieve that always pushed me to dance higher, to keep at it, whatever it was, longer. I felt like I could never be as good as Mac was. It was my secret that I envied him, this sweetness and serenity and placidity of his. I somehow felt guilty about being a go-getter, and even at that early age, a little bit ruthless. But it was the strength of my passion that would ultimately propel me toward success. If I hadn't been like that even then, I don't think I would have succeeded in the way I have.

On the front porch of the house was a big swing that Mac and I and my cousin Louise would spend hours on, its steady squeak setting the cadence for our childhood songs and secrets. One of my first object lessons took place on that swing, where my uncle, Cornelius Vander-

My brother, Mac, and me in 1945.

bilt Smith, Uncle Neal for short, would push us—but for a price. "I'll swang you, if you'll let me thump your big toe." And we would all squeal and say, "No, no, no!" "All right, I won't swang you then," he'd say. Finally we'd agree, and Uncle Neal would swing us and then, sure enough, he'd thump our big toes. Unwittingly, Uncle Neal taught me that nothing in life is free.

I well remember playing hopscotch or "Mother May I" in the dusty twilight roads that ran off the main highway going through Bascom. I loved "Mother May I" best. Someone was the mother and they first stood round and faced us kids. We would ask, "Mother, may I take two giant steps?" And whoever was playing Mother would say, "Yes, you may." But then they would turn their back on us, and we would race ahead as many steps as we could before they turned back around. I loved that game, racing ahead as fast as I could, wondering if I would be caught and have to start all over again. And we'd play paper dolls on the porch out back. The porch and those paper dolls were the first events I staged, creating elaborate and intricate lives for them. The stories captured my fantasy, and we would play until the sun went down.

When rain drove us inside, we would huddle under the bed where it was dark while Louise conjured up great, long, scary ghost stories. And when we ran screaming from the room, Aunt Phine would gather us up and tell her brand of tales, crazy misadventures of this one or that, which would leave us worn out from laughing. One day we all stumbled onto Olpa, stretched out and looking for all the world like death itself, his chest covered with something red. We were sure it was blood. Just before the wailing could begin, his eyes popped open and he leapt up grinning, sending us all into fits. The red turned out to be ketchup. He was nothing if not authentic in his horseplay. When I think about Olpa, my uncles, Aunt Phine, and Cousin Louise, I know that a part of my affinity for acting I come by naturally, a legacy of my Olpa's love for dramatic moments passed on generation after generation.

It was a rich mixture of playfulness and fun that I grew up with, from those big toe thumpings delivered by Uncle Neal, to Olpa's ketchup-covered shirt, the scary tales spun by Cousin Louise, and Aunt Phine's wonderfully crazy and colorful stories. All that went into my heart as a little girl, the sheer enjoyment of life in these very poor southern relatives of mine.

WHEN I WAS five, I started first grade. Bascom's grammar school was little more than three small classrooms and a tiny auditorium. In the spring each year, the students put on a talent show for the PTA, and I wanted to sing and dance in it. My mother spent hours making me a long green-and-white gown to wear. She pinned up my long curls, rouged my cheeks, and let me use lipstick for the first time.

On the afternoon of the show, just about everyone in town had come. It was standing room only and as I waited my turn, I could hear the rustle of the crowd and feel a knot of excitement and fear building in my stomach. When it was finally my turn and I opened the curtains and stepped centerstage, everything fell away. The faces in front of me blended into a quiet sea, my mother's whispering from behind the curtain ceased to reach me, and I felt completely alone, cut off from everything and everyone. But in a strange way, it felt comfortable, safe.

The melody suddenly spilling out of the gramophone brought me to life. "Doin' fine, doin' fine, I'm doin' just fine." The song was about a country girl who goes to the city to make her own way. I didn't know then I was singing lyrics of my own future. People who saw me that day tell me I seemed right at home up there. But when they say I loved the applause, that stops me cold.

Even then I didn't very much like the scrutiny that was an essential first step to the applause. I didn't like being on display; I didn't like being watched and judged. Maybe, when I was that little girl with my hair piled on my head like my mother's and wearing the strapless dress she made for me, and everyone clapped, maybe I felt like they all loved me. But what stays with me is the distance, and the comfort I found in being in my own world, playing. I was separate from reality and I was in the fantasy that was being created through me. I was intensely connected with all that I knew, and yet in a private world. Something the actress Shirley Booth once said has stayed with me— that it was only when she put on the mask that she was free to be the best of herself.

Living has not always come easy for me—finding a way to live that brings with it a measure of happiness. But then that is the universal struggle. I do know that my ambitions and my expectations have always far exceeded my own abilities and those of other people. I was encouraged as a child by my mother to yearn for a better world.

Being given the role, a character to play, is a gift. When I play that character, it gives me a sense of connection. Though I might be very uncomfortable in life, when I'm up there on stage or when I'm in front of a camera, or when I'm investigating the character, I'm strangely comfortable. It is the investigation that I love. When I'm asking the questions, Why does she do that? What's happening there? I love that process. Then too, I love going up there and being alive in the moment, carrying with me all the investigation I've made. Who is this character? And in the end, she is me, behaving at my most alive. Being there. Not worrying about anything but that moment. What's being said to me, listening to it, hearing it, and reacting. Somehow, all the work I've done is channeled and funneled in my reactions.

I always felt comfortable in that world, and I always felt safe.

More importantly, I've always felt that I belonged there. I never felt at home anywhere else, it seems to me. I never felt good enough, the poor southern girl from the wrong side of the tracks. Where I did feel comfortable was this place where a world was created and I fit into it as the character, and as myself.

But it is not always an easy place to live in. There are the times when you excavate the pain, you dig down inside and bring up all those memories you'd rather forget, and use them to help form the reality of the character. It all just kind of melds together and becomes its own entity. The rub is, on those days when you have brought up into the sunlight these chunks of your own pain, you're still left with some of those chunks in your hand when you go home at night.

It is why we actors sometimes can't rest. We have to walk around with these excavated bits of ourselves, still hurting. But you often find that in bringing it up, you have dealt with the pain a little bit more. As Aristotle says, "A tragedy is the imitation of an action that is serious . . . with incidents arousing pity and fear, wherewith to accomplish it is catharsis of such emotions."

There I'd be, walking around my house at night with these large chunks of my life that I thought were quite nicely put away in a place where I could handle them and not think about them too much. That's what most people do. But acting doesn't allow that. The craft demands that we actors investigate, we question, we bring up again. The aim is to hold the mirror up to human nature so that all of us can look at it. Then hopefully out of that looking will come an awareness and some kind of help in understanding how we all live our lives.

AFTER I STARTED first grade, my mother went back to high school to get her diploma. I loved going to school. My mother and I would study together each afternoon at the kitchen table. My mother, like any mother, wanted me to get straight A's. There was a real sense that she got from Olpa about the importance of education that she passed down to me. And I worked very hard to get top marks.

In recent years I've learned that in that little girl's head, I thought if I got straight A's and did everything my mother told me, that would make everything all right with her and my father. This was a concern in my heart and mind from early on. I thought with the omnipotence of a child, that somehow I would be able to fix what was wrong with my family. That my straight A's would keep my father from leaving and keep him home more and keep her happier, and most importantly, we could all be happy. All those emotions went into my achievement.

I have a deep, true love for my mother, and a real respect for the woman. She gave me my backbone and that's what I've tried to put into my roles. It's true that I was always looking for my daddy, but my mother, you couldn't mess with her. She was strong and smart and had a lot of get-up-and-go, and I have great admiration for her. She keyed right into the condition of womanhood in this country, that women do not sit down and accept easily, but get up and change their destiny. My mother did that. And she taught me to do it too.

The lessons she taught were infused with the distinctions between success and failure in life. In her mind, success didn't compromise or let anything stand in the way, and she made it clear I shouldn't either. I was taught to be a "good girl," and that meant excelling at anything my teachers gave me. At church, she would pray that my brother and I would have success in our lives. "Lord lift my baby high." It became her mantra.

Soon I never thought of being anything but the best, no matter how long it took to achieve it. She raised me right into the American Dream, and I grew up believing it. The deal that my mother made with me was that if I tried hard enough and worked hard enough, I would achieve my dreams. And I have. Whatever happened to me along the way, this is what I've made of it, and I'm proud of that.

There was much emphasis on achievement—sometimes clearly too much—but then I wonder what I would have been had I not been taught to aspire, to hope, to dream, to work hard. I've never regretted that she gave me that. When I was older, I learned that the rewards of success usually exact a high price somewhere along the way. But that was one lesson I had to learn on my own, though Uncle Neal had given me an early taste of that.

With parents and children, it is a mixed bag, and my relationship with my mother is a complicated one. I may falter, but we are joined at the hip and at the heart, my mother and I. I love her dearly and she loves me. That is one thing in my life I never questioned.

My father wrote fairly often from his army postings, and we would trace his travels through the postmarks on the letters he would send. He went to basic training in Alabama, then shipped out to Japan. His letters told of the burning ruins of Hiroshima and Nagasaki that he saw when he arrived. But if there were other horrors in my father's war, we didn't know of them. After the war ended, he reenlisted and stayed in Japan. I was three and my brother was still a toddler when my father left. We wouldn't see him again until I was seven.

TWO

I T WAS A HOT NIGHT, one of those summer evenings when the humidity is so thick it holds any breeze at bay. My mother had put her hair up and moved the ironing board to the living room, where it was a bit cooler. Mac and I were playing on the bare wood floor near her feet, so far having managed to evade all her attempts to get us to take our baths and get into pajamas. You could hear the June bugs slapping up against the screen door and the sound of crickets filling the night air. Just then a car pulled up, and a large man with a mustache bounded up the walkway.

My mother had described for years exactly how it would be when my father came home from the war. She would hear him coming and run out the door and just scream and scream. In the story, she would throw her arms around his neck and he would take her in his arms and lift her right off the ground, and twirl her round and round. It seemed like a fairy tale, and the only thing waiting to make it happen was my father's return.

Then the letter came saying he was on his way, and a real sense of excitement set in. Daddy was coming home. Olma and Olpa moved back to the farm to give us more room and my parents some privacy. My mother, who hadn't seen my father in four years, was jubilant. Mac, who had just been a baby when he left, wondered what his father would look like. In my mind, he was a tall, darkly handsome man who I wanted very much to love me. I couldn't wait and practiced being good and thought about all the things I had to tell him of school and grades, hoping that he would be as proud as my mother.

The man in the mustache turned out to be my daddy. Before he could reach the door that night, my mother ran out screaming, just as she had said. Mac and I watched from the porch as he lifted her up off the ground. Then I ran out too, while Mac hung back on the porch. I want to think that my father picked me up too, and swung me round and round. But the truth is I don't remember, though I've run the scene through my head a hundred times.

Eighteen years and a lifetime later, I was in Baton Rouge, Louisiana, filming *Hurry Sundown*. It was my second film and I took the role because the character, Lou McDowell, was very much like my mother, and her last name was eerily close to my father's middle name, MacDowell. Those weeks in Louisiana became like a psychodrama in a way. I was a dirt farmer's wife waiting for my husband to come back from World War II, just as my mother had waited for my father. There is a scene, just before my husband, played by John Phillip Law, comes home, and the script calls for me to cry. Otto Preminger, who was directing the film, yelled "Action!" and I started crying on cue. I knew what it was like to shed tears of joy at having someone so very dear to you come home after being away for such a long time.

MY FATHER, who had loved the army, did not take well to civilian life. Jobs near Bascom were not easy to come by in the postwar years, and the pay was poor. He started driving a truck, hauling logs to a nearby lumber mill. My parents were having a hard time making ends meet, and my mother worried that my daddy was spending some of his paycheck on other things. But somehow they managed. We stayed in Bascom until the end of 1948, when my father reenlisted in the army. He wanted to be a career man and by the fall was stationed at Camp Chaffee, Arkansas. Just before Christmas that year, we left Bascom to join him.

It was a big move, leaving Bascom, but we were all anxious to be with my daddy and were ready to go meet him as soon as housing was arranged. I realized later that this was the start of an episodic life for me—two years at one army base, then a new assignment, a new school, new friends, new experiences. It's always a mixture in life. The leaving was painful, but I did love the travel. It was always a great adventure. What was beyond the next ridge always intrigued and interested me. It did then and does still. Now I think the moving marked me more than I realized. The message my experience sent me was—this is going to end. Nothing was ever constant—except for loss. And too, it reinforced the message my father sent us, never being there really, physically or emotionally.

I sometimes think making movies suited me, in a way, because it is a business of putting up then folding the tents. Two months and three months of an intense drawing together for a project. Creating this kind of temporary world of solace, building a makeshift family, growing truly fond of the people you're working with, experiencing life in close quarters with them. Then it ends. Everything is disassembled, and on you go to something completely new. I lived for decades on a two-year cycle—as if there was always one more army post and one more two-year tour of duty. Work for two years. Try to have a relationship for two years. Then back to work. I look around at people with long relationships who've lived in the same house all their lives, and I'm sad that I don't have that. But the rhythm of my life was set at an early age.

I was in the third grade the year we moved to Arkansas, and Mother enrolled us in the Mill Creek Elementary School in Fort Smith. My father was a mess sergeant, and the job and Arkansas seemed to agree with him. We were living just north of Fort Smith in a rambling, wood-frame house near the base. He and my mother were getting along well and I loved my new school.

Arkansas brought me my first boyfriend, Tillie Dean Loudermilk. When my mother threw a party for my eighth birthday, Tillie Dean sat next to me all through the entire rainy afternoon. I remember his white, freckled face and curly red hair. And that name, it was wild, and must have been terrible for him at times, but I thought it had a certain poetry to it.

Fort Smith was just starting to feel like home. Things weren't perfect, but we were a family. But then my father was transferred in the fall of 1949 to Fort Hood in Killeen, Texas. Tillie Dean and I said a tearful good-bye.

My parents found a house for us that was about thirty miles from the army base in a small Texas town called Temple that sits near the shores of the Little Brazos River. Texas was hotter than any place I'd lived, and after the lush green of the South, it seemed barren and dry.

The year in Texas, though, was a good one for me, filled with afternoons spent playing in the backyard, coming in to bowls filled with steaming banana pudding. I learned to skate on the front sidewalk, and I still remember looking out of the upstairs window one day and seeing my daddy and my brother drive up with a new car. It was a Ford sedan, beige and white, colors that are still my favorite— uncomplicated, easy, anonymous and safe, not like bright colors, which draw attention to me, as if they are inviting scrutiny or judgment. Do I like beige and white because of their simplicity, purity, and understated glamour, or because they trigger that memory of my father? It is a complicated skein that I have spent a lifetime trying to untangle, to move a little closer to the sense of peace and reconciliation with my past that I still seek.

In November of 1950, my father's battalion was put on alert that they might be shipped to Germany, so we moved into Killeen to be closer to the base. We were there for Christmas, but when my father shipped out to Germany in January, we returned to Bascom.

I hadn't thought of Killeen in years, until 1993, when a local man went berserk, crashing his car into a Luby's cafeteria there, and shooting at anyone in range. Three people died and more were hurt. Several months after that, I was approached about starring in a proposed movie for television titled *Countdown to a Massacre*. If the script could be sold to a network, we would shoot on location in the town. I wondered how it would look now, and if I would be able to see any traces of my childhood there. But the project never got off the ground and I went on to other things.

WHEN WE GOT BACK to Bascom, the house seemed substantially smaller. Olma and Olpa had been living there. And my aunt Phine and cousin Louise were there too. Louise, Phine, Mac, and my mother slept in the front bedroom, and I slept in the back with Olma and Olpa, curled up against Olma's considerable softness.

We children had a great time, racing between front yard and backyard. We were old enough to trudge off on our own to neighbors, some who lived on farms beyond the town. There was always a nickel every Saturday for a soft drink and a candy bar at the Wise General Store in Bascom. The house was filled with laughter, and the furniture of three separate households now merged into one. Olpa would walk in every afternoon and declare that the house was so full of folks, it was bound to fall apart.

On February 2, 1951, everything did fall apart, but in a way I could never have expected. Just a few weeks after I had turned ten, it had become bitterly cold, a rare event even in northern Florida. It was still dark when Olpa got up to build a fire in the fireplace that had gone some winters without a single log being burned. Olma and I hadn't ventured from under the covers when we heard Olpa cry out and fall to the floor. My mother ran into the room and began to cradle my grandfather's head in her arms, crying hysterically "Papa, what's wrong?" He looked at her once, whispered her name, then closed his eyes.

Somehow, Olma and my mother managed to get him into bed. The house didn't have a phone, so mother woke one of the neighbors and sent him racing to call the doctor from the phone at Wise's store. But by the time the doctor arrived, Olpa was gone. The cause of death was listed as heart failure. He was seventy-eight years old. I cried for Olpa. I cried for Olma, and I cried for myself and the grandfather I had lost.

My mother was devastated. Olpa had been there for her at every bad curve of her life to help straighten things out. They had grown particularly close in these last months. Each Friday, they would take the bus together to Marianna to make a payment on the mortgage, and she told me how they'd talk the whole way there and back. With Olpa gone, I think for the first time in her life she felt she was truly on her own.

I don't remember ever seeing Olpa in a suit before the day he was buried. It was a double-breasted navy blue one. He wore a brand-new white shirt and a light blue tie picked out by my mother. If you can measure a man's worth by the people who come to pay respects, then Olpa was rich indeed. A steady stream of family and friends came to the house to say a final good-bye to one who had long been a pillar of the Bascom community.

I couldn't adjust to the fact that this man who had been the only consistent father figure in my life was gone. Death didn't seem to have the promise and hope that he had preached about for years. It seemed cold and harsh and unfair. I didn't want to go into the living room, where my mother had placed his casket for viewing. I don't think I closed my eyes the entire night.

At the funeral, some of Olpa's friends sang "Peace in the Valley," the a cappella harmonies filling Collins Chapel, next to the cemetery. The music was heartbreakingly beautiful. Mac and I sat on either side of my mother. After the service I put my arms around her. I wanted to say something, anything, that would make her feel better. "Don't cry, Mother," I said. "Olpa's gone to heaven." My mother stopped crying and hugged me tight against her. And then Olpa was laid to rest.

MY FATHER was in the middle of the Atlantic Ocean on a ship bound for Germany when Olpa died. Though my mother hadn't planned on joining him there, after Olpa's death she changed her mind. But it would be a nine-month wait while the army processed passports and papers, and Mac and I got the requisite shots.

We were going to the Methodist church now in Bascom and that summer, during Vacation Bible School, I wrote this poem:

> *My Mother*
> *There is someone in this world,*
> *Who, within me will never die,*
> *And will always comfort me,*
> *When I cry.*
>
> *Who is my dearest friend,*
> *And will always be,*
> *So kind and dear,*
> *And thoughtful of me.*
>
> *By this time you surely know,*
> *Just who I mean,*
> *My Mother, of course,*
> *Who to me is like a Queen.*

I look back on that poem and see something of the tangle of our relationship. I adored my mother. We have a connection that is very complicated, and the debt I owe her is enormous. Her guts and determination may be the best legacy she could have given me. As I was growing up, the bond with her was strong, unbreakable, and a fact of life. But as the years became increasingly turbulent, the bond that held us together became the wedge that would ultimately drive us apart. I was spared very little. The indignities my mother felt, she shared with me. My father's transgressions too were laid out in bold relief.

Every time my daddy left, I'd set out the only picture I had of him. Taken just after he was drafted, it showed a dashing young man in uniform, with the most captivating smile on his face. I was sure that smile was for me. I could put that picture on the dresser and stand anywhere in the room and it always seemed as if my daddy was looking right at me, that twinkle in his eyes and the smile beaming in my direction.

At some point though, loving my father meant betraying my mother—at least in her eyes—and I couldn't bear to do that. At times, I set my own feelings aside because hers would become overwhelming. The true legacy of those years may be the difficulty I still have in trusting and allowing myself to open up to another person. For years, I would let no one too close. If I let them in, as I did my father, I was sure they would leave, or like my mother, their pain would swallow me up. Yet as much as I pull back, when I finally move one step toward another person, I tend to plunge completely into them and lose all sense of who I am. I worry that if I ever look away, if I even blink, they'll be gone. To stave off the pain of losing someone, I rarely get close at all. When I do take that risk, I never stay too long, lest they leave before me.

WHILE MY MOTHER was hesitant about Germany, I couldn't wait to go. I wrote long letters to my father, telling him everything he was missing in Bascom. I wrote of the church missionary meetings, and the lemonade, pimento cheese sandwiches, and cookies that were served that day. I told him about the card tricks I had learned and wanted to show him. And I had a growing stack of comic books I was reading. He wrote me about the place we would live in Germany and how we would play cards together in the evenings. He wrote about the Easter snow they had and of streams where he and Mac would go fishing.

He had asked me to see about a birthday present for my mother. Though I was just ten, I already felt the bruises in my parents' relationship and knew this would inflict yet another. "Daddy," I wrote, "about the birthday present for Mother. I think she would like one from you because she would know that you were thinking of her, but she would rather you pick something for her I would think."

While we were awaiting our transfer to Germany, I started taking singing lessons. There were ten of us in the chorus, and we had two weeks to get ready for a concert. My mother drove me over to Malone, a nearby town, for the lessons each day. It had been five years since I had been in front of an audience. And though I shared the stage with nine other kids on a hot August night in 1951, I knew that it was where I wanted to be.

I had barely started the fifth grade when we got word that we were cleared to go to Germany. When my mother got the news, she drove straight to the school to tell us. We were to drive to New York, and then make an ocean crossing. I thought at the time it might be the greatest adventure of my life.

The trip to New York became quite a family affair. Olma drove with us as far as Columbia, South Carolina, where Aunt Phine was now living with her new husband, Farris. Then Uncle Gurney took over and drove us on to Fort Hamilton in Brooklyn. We drove on highways that seemed like rivers of ice. These were grim odysseys we took, always in winter, to each of my father's new assignments. When we got to Fort Hamilton, Gurney had to leave us outside the gate. It was all confusion and panic, and I could feel my mother's fear. In the cold and the dark I turned to her and said, "Mother, let's just go home."

After a shaky start, Fort Hamilton turned out to be an incredible place. It was almost October and already cold, and Germany would be even colder, so Mac and I got our first real winter coats that year. There was another, more important first for me. I had never seen a television set before, but there was one in the family lounge on the base. The images that moved on the screen absolutely captivated me. The World Series was on most of the two weeks we were there. Though I had no interest in who won or lost the game, I was fascinated by the power of that big electronic box.

The army base was huge, row after row of barracks that seemed to go on forever. There were concrete playgrounds scattered around for the children at Fort Hamilton, and I remember standing on the side, watching crowds of other kids playing. Though few people realize it, I was then and am today very shy by nature—though that is often lost to the side of me that feels compelled to rush forward when something needs doing and take it on myself, since only then could I be sure it would get done. But constantly moving from one place to another was in no way easy for me, and it took weeks for me to feel comfortable, to feel at home in a place. But eventually I would.

From Fort Hamilton, I could see New York in the distance, and it seemed like a never-never land, Babylon. Little did I know that it held my future, and that it would be the place I'd begin to carve out who I was in this world. It is the city I would come to love more than any other. For years, when I would return to New York, I would always turn down Ninety-sixth Street on my way from the airport to my apartment. Dim, grim streets would greet me and I'd break into a smile. I used to say how I loved that dirty old town. I did and I still do. It's a town I never feel alone in, and yet I always feel completely private. Maybe that's where I'll end up, walking those streets, just like Ms. Garbo.

WE SET SAIL for Germany on October 10 on the USNS *General William O. Darby*. The first night a terrible storm blew up, and both Mac and my mother fought waves of nausea, as the ship rode out the storm. But I took to the sea. Though I didn't venture out during the storm, as soon as it cleared I spent hours and hours roaming the decks.

There was shuffleboard, a library, church services, which my mother attended, card tables, and deck chairs where you could stretch out like a cat and let the sun warm you. Sometimes I would stand at the back of the ship and watch the huge schools of fish trailing behind, drawn by the garbage that would be dumped overboard each day. It was unlike any life I'd ever seen and I soaked up every minute of it.

Nine days later the ship docked in Bremerhaven, Germany. It was a Friday, already long after dark, and we looked for my father among the throngs of servicemen who had come to meet their wives and children. We kept looking, watching other families long separated rush into each other's arms. But my father never came.

Though she must have been frightened, my mother snapped into action. "I've got my children here and I've got to get to Munich," she told the first person she saw who looked to be in charge. All the dependents who had not been met dockside were being given rail passes and a few German marks, he told her. She got us our passes and we climbed on board. The train was crowded and we were crushed together for the ten-hour trip from Bremerhaven to Bavaria, where my father was staying in temporary housing in a town just beyond Munich called Bad Tolz. It was bitterly cold and I felt chilled to the bone.

We thought surely my father would meet us in Munich. But again, when the train pulled up, he wasn't there. It was awful. We came all that way and he didn't even meet us. Again my mother took charge of things, and we spent the night in a German hotel that had set aside rooms for the families of American servicemen.

The next morning my father came for us. He was at the bottom of a long staircase in the old hotel, and the three of us came running down to meet him. All of us piled into a tiny Volkswagen and we drove to a beautiful old four-story chalet in Bad Tolz in the Bavarian Alps, near where my father was stationed. It looked like it was right out of a Hansel-and-Gretel storybook, with its steep, pitched roof and shuttered windows, and the German boys we saw were all wearing lederhosen. Everything was covered in snow, and it looked even more magical than what my father had described.

We had a great, huge German shepherd named Lady. And Mac and I made our first snowmen and waged endless snowball fights. One Sunday, my father bundled us up and took us to ride a cable car that sat at the foot of the Alps. My father said if you looked in the distance, you could see into Switzerland one way, Italy another, and Austria still another. I was in a new country, and I could see three more. I promised myself someday I would see them all. At the top of the mountain was a small ski lodge, and we had hot cocoa and a dinner of German bread and sausages. It was a near perfect day.

WORD CAME that the 1950 dark green Hudson we had driven to New York had finally arrived, and my parents went to Bremerhaven to get it. After that, Germany truly changed for us.

We were assigned family quarters in Mannheim, close to Heidelberg it was, and just before Christmas we moved into an apartment, No. 28 Agusta Anlage, fourth floor. There was a living room and a dining room, a bedroom for my parents, and Mac and I each had our own rooms. With the move to Mannheim, we switched schools.

My parents would sometimes quarrel over money or my father's late nights. On those nights, I would wait with my mother on the balcony for my father's return, watching for the Hudson to turn up the drive. I would hear his key in the lock, and the door close behind him, and my mother would be there. And there would be the lipstick on the collar of his white shirt. I see it to this day. My mother would begin to cry and I would think to myself, "If only she wouldn't do that. He'll never, never change, if she keeps on nagging him."

I would go back to my room and the next day, I'd go to school vowing to get straight A's, believing somehow that would make things better. And I did get straight A's. It wasn't enough. But I was just twelve then, and didn't know that I couldn't possibly save things.

AN ARMY SERGEANT'S paycheck is not large, and there were things that my mother wanted Mac and me to have. She would sell the cigarettes, tea, and coffee the family was allotted but didn't use to the Germans she met on the base. The extra money went to buy a piano and pay for lessons for us. In one of the recitals, I played Brahms' "Hungarian Dance."

I started taking tap and ballet lessons too. It was in these classes that I began to understand what my mother meant when she would tell me that she wanted me to be with the "nice people." There was a clear separation between officers and enlisted men, and that distinction extended down to us. In my ballet class, most of the other girls' fathers were officers, while mine was a cook.

I felt it, but my mother gave it a name. She would pick me up after ballet and tell me to hold my head up high, that I was just as good as anyone in that class. But I knew, that to be just as good, what I really had to be was better than anyone else.

My mother made my costumes for the dance recital the year I was twelve. In one, I was a Spanish dancer and the other, a clown. I practiced each dance for hours and hours. The night of the recital I stood waiting in the wings to go on. There were three of us who danced together that night—Brenda, Sue, and me—the daughter of a lieutenant colonel, the daughter of a colonel, and me, whose father cooked for theirs.

Even then, I loved the process of rehearsing, and then, when everything was as near perfect as it could get, performing. I had a knack about dancing. That night, as I twirled round and round in my Spanish dancer's dress, the long train spiraling behind me, I knew once again that this was what I wanted to do. But I was a long way from being a star. I was just one of three young Spanish dancers on a stage.

I've always liked the idea of achieving, even in simple things. One night, my mother left for a PTA meeting and my father stayed home with us. Mac and I were playing on the stairs with some of the other kids who lived in the apartment house on the base in Germany. The game was to see who could jump the most stairs.

I took my final leap, clearing enough stairs that I was sure would make me the winner. But when I landed on the bottom stair, I heard a crunch and my leg collapsed underneath me. Pain shot through my leg, as Mac went running for our father. "I'm okay, Daddy," I said as he picked me up and carried me upstairs. "I promise, I'm okay."

My mother wanted to take me to the hospital that night; my father was sure that I was all right. I had barely cried and was sure I had just twisted my ankle. But when the doctors X-rayed my leg the next day, they found my ankle had been broken, and I was in a cast for eight weeks.

AS TENSIONS between my parents grew, my father spent more and more nights away from the house drinking. Most of those nights, he'd end up sleeping it off in the barracks, since he had to be up and at work by 4 A.M. But one night he didn't do either, he simply disappeared.

The next day, the MPs showed up at the apartment asking where my father was. No one knew. He was officially listed as AWOL, and the military police throughout Germany were alerted. A day later the base chaplain called my mother. They had found my father in Heidelberg—drunk and driving—and now he sat in the stockade for that, and for resisting arrest. He was facing a court-martial. Though I had no real idea of what that meant, the idea of my father sitting in a jail cell simply stunned me. I would sit in my room and try to imagine what that must be like.

My mother quickly found out that if convicted, my father would spend time in jail, and lose his sergeant's stripes and any future in the military, something she knew meant so much to him. She wrote a letter to the base commanding officer asking him to reconsider, to give my father another chance. But a hearing date was set for my father's court-martial, and the military justice system ground forward.

As I think back to it, I've spent much of my life acting. All I knew as my father's court-martial hearing approached was that I couldn't let down for a minute or the weight of it all would surely crush me. I look back on that time now and the great sadness of it, this man, who couldn't stop drinking and became not himself when he drank. I don't know what Mac was thinking, but each day we came home and saw my mother's eyes sad, red, swollen, and fearful. We didn't hear from anyone for weeks. Then one night the MPs brought my father home for the night.

I was torn between the relief of seeing him again and the knowledge that some of my classmates would surely have seen the MPs deliver him and pick him up the next morning. My mother's anxiety about our future grew daily. She would come into my room at night, sit on the bed, and talk about her fears. On the night before the trial, I made myself a promise. When I was grown, I would never depend on anyone else to take care of me. I determined that no matter what I did, I would never allow myself to be in the position of needing financial support from a man. And I never have.

In October 1952, my father was convicted of drunk driving and resisting arrest. The more serious charge of AWOL was dropped. He was sentenced to six months in the stockade, ordered to pay a fine of $300, had his driver's license suspended for a year, and was reduced to the rank of private.

IN TWO WEEKS, the base commander finally responded to my mother's letter. He set aside my father's incarceration and allowed him to keep his sergeant's stripes. But the fine and the driver's license suspension remained. That meant for the next year, my mother would get up at 3 A.M. to drive my father to work. She'd get back home by 5 A.M. and get us off to school by 8. Every afternoon she'd make the drive back to pick him up. Sometimes it would be evening before he'd get off work and we'd go with her.

One night, it had grown particularly cold and icy. The snow was piled high on either side of the road. The gray-black slush had started to freeze as we set out to fetch my father. My mother never felt comfortable driving even in the best of circumstances, and driving the dark, icy roads was an exercise in terror for her. Every terror my mother felt, we felt too, and as the darkness closed around us it would feel desperately full of unknown dangers.

We drove through that snowstorm with the flakes coming down so thick the road disappeared completely into a white haze. The only sound was the slow crunch of the tires on the snow as Mother drove more and more slowly, her hands gripping the steering wheel for dear life. I turned round and watched the flurry of white flakes cover any trace of our travels. If we wandered off the road, no one, I was sure, would ever find us.

"Don't worry, children, God is leading me along," my mother told us. She began singing "Alexander's Ragtime Band" in that dark and lonely night, and one by one, Mac and I joined her until all three of us were singing. We drove through that snowy, silent German night, the three of us singing at the top of our lungs.

With his license suspended, my father spent his nights at home now. Life became predictable, and my parents entered into a sort of truce, with my mother spending her nights cooking dinner, then cleaning up, while my father lay on the living room couch drinking the German beer he'd become partial to. As the weather got warmer, he moved his evening ritual to the balcony where I had spent so many nights watching for his return. I think he spent those months trying to repair the damage that had been done. He began to go with us to school events and occasionally to church. We had a vacation in Holland, and both Mac and I made it back to Germany with wooden shoes.

The Christmas of 1952 seemed almost normal, but I wanted it to be perfect. At Christmas time, I would look in the windows of the houses we'd drive past and always see the Christmas trees inside and pick the one that I thought was the most beautiful. Once I saw a tree that looked as if every single icicle had been put on separately, and it just captured my heart. That year in Germany, we had a huge tree that I covered in icicles, one at a time. At least the tree would be perfect.

Years later, I was costarring with Frank Sinatra in *The First Deadly Sin*. In the movie, I was Frank's wife and I was slowly dying. It was Christmas and destined to be our last. I remember one scene that was supposed to touch on the painful irony of the holiday coinciding with my descent toward death. But the moment just felt flat. As I was searching for a way to layer the scene with a subtle poignancy, I thought back to years past, to that Christmas in Germany and the perfect tree and the imperfect family, and asked if we could add a line to the script. When I watch that scene today, the sadness of those holidays flashes through my mind, as I ask Frank to put the icicles on the tree for me, as I had done at twelve, one silver strand at a time.

WE LEFT GERMANY in January 1954 and arrived in New York two days before my thirteenth birthday. My father bought a black Plymouth and we set out for Dugway Proving Ground in Utah, my father's next assignment, by way of Bascom and my Olma. When we crossed the Florida state line, my father honked the car horn for miles, and we all whooped and yelled like it was New Year's Eve.

Our house in Utah was on the base, a brick duplex just down the street from the mess hall my father was assigned to cook for. My mother went to work at the base dry cleaners, and I set about making a place for myself at Dugway. I was in the eighth grade now and found a new circle of friends in the Skull Valley Players, the neighborhood theater group. We did *Harvey* that year and I was cast as Nurse Kelly. I was barely thirteen, playing a twenty-two-year-old woman. I look at the photo from that play, and I see the face of a woman, with few traces of the innocence of early adolescence that should have been there.

Thinking back on it now, I know that there was sadness in my childhood. Though I had a good time playing Nurse Kelly and was quite proud that I could play beyond my years, I see now that I never played the ingenue. I don't think I was ever young and innocent; perhaps I was born an old soul. Some of those carefree, childish years were just lost to me. Now, as a parent myself, I see my son having a good time, and I learn from him. He has taught me to laugh more, to just have fun. I'm still not too good at it, but I'm getting better.

BY THE TIME I was a sophomore in high school, I was spending so much time with the drama club and with friends, I didn't notice the growing distance between my parents. They weren't fighting as much and I took that as a good sign. I started spending most of my evenings at the Teenage Club they had on base. They had a shooting range and I learned to shoot there. The club room had a jukebox and a Ping-Pong table, but we'd mainly just stand around listening to music and talking for hours, though one of my friends taught me to jitterbug.

Things seemed pretty much status quo with my parents then. But after years of putting up with my daddy, and doing the best she could, my mother finally began to see someone else. My father discovered it and there was an ugly scene. After that, a terrible pall settled over the house. Mother sent Mac and me on to school each day and we went, knowing all along that something was terribly wrong. One day we came home and my mother told us we were going back to Florida without my daddy.

One of the last things we did as a "family" was to drive together in almost total silence to the airport, where my mother and Mac and I would catch the plane to Tallahassee. I had gotten dressed up for the plane ride and was wearing a two-piece suit, black pumps, and white gloves. I remember being in the backseat of that car, staring out the window at the desert, an endless stretch of snow-dusted sand, and then at the back of my parents' heads. The one thing I had tried to keep from happening my whole life was finally happening. I must have known in every fiber of my being that it was going to happen. That one day it would take place. And now it had. We would lose my father. We would split apart as a family.

LEON HIGH SCHOOL in Tallahassee. I headed up the front steps of the school and thought, it's just another mountain to climb. I remember thinking, just grit your teeth and get through this. Just find a way to prevail. And I did.

I finished high school there, graduating in 1958. It may have been a record, more than two years in the same school. I joined the drama club and was elected a member of the cheerleader squad. We moved into a small apartment on North Adams Street that was close to the school. Most of my friends lived either in the suburbs or a better part of town, and I avoided catching a ride home with them when I could. In the South, so much was dependent on outside appearances, and I was very much aware of that. It is one of my most painful teenage memories that we lived in this rather broken-down apartment.

Our first Christmas there, we took a bus to Maryland, where my father had been transferred. My mother had decided she should try for a reconciliation. My father picked us up at the bus terminal. It was a sad, dreary Christmas. We had Christmas dinner at the base, and there was lot of talk between my mother and father. Hours seemed to drag on forever. We left the day after Christmas.

Mac and my mother never saw John MacDowell Dunaway again. I saw him once in New York. I had graduated from college and had gotten a part in the Broadway production of *A Man for All Seasons*. He wrote and said he was coming through town. We met at a bar not far from the theater at Fifty-second and Broadway. He was drinking coffee, coffee with ice in it. I was drinking scotch; only later would I graduate to the perfect dry martini.

It had been seven years since I had seen him. I'd gone from being a sulky teenager, very unsure of myself and my looks, to an adult focused on a Broadway career. I had written him letters while I was in college, just to stay in touch, though he rarely wrote back. He was quiet, didn't say much. He kept looking at me, and stirring his coffee, the ice cube clinking against the side.

"They told me I was a daddy's girl," I suddenly said to him. I wanted to know. "Was I a daddy's girl?" I hadn't planned on asking that. I don't think I'd planned anything, though I had seven years of a life stored up that he knew almost nothing of. He looked at me, startled, then smiled and said, "Yes, you were, and I'll tell you something, honey, you still are." I wanted to believe him, that for that one moment he did truly love me and he was proud of who I'd become. But it was difficult to trust this man, who hadn't always taken care of his family, who had never been there for me.

We didn't say much more and before long he left. I watched as he walked out of that bar. I never saw him again. We talked once again on the phone. By then he was working as a cook in a boys reformatory. He sounded quite ill. "Daddy, you have a cold?" I asked. "Honey, I keep a cold," he said. "Going in and out of the refrigerator all the time, I keep a cold." It broke my heart.

He died in 1985. I was living in London then, and my son was still a baby, and I couldn't get back for the funeral. The broken connection with my father remains one of my great regrets. Mother never stopped being angry at him, and I felt to see him again would betray her. For many years when I thought of my relationship with my father, I got this wintry feeling. That place where there's a fault in the earth, and the earth opens up and you fall into it, and everything is wintry and endlessly bleak.

From my childhood on, I always tried to understand why my father was the way he was. After I was grown, I went back to see if I could uncover something in his childhood that might explain it. That's what made me an actress, probably, trying to find what it was that created the man who was my father. When I heard that he had been beaten severely by his father, it helped me understand a bit more. But, you know, as Albert Camus said, a human being is responsible for his face. Childhood experience can help those who love you to understand, but each of us is responsible for who we are.

But for all his flaws, my daddy was not a cruel or hateful man, and I knew he loved me. I could see in his eyes a kind of mute love, even when he stumbled to find words to tell me he cared. He was buried by his second wife in Sarasota, far from where he was born and raised. I knew what my mother's dreams were. I still wonder what my father's were. I know somewhere along the way, he must have had dreams too.

THREE

T HE BATHROOM IS TINY, hot, and steamy, and the air is stale
and still. I've been submerged for what feels like hours in a bathtub
filled with milk to cover the fact that I'm sitting there without a stitch
of clothing on. It's 1986 and we're shooting a scene for *Barfly* in a
decaying hotel on a lost street in a dreary, run-down section of East Los
Angeles.

Mickey Rourke, my costar in the movie, is wedged into the bathroom next to the sink. If he takes a step in one direction, he'll hit a
wall, the other, a door. The space is so tight it allows for only the
smallest movements. The lights, positioned to keep us from fading into
the background, have raised the temperature at least twenty degrees
above an otherwise mild Southern California, 72-and-clear kind of
day. The director, Barbet Schroeder, who treats us like treasured children, is squeezing in and out of the room making last-minute adjust-
ments and fussing over us.

There is a drone of noise in the background, the mindless conversations that fill in the gaps between takes. But I can barely hear it
over the sound of the blood whooshing through my veins. My head is
throbbing. Breathe, Faye, focus on the scene, I tell myself. Breathe.
The wall next to me feels like it's growing thicker, heavier, closing
in. Breathe. My heart is pounding, faster, then faster still. I can't
breathe. Breathe. Breathe. The air. It's all smoke and steam. No oxygen. I . . . can't . . . breathe. "Can I get out of here? I gotta get out
of here for a minute." It's Mickey's voice. Thank God, he's as claustrophobic as I am.

Barbet calls a break, and Mickey and I both scramble out of our tile-and-porcelain torture chamber. I don't remember who made it out faster. It made filming the scene both horrible—What's worse than one claustrophobic?—and hysterical—Two. We did what we needed to do, taking deep breaths and walking back into that coffin of a room more times than I want to remember. We suffered; thankfully the work didn't, though I think the scene was far edgier in an already edgy movie than even Barbet had planned.

The feeling of claustrophobia that makes my heart pound and takes my breath away is a page out of my own private high school yearbook. If I close my eyes, I see myself walking down a long tree-lined road in Tallahassee. The trees tower above me and their limbs stretch across the road, leaving it perpetually in shadows. It is an old, stately street and huge plantation-style houses are just visible at the end of long, winding driveways. The air is warm and thick with the smell of magnolia blossoms. Spanish moss hangs from the limbs. From a distance, it has the look of a chorus line of ancient women with long gray feather boas tossed carelessly round their necks. The moss is so heavy that only a strong breeze will set it swaying. The houses, the moss, the trees, everything on the street is saturated by age.

As I walk along, the moss brushes my shoulders. It feels like it's on me, all over me. My skin feels damp. Dread more than fear squeezes my chest tight. My breath comes fast, shallow, like a sprinter in the final moments of a desperate race. Such a deception of nature, this lacy, graceful garnish that slowly kills the trees. I know when I am only sixteen, if I don't get out of Tallahassee, just as surely as the Spanish moss does its work on those ancient trees, this place will suffocate the life out of me.

TALLAHASSEE was full of contradictions for me. Though I was forever searching for an escape hatch, for the first time in a long time, I felt a part of things. At Leon High School, I had my first serious boyfriend, a football player named Gene, Edward Eugene Page III, and I was a cheerleader.

In the fall afternoons, Gene would be at football practice. I'd be with the other cheerleaders on these great green banks of grass that lined the football field, practicing cheers for the games. He was a football hero, made straight A's, looked terrifically handsome, and, just for good measure, was an incredibly nice person, a southern gentleman in the making. On the weekends, we'd go to games, where Gene would invariably make a crucial play. I'd be with the other cheerleaders along the sidelines cheering the Leon Lions on: "Gimme an L . . . ." Our school song still brings tears to my eyes: "The red clay hills of Tallahassee, harbor memories dear. . . . Memories of our dear old high school, that we all hold near." Really the stuff American dreams are made of.

There were dances at the high school and movies at the old State Theater. In what quickly became a weekly ritual, Gene and I would go to the Episcopal church with his family each Sunday morning, then over to his house for Sunday dinner. The table would be covered with traditional southern dishes and there were always fresh flowers in the center.

His was a beautiful house on Old St. Augustine Road. I adored Gene's mother, Dorothy Day Page, who was one of the last of the true southern belles. A very ritzy woman, and as smart as she was sophisticated, with a wonderful smile and a laugh as delicate and rich as real whipped cream. Her gracious, easy style, my first close encounter with casual elegance, gave me a window into another world, of how a home and a life could be.

At school, Mina Cubbons was the drama teacher and my first real acting mentor. She was short, and quite round, with matching round cheeks, and she bustled as much as walked through the halls. Miss Cubbons began to make me believe that I might have a real talent for acting, and I took on everything I could. I was Cornelia Otis Skinner in the junior class production of *Our Hearts Were Young and Gay*, and directed ten of my classmates in *The Pajama Game* for thespian night in the fall of my senior year. There were speech tournaments around the city that I always competed in, and I usually came home with a ribbon.

The senior class play in the spring of 1958 was *The Remarkable Incident at Carson's Corner*, a dark courtroom drama, and though I had a major role, I remember other, more important dramas in my life that year.

Though we were always hard-pressed for money, it really weighed me down that last year in high school. There was not much work a teenager could pick up in those years before there was a fast-food restaurant on every corner. Baby-sitting didn't pay much, particularly in the neighborhoods we tended to live in. My options seemed to boil down to retail, as in the dimestore down the street. I rebelled at the idea. None of the other cheerleaders were faced with working at all, much less in that sort of job. But it was Sears that caused one of the biggest fights I had with my mother. She thought it would be a great place for me to make a few extra dollars to help with expenses. All I could envision was the time when someone from school would walk in to find me behind a counter selling overalls or farm tools. I just felt I couldn't bear it.

One of my teachers told me about a local essay contest. Students were being encouraged to write an essay on their view of democracy. The winner would get fifty dollars and a certificate of achievement. I worked for days on the essay, writing and rewriting it. When I won the contest and got the check, I remember telling my mother that this was the way I was going to make money, in some sort of creative way, not as a salesgirl at Sears.

GENE AND I were still dating and by this time, everyone expected us to get married. There were moments when I probably did too. But one afternoon we had a terrible argument. I forget exactly what it was about, though it could have been sex. I was very reluctant to lose my virginity, having been raised in the shadow of Olpa's unshakable belief that it was better to marry than burn. At this point in my life, I wasn't interested in condemning myself to either.

On my way home from school the next day, I drove past the State Theater. Gene and a classmate of mine were just walking inside, very close they were, laughing in that way that makes intimacy seem intense and new. She was blond, had short hair, new clothes, the latest style, was from a very good family in town, and was one of the smartest girls in the class.

I drove home and flung myself on my bed and cried through the entire afternoon. My mother kept coming in trying to get me to stop crying. My eyes were almost swollen shut, my nose was painfully raw, but I couldn't stop. She said, "You love that boy." But it wasn't just Gene, it was my father, the breakup of my family, the hard time it was starting another new school, it was my whole life I was crying for.

I waited and in a day or so Gene called and we soon patched up our differences. But I knew then I was never going to stay in the South, or with Gene. I was never going to have a life that was ordained by the strict social conventions I found there. I was going to strike out on my own. I had places to go and things to do. I had a life to live where I wanted to make a difference.

In the late fifties, winning a beauty contest was still *de rigueur* for anyone growing up where I did. I faithfully entered every beauty contest I could. Miss This, Miss That. I was always the runner-up. I'd always win in the talent category—there was nobody down there that did dramatic readings as well as I did—but it took me a while to win outright.

The name of the game in high school, certainly in Tallahassee, was being the most popular girl. And that was measured by whether or not you were a cheerleader, if you were chosen for the May Court, even how many people knew you and said "Hi" as you walked through the hallways. It's a terrible thing we do to girls as they reach their teenage years—suddenly they're expected to be a sweet, nice, cute girl, nice to everyone, particularly boys. Then comes marriage and the rest of it. And I was no exception, certainly not in the South.

Each year, the most popular girl was picked as May Queen at Leon High. It usually went to a girl whose family roots in Tallahassee went back a century or more. Girls who lived in my neighborhood rarely broke into the long-established society cliques that had provided the social underpinnings for the school, and the town, for generations. Family, in the "My great-grandfather was a general in the Civil War" sense, mattered.

I had made it "in" through my own grit. Since coming to high school in Tallahassee, I had gotten to know just about everybody, between being in the drama club, getting elected a cheerleader, and dating the star football player.

The votes were cast and counted. It was the closest anybody had ever come to being May Queen without winning. Six votes. My dress for the dance was aqua and covered with big pinwheels of tulle. My hair was shoulder-length, and still its natural shade, the color of Colombian coffee with a splash of cream, and I wore it loose and down. Gene and I looked the perfect couple. We were not close friends, Linda Gormley and I, but we knew each other. Both cheerleaders. I acted in all the class plays. She was a star diver. And that night she wore the crown. I had come so close.

For most of my life, I believed that when things didn't work out, in some way I had fallen short. Had I only been better, prettier, tougher, whatever the situation called for, everything would have turned out differently. It has taken time, and much painful soul-searching, for me to let go of that notion, and realize that there are dynamics far beyond me on which so many things in life turn—just as all my straight A's in school couldn't make my daddy stay. Such a strange thing ego is—that you can feel so inadequate and at the same time so important as to believe that the ability to change a situation or a relationship lies solely within your power.

But at seventeen, I was a long way from understanding either my potential or my limitations, or all that much of life for that matter. There was something imbedded deep down in my psyche through the steady diet of axioms about class and social standing and success that my mother raised me on that would not let me leave Florida until I won a beauty contest. I don't know precisely why I linked my departure with that, but I did. Maybe it was the final validation I needed to believe I had conquered all that I could there, and only then could I move on. Looking back on it now, I believe it was, in part, a final gesture, a tip of the hat to my mother's hopes and dreams for me.

THERE WAS no money at home for me to go to college, but I was at the top of my class scholastically, graduating third in a class of 289, and was able to qualify for a teaching scholarship at Florida State University in Tallahassee. I was already serious about becoming an actress when I accepted that scholarship, and I knew I might have to pay it back. But I had won it and it was the only way I could afford to go to college.

I had no sense of the roads I needed to travel to make a different life for myself, beyond a strong belief that it required a good education. What I hadn't been born into, I determined I would learn. Art, architecture, literature, philosophy, psychology, history, language—these would form the pillars for the life I was set on creating for myself. From the outset, I knew that I wanted more than the cosmetics of success—I wanted to become someone of substance. I wanted to be an educated woman.

The scholarship brought with it a room in the dorm. Though it was the first time I had not lived under my mother's roof, I didn't feel the same carefree sense of freedom that seemed to come so easily to other girls in the dorm. The scholarship was my shot and if I botched it, I wasn't sure that I'd ever be given another chance.

I pledged one of the top sororities, Pi Beta Phi, got A's in my classes, competed in a few beauty contests, worked for extra spending money, and as always, tried out for all the plays. I tackled Shakespeare for the first time, as Olivia in *Twelfth Night*, which had a four-day run at the Conradi Theatre that spring.

I found a measure of comfort in college in the often aggressive give-and-take between professor and student. I've never been one to just accept things and have spent a lifetime seeking the answer to the question "Why?" That unflinching need to understand landed me in a ditch when my mother was first teaching me to drive. I was backing up the car, quite nicely I thought, and she told me to put on the brake. "Why?" "Just put on the brake, Faye." "But just tell me why?" The ditch answered my question. It took a neighbor, a pickup truck, and a couple of hours to pull the car out, but that didn't stop the curiosity or squelch my need for explanations.

Gene, who had graduated a year before me, was at the University of Florida in Gainesville, where he played football. He came home to see me on the weekends when he could, but we were apart more than we were together. He was talking more seriously about marriage, and my sophomore year I transferred to the University of Florida in Gainesville to spend more time with him.

I was still on a teaching scholarship, but at the same time I knew that I was closer than ever to leaving the South. What I hadn't faced yet was what I would do about Gene. He was very much a necessary part of the puzzle. I loved him—he was a terrific man—but I knew the prescribed life in the South was not for me. I look back with regret that it couldn't work out for us. Gene went on to become a distinguished doctor. He would ultimately marry a sorority sister of mine, Pat Doepke, and they had three boys. I still speak to Gene on occasion and I'm always reminded of what Arthur Miller said in *After the Fall*, "You never stop loving the people you loved."

In Gainesville, I checked into the dorm, registered for classes, and immediately sought out the professors and students involved in drama there. In the fall, I was Daisy Diana Dorthea Devore in the Elmer L. Rice play *The Adding Machine*, and later that year played the lead in

Medea. But more importantly, I began to hear about Boston University's theater department.

Boston had an extraordinary reputation, with renowned visiting directors and top-flight lecturers drawn from the ranks of those in New York and Hollywood who were defining a changing industry. Many of the professors had been among those in entertainment who had been blacklisted during the McCarthy era. Whatever sacrifice I was making to feed my very raw talent felt quite insignificant in the face of what they had undergone. At the same time, the idea of having principles that were invoked despite the cost made me want very much to have that sort of mettle.

Each year, Boston University invited two prominent directors from New York to direct the university's theater students in a play. There were casting calls, two and three auditions, rigorous rehearsals. These directors were well known for their uncompromising standards, for asking as much from students as they would from a Broadway cast. It was about as close to a professional production as you could get, and still be a student.

If any questions as to what I should do remained in my mind, those disappeared the night I was chosen as the runner-up in the "Miss University of Florida" contest. A Hollywood talent scout was in the audience and asked if I'd go out with him after the show. We had a long dinner and I grilled him endlessly about acting and the business, from theater to film. Walking back to the dorm that evening, he told me if I was really serious about acting, I should find a school with a well-known drama program and get into it.

Now I knew with certainty that I had to go, and where I had to go. But when? That was answered in the spring when I was named the Sweetheart of Sigma Chi. Finally I had won my beauty contest. The next bus, and I was out of there. Well, almost. I did go down the next day and buy my ticket. Talking to Gene about leaving, about not getting married and the rest of it, was more painful than I had ever imagined. He was and is a wonderful man, but I knew I couldn't stay and I knew he couldn't go.

That year was another of losses deeply felt. I saw the Douglas Sirk film *Imitation of Life*, starring Lana Turner as an aspiring actress determined to find fame and fortune. But it is just as much an examination of the bonds between mothers and daughters, and all the ways in which they can be torn apart. The character who moved me so on the night I first saw the movie was Sarah Jane, played by Susan Kohner. Though her mother was black, and mine was white, our stories were not all that different. As the daughter of Lana Turner's black maid, Sarah Jane is both very beautiful and very light-skinned. She finds as she grows from a girl into a woman that she can pass for white. As Sarah Jane slips into this other world, the white world, she sheds the old, disowns her mother, and leaves behind anything that would connect her to her black ancestry.

The guilt was tearing at me as I watched the story unfold, because I knew in my heart I wasn't that different from Sarah Jane. I was ashamed of my mother and trying desperately to compete in a world of which she had no real understanding. I had seen it in high school. Those were years of bitter arguments between us. I blamed her for losing my father. I blamed her for nagging him so that he wouldn't want to stay. It was made worse by the fact that along with the normal pulling away that comes with being a teenager, I wanted more than I had and I blamed her for not having it.

Watching *Imitation of Life* fed all that pain and guilt. On this night, it hurt more than I can say, the knowledge that she was hopelessly out of place in the polite, educated society that she wanted me to travel in. Because in my heart of hearts I adored my mother. I loved her deeply and dearly and still do. As the lights went up and the theater emptied out, I sat in the back of the theater sobbing. In leaving the South, like Sarah Jane, I was also leaving my mother behind. I wondered if every step I made to pull myself out of the poverty of my past would come with its own heavy measure of loss and grief.

During finals that year, I lived on No Doz and coffee. I got A's in every class except Geology. I remember hallucinating during the exam. All I could hear, as clear as if they were in the room with me, were The Four Freshmen singing "I wish I didn't love you so. My love for you should have faded long ago." That's what I'd listened to on my study breaks. I got a D, the only one I've ever gotten. Then I packed up and went home to Tallahassee.

There was much to talk about with my mother. I was leaving for Boston, I was going to be an actress, and I was not going to marry Gene. It wasn't really up for discussion, I had already made up my mind. I know my breakup with Gene was a great disappointment to her. Everything she had wanted for me seemed to be disintegrating in the wake of this dream of mine. But through it all, she believed in me and let me go my way. The irony is that while she taught me to reach high and strive for my dreams, that reaching high and that striving took me away from her. And that's the sadness about my mother and me.

Though there had been music and dancing lessons through the years, my mother saw those as accoutrements that a truly refined lady should have. It was more her attempt at a crude sort of finishing school for me than it was an effort to steer me toward the stage. And though she had faithfully attended each of the school productions I'd been in, she was never a stage mother and never envisioned that sort of life for me. But where my mother may have seen the end of my future, I saw the beginning.

THE SUMMER before my junior year was magical. I spent the months working as a waitress in one of the resorts at Lake Saranac in upstate New York. It was a gorgeous place, a white-clapboard, Adirondack-style hotel that said old money. The dining room was run by a very charming Italian maître d', with a minuscule white mustache and very tightly groomed white hair. He would greet everyone as they came in—"Helloooo, how are yooooo? Cooom in. Your day—it was a nice ooone? Wooonderful, I am so happy. And tennis, was there tennis today?" Each word was treated like a single pearl in a long, perfectly matched strand. The people staying at the lodge absolutely adored it and him, and I was fascinated by the daily performance.

The guests would have three meals a day in the dining room, and I served the same family, Mr. and Mrs. Trifari, of Trifari Jewelry. And then in the alcove were the Arthur Murray Dancers. There was a tall one—he was endlessly tall, and for some reason he didn't have a partner. When I could, I would go and dance with them, and he, the endlessly tall one, would dance with me, teaching me steps along the way.

On weekends the Arthur Murray Dancers would go, and take me along, into the Adirondack Mountains to the estate of Marjorie Merriweather Post. We nicknamed it the Post Toasties Palace. The estate went on for miles. It was filled with wonderful pieces of art that left me humbled by their beauty and lingering as long as I could to drink it all in. Its passion moved me in a way that began the need for art in my life. An afternoon in a gallery never fails to leave me nourished and in some deeply visceral way, restored, whole.

We were there at the Post estate to teach whatever guests might be there to dance anything from the mundane to the exotic, the paso doble, the rumba, the waltz. Those were strange, gossamer nights, floating around on a ballroom floor, with people whose sophistication and culture fit them like old clothes. I would close my eyes and imagine what it must be like to be one of them, where there were so many dollars you've stopped ever wondering where the next would come from, if you ever had. But money has never made me happy, as I thought it might have that night. It is in connecting with other people that I have found happiness, and in my work, of course, always in my work.

As with Cinderella at the stroke of midnight, the weekends at the Post estate would always come to an abrupt end. I'd find myself back at the lodge, serving three meals a day, tea in the afternoon, and picking up evening shifts at a local pizza place, the Dew Drop Inn. And though there was never a day I didn't worry about making enough money to pay for room and board, and school for the next year, it was in all a carefree summer.

Beyond the Arthur Murray dancer, there was a dark, edgy guy named Jimmy that I fell for. He was the sexy guy-about-town, with the swagger of someone used to having the best-looking girl as his girlfriend. The darkness, the unpredictability, and the fact that every other girl wanted to be with him made him extremely attractive to me. I was drawn to Jimmy for absolutely all the wrong reasons—the first echoes of a search for my father.

We'd spend our nights going to the local roadside nightclubs, where the music was live and loud, the crowd was young, and the lights were dim, and we'd dance until we couldn't bear to stand up any longer. The theme from *The Unforgiven* was big that summer. They used to play it over and over again on the jukebox. I still think of Jimmy whenever I hear that song. It was an easy romance. Like me, Jimmy wasn't looking for commitment, and at the end of the summer it wasn't hard to say our good-byes.

It was a summer of firsts. I had my first hangover, a perfectly horrible experience and one that I vowed not to repeat, though of course, like my friends who vowed with me, I did. And I saw Broadway for the first time. It was the tail end of the summer, and a group of us from the resort, all on our way back to college, decided to make a quick detour through New York. We spent the day roaming around the theater district, looking at all the playbills. I wondered if I would ever see my name on one, something I didn't dare say out loud. That evening we managed to get some cheap seats to see Robert Preston in *The Music Man*. It's still funny to me that my first Broadway play was a musical, since my preference for drama was already ingrained. But in its way, *The Music Man* was the perfect ending for a near perfect summer, the first in a long time where there actually was no trouble in River City, at least for me.

BOSTON, another place with old families and old traditions. At least in the South, I could rightfully claim family roots, humble though they might be. I stepped off the bus and got my suitcase and a cardboard box that held my books from home. It is a habit that has stayed with me—not the bus, the books. Bad or good, for better or worse, once I have a book, it's usually forever. The difficulty comes in moving countless boxes of books, enough now to fill a good-sized piece of a moving van. That also means any place I live for long must have lots of big, empty walls that can be lined, floor to ceiling, with books.

A new house starts feeling like home when the books are organized. It's nothing as formal as a library, though I do catalogue things so that I can put my hand on any book I want in a manner of seconds. One of my dreams is to have a library like Susan Sontag's. I once read that hers is organized chronologically, so that everything is arranged by time period. So you have the 1900s, and in that section the plays written then, plus the books on architecture, history, everything. I've been entranced with the idea since I read about it and have begun to organize my library that way.

There was no scholarship waiting for me at Boston University and no dorm room. I found a rooming house for young unmarried women, Franklin Square, and rented what they called a room, though it was more a cell. Colorless, lifeless, as dreary a place as I could imagine. I would lie on the bed and look up and it was as if there was a camera on the ceiling recording this gritty black-and-white movie. The place felt perpetually cold, as if a chill had crawled into its bones during the Revolutionary War and refused to leave. The radiator hissed moist heat through the bitter winter, but the cold stalked the room anyway, and in the night, it would steal its way back in.

I don't think I have ever felt the depth of loneliness that I felt in Franklin Square. There were nights, late long nights when I seriously debated leaving. This place felt so foreign to me, and though I've often felt an outsider, I felt positively alien here. The North can be hard and unforgiving of southern people. I was very much a product of the South, trained as most southern women are from the time they are little girls that if something is wrong, it falls to you to make it right. What is taught as gentility and grace seemed to me a lifetime of accommodation that I wanted to avoid. Yet here was a world without that gentility, warmth, hospitality, and I found I missed it dreadfully.

I went to classes all day, then worked as a cocktail waitress at the Somerset Cocktail Lounge in the evenings. The hours were long but bearable due only to the Somerset's jazz pianist. He had a style very much like the legendary Erroll Garner's, whose left hand and right hand would create intricate opposing melodies, only to fuse them back together somewhere along the way. I had left behind my interest in pop music when the bus rolled out of Tallahassee and was very much into jazz, drawn to the last remnants of the beat generation, black clothes, drama, and dark poetry.

The Somerset was a different landscape than Lake Saranac, and I got a quick lesson in how to handle difficult customers. On my first day off, I took a couple of dollars in tips that I didn't need to pay the rent and bought myself a cheap wedding band. It probably reduced my earning potential at the Somerset, but it also reduced the number of men who had visions of going home at 2 A. M. with the "little southern gal" who was serving their drinks. I also began working on refining my speech, reserving the soft liquid drawl for those times when the role demanded it. On Saturdays I picked up a little extra money working at the Kenmore Coffee Shop nearby. My life that year was nothing but school and work.

There were generally four productions each year at the university. During my junior year, Word Baker, who had directed *The Fantasticks* off Broadway, was there. I auditioned for anything, but didn't get much in the way of big roles. I was up for the lead role in one of the productions, but it went to another girl, and I played a supporting role instead. This girl seemed destined to be a star. She was very thin, waiflike, almost like Audrey Hepburn. I don't know which I disliked more, that she always got the leading roles, or that she was so effortlessly thin. I was later told she had an eating disorder.

I never was bulemic or anorexic, thank God, but at points in my life, I've done battle with my weight. In Boston, I had a weakness for Howard Johnson's clam rolls and pistachio ice cream. There were nights when I felt so overwhelmed by the solitude that I would find myself slipping into a seat behind the counter at Howard Johnson's, having my clam roll, smothered in tartar sauce, only to finish off the meal with a double-dip of pistachio ice cream on a brown, crunchy sugar cone.

Now I work a very careful food plan. Grilled fish, chicken, salads, steamed vegetables, and some grains. White flour, sugar, and desserts, beyond a very occasional sugar-free frozen yogurt, are a thing of the past. I am thankful that I have found better and more healthy ways of dealing with the sadness.

When I was cast as Bonnie in *Bonnie and Clyde* I was still trying to lose the twenty-five pounds I'd put on during the filming of *Hurry Sundown*. It was a measure of my anguish at having to walk in my mother's shoes and go back over that experience myself, which is what we do—relive that experience. So the weight came on. Arthur Penn told me he absolutely wanted me and no one else as Bonnie, but he also thought I should lose the weight. I said, "Don't worry about that, I most certainly will."

At that point in my life, I ran a lot on will, and it was pretty strong and healthy, my will. I spent weeks walking around my apartment and working out wearing a twelve-pound weight belt, with smaller weights around my wrists to help me burn the pounds off faster. I only took the weights off to sleep and bathe. By the time I headed to Texas, where we were shooting the film, I was gaunt.

I CAME to one painful conclusion very quickly at Boston University, with its connections to the New York theater, its serious drama school, and its cadre of widely respected visiting directors: I didn't know how to act. I had the will, the inclination, and some measure of talent, I suppose, but it was raw and unschooled. I hadn't begun to learn the craft. I threw myself into trying to absorb the process, and I began to get a notion of character development.

The world of the character I was playing had to be totally exposed and explored before I could step into her life. While that might sound obvious, slipping inside someone else's skin and getting all the right nuances, from how they think to how they move, doesn't come naturally for me. The play might have a character in her thirties, but if I was to make the moment true, I had to know everything that had come before.

The invention of it, creating a history for each character along the way, is something I came to love. Some of my fondest memories are of sitting around with directors and other actors and going at a play, or a script, as if it were a giant psychological jigsaw puzzle, with the picture, the people, and their stories emerging in bits and pieces. Sometimes as you come to know your character, the story will change because instinctively you know they would not react as the script has it.

I began to truly get a grasp of the process of character development for the first time while I was at Boston. It was during Christmas break of my junior year, and I was on the bus bound for Lake Placid to work at one of the ski resorts. The bus was a confined space where I could really focus. I sat there as we bumped along over the winding, icy roads, trying to understand the Second Girl in García Lorca's *Yerma*. The production was being directed by Peter Kass, who had just come from directing the Broadway production of *Marching Song*. Peter had been a member of the Group Theatre of the thirties. It's what Clifford Odets came out of, Elia Kazan, Harold Clurman, many of the greats. It was a small part, and Second Girl—well, it felt like the story of my life. I'd tried out for Yerma, and the lead had once again gone to someone else, but I threw myself into my role even so.

I went through her speech—about a half-page long. Yerma asks me, "Then why did you marry?" and I answer, "Because they married me off. They get everyone married." I began to think about the subtext, which really is an important part of the way I work. My subtext that night became so intricate and so dense. When she says they marry you off, feeding into that is every thought I ever had when I read that line. Over and over and over again. I discovered on that bus how fast my mind was able to move from action to transition to the next action. It was like championship skating—fluid and fast. The more you look at it, the more you repeat it—*répétition*, the French word for rehearsal—the more it becomes a part of your muscle memory. That speech, by the time I got to my destination, was chock-full of actions and transitions and new actions. That was the fun of it really, to be able to do that, to move so quickly.

There is something about the quickness, the transitions and the mental agility to make them, that's one aspect of really good acting. I look at Marlon Brando and I say, "Why is he a genius?" And Anna Magnani, who was in *The Fugitive Kind*. They play something with a purity and a density and a focus of concentration. Some actors you look at and it's light, what they're doing. And other actors you look at and it's dense, because they are consumed with what they are doing. Somehow it's coming from the deepest part of them as well. There is an intensity of truth in Brando's and Magnani's work; you are compelled to watch them and there's never a false moment.

On the bus that day, I was just putting in spade work. I was reading the whole speech and fantasizing and using my imagination, both about the character and how her experiences connected to mine. "Because they married me off." Who are "they"? Then you find out who "they" are for the character, and how you can personalize that. You've got to personalize it. What in my life is like that? Who do I know that I've had that feeling toward? The minute I remember a feeling I had toward Gene Page, say, I'm in the moment of that feeling in a way that I could never be if I only tried to "be" the Second Girl with these feelings about some unknown character. By substituting my experience, which was a parallel experience, with the experience of the character, I find my home in the feeling.

There are some actors who are able to simply let themselves be taken over by the role. It's a bit like being on a trapeze and not caring if you fall. I was always too anxiety-ridden or too frightened for that sort of free fall. Very early on, I had an enormous fear that there would come a point when I wouldn't know what to do next, and of course those moments do come.

In George Bernard Shaw's writing on the theater, he talks of a wonderful moment in Eleonora Duse's performance in *Magda* and Duse's incandescent power on the stage. In the scene, her marriage is breaking apart. Though she says nothing directly, throughout the scene Duse nervously twists her wedding ring, unaware that she is doing it. Wordless, the moment is drenched with a fear that she is not yet aware of. It's the layers, exposing the subconscious, that brings the actor and the audience closer to the soul of the character—a different pathway they take to what is hopefully the same point of truth.

To illuminate the subconscious of the character, you've got to have the actor know things about the character that the character doesn't know about themself. If Magda in that moment is terrified she's losing her husband, and the character doesn't know it, she'll twist her ring in a different way. Then there is a moment of enlightenment where she sees what she's doing. The terror of losing her husband suddenly becomes conscious. That's a heart-stopping moment, a moment of recognition for the character, where you see her discover something that she didn't know about herself before.

To so many actresses of my generation, Duse represented the ultimate in acting genius. Acting for me was never mere performance—it was about the art of it, the expression of something larger. Eva Le Gallienne, in writing of Duse, said that she had an immense reverence for art in all forms: "She was a great force capable of spreading beauty and understanding."

Creating beauty wherever I can, in my life and in my work, is really a need, a passion that I have. And you always hope when you do create beauty in your work that it will connect with people, and in that connection they will become more aware of the mystery and the wonder of the human spirit. Though I may not always succeed at it, I never stop trying to raise whatever play I'm doing to a higher spiritual level.

Duse's acting has always struck me as sacrificial. It was as though each time she played, she immolated herself upon an altar. This reckless annihilation of self was what made her unique among actresses. Through the years, acting became like a crucible into which the sufferings and sins of all the women I have known were sublimated, there to be forged into the pure essence of pity, terror, and pain. I studied Duse, I studied human behavior, I studied my own emotions and thoughts. And so it was that I began to learn about acting.

I SPENT the summer in Boston and became one of the Harvard Summer Players, winning the role of Hypatia in George Bernard Shaw's *Misalliance*, one of several summer productions. *Misalliance*, one of the first comedies in which I had a leading role, opened in late July at Harvard's Loeb Drama Center in Cambridge, where $1.50 could get you the best seat in the house. Jane Alexander, who now heads the National Endowment for the Arts, was in that play too. She played an aviatrix who was used to standing up and taking a bow with her hand flung upwards in the air. There was a moment in the play where she was dozing off on the sofa and someone said her name, the Great Aviatrix, and she leapt up with her hand in the air as if she were taking a bow—and she was so funny. The audience always loved it. I saw her again a year or so later when I moved to New York. I remember staying at her apartment while I was trying to find a place of my own, so we were roommates for a while.

DURING my senior year at Boston the snows and the cold came just as relentlessly, but it felt warmer somehow. Emotionally I was thawing a bit. I was out of the dreaded Franklin Square and rooming with a couple of other people who were in the theater department too. One of my roommates, Tanya Berezin, went on to become an artistic director at the Circle Repertory Company in New York for a time.

We lived in an apartment behind the Symphony Hall on Symphony Road. I was in the front of the place. There was a room where I studied, and a tiny alcove off it, where I slept. The curtains were orange and there were huge windows that always caught the morning sun. The light streaming through those curtains, and the way it never failed to lift my spirits with its simple beauty, I will never forget. I started to feel almost human.

I began going to see whatever plays I could anytime I could afford tickets. I saw Donald Pleasence in *The Caretaker*, the first Harold Pinter play I ever saw, and it blew my mind. I fell madly in love with Pinter. Later I would act in one of his plays, and ultimately I would meet the playwright and he would direct me in a play when I was living in England. As a student you seek out ways to learn how to do what you do better, and I began that in earnest in Boston.

I did the same when I moved to New York. I was so struck by the performance given by a Kabuki troupe there. It was my first exposure to that form of theater, and I was stunned by the artistry of the leading lady, who was, in a tradition dating back to seventeenth-century Japan, played by a man. The music, a high haunting wail, cast a spell over me as the young girl began to tell the story of war and a lost love. I watched as tears began streaming down the masklike face.

It was the daunting nature of what this man achieved. He sang in a very high voice. He walked and danced on high wooden shoes, and there was this constant sinuous writhing movement of his body that seemed almost choreographed; it was a dancelike thing. At the same time, tears were literally streaming down his face. Now, you often see actors shed one or two tears, and you see crying, but you don't see that concerted thing with the tears just falling and falling and falling. It seemed like some of the best acting I was ever likely to see. I felt if I could just approach that one day . . . Just the skill of it was so amazing.

THERE WERE four productions that year, and I finally won major roles in three of them. I was Loraleen in *Cock-A-Doodle Dandy*, which Ted Kazanoff, my chief acting professor, directed, then Jack Manning cast me as Viola in *Twelfth Night*. But the play that was to set me on the road was due to go into production in the spring.

The department was going to stage Arthur Miller's *The Crucible*, directed by Lloyd Richards. Lloyd was best known at the time for directing the 1958 Broadway production of A *Raisin in the Sun* and he later went on to be dean of Yale University's prestigious school of drama, originating on stage all of Lanford Wilson's plays. One of my classmates had been recommended to him for the part of Elizabeth Proctor, one of the two principal female roles in the play. For some reason, she couldn't take the part, and my name was given to him. I auditioned and was cast as Elizabeth.

The play was set for a grand old theater that had been used for years by the Boston Repertory Company before the university took it over. The production, as designed by Richards, was going to be the first to use Miller's play untouched. There had been a Broadway production of *The Crucible* in the fifties, but it had been greatly abbreviated. Since Miller had yet to see his play produced in its original form, he made plans to be there. Word began circulating in theater circles, and a contingent from New York also came to see it. Robert Whitehead, who was having a very successful run on Broadway with his production of the Robert Bolt play A *Man for All Seasons*, starring Paul Scofield as Sir Thomas More, was among those who came, as well as Kermit Bloomgarden, who had produced the Broadway version of *The Crucible*.

My role was that of a wife whose husband is in love with another woman, an agony I had witnessed through my father's various liaisons in the years he and my mother were together. I understood clearly how one person's moral dilemma can become a wrenching pain inflicted on someone else. The play was a success, and Miller stopped by after one performance to say how much it had pleased him to see it this way.

That role changed my life, because I was able to work with Richards. He watched me through the long hours of rehearsals, and saw where I took the performance on stage. Richards told me later that by the end of the production, he knew I had talent and determination, but beyond that he knew that I "would be willing to pay the price" to do whatever it took to get where I was headed. He was right—there was a price to be paid, and I was willing to ante up. I had learned that all those years ago on the swing with Uncle Neal.

Richards was impressed enough with my performance that when the Repertory Theater of Lincoln Center was being formed and Elia Kazan asked him for the names of two students to consider for the training program, mine was one of them. I auditioned for Kazan, with a piece from *Twelfth Night* and a selection from *Orpheus Descending*.

It was a heady time as I moved closer to graduation. I had an offer to join the Lincoln Center training program, but I'd also won a Fulbright Scholarship, which would let me study in London at the London Academy of Dramatic Arts for a year. I really deliberated on whether I should study in London for a year or stay here. And as I have always done—the habits of a lifetime—I went to the experts, any expert I could find. Elliott Norton, the dean of American theater critics at the time and one of the professors I studied with, was one of them. I said, "What do you think I should do?" He told me that Lincoln Center was the most important thing happening in the American theater.

Then I thought to myself, the bottom line is I'm an American actress, that's what I am. That's where I want to make my mark. And Lincoln Center was just too important not to be involved in. At the time, the Lincoln Center project represented the formation of a major national repertory company in this country. At that moment in my life I wasn't thinking of movies. I wanted to be in the theater and become a great stage actress in the tradition of Duse, and I still want that. Soon, becoming a great film actress would become just as important to me.

Some of the best advice I got that year was from Robert Whitehead, who told me not to go to film until I truly had something to bring to it, to learn the craft first on the stage. He was right. My heart

My Broadway debut in 1962 in A Man for All Seasons *only days after graduating from college.* Courtesy New York Public Library

goes out to young hopefuls in Hollywood who come out here hoping to be actors when they know nothing about the craft. When you get flung onto a soundstage with everything happening at once, and makeup and camera and "How do I look?" you're lost if you don't have a very strong technique to hold you, to keep your acting intact. That's why whenever I've been doing a lot of films for a long time, I want to get back to the stage, because it's there that you get solid in terms of who you are as an artist. Film is taking out, theater is putting in. I've always felt that.

I WAS STUDYING for finals and trying to figure out how I could manage to make enough as a waitress in New York so that I could attend the Lincoln Center program, when Olga Bellin decided to leave

A Man for All Seasons. She was playing the role of Lady Margaret, Sir Thomas More's daughter. Whitehead, who was also involved in the Lincoln Center project and knew I was coming to New York, called me in to audition for the role.

There were seven other actresses up for Lady Margaret, none a green recruit just out of college. I had absolutely no chance. *A Man for All Seasons* was the talk of the town at the time, having just gotten a Tony Award as the year's best play. The cast was made up of seasoned performers. Somehow I made it to round number two. This time there were only two of us in to read. I walked out convinced that she had gotten the part. I was the perpetual runner-up, with images of being Second Girl, and six votes away from the Leon High May Queen, running through my head. So I couldn't quite believe it when I finally got the call. I was to play Margaret.

I graduated from college on June 3, 1962. On June 5, I signed a contract to play Margaret for the run of the play, a full year, and started rehearsals. I was making my stage debut in New York at the ANTA Theater, at Fifty-second and Broadway. On June 25, my opening night, I entered in act 1, wearing a simple deep blue velvet dress of the kind a nobleman's daughter would wear on an ordinary day. It had long sleeves and laced up the back, with the skirt falling to the floor in soft folds around me. I wore an Alice in Wonderland–style headband, and though my hair was quite long, they added a fall so that it came nearly to my waist.

I took a deep breath and stepped out onto the top of the stairway. A moment's pause at the top and a glance at the room below. Emlyn Williams, who had just taken over the role of Sir Thomas More, called up to me, "Come down, Meg." I smiled at my father and began to walk down the stairs. Gatsby.

Though I would never have allowed myself to look, I knew beyond the footlights there was an audience. That it was my Broadway debut was of little interest to anyone there. They had come for the play—to be entertained, to be moved in some way, to laughter, to tears, to reflection, if the playwright and the actors had done the job right. I could feel it, this living, breathing organism and the strange field of energy that suddenly bound us together. I wanted very much for them to believe that I was Lady Margaret More, Meg.

I slowly descended to the room below where my mother, father, the steward, the Duke of Norfolk, and a few others were gathered around a table discussing the extraordinary flight of a falcon, who had come from the clouds and mists that morning to make a stunning dive, hundreds of feet. I stood near the table. The Duke poured a goblet of wine and handed it to me. It was time for my first line, and my stomach felt a bit like that falcon, plunging hundreds of feet, as I asked, "Did he kill the heron?"

Hours later, I sat in front of the mirror in a tiny dressing room backstage and slowly took off my makeup. The face that stared back at me hardly seemed familiar. The agony had already set in. I was my toughest and least forgiving critic. My mind ran through every moment onstage. I wanted to take it apart, I wanted to do it better, I wanted to do it differently the next time. A minute of solace. There would be a tomorrow and I would once again be on a Broadway stage. I was on my way.

FOUR

L ATE ONE NIGHT in the fall of 1962, I dropped by the Village Vanguard, the wonderful old jazz club in the West Village. I'd taken to roaming New York on my own a lot. There were nights when I didn't need company, didn't want company, and resented terribly anyone who suggested otherwise. The Vanguard and the Village Gate, which nearly always had great jazz, had become fairly regular haunts for me. But it was Lenny Bruce who was playing the Vanguard that night.

Everybody knew about Lenny by then. His scathing brand of comedy was drawing big crowds wherever he played, and when he wasn't onstage, he was in court fighting obscenity charges around the country. It's the essential anger of a rebel in Lenny that I was drawn to. I have it myself, a rebel literally from the South. I never want to lose the fight, that courage to go to the mat for what I want, and he had it in spades.

That night, I was wearing the couture of the counterculture, all black, and I managed to get a table to myself. Even then I hated the notion that a woman, unlike a man, shouldn't be out on her own. I have always liked it, a table, a book, and the freedom to observe people. It's the life-blood of my work. As the show opened, I was a lone figure fighting my own angry demons of self-worth, slowly smoking a cigarette, nursing a scotch, soaking in the scene and waiting for Lenny to work his magic.

That night he was amazing. There was something really seeking and troubled and very dramatic about his eyes. He had a great face, really quite handsome in a dark exotic way, and the comedy was brilliant. There he was standing on the stage, wearing a raincoat like some panhandler who had just drifted in off the street, delivering a stinging indictment of life as we knew it. I'll bet money that Lenny was the inspiration for Peter Falk's wrinkled trench coat that became his signature as Columbo years later. Peter is a formidable actor who would have dug Lenny. Lenny's comedy gave you a way to look at everything that was so funny and incisive and true, that it made you comfortable with the moment and the place and the time. It was as if he threw a line into your field of vision and said, "Hey, look at it this way." That's what Lenny did. *He was a great artist.*

About halfway through the show, I decided that Lenny was as much an actor as he was a comic, with an incredible ear for dialects. He could slip from Irish priest to Jewish rabbi to southern black without a breath in between. If there were undercover cops planted in the audience that night looking for something racy—and by then there usually were—Lenny didn't disappoint. Sex, race, religion, and just life in general—he exposed the hypocrisy he found there and then would savage it from every direction. It was the first observational comedy I'd ever seen, maybe the first of that sort of comedy that was being done, and it was painfully funny. The absurdity of real life became his setup and his punch line, and he pounded away at it for hours.

The room was packed, but Lenny had a way of making it all feel very intimate. When he said, "I'm not a comedian. I don't have an act. I just talk. I'm just Lenny Bruce," you believed it. The two-hour diatribe began to feel like a dialogue between the two of you. And I didn't want the dialogue to stop. I reacted to Lenny just like I had to Elvis when I was about thirteen. I was an immediate fan. I thought he was great and I wanted to be around him, to see how his mind worked. I asked the bartender how I could meet Lenny, and after the show it was arranged.

That began a romance between the two of us, though the drugs he used had taken a toll and it wasn't a torrid romance as it might have been. I don't know if he was using heroin at the time we met. I never saw it. But I was only twenty-one at the time; he was nearing forty and had a lifetime of hiding his drug use from those he wanted to. We would talk, though, for hours, about his court cases and about his comedy, the process, how he made it happen. And he would listen to the litany of my own anxieties. It was his work and his mind that I loved, and that he made me laugh. Laughter for me was like Christmas. It didn't come around that often.

After that night, Lenny would usually call me whenever he came to Manhattan. If he wasn't staying with friends, he'd check into the Hotel America, a place off Times Square that was so seedy I almost wondered if Lenny had staged the whole thing. The lobby—and that's being generous—was absolutely bare. Not a chair, much less a couch in sight, and the most awful yellow tile you could imagine. Except for Lenny, the other occupants tended to be couples who were renting by the hour, or folks who'd been down on their luck for more years than they remembered. It was a microcosm of society's underbelly laid out for Lenny to poke and prod at will, like the self-appointed social scientist that he was.

His suite was always stacked with law books and legal papers, and it smelled musty and old. The court cases obsessed him; he believed that if he could somehow really explain his position to a jury or a judge, he could make them understand what he was trying to do. He began the process of taking over his own defense. Over time, the court papers became the core of his act, and most of what we'd talk about as well. He'd read long passages, then go into endless existential riffs on the flawed logic of the arguments against him. But having been raised in the South, I knew well who would likely win in a clash between logic and convention, though I thought he was brilliant and brave for trying.

I saw his show enough times that I can still remember bits from some of the routines. Years later, on the set of *Bonnie and Clyde*, Michael J. Pollard and I would pass the time doing Lenny Bruce bits. We would act it out as if it were a script, because I knew them backwards and forwards and so did he. And we would use them as comments, interspersed in normal conversation. "Why don't you go get King Kong?" we'd say when somebody would be challenging us or pretending to be great. It was from Lenny's *White-Collar Drunk* routine. The white-collar drunk was just what it says, a guy who worked in an office. He's in a bar getting drunk and very obnoxious, talking about how he'll get his dog to just—Kill—the bartender if he doesn't bring him a "drinkie-winkie." A big burly guy, who claims to be an FBI agent, finally has had enough of this "vicious dog" story, which he clearly doesn't buy, and says to the guy, "Why don't you go get King Kong?"

We did a lot of *White-Collar Drunk*, Michael and I. And I loved Lenny's riff on the old prison-break movies—with Dutch and the rest of the boys on Death Row; the priest, Father Flotsky; and Kiki, the gay male nurse who wants to be the Avon representative for the prison. It remains one of my favorites. It was outrageous. Lenny was outrageous. I wanted to be like him, at least in attitude. I wanted to challenge it all, too—conventions, the establishment, the status quo. I didn't want any compromises, I wanted to go right for the truth, whatever that was. It was a time of extremes in my life, and I wanted to push everything to the edge. Lenny couldn't skirt the edge, though. He flew right into the flame.

THE LAST TIME I saw Lenny was in the spring of 1963. He had gone to London by way of Ireland to escape the growing pressure here and to try to get a work permit there. But the British deported him and put him on a plane back to New York. There was a pretty close circle of people who tried to watch out for Lenny, definitely a lost soul in need of more than a few guardian angels. A couple of us kept up a vigil, waiting for him to return. When I did see him, just hours after he'd gotten off the plane, he was completely broke, desperately sick, without a penny to his name. The system had beaten him down.

At that moment, I looked into the eyes that could pierce you to the bone and saw nothing but defeat. Tears starting welling up, but before they could spill down his face, he shoved some of his clothes at me and asked if I'd drop them off at the Chinese laundry around the corner. He didn't want me to see him in such bad shape. "Sure," I said. I took his shirts. I would have done anything for Lenny. I adored him. He was a genius, I truly believe that. Lenny and Peter Sellers are perhaps the only two comic geniuses I've ever known.

But that night left me feeling like it was over. Lenny was gaunt and edgy, twitchy, the bags under his eyes so dark it was as if someone had worked him over in a back alley. I realized that life for him was all about the heroin again, not about me, not about his work. He blinked back tears and turned away. The thought of the physical and emotional price of his desperation scared me even more. I saw the power of Lenny's addiction and how profoundly it held him.

When I picked up the paper a couple of years later and saw that Lenny had died, I was sad but not surprised. I'll never forget that final picture of him they ran. He was naked, sprawled out on the bathroom floor. It is an image seared in my memory. I wanted to rage at the stupidity of what he had done, but it was the first time I'd seen his face look peaceful, like a boy just fallen asleep.

I still feel a profound sadness in Lenny's death. The great truth of Lenny Bruce is that he was a brilliant comic. The greater truth is that he was addicted to heroin—it took his life and cut short the legacy of his art. He couldn't save himself. The drugs killed him as they have many people in my business. It takes a lot to survive, and far too many don't. But Lenny was a modern Messiah, and his was a brilliant talent that is now lost to us.

ELIA KAZAN, who was running the Lincoln Center training program then, said I moved through life with clouds of drama about me. New York in those early years did feel dark and drenched with drama. I was battling a lot of fears about my ability, yet at the same time I was still driven to learn all that I could and determined to succeed at all costs. I found a lopsided little apartment on Spring Street—the back wall was literally about a foot lower than the door. Walking from room to room, the sensation was either downhill or uphill, only peaks and valleys, a bit like my life then. It was in Greenwich Village, way down in the far south end before that was called SoHo, and at thirty-five dollars a month it was all I could afford.

There was a tiny sleeping alcove with just room enough for a single bed, a living room, and a little kitchen—well, a stove and a sink along one wall. Every morning I would go uptown on the Eighth Avenue subway, get off near Fifty-seventh, stop at Schrafft's, and pick up a coffee to go. It was great coffee, strong and milky, and I'd take it with me to Carnegie Hall, where the Lincoln Center classes were held in practice rooms above the auditorium. Carnegie Hall was badly in need of repair then, but I loved the graceful architecture and the charm of the place, and I could feel the history as I walked through each morning.

Anna Sokolow, already a renowned choreographer, taught dance and movement, Bobby Lewis taught acting, and we had Arthur Lessac for voice. They'd let me off early on Wednesdays so that I could make my matinee performance in A *Man for All Seasons*, which I stayed with until the summer of 1963.

As a teacher, Anna was really my cup of tea, very serious about the work, a great choreographer of modern dance still working in New York. Bobby was a witty, roly-poly sort of guy, a good acting teacher in the Stanislavski tradition. But he wanted it all spelled out. His was a strict, by-the-books method. He went at acting like you were diagramming a sentence, very rigid I felt. By the end of class, I would be so aggravated with him. I didn't want to write everything down. I wanted it to exist in my pores, not on paper. I wanted to analyze the character and the action, but in a jazz fusion sort of way, rather than his highly structured technique. But, you know, he had a point. The more specific I am in the choices and the clarity of what I'm doing— the bull's-eye of the action—the better it is. I, in my youth, was a little impatient with it, but he made his point and he was right, in his way.

Kazan used to say you tap into the river of your experience. There are moments when bam! You're in the river. If you can get the character's experience into your own, the parallels coalesce, they come together, and only then will you finally give the character life. I consider myself a Method actor, for sure. The bottom line on Method acting is just that you experience the moment rather than indicate the moment.

I would spend my days at the training program Monday through Friday. Then the play on Broadway meant eight performances a week, six nights, two matinees. It was exciting, intense, but it was also lonely. I had never wanted a conventional life. I didn't want to find a man and marry and be consigned to a world where he made the money and my role was wife. I had a chance at that in Florida and ran from it.

I know there are people who are happy in marriages that have lasted a lifetime. But looking from the outside, it often seems that it exacts a kind of compromise that I wouldn't be able to live with. Though I was confused about many things, I knew myself well enough to know that I would not be able to give that much, to be so self-denying. I chose to go this way, to go for achievement and creative pursuit, not of fame and fortune as much as I wanted to be good at my art. But that didn't make it any less lonely.

Bette Davis talked about the isolation one feels as a woman in this profession in her book *The Lonely Life*. I read it that year and didn't want to believe it. I hoped that there would someday be enough room in my life for my work and a long-term relationship, a commitment. At times I've had one or the other, but never both together. But I'm enough of an optimist to believe there is time enough still.

Sometimes I feel the choices I've made have condemned me to this lonely life. Increasingly I enjoy my own company and I love the solitude of study and reflection, the private time necessary for my work. I need a lot more of that than most people because I am trying to achieve in my work something very detailed and very deeply thought out. But I still yearn for walking on the beach with a man that I adore. What I think I miss most is sharing the little moments of life with another person; the companionship and the sharing of fun and good times. Along the road, as I fulfill myself in my life and my work, I hope that I will meet my own Gatsby, the man that I'm destined to be with.

KAZAN AND WHITEHEAD had picked three plays that would be the first offerings of the Lincoln Center Repertory Theater. All three would be staged in the spring of 1964. Arthur Miller's new play, the auto-biographical *After the Fall*, was to be the first, followed by Eugene O'Neill's *Marco Millions* and S. N. Behrman's *But for Whom Charlie*. The entire company, including the fifteen of us who were students, gathered in a big rehearsal hall down on Second Avenue above Ratner's Dairy Restaurant for the first reading of *After the Fall* in late October 1963. It felt like a momentous time. We were part of what would be a new tradition of theater in this country.

The day opened with Kazan trying to give us that sense of history. This was our chance to reignite theater in this country, he told us. "People like ourselves are only rarely in control of our own lives and destiny," he said. We could either choose to make something happen or end up like the playwright Clifford Odets, who later in his career was always on the verge of writing another play, but never quite got around to it—and then death intervened.

The room felt electric by the time Miller came to the front to read us his play. It's rare, but it's quite unlike anything else, to hear a playwright read his or her own work. Though the voice is usually untrained and doesn't carry the kind of texture and resonance that you hope you will ultimately bring as an actor, there are nuances of meaning that emerge and emotions that seep through and bring you a deeper understanding of what lies behind the words on the page.

Essentially this play is one man's internal examination of his conscience, his values, his own actions, and the pain of how we let each other down as human beings. The set was to be minimalist and somewhat surreal as the production was designed to be played on a series of stages that were of varying heights, echoing the caverns of the mind. The second act focused on Miller's tumultuous relationship with Marilyn Monroe. Miller's character, named Quentin, was played by Jason Robards, while Maggie (Marilyn) was to be played by Barbara Loden. When Miller read it, you could hear the authenticity, the pain, the emotion of it coming off the page. When a playwright reads his own play, it is *him*. It never can be that again when it's performed. Then it's a company of actors interpreting what was originally written. So hearing Miller, or any playwright reading his work, is truly a unique experience.

We were about four weeks into rehearsing *After the Fall* when someone walked into the rehearsal hall and pulled Kazan aside. He came back, his face drained of all color, and called us all together. President Kennedy had been shot in Dallas. Everything stopped. He tried to send us all home for the rest of the day, but I don't think anyone left. There was a sense of complete disorientation, as if you might be lost forever if you walked out the door.

I sat in a chair feeling numb and full of pain at the same time. Tears began streaming down my face. Someone found a television set and hooked it up, and most of us spent the afternoon and into the evening in front of it. It was eerie. The voice of Walter Cronkite sounded small and very far away, lost almost within the cavernous room. For a while, as day turned to night, the room was lit only by the television, the only sound that of the newscasters narrating the unfolding events as if even they could not believe it was reality either.

Though I had never been much of a political animal, for me the Kennedys were an exception. Camelot and this beautiful, intelligent couple trying to reshape the country into something better was a dream, in a way, for someone with my background. He seemed to be reaching out to all the disenfranchised who began life on the other side of the tracks, and she brought an elegance and sophistication that was transforming the image of American grace and style around the world. For me, the Kennedys represented everything one should aspire to. I thought it impossible not to feel their magic, and always I felt a surge of patriotic pride that he was our leader.

I grieved along with the rest of the country. In this death, it felt as if something intangible had been lost as well, something that we would never be able to recover. Though the company began rehearsals again the next day, a kind of uneasiness set in. The weather was bitterly cold and gray, the death of the president lingered in everyone's mind, and we huddled around the fire of this theater led by Kazan and Miller and Whitehead, and it warmed us.

It was to be a season of death. Two weeks later, when things were beginning to return to normal, Kazan's wife, Molly, had a stroke and passed away. Though Kazan had been involved with Barbara Loden for some time and they would later marry, he had stayed with Molly and stayed close to her, and her death tore him apart. But you go on, you just do, and we did.

In the midst of all this grayness of death, Miller's characters, so beautifully observed, touched us. The rivers of these plays I work on always flow through my life as little streams and rivulets. *After the Fall*, and the humanity held within its pages, became a part of the stream running through me. Every play I've ever done, the words of it and the things I love in it, are with me still. That November, we all worked on with great pain, but with great beauty as well.

AFTER THE FALL opened in January of 1964 to generally good reviews. Early in the run of the play, I started climbing up on the catwalks that ran high above the stage. There I'd lie, stretched out on the narrow walkway, and watch Barbara Loden. Hers was a demanding role anyway, trying to plumb the depths of Marilyn Monroe's descent when she was going out of her mind with alcohol. But Barbara was a wonderful actress and her performance was chilling. I'd first seen her work in the film *Splendor in the Grass*. The role had been a small one, but she was brilliant in it.

Every night of the play, Barbara was able to pull out this incredibly tortured, wrenched performance, with never a false moment. And I mean never. I would watch from above and wonder how she did it, how she got there every night, and how I could find my way there. I watched and I learned, as if by osmosis. By absorbing everything I could, when it was time, I gave it all back.

I was understudying the German wife and playing various walk-ons—a nurse, a governess, an ugly girl—with the other young lights of the company: Jack Waltzer, who's a well-known acting teacher now in New York; Jessica Walter, who may be best known for *Play Misty for Me*; Joanna Pettet, who went on to films, including *Casino Royale*; Stanley Beck, who would go on to be in the 1974 film *Lenny*; Clint Kimbrough, who would get a major role as did I in one of the later plays, *But for Whom Charlie*. I was really in heaven—this was what I wanted. And yet I was agonized as well. I did not feel comfortable in my own skin.

Ralph Meeker was going out with Salome Jens at the time. They both had principal roles in *After the Fall*, with Salome playing the role of the German wife that I was understudying. Ralph, who was one of the central figures in the company, had decided to throw a big party at his apartment and invite the entire Lincoln Center crew. He was building a substantial career for himself, getting good notices for his work onstage, and he had been in a couple of movies already. Ralph was probably best known then for playing Mike Hammer in *Kiss Me Deadly*, the 1955 film adaptation of a Mickey Spillane mystery. He was definitely one of the more successful members of the group, pursuing both film and stage careers.

I always felt somewhat nervous around these people like Ralph, who had a measure of career success. I thought that I had talent; by then enough people had told me so. But I was frightened that I wouldn't be able to shape it into something that was exceptional. I wanted to be a great actress. I was determined to do that. But I was scared. In those early days, I was working too hard to make it happen, and you can't do that with acting. *It* happens to *you* as a result of your thoughts and feelings. I never trusted that in myself, and I always tried to make it happen. Pushing, we call it. But you can only think the thoughts, have the feelings, and that is what creates the emotions. Kazan taught me that. You have to be available to the moment. Great acting is very interior—you don't force anything to happen—and that's what I saw when I watched Barbara, and it's what I didn't see in my own performances yet.

I was finally miserable enough that one day I asked Kazan what he thought about analysis and did he know of anyone I might see. He put me on to a wonderful man who was actually his wife's, Molly's, analyst, Isidore Portnoy. Kazan said Molly had done a lot of work with him, and he thought it had been quite helpful. Then just a few weeks later I overheard Kazan tell Clint Kimbrough the exact opposite, that you could do years of analysis and accomplish nothing. But it was said in the service of interpretation, of helping Clint with his character. I immediately distrusted Kazan. I went to him and said, "Does it work or not?" He said, "Sure it works, of course it works." And it does. But Portnoy's name and number stayed tucked in my address book.

Each day I found myself growing more frightened. The emotions were all just so much in me, with me, that there wasn't a moment that I didn't feel saturated by them, drenched in them. I couldn't shake those negative feelings. But for me, at that time, I didn't understand what was triggering this deluge of emotional darkness. I knew even less about how to begin to deal with it. Kazan once said to me, "You think your emotions make you weak. They don't—they are your strength. They're who you are." But I couldn't get beyond the image of my mother's tears—they seemed to me those of a victim. And so, until I had reached the point where I could no longer bear it, I could not, would not cry.

THERE WAS A NIGHT when the fear and depression just swept completely over me. Emotionally I was exhausted. I didn't know if I could grit my teeth and get through yet another day. For a long time, since those days at Franklin Square, my life had been about work, and I really didn't find it easy to go out and find friends. I had a few, but we were not yet very close. Those connections were always difficult for me. There was no one to talk to in New York yet whom I truly trusted. I was still very young and I was very much alone, and on my own.

When you hit that level of depression, thoughts of suicide start creeping in. I thought about it, wondered what it would feel like— death, the road there. I took a razor blade and watched, transfixed, as I sliced it across my leg. It was an easy stroke, just a sting, and then the sight of that line of red oozing out, perfectly straight, against the white skin. I felt removed from it all; it was a drama to which I was the only witness. I was writer, actor, and director—with the final scene still unfinished.

My hand started trembling, and I couldn't stop shaking. I dropped the razor and reached for a washcloth with one hand, turned on the faucet with the other. Water splashed into the sink. "Here, Dorothy Faye, let me show you. Take the cloth in each hand and wring it, like this." My Olma's words, there in the night. Dorothy Faye. Where had I lost her? "Now here, you try it. You'll learn how to do it for yourself." I had to work through these fears and get to the other side of them. But I knew that I couldn't do it alone anymore. I needed someone to show me how. I called Isidore Portnoy.

When I told Portnoy about it, he got furious. "That's a pretty puny attempt," he said. I think it was partially a ploy to make me feel I was stupid to ever try such a thing. But nonetheless I can't pretend I'm in the ranks of great suicide attempters. There were some very low moments, but I was then and still am too much of a fighter for that. There was too much of a life force at work in me.

Portnoy told me sometime later that he would never forget the first time I walked into his office. "You were twenty pounds overweight, dressed completely in black, and in the throes of self-hatred." The weight was just one part of the struggle. Why was I so unhappy? I had worked hard for everything, nothing had been handed to me. Why did I hate myself so? I wanted to find an answer.

It was during this period in my life that I began my long foray into analysis to see if that would help. And it did help. For a good portion of my life, I saw analysts off and on. It was the thing to do, and I was as fascinated by the psyche in general as I was concerned about fixing mine. Some analysts helped me to better understand the dynamics of my life and the unresolved pieces of my past that were eating away at me, and some, I think, helped me not at all.

At times it seemed I was facing an impossible catch-22. The very things that drove me to succeed as an actress—my need and wish and desire for perfection in life—were also the things that worked against me in my trying to find my own happiness. It took a long time for me to learn the craft of acting. This fear and this need to do it great, to do it perfectly, and the feelings and patterns of behavior that go right along with all of that, are the internal struggles that I wrestled with for years.

Analysis is not what I do now, but for a long time, I thought it was a real salvation. And I do think that the discoveries I made there made a big difference in putting me where I am today. It's not nothing. Analysis is a very important science . . . and an art. I talked to Robert Coles, the psychologist, for a while, who is a genius at it, and others also helped. I never will forget sitting long afternoons in the study of Bob Coles out there in Concord, Massachusetts, in this room filled with books and photos of people who were important in his life. Bob and I would sit there for hours on end. It was as if he could weave words from the air, and the way he spoke was a tapestry. He'd go from one thought and one connection, and that would swing into another, and he never once lost a thread. I am amazed at the understanding this man has of human behavior, how it connects, where it comes from, and what the truth of it is. For me, what I do, what any artist does, is really an inquiry into human behavior. I was grateful that I had these long afternoon moments, drinking cups of tea, listening to Bob and trying to figure out who I was.

IT WAS A BIT crazy once we began rehearsals for the first season of the Lincoln Center productions. We were rehearsing all three plays at once, each play on a different floor. *After the Fall* was on the fourth floor, *But for Whom Charlie* was on the third, and *Marco Millions* was rehearsed wherever we could find the space.

Step onto a different floor and you were immediately in a different reality. Underneath it all, no doubt shoring up a good portion of our far-flung troupe, was Ratner's Dairy Restaurant and dear Bernie Birns. He was a patron saint to all actors, and there were many days that I lived on nothing but Ratner's hot onion rolls and the mushroom-and-barley soup. Bernie had very wiry gray hair, was always quite well-dressed, the proper landlord, and a real soft touch. I think he considered all of us as part of his extended family. Sometimes I'd wander in there at the end of the day, really low, and Bernie would buy me dinner. There were a couple of guys in the company who were forever fighting hangovers, and Bernie was usually the one to help put them back together again the next morning. For years, every time I went to New York, I couldn't leave until I'd stopped by Ratner's for mushroom-and-barley soup and onion rolls.

I had a role of some size in the final production of that first season, Behrman's *But for Whom Charlie*, which opened in March. Kazan was directing. Years ago his wife Molly had nicknamed him "Gadget" and we all called him Gadg. He was the sort of director who is always accessible to the actors; there was never a feeling that he was unapproachable, or that everything was written in stone.

The man had a level of energy that could leave you breathless trying to keep up. One of his greatest gifts, though, was his instincts when it came to people—he knew what roles they could and couldn't handle, and he knew what to say to get the performance he wanted out of them. It is widely conceded that he wrote the book on the relationship between directors and actors. Everyone knows you look to Kazan to learn what is the best way to get great performances.

His was a magic touch and I never saw a time when it didn't eventually work. I'd finish a scene and he'd say, "That was so wonderful! I love how you did that. Now, just try it this way." Years later when I did *The Arrangement*, the film adaptation of Kazan's autobiographical novel, he would do the same thing with all of us, scene after scene. After one scene that I knew wasn't working, I finally said, "Gadg, it wasn't wonderful—you know it wasn't and I know it wasn't. Why do you keep saying that?" He shot back at me, "I've tried telling people the truth, and I've tried praising them, and it's always better to praise them." I said, "You're right." You usually know when your performance is awful, but it still helps to have somebody saying it was great, and at the same time allowing you to do it one better.

It's a little like love. Or like in the song "Paper Moon," as someone dear to me would suggest some years later: "It's only make-believe . . . but it wouldn't be make-believe if you believed in me." The thing is, Kazan believed in us, you see. So we were allowed our latitude to be bad, and still be told that we were good. We could go way out there and jump off the cliff, and he'd still say, "Hey, that was good." We'd still be loved, really, and that was the trick.

I loved *But for Whom Charlie* for its satire, where good, old-fashioned honesty is pitted against the rising economic opportunism of the day. As Faith Prosper, an aspiring actress, I was able to spend the evening falling in love with just about all the men I came in contact with. I might not allow myself to be flirty and frivolous very often in life, but at least I could throw myself into the role onstage. I closed out the first season of plays feeling like much had been accomplished. I was still struggling, but gaining confidence with each new role I took on.

MICHAEL O'BRIEN entered my life in the summer of 1963. On Sundays, I would go to brunch at a friend's house, where a lot of struggling New York actors made a habit of dropping by. Uptown, it was. All these out-of-work actors, all of them geniuses. Michael was there with Robert Duvall and Dustin Hoffman, whom we called

"Dusty," and as I recall I first noticed him when they were in the midst of acting out dirty jokes. It turned into a rather blue impromptu farce, in a Three Stooges kind of way, and everyone in the room was breaking up over punch lines that you could not only hear but see illustrated in somewhat graphic detail.

Michael did this incredible mambo routine where the character he was playing was always just off beat. All the time during the dance. And yet this character believed that he was on the beat—more than that, that he was the best dancer in the world. So on the face you have this look of complete authority, but the body was going just off the beat. Now that's chillingly hard to do. He was brilliant. And it was brilliantly funny.

Michael would have been hard to miss in any event. An extraordinary face that looked as if it had been fashioned by a sculptor, good bones he had, and eyes, great deep caverns that you could wander around in forever. He worked at a club, Upstairs at the Downstairs, where he waited tables. He lived just down from the ANTA Theater on Fifty-second Street, where A Man for All Seasons was playing. We were truly soulmates. There were a few people in my life like that, people easy to be with, as Bob Dylan put it, "when you want someone you don't have to talk to." Michael was like that. I didn't have to talk to him. It still felt comfortable. He always seemed to know what I was thinking, and I knew what was on his mind. We just accepted each other, as is. It was a very nice feeling, and I felt like I had found a port in the storm.

His stepfather was Cuban and was a strong enough influence that by the time I met him Michael had a definite Latin streak to him. It was a charming kind of sexy-machismo. Between his charisma, his intellect, and his drop-dead good looks, Michael O'Brien was hard to resist. He used to call me Niña. Little Girl. He would take me dancing, and to Cuban restaurants, and everyone called him Miguel.

Though the relationship began with dancing and dinners and talks into the wee hours of the night, perhaps what bound Michael and me together so tightly from the beginning was our shared pain. We both had felt the depths of depression, and there were wounds, still unhealed, from our past. I was starting to find my way out of the darkness, but life was only growing darker for him. In his mind, there were huge pools of depression that worked at him like quicksand and would just suck him under.

Michael's walk-up was so close to the theater I was performing in that I would often drop by. But I started dreading those stairs. Many times I would climb them not sure if I would find him alive or dead. Sometimes I'd get halfway up and just sink down on the step, holding on to the handrail, unable to go any farther. He really wanted to kill himself, and I knew that.

As much as I feared otherwise, I wanted to believe that his talk of death was not truly serious. There was just too much brilliance and too much good to throw it all away. Though I didn't see it at the time, in Michael I was repeating the role I'd taken on as a child with my mother. I believed that somehow it was in my hands to make everything better. If I made A's, my father would come back; if I only loved Michael enough, he would want to live. He believed just as strongly that there would come a day when it was all too much, when he couldn't stay here any longer, even for me.

By the time my career had begun to take off, a few years later, Michael and I had already begun to drift apart. I couldn't go through each day wondering if he was going to be alive at the end of it. He came to see me in Miami, where I was shooting my first film, in the spring of 1966. My room opened out on to a little balcony. I remember he sat there in the doorway, his back resting against one side, his feet propped up against the other, just staring out, saying nothing, completely unreachable.

I was back in New York several months later, when a friend called one day to say that Michael couldn't be found, he was missing. The night was chaos—calls to friends, to his apartment, to the club. The next day someone managed to get into the apartment. Michael had committed suicide. He had taken sleeping pills, then downed a bottle of Kaopectate to make sure the pills stayed in his system. I began helping to organize the funeral, which kept me from falling apart. As soon as I had nothing to do, that was when I crumbled.

I don't know that I ever felt we were going to make it; there were not enough good times. But Michael had been my first real love after Gene. Sometime during the night after his wake, I ran out of tears, but I still couldn't fall asleep. I wanted to lock all this up in a box and put it in the attic, let it gather dust. I didn't want to look too closely. What had made life too much for him?

Once Michael told me he thought the profession of acting was more suited to a woman than a man. I thought he was completely wrong, and told him so. But he was raised by his stepfather to have a certain Latin male dignity. To be a struggling, out-of-work actor was, I think, more demeaning for him than it might have been for other people. This was an accomplished guy, he was smart, he was great. But there was a lot of fear. And though we shared a lot, there were fears that he had that he kept private. Fears of his that I never saw.

WHILE THE Lincoln Center Repertory Theater had been started with the idea of serving art, it soon ran headlong into the great god commercialism. That was my first encounter with art and commerce. Commerce and art. Of the first three plays the company put on, only Arthur Miller's *After the Fall* made any money. The next year, 1965, we staged *The Changeling*, in which I played Beatrice's maid, and *Tartuffe*, and we had no better success in ticket sales.

In this country, even in theater, it's about having a hit. You either have a hit or you don't. But that's not the fundamental purpose of a repertory theater company, which is supposed to be about something larger, to nurture the art form. It is also to bring to the audience plays that will make them think, great works of art, classics, as opposed to the latest rage. But we were judged from the beginning as if we were putting on a Broadway show, with all the razzamatazz and currency of something topical, designed to make money hand over fist.

Kazan and Whitehead were fired after the 1965 season ended and were replaced by two new artistic directors, Herbert Blau and Jules Irving. The two had cofounded The Actor's Workshop of San Francisco and had long been partners. Blau had written a book called *The Impossible Theater: A Manifesto*, in which the first paragraph closed with Blau likening himself to a crazed Lear shouting the words, "Kill, kill, kill, kill, kill, kill," which certainly seemed to be the attitude about the Lincoln Center company.

We who had loved Kazan and Whitehead were horrified at the sensibilities of men like this in the theater, which ought to be a place of love. They seemed gross and not very great men, whereas Kazan clearly was a great man of the theater, as was Whitehead. Blau and Irving were not cut from the same cloth as Kazan and Whitehead by any stretch of the imagination. There was a revolt among the actors in the company, petitions were written, and letters of protest drawn up.

The Russian Tea Room, then as now, was a great hangout for

people in the theater. Harold Clurman, the legendary theater critic and a member of the Lincoln Center board, lived just across the street and used to go there all the time. At one point, a group of us actors were huddled in coats walking around New York City trying to find these board members to talk to them directly. Maureen Stapleton, who was one of our little band, said, "Well, where do we go to find Clurman, the Russian Tea Room?" So we tracked him down there. This delegation. All of us were wandering the streets of New York trying to change this situation. But Blau and Irving stayed.

As WE MOVED toward 1966, I was feeling really good about what I was doing at Lincoln Center, despite Blau and Irving. With a steady two hundred dollars a week now as a member of the company, I had moved to an apartment on West Fifty-fifth. Leaving Spring Street, where life was lived on a 35-degree angle, was a relief, and the move put me much closer to the theater district, which had become my life's blood. I'd turned down the offer of a spot on the TV soap opera *The Guiding Light*, because I was convinced the stage would be where I would spend the next few years of my career. I was intent on being a serious actress, and though the salary was tempting, I was worried that a soap opera might lock up my prospects for good. If I took the part, I knew there were those who would never take me quite as seriously again.

But most importantly, I was worried that a soap opera might push me into habits of working that would be awful. You had to do all these stupid lines and learn them all every day and go and do them the next day. I just knew that wasn't the kind of work I wanted to do. If you work on a soap opera, that's the ball game. You're forced into doing this very superficially observed work. I didn't want to play that kind of ball.

We were scheduled to do Jean-Paul Sartre's *No Exit* at Lincoln Center as a workshop. In preparing for the play, I had begun working with an acting coach, Andreas Voutsinas (he now has his own theater in Paris). He had had a close liaison with Jane Fonda for a number of years and I think had influenced her early work. Andreas and I were not romantically involved, but I credit him with teaching me some of the most important things I ever learned about acting. Working with Andreas, it all started to coalesce as a way of working for me.

We really went into the subtext of it, discovering the details that would fill each moment, uncovering what was happening each step along the way. Often once you're onstage you completely forget everything you've detailed, but it's all stored in your memory bank. You can then go into the moment and react purely and completely instinctively. I remember working with Frank Langella at Lincoln Center on a scene, and he just kind of showed up and went with the flow. He's a wonderful actor, but he was a different kind of actor than me. More trusting. I was too fearful to leave a given moment onstage to fate. I needed to know what I was going to do moment to moment in order to feel secure enough to go with the flow, to sit in the lap of the gods.

I always think it's kind of fun that the top balcony in the theater is called "the lap of the gods," because that's where you put yourself when you act. There are actors like Frank, whose work when we were both young actors at Lincoln Center together was more emotional and instinctive, but my taste has always run to those whose acting shows intellectual cragginess. I've always loved Christopher Plummer's *Hamlet*, because it was smart. And the choices were really intellectual choices, and unusual. I always like the mind that tempers the emotions.

My work with Andreas was an extension of what I had first tried to do with the Second Girl in *Yerma*, but Andreas helped me to do more than understand the process—he helped me finally to apply it. It was like French. One day I reached a point where I simply heard the words and responded in kind. I was no longer translating French to English in my mind, I just understood.

Years later, Sharon Stone introduced me to Roy London, a great acting coach, who was also in the tradition of Andreas in terms of these choices, which were very far-out choices. And the ability to make the interior choice that is a shocking choice will get you going. Rather than just thinking, I want him to open the door for me, think, Well, what do you really want him to do? What, in the deepest depths of who you are, do you want that person to do?

These kinds of choices can get to the subconscious things at work in you. Andreas and I worked in this very specific way. It made me realize the kind of embroidery that could be *behind* the lines. And that's what is played. You never play the lines. So Andreas helped me find this fabric. The lines are just the tip of the iceberg. What is underneath is what you play, what's really going on. It's like that wonderful line from Miller in *After the Fall*, "We're not talking about what we're talking about." And that's true of acting. And life. You're never talking about what you're talking about.

In the fall of 1965, I was working on *No Exit*, and I knew that I was good, that I was starting to know what I was doing. I felt alive on the stage and things were happening as I was doing it. It was the best work I had ever done. Irving and Blau didn't agree. They called me in and told me they didn't think I was right for the company anymore. A line from *No Exit* flashed in my mind as they were handing down my fate: "Hell is other people!"

As I was a member of the old company, the situation was a bit like that at a movie studio when one studio chief is replaced by another; usually the new studio head wants to surround himself with people of his own choosing. Irving and Blau made a pretense of keeping us on, but eventually all of us either left or were fired.

I felt cheated out of a chance to perform *No Exit*, to show at last what I was capable of, but I was determined that I would succeed despite them. One opportunity had been snatched out of my hands, but I would find another. Two weeks later I walked in to audition for *Hogan's Goat*, an off-Broadway play by an American playwright, William Alfred. And nothing would ever be the same again.

THERE ARE turning points in everyone's life, though we often don't recognize them until later. But I knew that somehow this play was going to make a difference for me.

The role of Kathleen Stanton was the most beautiful I'd ever read. The lines she is given are as finely drawn as any I would ever read again. I desperately wanted to get a chance at this role. It's always really something close to mystical when you find a character with such dimension, and such possibilities. You read it and you know in your very soul that you can give it a shape and texture that is unlike what anyone else would do, a unique concoction of your experience and your craft.

The play was set for American Place, an off-Broadway theater that had only just been founded a year earlier to feature the work of living American playwrights. It wasn't actually a theater yet, but St. Clement's Church, which had been converted into a temporary home for

A scene from Bill Alfred's Hogan's Goat *in 1966—the Off-Broadway hit that gave me my career.* C. Martha Holmes

American Place. *Hogan's Goat* was to be staged during the second season. The theater was in the sanctuary, and it had a mystical beauty that was an ideal backdrop for this morality play.

I walked into a rehearsal room and read from *Hogan*. But I didn't get the part that day. The director, Frederick Rolf, wasn't sure I was right for the part, but the artistic director, Wynn Handman, wanted me to come back again. I came back another day and read once more. When I had finished, William Alfred, who was sitting in the back of the room this time, leaned over and told Rolf, "Don't let her get out of the building." They didn't. I signed a contract for the run of the play, seventy-five dollars a week, with the premiere set for November. Ralph Waite was cast as Kathleen's husband, Matthew, and Tom Ahearne, who had been forever on Broadway in *Guys and Dolls*, was Edward Quinn, Matthew's nemesis.

I don't know how you can look at those who are close to you and determine who's more important in a life. Each person is on a different axis. But with the exception of my mother, and yes, my father, my brother, and now my beloved son, Bill Alfred has been without question the most important single figure in my lifetime. A teacher, a mentor, and I suppose the father I never had, the parent or companion I would always have wanted, if that choice had been mine. He has taught me much about the virtue of a simple life, about spirituality, about the purity of real beauty, and how to go at this messy business of life. And to top it all off, our time together was always punctuated with howls of laughter. As well as being known as the Saint around the Harvard campus, he was hilariously funny. Bill has also taught me about great literature and great art. He is indeed my mentor.

When I first read *Hogan's Goat*, it gave me the measure of this man. He had woven the nature of good and evil into a complex tapestry. Even those characters who are driven by hate and revenge are treated with a gentle hand. Kathleen is a young bride from Ireland, come to Boston with her husband, and deeply troubled by the circumstances of her marriage. A devout Catholic, she's been wed three years, but the service was a civil ceremony, not sanctioned by the Church. When the play opens, this secular wedding, she thinks, is her sin. But scene by scene she discovers there are greater transgressions, that the brick and mortar of her life has been a web of lies.

It is an emotionally taxing role, with Kathleen spending much of the play in a series of drunken rages as she fights it out with Mattie, a man she loves even as she rails against his deceit. In the final scene, I'm to tumble down the stairs to my death. It took us days to choreograph the fall so that I wouldn't break a leg or be bruised and yet still give the audience the sensation that I had truly fallen, or perhaps even been pushed by my husband. No stunt doubles here. We worked it out so that my ankle would hook around the banister at a couple of points to help break the fall. I had to know at each moment where I was and find places along the stairway that held me secure. But I had to do it quickly, like any transition in acting, so that the audience never sees me catching myself.

This was the first time the play had been produced, so everyone was feeling their way along, trying to find the right notes. We were deep into rehearsals and I knew Kathleen well. Rolf was working with us on blocking one of the final scenes. I'm on the back of a steamboat, and have been drinking heavily. Quinn is the corrupt aging mayor who is out to destroy my husband and has picked this moment to do it by destroying me. He tells me my husband has committed the sin of bigamy. That indeed he was married to a woman named Agnes Hogan, much older than he, a powerful woman in the Irish community of Boston. Hence the play's name, *Hogan's Goat*. I sit there lost in that flood of words, suddenly knowing that I'm living in mortal sin, and I'll be excommunicated, with no chance of going to heaven. And worse, that Mattie has lied to me all the time I have known him.

At that moment, Kathleen is a woman in a place of great tragedy. I'm standing there swaying in the wake of Quinn's words, as if their very force will not let me stand any longer. Tom, playing Mayor Quinn, wanted to come over and take my arm and comfort me. And God bless him, Rolf thought that was a good idea.

It was, I thought, an exceedingly bad idea. "If he comes near me, something awful would happen," I told Rolf. "I would have to hit him, I would have to kill him . . . he daren't touch me now." Rolf was shaking his head, Tom was shaking his. It was clear that I was not winning my point, when Bill, a distinguished Irish-American poet and playwright, got up in a very quiet, gentle way and walked over to the director, and said, very delicately, "She's right." Then sat back down.

Bill knew how one's heart beat. Sometimes it's very difficult for people outside to find their way to the interior of those kinds of moments. But when you're both inside the same moment and see it the same way, there's an amazing kind of communication that occurs. Bill Alfred was to become my greatest teacher.

We began talking about how one looks at material as an actress and as a playwright. He really taught me how to work. We talked first about Kathleen, then other characters, then other plays. It is a discussion we have not yet completed. Bill and I collaborated again in 1971, when *Hogan's Goat* was made into a television production for PBS. After that, I began sending him all my scripts. We would look at them together, sometimes spending days building a character's story. In my various roles over the years, when my dialogue did not work, when a scene seemed to have reached a dead end, Bill would come in and rewrite it. He has a keen understanding of great writing, which helped me as an actress to try to make great characters. It was a search for quality that we embarked on long ago. I trusted his instincts and his writing. He's the greatest artist I've ever worked with.

HOGAN'S GOAT opened November 12, 1965, and was very quickly a hit. A few weeks after opening, American Place held a benefit show and invited Jackie Kennedy to attend. Though we were beginning to get our share of celebrities and dignitaries in the audience, it was an extraordinary night to be performing for the former First Lady. I couldn't help but think back to that November day just two years earlier.

At the party later that night, she was everything I had expected, elegant and articulate and exceedingly generous with her time, talking to all the actors. About an hour into the party, Tom, who was of pure Irish stock by way of Brooklyn, had cornered her for a few moments. He spent the rest of the night going from one group to another replaying the conversation: "Jackie said it was the best acting she'd seen. You know what that's worth? That's worth seven Oscars." For the rest of the night, the words "seven Oscars" echoed through the hall. It was high praise indeed.

The play was drawing such crowds that the run was extended for a few weeks. Finally, with another play already scheduled at American Place, *Hogan's* was moved to the East 74th Street Theater, where it ran for two years. There were other Kathleen Stantons to follow me during that run, but it has been my blessing to have originated the role.

FIVE

T HE NIGHT IS COLD and I have the deck of the *Malahne* to myself. The water has turned suddenly rough and my cheeks are stinging from the salt spray. The black wool shawl, which covers me nearly from head to toe and keeps the chill at bay, is from an earlier excursion to northern Italy. The design is simple, utilitarian, a coarse weave with long peasant fringe, the kind that has been worn for generations by the wizened white-haired women who populate the rural villages there. I loved it and knew one would not be enough. I bought three. Only one remains now that is not threadbare from years of use.

This yacht, I've decided, is Sam Spiegel's true love. He dotes on it, calls it his "boat," and once you set foot on board you know you've entered Sam's kingdom, and it is an opulent one. Tonight, the *Malahne* is plowing through the Mediterranean headed for Saint-Tropez, where some of the guests want to spend tomorrow browsing the shops. Sam has a smaller launch that will take us in. One of my favorite shops, Choses, has wonderful French lisle knit button-downs, terribly thin, and they feel like cotton cashmere. I had intended to pick up several for myself and for someone in my life, but as it happens, he and I are at odds right now. Though I usually love these excursions, I am debating whether or not to make the trip to shore.

There are nearly a dozen of us here, an eclectic mix—European dignitaries, Yul Brynner and his wife, a foursome of young beauties each hoping that Sam will make her a star, a couple of Hollywood money men, and me. To create the easy luxury that Sam demands, it takes a crew of about twenty, and a chef, no doubt with *cordon bleu* ribbons stashed away, who delivers the most extraordinary cuisine night after night. But I am in a stormy place, and not much matters to me.

When I step into the main cabin below, the wind whipping at the edges of the shawl, Yul tells me I look like King Lear come in from the heath—dark and troubled. Sam is there, with a girl on either side. He has grown to tolerate my indifference to his advances, and finally, this trip, seems resigned to the idea that we really are going to have a professional relationship and nothing more. This truce has taken me six years to negotiate.

I probably took our stalemate more seriously than Sam, whose affairs were as well chronicled as his films. But Sam had the capacity to treat one with a benevolent paternalism that was very seductive, and that was enough to keep me on edge most of the time I was around him. I was forever looking to make things right, but I didn't want to turn Sam into the father I felt I'd lost. I had spent enough time in analysis to know that was going to be my eternal Achilles heel, a broken connection that would color and cloud all of my relationships with men, both personal and professional.

Sam intrigued me, though, and I loved to listen to his stories, which he told with a great deal of charm. He spent some of his time living and working out of London, and kept an apartment on the top floor of Grosvenor House until the end of his life. The life he made for himself was one that was filled with both luxury and art. He knew how to live well and he treasured beauty. His wonderful collection of impressionist paintings that he added to through the years was ultimately given to the Israel Museum. Until then, they looked at home on the walls of his Park Avenue and other apartments, like art should be, a part of life. Sam never lost his sense of the value of something that was rare and beautiful.

When I first met Sam in 1966, he was already a legendary movie producer, having made *The African Queen*, *On the Waterfront*, *The Bridge on the River Kwai*, and *Lawrence of Arabia*. I was a young actress with a promising stage career, and Hollywood had just begun to nibble. Joyce Selznick, who worked with Sam's production company, had come to see me in *Hogan's Goat* because the reviews, which had been quite effusive, piqued her interest. A buzz was building up around the play and my performance in it. She called to see if I would come over to the production company office.

I met first with Joyce and Elliot Silverstein. He was a hot young directing talent, just come off the surprising hit *Cat Ballou*, which had gotten five Academy Award nominations and earned Lee Marvin an Oscar for Best Actor. Young and intense, he was set to direct one of Spiegel's next projects with Columbia Pictures. The movie would be a smaller one, by Spiegel's standards. At the time, the working title was *Mr. Innocent*, and Anthony Quinn was signed as the principal star. I had gotten the script the night before. The character was named Sandy, one of a gang of disaffected college-aged kids. After I met Elliot, we began to read. We read for two hours. I think we must have come close to going through the entire script, which I took as a good sign.

Joyce scheduled a screen test, and if they liked what they saw on film, they would call. It was strange being in front of a camera, wondering whether or not I should play to it, how it would see me. Other than a small part on an episode of the TV series *The Trials of O'Brien*, starring Peter Falk as a rumpled detective (early shades of *Columbo*), and the family photos my mother insisted on as we grew up, I had not worked in front of a camera. Film can be a very unforgiving medium; flaws that are blurred in normal life are magnified under the lens. I would learn over time about lighting and angles, all the elements that can work either for you or against you. The camera would become one of the more significant relationships in my life. But on that day, I was a novice.

It is the intangible that is so crucial on film, that spark of energy—does the camera read it, does it capture life and breath as well as flesh and bone? A young acting colleague of mine, Jimmy, at Boston University, had called it "the shine." After that, I would scan the faces in all the productions I worked on, looking to see who had the shine. People said I had the shine. But now I stood there, wondering, as the camera kept rolling. I turned this way and that, walked around, followed assorted directions, read some lines, and in general felt quite foolish and awkward. Walking back to my apartment on West Fifty-fifth afterward, I couldn't get away from feeling that all the skill in the world wouldn't help me if the screen test was flat. But the call came, the film looked good. Sam was to tell me sometime later, "The camera loves you."

I walked into the office to finally meet the great Sam Spiegel and there sat a rather portly older man. He was already in his early sixties then, balding, with a few strands of hair carefully combed over the top. Sam was nothing extraordinary to look at, but there was a kind of charisma and intensity about him that absolutely filled up the room. Sam had a worldliness and sophistication about him too. He was a tough man and smart, but he had a real sweetness to him, Sam did. And I responded to that. He loved paintings, sculpture, films, all art. And he knew how to catch your imagination and run with it, send it soaring. He had a grin on his face, a cigar in his hand, and a grand plan in mind.

As Sam spun his tale, I sat there barely believing what I was hearing, but willing my face not to give me away. I was star material, he said, the kind of actress that could expect a thirty-year career, which seemed like something close to forever. Sam wanted to sign me to a five-picture deal. We'd do one a year, and then see where things went after that. The details would be worked out with my manager, Simon Maslow, and my agents. The first, *Mr. Innocent*, would pay me about $25,000 for six weeks or so of work, which was more than double what I had ever earned in an entire year. The title credits would include a separate line: "Introducing Faye Dunaway." I was already scheduled to fly to London the next weekend to test for another film, *Funeral in Berlin*, starring Michael Caine. But Sam was offering a sure thing, a multipicture deal with a contract already drawn, just awaiting my signature. The decision wasn't a difficult one to make. Once again I would turn down London for a job in the States.

After I called my mother to let her know, she hung up the phone and composed this poem. There is no title, just this notation: "Saturday night, February 12, 1966, 11:30 p.m. Faye called from New York to tell me of signing her first movie contract with Columbia. My thoughts:"

> *O! Lord, hold my Baby high,*
> *With feet in hands, up into*
> *The starlit sky.*
>
> *Let not man deter her height,*
> *But gaze upon the lovely sight.*
> *Would they know the road*
> *She trod to gain this height;*
> *They would respect with all*
> *Their might!*
>
> *Some day when the Star shines*
> *With heavenly bright;*
> *The world will know the ray of light.*

O! Time burns away the years;
Bringing her destiny so near, so near.
Hold her Lord with upward arms;
And keep away all hurt and harm.

My first movie, and what exotic locale had they chosen to shoot it? Florida. I was going home. Before I left, I borrowed two thousand dollars from a friend to buy a new wardrobe and gave her a stack of postdated checks to pay off the debt. I knew I needed something that wasn't off the rack of the 99-Cents Store if I was going to be the star that Sam Spiegel was predicting I would be.

WITH SAM IN CHARGE, I entered the star machine at warp speed. One day, I was a starving artist in New York who barely made enough to pay the rent on a walk-up. The next day I was in a first-class seat on a plane to Miami for the start of production. A car and driver was there to meet me at the airport. They would stay with me throughout the production, transporting me to the set and back to the hotel and anyplace I chose in between. The next day I was assigned a makeup man and a hairdresser. The production people took care of everything. They fed me, they dressed me, they poofed and polished. I came South with dark brown hair and wound up a honey blonde to accommodate the way Silverstein and Spiegel envisioned Sandy. It was almost a Brigitte Bardot look, brushed back and teased, the cookie-cutter blond bombshell.

The costumer promptly put me in a push-up bra and hip-huggers. My entire wardrobe consisted of less rather than more—miniskirts, minishirts, and acres of bare midriff. My navel got almost as much exposure as my face in this film. I was in a thin phase, not much more than skin and bones, 115 pounds on my 5'7" frame. But I did 150 sit-ups religiously every morning to keep my stomach taut and only allowed myself to munch on salads and lightly at that.

The production company booked the cast into the Palm Bay Club, a small, elegant old hotel that catered to the Miami jet set. There was a balcony off my room overlooking the pool and tennis courts. I woke up at five o'clock most days before the early morning tennis games began. We were nearly always shooting by eight. Everything in my life was changing and at a dizzying pace.

Within weeks, I had a six-picture deal with Otto Preminger, another legend, which topped my five-picture deal with Spiegel. Both deals were nonexclusive, it was just a matter of juggling shooting schedules. Preminger was a serious director whose work already included films that were classics—*Laura, Anatomy of a Murder, Exodus.* He'd seen me in *Hogan's Goat* and ordered up a screen test, about the same time I had tested for Spiegel. First on tap was to be *Hurry Sundown,* a meaty story of class and race set in the South. I wondered briefly if I was destined to only be in films shot below the Mason-Dixon line.

First Sam Spiegel, now Preminger. Boom. It was all happening so fast. It's exciting, it's invigorating, it's life on the edge and in the fast lane. As Bill Alfred's mother said to him when he was a boy, "Show me some speed." And I loved it. But life in the star chamber is made of very dangerous stuff. It's easy to get used to it, this life, and the truth is you're damned lucky to ever get out alive. A lot don't. But if you handle it right and you become an Oscar-caliber actor, that buys you options in Hollywood's futures market. Suddenly you have the chance to make of your career whatever you will, to ply your trade in any medium—theater, film, television. I was given that chance. I've made good decisions and bad ones, but remain forever grateful that I had decisions to make.

Fame. It's easy to get drunk on it. Not so easy to keep life in perspective in a world where reality is temporarily set aside. On the first few films, you might eat at the tent with the crew and the extras. But before long there is someone who brings your meals, prepared to your specification, on the china of your choosing. The car that picks you up and brings you back home is replaced by a limousine; the cubicles you dress in become trailers, and trailers grow ever larger and more luxurious. It so removes you from the details of your own reality that it's just scary.

In recent years, I have purposely stripped my life of many of the trappings of stardom. I live simply. I have taken charge of the details of my life. No press agent. An agent, and a little mafia of assistants— but no longer any one person who "runs" my life.

For so long, everybody else took care of my life and I was left in the air, unmoored, not connected to the basic realities which organically create the real world, which create my life. That's the danger.

You're out there in some rarified atmosphere, and you're tempted to turn over to somebody else the details of your life. One fine morning you awake to find you don't have a life anymore because you've turned it all over to someone else.

I reached a point where I said, "How does my life work?" In the early nineties, I began to fastidiously and zealously and in a very determined fashion take back my life so that I know how it works from the ground up. Now I know who to call when my electricity goes out or when I have to get a parking permit. Those little "mundane" bits and pieces of a life are very important to my sanity. I don't live in a rarified atmosphere where "it all happens elsewhere," as Pinter says in *Old Times*. It happens with me now. I touch everything in my life. I connect with the truth of my life. And only from that position of real reality and connection can I go to anything else, whether it be a relationship with my son, a man, or my work.

Then, too, as times change, you change. One day, you are not the person who gets the limousine all the time. As Mary Pickford said, "I've been rich and I've been poor, and rich is better." It was so fast for me in the beginning. College. Broadway. Movie star. I never, they say, paid my dues. But I never saw it that way. I happen to think that all my life up to the moment of *A Man for All Seasons* was dues-paying. And I paid a heck of a lot more during my career.

I took long hiatuses from the pressure of the business, and an entire decade in the eighties in London to get away from it and live a "normal" life with my infant son. I think I lost ground when I stayed in England, away from the business, which would not have been so had I stayed here and stayed on track and in the ball game—out of sight, out of mind. I'm still regarded as a big star, so I still get the perks of stardom. Yet for all the bumps, I wouldn't have missed the ride for all the world.

ONSTAGE, what had mattered was my performance. Until this first movie, publicly, I was the sum total of a handful of newspaper clippings, a line in a review mentioning my name, and if I was lucky, a kind word or two about how I had handled the role. Even with the success of *Hogan's Goat*, the play and the performance were still the thing. Now I was facing a steady stream of reporters coming to the set wanting to talk to me. Who was I? Where had I come from? They wanted to know about the life that I had been trying to forget. The entire enterprise took me by surprise, so when I was asked about my ambition and drive, my reactions were uncensored.

When I look back, what I see in those interviews is a picture of raw emotions and a younger me, patently hungry for fame and attention, and brutally honest. "I became an actress because I have a desperately pathetic wish to be loved, to be admired, to be respected," I told *Parade* magazine. "I want to be a star, I want to be famous, I want to be rich, but most of all I want to be a healthy human being." It took me a while to figure out this was just another role, another performance; the trick was in keeping Dorothy Faye in the background, protecting her, and letting Faye Dunaway take center stage.

My instincts told me I had to look great, get the makeup and the hair perfect. At the same time, I had worked so hard at the craft of acting, at getting a proper education, that I didn't want it all lost behind the fake bosom and the blond hair. I remember asking the director, Elliot Silverstein, if the padded bra was really necessary, we were artists after all. He looked at me and laughed. "Yes, I think it is." Sex and commerce had won. But I worried that I was losing whatever was left of the real, authentic, genuine me. Once your image is on the big screen, larger than life, it's not completely your own anymore. Anna May Wong, who appeared in *Shanghai Express* with Marlene Dietrich, said the camera takes a piece of your soul. I began to understand that, to feel less real, and more a creation of other people. It took me until the third film to get rid of the pushed-up bosoms. The blond hair's hanging on, though. I wrestle with it still.

Even now I look back at the pictures taken of me in these roles through the years, and the last one where I really looked like myself was taken on *Hogan's Goat*. I look at me as Sandy in *The Happening* and already, baby, the transformation was in place. Like Dorothy in Kansas, I was picked up by the tornado, whirled around, and finally spat out. When we finally spiral to our bottom, to the lowest point, that's just a way of getting us back up again and back to who we are.

WHILE OTHERS wanted interviews, *Esquire* only wanted pictures. The magazine sent down Jerry Schatzberg, who was a very hot fashion photographer at the time. It was the Antonioni *Blow-Up* era, where photographers were stars, and Jerry was one of them. He searched out and found a secluded strip of beach and we set out for a day of shooting. One of the myths that still lingers is that I began my career as a fashion model, not an actress. The photos that Jerry took of me on the beach in Miami were the first shots of that kind ever taken.

Jerry told me *Esquire* was in the business of finding new stars and showcasing them in the magazine early on. Even though I'd left the New York stage and *Hogan's Goat*, there was still a residual buzz surrounding that performance, which had been pumped even higher by the Spiegel and Preminger deals. The editors had decided that I might be "the" new star on the horizon, the one to watch. There is pressure in that sudden glare of the spotlight. What if you don't measure up? Once again I was torturing myself with "what ifs."

The photos ran in October of 1966 along with a short essay called "The Line of Her Back." In the opening shot, a grainy black-and-white, Jerry has me sitting as if I've just awakened. My eyes are still closed, my head is slightly turned, cheek against my shoulder, hair loose around my face. I'm leaning on one hand, a sheet pulled up with the other. The curve of my bare back is what catches the eye. I still love that photo for its drowsy sensuality.

The other shot is pure beach baby. I'm lying stretched out on my stomach on the sand in a blue-and-white checked bikini with the top unfastened—no tan lines—and my hair in loose swirls in the sand. Although I think the effect was supposed to be sun-drenched languor, to me I look as if I might jump and run at any moment. There is a line of tension across my shoulders that I know is there, even if no one else does, and a wariness in my eyes.

There was a real gentleness about Jerry. He sensed what was cool on the outside was terrified within. At one point I began crying because he was being heartbreakingly kind to me. All my life, I've been the sort of person who could shatter easily. I've never been able to bear being hurt, so rather than feel any kind of emotional pain, I've usually snipped off that kind of relationship, even friendships, and just closed myself in and everyone else out. It is why people have thought of me as cool, removed, even cold. It is my only protection for this painful tenderness that I felt inside. I'm not saying I wasn't strong. I was. But I was also very fearful and very vulnerable. But Jerry somehow managed to reach me, to let me know that in this I could trust him, that the photos would be wonderful, that it would be okay.

I HAD BEEN in Miami only a few weeks when I learned that David Begelman and Freddie Fields were interested in me. David and Freddie were big ol' Hollywood agents, I knew that. The two of them had masterminded the career of Judy Garland and just about every top movie star that had come down the pike in recent years. And I knew this was my boat to get on and get there in.

David had seen me in *Hogan's Goat*, and wanted to meet me for a couple of hours over lunch at the Palm Bay Club to talk about my future. It was a Sunday and he was flying down from New York for the day. David, who was with one of the top talent agencies, CMA, Creative Management Associates, flew in that morning and found me at poolside. I was wearing a white two-piece bathing suit, and with the new blond hair felt like I looked pretty terrific. He said when he spotted me that I looked like 250 million bucks sitting there by the pool.

I knew very clearly, long before David had called, exactly where I wanted to go and how fast I wanted to get there. I wanted to be a great American actress, to conquer the stage and film and television. There were actresses who had come before me whose work inspired me, moved me, but I never wanted to look or sound or act like anyone else. I wanted stardom and I wanted a unique identity to go along with it. Just as years earlier I had hidden my dreams from my mother for fear, as illogical as it was, that she would somehow take them from me, this career was going to be mine, no one else's.

David was a tall, elegant man—intelligent, charming, and knew the business absolutely. The movie industry was completely virgin territory for me. I didn't know the producers, the directors, or the intricate web of relationships that binds Hollywood together. What I needed then was a navigator. By the end of the day, when David was finally leaving to catch the last plane out that night, I was convinced he and Freddie could chart a path to get me where I wanted to be. I nicknamed him "Lightin' Begelman" later. Once I signed a contract and was in the elevator before I realized what I'd done—he was that fast, and that good. This summer, his production company in dire straits, David became depressed. In August, he ended it all with a single gunshot. Yet another crushed by the pressures of this world.

I TOOK TO MOVIES, and everything about them, like a duck to water; I was truly in my element. The cadence of the work, and the structure of it, just fit my sensibilities. When you're doing a film, you're not doing much else. The movie set becomes the world, your entire world for a while. And I loved that kind of focus, that necessity to concentrate all my energy on a single set of demands. Troubles could be put on hold, at least for the moment, because the film absorbed all the attention.

The Happening, which is what *Mr. Innocent* was ultimately titled, was a fast-moving caper story, not an art movie at all. The pace of the film was set to the beat of Herb Alpert; even some of the dialogue sequences were written with a very specific rhythm to them. It was a sort of rap, long before there was rap. The director's idea was to examine what would happen when establishment and antiestablishment forces clash, to see what truths would emerge on both sides. The story was also one of generational differences, only a few years before the country would be torn apart by a generational war where the rallying cry was "Don't trust anyone over thirty."

The establishment is represented by Anthony Quinn's character, Roc Delmonico, an ex–mob kingpin who has become a respectable businessman. The antiestablishment piece of the equation is made up of Sandy, my character; Sureshot, Sandy's love interest, played by Michael Parks; George Maharis, as Taurus, the self-appointed leader and ultimately a loose cannon; and Robert Walker, as Herby, a sweet, nebbishy kind of hanger-on who's trying to keep up with us faster kids. We're bored, rich college students and have far too much time on our hands. I remember Elliot telling us we should be absolutely saturated with the decadence of it all, to the point where there is no feeling. I kept trying to just think those thoughts, trying to reach for a kind of emotional numbness to provide the nuances of each scene.

I begin the movie with the words "I'm hungry." A little more than an hour and a half later, the movie essentially ends with us in a burned-out shack buried deep in the backwater, with the same line, "I'm hungry." Bookends. I loved that. This is a character who is never satisfied. Not at the beginning. Not at the end. Food, kicks, college, nothing is enough to really engage her. I knew something about that kind of hunger.

In the opening scene, Sandy and Sureshot are making their way

My first movie, The Happening, *with Tony Quinn in 1966.* Copyright © 1966 Horizon Dover, Inc.

through a Dante-esque vision of the Garden of Eden, the aftermath of an all-night party where the human foliage is as thick as the Florida Everglades, aspiring stars all of them. I am thinking of my constant internal tug of war—the part of me that believes that I have talent, and the part that fears I'm replaceable. That night I had a dream that I walked onto the set, and my name was still on the canvas back of the director's chair, but it had been printed upside down. My topsy-turvy world.

THE HAPPENING also turned out to be a crash course for me in making movies. I watched, I asked questions, I learned. Tony Quinn was a wonderful, generous teacher. He really introduced me to the etiquette of acting in film. On one occasion we were working on a scene together and they were setting up to get a close-up of Tony's reaction. It was a fairly poignant moment when he learns that not only will his wife not pay for his ransom, but that she's rather delighted that he's out of her life, possibly for good.

"You're off-camera, but you have to work even harder, Faye," he told me. It's true. When the camera's on you, it's much more frightening, and you need the other actor in the scene to really be there for you to play against. If they relax because the camera's not on them, it's far more difficult for you to keep up the intensity level so that your reactions are true, so that the emotion isn't forced. Otherwise the moment is false, and with a close-up, there is no room to cheat the lens.

What I learned then, I still do today. When I'm not in the shot, I'll stand with my face very close to the camera and play the scene, so it pulls the eyes of the other actor close to the lens. I play the scene fully, so that the actor who's the target of the camera is able to get as much help as he can off-camera. He is responding to what I'm giving him. I've always said, you can only be as good as the actors you're working with. You can't act in a vacuum. Too many actors now don't know these things, don't care about them either. I can understand not knowing; I can never reconcile not caring. When the close-up's mine, I need that reality across from me. The eyes of my partner become my anchor, my safety net, so that all the other distractions can be blocked out.

I started watching the takes very closely and the rushes each night. I began to realize that in film, even more so than on the stage, performances are tied together. A single weak link can destroy the essence of a scene. Forever after, the talent and the skill of the people attached to a project became a real consideration for me. As I began to learn this very considerable craft of moviemaking, I found I was fascinated by it. I always want to know how something works, possibly because I can then hope to control it so that I'm not at the mercy of it. It's a blend of curiosity and a need to master it all.

WHILE I BEGAN to soak up the details of filmmaking, Elliot Silverstein talked to me about the aesthetics. Elliot was not what I expected a movie director to be. He was not much older than most of the cast, and we were, for the most part, in our twenties. He had completed graduate school at Yale and taught for a couple of years at Brandeis. He brought the sensibilities of a philosophy professor to moviemaking. *The*

Happening might be a caper, but that didn't mean it couldn't be layered with meaning.

This film mattered a great deal to Elliot. After the wild but completely unexpected success of *Cat Ballou*, he wanted to prove that he was not a one-trick pony. With some directors, a film becomes a proving ground, and the director will turn autocratic and inhuman. But that was not the case with dear Elliot. With everyone working together, this was a comfortable, trouble-free set.

That's not to say there were no problems. Most of the film was shot on locations around Miami, and there were elaborate action scenes that needed certain concessions from the local authorities. In one, a helicopter was to land in a shopping center parking lot during rush hour. That got a quick no. Then Elliot had his eye on the city's North-South Expressway for an elaborate chase scene that takes place near the end of the film. He wanted to borrow the expressway for a few hours—rush hour again—and that was nixed as well. We ended up staging the chase on what was a four-lane side street, but it never had the visual impact that the expressway would have delivered.

But moviemaking, I was learning, is often about invention along the way. You want the best of all possible worlds—locations, actors, dialogue, directors—and you rarely get them at the same time. So you adjust, you alter the scene, you massage the dialogue, you turn a deserted trailer park into the Everglades, which was done with amazing attention to detail on this film. Essentially, you work with what you have to make it the best that it can be. At times, it is the ultimate shell game.

THE JOKE on any Hollywood set was "the girl," sadly, and *The Happening* was no exception. We women are called "the girl." So I began to make a joke out of it. To say, in an ironic way, "Well, 'the girl's' here." "Are you ready for 'the girl'?"

At the same time, I liked playing around with the notion of creating a sexy character. For once I wasn't someone's wife or daughter. I took my voice down a register, a lower husky sound. The acoustics were so different from a theater too. I could turn down the volume, use softer tones to create different effects. And one's body moves differently. There is more room for subtlety. I wanted to get to the kind of latent aggression that exists when you know down to your bones that you look terrific. My eyes look heavy, languid in most of the shots. I wanted to create a certain presence on-screen with Sandy. *The Happening* wasn't just a movie, it was a shot at the big time. And when I watched the film later, once I got past cringing, which I always do, I thought I'd hit something in the performance that was quite unusual.

Ironically, the look that caught the fancy of photographers had nothing to do with my bare midsection, and even less to do with any sort of subtlety. It was a tight black leather skirt that came just above my knee, with a wide silver zipper running all the way down the front, a black turtleneck, with the sleeves cropped very short, then black leather gloves. The outfit was all topped off by a cap in an old newsboy design, made out of black-and-white wool houndstooth. From the neck down, the design was theirs, but that cap—which one photographer after another wanted to perch atop my blond hair—was one I'd picked up when I was in college in Boston. I had been stuffing my hair up into its puffy recesses for years. That cap had guts and sex appeal and I knew it.

The cast was a set of walking contradictions. Tony Quinn was by then a formidable actor, who had begun on the stage and was forever going back to it. He gave very deeply dramatic, textured performances. George Maharis was a Hollywood sort of guy, terribly nice, a television hero whose acting was very much drawn from his experience there. The two acting styles could not have been less alike.

Michael Parks, who seemed locked forever in a James Dean sort of anguish, was the resident *enfant terrible*, at one point walking off the set in a funk. But Michael was a very good actor, trying to do good work. It was just a difficult process at times, with a lot of clashes. I was trying to do the best work I could; at the same time I didn't want to make a wrong move. I didn't want to lose this chance. When there were fireworks, Robert Walker and I became sort of partners in crime, much the way Michael J. Pollard and I were soon to be on *Bonnie and Clyde*, the repetition of the little brother in my life. He was a funny, easygoing guy, who made the long hours seem a lot less tedious.

There was a lot of running either from or after someone in *The Happening*. In fact most of the scenes were quite physical. Elliot would play Herb Alpert tunes as we were shooting. I thought it very clever. Having a musical playback will do something to the rhythm of the scene; you begin to intuitively shift your actions to be in sync with the beat. It gave the running and jumping about a syncopation that helped to create the kind of surreal human landscape Elliot was looking for. The music was ultimately more of a hit than the movie, with Diana Ross and The Supremes singing the title track.

The love scene between Sandy and Sureshot was kind of hot too. Very hot. It was a real sort of player performance. Michael was wonderful and I got to be quite aggressive about it all. Creating that kind of sexual tension in a series of takes from a variety of different camera angles very quickly becomes a lot more work than fun. But it is fun.

The crew really become your friends, your family, and your audience. And if they like you, you know you're in pretty good shape. They're your fellow workers. If I'm standing somewhere and a table's got to be moved an inch, I'll move it an inch. We're all in sync with each other. It's a team. That was a new sensation for me, playing to this intimate audience that—unlike in theater, where the audience is at a distance and filled with strangers—gets to know you very well. It becomes a close-knit group. And you joke and you laugh.

I thought the relationship between Michael and me was a very interesting if conventional screen relationship. I do concede to thoroughly disliking the final twist on their affair, though. As soon as I want Sureshot to tell me he loves me, he leaves. It's the old cliché of the guy wants the girl, and when he gets her and she falls in love with him, he leaves. It's the male chauvinist formula, "don't get trapped." We think that's what men have to do. That a man can't say, "Gee, I'm glad you want me to stay, I'd love to stay." A sad comment, though true for the world of these characters, perhaps.

One of my favorite scenes was toward the end of the film. We're all standing around in the old burned-out shack. We really burned it while two fire trucks, firemen with hoses in hand, stood by. But the caper is over, the money rests in a charred heap on a table inside, and there is a strange mix of light and shadows playing across my face. Moving, reacting within the light and shadows, made it something other than ordinary. It was telling, tragic stuff, a moment of reckoning for Sandy.

Sandy was a strange sort of reckoning for me as well. I had never had the luxury in college to be rich, bored, and cynical. Much of the revolution that was just beginning to ferment on campuses around the country had blown right past me. Between my ambitions and my long-distance run from the past, I hadn't the time to be disaffected. Though I was rejecting the lifestyle of my parents, it was their poverty not their affluence that I wanted no part of. It was amusing being inside a rich world, but look out, Faye, look out.

I SPENT most of 1966 setside, as one of my very chic New York friends, Ara Gallant, was later to call the process of going and hanging out on a set. Setside. As opposed to, I don't know what else. Setside, though, is what he called it, very chic like on an ocean liner. He was nothing if not chic. After production wrapped on *The Happening*, it was just over a month before I was due on location to start filming *Hurry Sundown* with Preminger. The story was a volatile one that touched just about every southern sensitivity when it comes to social class and race relations. Otto had planned to shoot in Georgia, but then-governor George Wallace apparently didn't take too kindly to a story in which poor whites and blacks were the good guys, and rich white families were the villains. After a lot of back and forth, the production was finally set for Louisiana, near Baton Rouge.

How Otto and his staff ever thought Louisiana would be better than Georgia I'll never know. We had landed right in the heart of Ku Klux Klan territory. There were threats before we showed up and they continued throughout the production. A few times the threats turned into reality, though thankfully no one was hurt, at least not physically. Guards were with us at every location, from farm fields to small towns. And after one homemade bomb exploded at the motel, guards were posted there too.

Even finding a place there that would house all the members of our cast, black and white alike, had taken a series of negotiations. A deal was finally struck with the Bellemont Motor Hotel, its claim to fame being that at the time it was the second-largest motel in the U.S. I don't think anyone was sufficiently curious to ask who was number one. It was a huge complex reaching in vain for an antebellum look, with big white pillars lining the front. We were all put in a wing, with the staff trying to segregate us from the other clientele as much as they could.

Otto refused to make any concessions when it came to race; it was either all of us or none of us. When someone in the governor's office called to invite the cast to dinner, or at least some of the cast, Otto declined. When it came to the pools at the hotel, we managed to integrate them, or at least one of them. The motel management tried to force Otto to keep the black cast members from using the pools, but he fought to have one set aside exclusively for the movie company. Unfortunately some of the locals got wind of it, and a crude bomb was tossed in the pool late one night. Thankfully the damage was minimal. Though Otto and I were to have a major run-in of our own, in this one thing I admired his willingness to go to the mat.

This was small-town Louisiana—there weren't too many diversions where we were filming. Jane Fonda set up a jigsaw puzzle in her room, and it turned into a hangout, with people stopping by and playing to pass the time. On weekends, when we could, a gang of us would make trips into New Orleans. There were long summer evenings in the French Quarter spent drinking Ramos gin fizzes and wandering down Bourbon Street. My first brush with the fickle nature of fame happened when Jane, Michael Caine, and a bunch of us were sitting in this bar. People were coming in off the street, their hurricane glasses in hand, weaving in and out, looking over to see all the movie stars. Finally one of them lurched toward us, stopped at the table, and said, "Which one of you is Troy Donahue?" Finally we realized he was referring to me. Troy Donahue. Faye Dunaway. A star is a star is a star—much like a rose.

HURRY SUNDOWN dissected all the notions of race relations in changing times, in a way that I felt was brutally honest. I'm a southern girl and I had witnessed the rise of racial tensions as I was growing up. There were the patricians in town, who were not at all threatened and tended to maintain friendly relationships with the only blacks they generally had any contact with, those they employed. There were whites at the bottom of the socioeconomic scale who were terribly threatened by any emerging economic and political power in the black community, and many of those did end up either in the Ku Klux Klan or siding with them. There were lower-middle-class whites, which my people were, who were more worried about putting food on the table than about racial problems.

My mother's side had a very deeply ingrained sense of integrity and fairness coming from my Olpa, who always went to the Bible for his inspiration. The word "nigger" was never used in my house and I'm extremely uncomfortable even making the reference. Where I would see the prejudice in contemporaries of mine and their families, I did not see it in my own. I don't know quite why. They were farmers and it seemed that you worked in the fields, everyone else you knew worked in the fields, and people were black or they were white, and you were treated more or less the same. I was raised never to judge the color of their skin. The changing dynamics of race and class that I had seen growing up in the South were all dissected in *Hurry Sundown*. The film was destined to be haunted by controversy.

THE CAST included Michael Caine, whom I'd met during my *Hogan's Goat* run in New York, and had just missed working with on *Funeral in Berlin*, and Robert Hooks, whose work on Broadway I knew by reputation. John Phillip Law, a colleague from my Lincoln Center days, was set to play my husband.

Though there were three major roles for women, Jane Fonda really had the lead, as the rich girl in town and Michael's wife. Jane was the May Queen in this film. She was the bigger star, and Otto wanted her to be the main star of the movie. Jane was always a slightly bigger star than I was. She came in before me and I was always kind of in her footsteps, in an odd way. We shared the acting coach Andreas Voutsinas, and when I was in England in the eighties, beginning to look back on the American shores, I watched what she did with her career and how she reinvented age for women on film. She was fifty and she played late thirties. She carved that out for herself, as a very important leading lady well past the age that leading ladies normally are. I still admire her and count her as a role model.

I took on the role of Lou McDowell, a dirt farmer's wife who has to walk as dark an emotional tightrope as Kathleen Stanton had in *Hogan's Goat*. I finally agreed to take the role because the character was very much like my mother. At the time, I was in the middle of filming *The Happening*, and there was no time to concentrate on anything but the moment. But as soon as I got back to New York and began to really look at this character I had committed to doing, I knew it was going to tear at my emotions. I knew Lou McDowell. I knew what it was like to be a farmer's wife, to be that poor and to be waiting for a husband to return from the war. In that sense, I was home free. But it really wreaked havoc with me emotionally.

Hurry Sundown became a psychodrama that left me feeling damaged at the end of each day. Lost in the past I had fled. The danger in finding your way deep inside a character is that you can get lost in there. Some get so close that they come and live with you a while. Years later when I was doing *Mommie Dearest* there were nights I could feel Joan Crawford's presence in the room, sitting in the window.

It was anguish walking around in Lou McDowell's shoes. She was so like my mother. I remember hearing as a child how she hated going to school with holes in her socks—dogged by feelings of never measuring up to the kind of women represented by Jane's character, the archetype of all those "nice folks" my mother felt looked down on her. There were moments, sitting through some of the hot summer afternoons waiting out a slow soaking rain, that I felt absolutely caught in this time warp from my past. Although I had wanted to play Jane's character, in the end I was happy to play the role of Lou. It was really a homage to my mother I was doing, because it really was my mother.

And in the sometimes agony of living through a life that was very much like my mother's, the weight came on again. You can look at many of my films and literally see it, from the beginning to the end, that slowly I start the descent from thin to, well, thicker. I'd use food to counter the stress of the filmmaking, which of course never worked. I've never stopped guarding against a return to that kind of emotional reliance on food, and as I grew into this sophisticated world, alcohol. I'm finally beyond that now, but it was the pendulum I would swing on for years.

LONG BEFORE *Hurry Sundown*, Otto had become legendary for his clashes and his temper. He was known as a brute and a tyrant. There are those directors who believe the best work comes out of conflict, but I think it was just Otto's nature to be confrontational. When it came to our particular row, I know it was ego rather than art that was at question.

Otto knew from the first day of shooting what he wanted *Hurry Sundown* to be. He had a very tightly conceived notion of things and tended to work at imposing his idea of how a performance should be done on the actor or actress. Otto is an example of one of the many directors I've survived. Barbara Hershey once said to me, there are three kinds of directors: one who will help you, one who doesn't hurt you, and one who will drag you down. Otto was one of the ones who dragged me down.

Otto was one of those directors you can't listen to because he doesn't know anything at all about the process of acting. I didn't think he was ever right. My eyes would glaze over and I would do an interior monologue so that I wouldn't hear what he was saying. You're in such a sponge state when you're gathering a role, anything said goes into that sponge. So it was a difficult process because I was having to stand there and say, "Yes, of course, uh huh, uh huh, okay," then go ahead and do it the way I wanted to anyway.

Otto was so autocratic and dictatorial, I suppose he thought he was being an auteur. Later I was to work with Roman Polanski, who *was* an auteur, who was just as autocratic and dictatorial in many ways as Otto, but he was a good filmmaker. And Otto wasn't.

There were days on the set when the tension came in waves. You could feel it, and I swear there were days you could see it. We were shooting one groggy Louisiana day when the sun was dodging in and out of the clouds. After hours of trying to get a take right photographically, with no light change in the middle of it, a bus had passed or somebody had dropped something so that the sound track was not usable, and the soundman said, "No, no, no, it wasn't good for sound." Otto shot back in his heavy German accent, "Mr. Jones, we cannot dub in the sun!" Freddy, whom I was later to defend, piped up, sotto voce, "It was good for hair."

Michael was one of Otto's favorites on the set. Their cordial relationship was a result of Michael making it clear very early on that he was not to be bullied. He came to the set knowing of Otto's temper and determined to do an end-run around it. I think most people think of Michael Caine as Alfie, that sort of persona. And off-set there is a bit of it there. But when he works, it's clear that he feels that every take matters. You could see the change in his face; once the camera started rolling there was nothing going on but the work. He was very determined about getting it right, absolutely right.

It was the first day of filming and before the first scene was shot Michael walked over to Otto and said, "If you're going to say anything rude to me, I'll go to my trailer and I won't come out." I'm convinced that if Otto had tried to call him on it, Michael would have shut the door to the trailer and not emerged without first getting an apology.

Otto backed off and as far as I know he made it through the long, relentlessly hot weeks without being "rude" to Michael.

It was not so easy for John Phillip Law, who was playing my husband. Otto never let up. There are times when actors and directors go through an entire film and never connect, never truly understand what the other wants. That was the case with John and Otto. John was sometimes slow to catch on to what was wanted, and Otto had no patience with him at all.

One incident occurred when we were shooting the homecoming scene, when John's character has just returned from the war. It's the one I played like my own father's return from his tour of duty in Japan. I'm a young wife seeing him again for the first time in a long time, and I'm feeling very tentative. But in his absence there has still been the farm, and the work there waits for no man. So while he was off at war, I'd been left to hold it all together. And now with him come home again, I had the license to break apart. This woman loved this man deeply, as my mother had my father, and had been without him for so long, so the tears just started to come. We went on, and on, and on, take after take. It never occurred to me that I wouldn't cry on cue, I just did it.

I was crying time after time. After a while my makeup man was going crazy between takes trying to get my nose and eyes back to normal. Whatever John was doing with his performance, it was not what Otto wanted. He finally called out at him, "Mr. Law!" Otto always called him "Mr. Law." "She cannot cry all night, and you must get it right!" But he didn't stop there. Otto went after John, tearing him apart, and the words were stinging. We had heard that there was always one scapegoat that Otto found in the cast whom he was merciless with, and John was it. It's difficult to understand the depth of the rage until the full force of it is turned directly on you.

I was in a little plaid sleeveless blouse. We were at the farmhouse set. It was late enough in the day that I could hear the hum of the crickets in the background. It was steamy hot, and Otto was drenched with sweat. Nothing was going right with the scene. Freddy Jones, the hairdresser and a very sweet man, said something. Otto went crazy and began yelling at Freddy.

I had witnessed Otto's anger for weeks now, but his attack on Freddy just struck me as so unfair, and Freddy seemed so defenseless.

I said, "Otto, it's not his fault—" Otto turned on me like a mad dog and went at me. His face turned red, his eyes were bulging, and with his shaved head, the effect was extraordinary. I didn't say anything; I just watched him. Watched while his eyes glazed over, the saliva gathering in the corners of his mouth. His hands squeezed into fists so tight that the knuckles turned white. He was no longer focusing on me or anybody else. I think it was the only time I've really looked full in the face at somebody who's gone into that sort of complete state of rage, unblinking and refusing to react. I just froze.

The words shot round me, hurled with machine-gun-like speed. His body was shaking. I looked at him and thought, How strange, he liked me in the beginning. I don't guess he will like me so much now. At some point, the sound just went; I stopped hearing anything and all I could see was this face coming at me, wild. All I could think of was that I could not imagine doing another five films with this man. I looked at Otto and said as slowly and as coldly as I could, "I don't want to work for you if you're going to behave like this." Otto railed back that it was fine with him. If I didn't want to work with him, I didn't have to work for him ever again.

We both left the set. I made some calls and ended up talking to an attorney in New York, Gideon Cashman. Otto apparently made calls to his lawyers as well. Because by the time that Gideon put in a call to an attorney in Baton Rouge to find out if what was said on the set would serve as a binding contract according to Louisiana law, the fellow just laughed. Seems that he'd just finished talking to an attorney from Hollywood who had asked exactly the same question. What was amazing, they both had just picked his name out of the Yellow Pages.

For the duration of the film, Otto never raised his voice to me again, though there was no attempt to smooth things over either. There was only that one time, but that's all I needed. Once I've been crossed, I'm not very conciliatory. While I never retreated from my position that day, Otto did. He did not want to release me from my contract with him, as he had said that day on the set. I was not going to change my mind about working for him. I thought he was awful to work with, and that he didn't do very good films. It was widely accepted that he was an excellent producer, but never a very good director, *The Man with the Golden Arm* notwithstanding. So I went forward with the suit. I didn't realize just how difficult, and how protracted, that battle would be.

This was my first encounter with lawsuits. And I daresay they riddle the horizon in this business of mine. I've had two others since then, but this one taught me that normally you do always end up settling, no matter how much you've paid the lawyers already. If you can avoid it, do so. They are so time-consuming. We went through the process of taking depositions for an eternity. There were months when it seemed that every lunch I had was with an attorney, answering another round of questions. In the final analysis, what was said on the set wasn't enough to get Otto to release me from the other films he wanted me to do. I still wasn't going to work for him again, and I told my attorney to find a way to get me out of the contract.

The answer was money. It cost me a lot of money not to work for Otto again. I paid him. I paid his attorneys. I paid my attorneys. I regret paying him, but the money didn't mean anything to me then. My freedom meant something, my art meant something. It didn't matter that I paid Otto not to work for him again, or his attorneys. I like what money buys, I liked Sam Spiegel's boat, and I love travel, and I do love luxury. But not at any cost. I now have a simple flat in New York as well as my house in Los Angeles. And I find that the way I really love to live is the way my friend Bill Alfred lives, surrounded by very beautiful old things and books. Always lots of books.

What is more difficult to assess is what might have happened to the course of my career had I not fought to get out of working with Otto. *Hurry Sundown* was very long and not very well received by critics. Not many people made it to the theaters to even see the film. By that time, I had gotten good notices for my work in *The Happening* and I was on to other pictures. It didn't hurt my career and it didn't help it. Of all the movies I've done, *Hurry Sundown* had perhaps the least impact.

Otto never had another big hit. He was constantly fighting with one actor after another. There was a long list of people who had worked with Otto once and then refused to work with him again before I ever arrived in Louisiana. Irving "Swifty" Lazar, who would later represent me, told me he once came to blows with Otto, who left the scene with his head bloodied, but unbowed. He was forever threatening—to throw you off the set, to never work with you again. I just happened to take him up on it.

Had the deal with Otto gone forward, the next movie that he had in mind for me was *Skidoo*, a satire of gangsters and hippies. The plot had the hippies converting the gangsters to the peace-and-love move-ment. The script was sent to my manager or my attorneys, but I never read it. When the movie finally came out in 1968, it was savaged by the critics, and was quickly shelved.

As much as it cost me to get out of the deal with Otto, if I'd had to do those movies with him, then I wouldn't have done *Bonnie and Clyde,* or *The Thomas Crown Affair,* or any of the movies I was suddenly in a position to choose to do.

Beyond the movies I might have missed, it would have been a kind of Chinese water torture to have been stuck in five more terrible movies. It's impossible to assess the damage that might have done to me that early on in my career. There are many in this profession who begin with so much promise, and disappear before it is realized. While I learned on *The Happening* to watch for the caliber of the people I worked with, Otto taught me to not always believe the pedigree.

David Begelman and I had talked about *Hurry Sundown* the first time we met in Miami. I told him then I had a very bad feeling about doing the movie. There was nothing specific, just a growing sense of foreboding about the project. That day we agreed that after *Hurry Sundown* if ever I felt that way about a film, I would not do it. Even if he thought it was good for my career, he told me, the agony was not worth it and he would not put me through it. In the nearly eight years we worked together, he never did.

SIX

THE STREET OUTSIDE the Cinématique in Paris is a sea of people, and the limousine has to slow to a crawl to make its way to the front. All I can see out the windows is a wall of headless torsos, though occasionally one bends as a face attempts to peer through the darkly tinted glass. As I duck out of the limo and step onto the red carpet, I turn around, planning to give a quick wave to the crowd that is chanting "Bon-nee, Bon-nee," then dash inside for the Paris premiere of *Bonnie and Clyde*.

The sight of the crowd absolutely stuns me. As far as I can see there are people. Many are young girls, teenagers; all are wearing berets, their hair styled in variations on the loose pageboy of Bonnie Parker, and wearing knockoffs of the long, slender thirties-style clothes that Theadora Van Runkle designed for me to wear in *Bonnie and Clyde*. There are close to 150 photographers, paparazzi, jostling for a spot. For a brief moment, I'm completely blinded by the flash of a thousand bulbs, seemingly going off at once.

This will be the first night that the movie has been shown in France, and yet it is already a sensation. Word of its success in London made the Channel crossing months ago, and designers from the haute couture houses who have seen the fashion interpretations in New York and London have begun to put their own particular signature on the Bonnie look. Berets, which had been cast off as horribly old-fashioned in recent years, are once again in vogue. Then on New Year's Eve, just a month before tonight, Brigitte Bardot had a special on television. For one of the numbers, Bardot dressed up like Bonnie and crooned the "Ballad of Bonnie and Clyde." All this I knew, but still I wasn't prepared.

As I blink, things come back into focus, and they surge toward me, this crowd, arms stretched out waving, shouting still. I am drawn to them, and frightened by them. I'm frozen, transfixed by it, overwhelmed by it. There is one girl whose eye catches mine, and I smile. Tears begin streaming down her face. I am just two weeks past my twenty-seventh birthday, and most of my life has been spent in an excruciating battle to prove myself, growing up feeling I had never quite done enough, would never be good enough. Here, in this Paris street, I am completely awash in an outpouring of love, affection, respect, adoration. This night is unlike anything I have ever experienced. For a moment I feel like maybe I *am* enough, maybe it will all be all right after all, this life of mine. I'm not sure I'll ever completely understand what it is that fans give you, but it is a powerful potion that I wanted to bottle up and hold onto forever.

BACK IN OCTOBER of 1966, I could not even begin to imagine the possibility of such a moment. It's the first week of shooting *Bonnie and Clyde,* the third movie I've shot this year and I haven't even set foot in Hollywood yet. I'm sitting in the middle of a field of freshly mown hay just outside Midlothian, a small town north of Dallas. The bales, which are scattered around the field, are drying to a golden brown in the Texas sun. My arms are hugging my knees up close against me. If I could disappear, make myself somehow smaller, I would. We've all just come from an old movie house in downtown Dallas where we watched the first rushes, and I am absolutely distraught. I look ugly, I feel ugly. Hoping for solitude, knowing there will be no peace, I've come to the middle of the field.

I don't know why it hit me so, but it was like coming face to face with myself, seeing those rushes. And I hated it. I couldn't stand how I was—my manners, my gestures. It was the first time I really got a sense of how I must look to other people. This was the first time I had seen myself on this big screen, with its millions of silver dots, and I just thought I was sadly lacking. I'm sure that I didn't like my work much either.

I had sat in the aging theater that reeked from years of popcorn, my feet on carpet whose design had long ago lost the battle to spilled soft drinks and crushed candy, and tried not to throw up as the images flickered by on the screen. Michael J. Pollard, who plays C. W. Moss, mechanic, getaway driver, and comic relief to Bonnie and Clyde, tried to nudge me out of my doldrums. Michael has a great, funny face. We have become fast friends already, and usually he can make me laugh with an imitation of Mel Brooks' 2,000-Year-Old Man, or something from a Lenny Bruce routine, "Fer-git-it, Faye." Nothing worked today, but he is dearer to me still for trying. Warren Beatty, my costar and one of the film's producers, and Arthur Penn, the director, were a few seats away talking, analyzing some fine point, but it didn't penetrate the place where I was.

When I saw these early rushes and how I looked, right away I was gone. Right away I was a dead woman. It was like, God, do I really look like that? Every woman has felt that. But then you are also trying to do good work. For three days afterward, I would come to the field and sit there, cut off from everyone, not speaking to Arthur. It wasn't his fault, the way I looked on film, but boy, did I blame him. Somehow it was all his fault. Silent, sullen, morose, there I sat. And finally, one morning, it lifted. I adjusted. I accepted that's who I was and that's how I looked, and it was okay, and I went on. Something about the rhythms of what it takes to live life and to accept who you are, and then change what you don't like and to go on—just the rhythms of life kicked in.

Since then, seeing the rushes has been so important to me. And it still is. I suffer terribly when I can't see them. For me to see the work connects me to it. It's as if I had performed it in front of an audience. Because the audience gives you back what you're doing somehow. Their reaction, whether it's a silent reaction, or a breath, it keeps you alive. But with movies you don't stay alive. You give, but it's dead out there. There's nobody out there. Yes, you have your crew and you have your director, but that's the team working together. Those are your stage people. Out of desperation I make them my audience sometimes. But basically, you don't have anything coming back at you.

The rushes function as an audience. Watching them, I become an audience, my own audience. It's the normal way of relationships, that if you give something, something comes back to you. With movies it's weird. You're in this time warp where you give and give and give, and there's a camera there, this fascinating, sumptuous, sexual thing. I think it's ironic that I've had two very important lovers who had cameras. Because there is a love affair. That's the thing

I perhaps wanted to marry. It's the thing I made friends with, because I knew I had to. If I was going to be an actress, I had to. But that first time when I saw the rushes, I just wanted to run and hide and not be an actress.

If you don't see those rushes, it's too easy to think that what you're doing is the most important thing, when in fact what's up on the screen is the most important thing. It humbles you to see the rushes. Beyond that, it literally puts me in touch with what I'm doing, otherwise I'm lost. I'm so hard on myself that my head will tell me at night that my work was no good during the day. I hate to see myself, because of the pain of thinking I'm not going to be good—that scrutiny, the criticism that comes from inside of me. But I make that adjustment, cross the Rubicon, and it never fails that when I finally do look, when I walk through the fear and trepidation, I can say, Hey, it's not that bad. Then I can look at it, study it, say to myself, Do it this way next time, try that. The rushes are like class for me, I learn from them. I learn what I'm doing and how I can change what I'm doing to be more effective. Watching the rushes each day became yet another piece of the process for me in Texas that I would continue from that movie on. As the days went by, I kept working on Bonnie, and slowly, under the warm sun and through the dusty days, Bonnie worked on me.

I had just missed meeting Arthur Penn when he was directing *The Chase*, screened out by the casting director, who was convinced I didn't have the face for movies. This time around Arthur wanted to meet me. He and Warren were still at loose ends looking for someone to play Bonnie. Warren had bought the story with the idea of costarring in it with Leslie Caron. They were involved when he first found the idea but had a difficult breakup before production began when Warren decided she wasn't right for the role.

After Leslie, there was a list of actresses who were being considered for the part, and my name was not on it. Warren and Arthur talked to Natalie Wood, Carol Lynley, Tuesday Weld, even Warren's sister, Shirley MacLaine. Finally it looked for the world like the part was going to go to Tuesday Weld, but she was pregnant and decided she didn't want to go to Texas. Though *The Happening* wasn't released yet, Arthur had seen some of the film and called David Begelman and said, "Tell me about Faye." David did and then set up a meeting in New York, at the Plaza Hotel. Arthur and I hit it off, and I had read the script and knew I wanted this role. He asked me to fly to California and meet Warren.

This is a game, this is moviemaking, this is deal-making. Freddie Fields, who was in CMA's Los Angeles office and working with David on the deal, made a play to get me above-the-title billing. Warren didn't want to do that at first. Freddie was angling for it because billing was terribly important. To get you above the title means you're a star. It means you get more money. It means you get better parts. But Si Maslow, my manager at the time, became fearful. In the end, I found Si to have feet of clay. One day, as the *Bonnie and Clyde* negotiations came down to the wire, I heard Si race up the stairs toward my apartment. "Oh no," he said, as soon as he was in the door. "They're going to blow it."

This wasn't about the creative process, it was about the deal-making process. And they're whole different rules. This was the commerce part of it. I realized then that Si was a little out of his depth, quite frankly. These were big guys. Whether they would have blown it or not, who knows. I doubt it. I don't think I would have let anybody blow my chance at that moment. And in the end, long after the movie was shot, Warren gave me the billing. That's because he's got a lot of class.

My friend Sharon Stone had the same battle not all that long ago with Michael Douglas on the film *Basic Instinct*. I like Michael and I know him around town, and I've worked with his father. But he did not give Sharon above-the-title billing and the woman became a star. And he should have. It hurt Sharon at the time. And it was a very nervous, fearful time for her. I was with Sharon when the film was first shown at a private screening at Columbia. Moment by moment, I tried to give her my insight into what was going on for her, what was happening, how I handled it when I was at that moment. I felt I was able to give something back to her. She'd admired my work. We'd met. And now she was where I used to be, the baton was being passed.

Everybody who's ever helped me all along the line, I've always vowed to pass it on, give it back. It's a particular joy to me that I was able to give a small amount back to Sharon. She's a bright, courageous actress who has her best work ahead of her.

Warren gave me the billing on *Bonnie and Clyde*, because clearly this was a story about two people. Warren also knows—and this is what makes him such a brilliant producer—that's what people go to the movies to see. They'd much rather see a movie about the relationship between Bonnie and Clyde than a movie about Clyde. That's what we're all interested in. How do we fall in love? How do we connect with other people? I was working with Portnoy, my analyst, at the time, and this was a subject I talked about with him as well. Warren was smart enough to know that the connection between two people is what brings the audience in. And Warren was also smart enough to know that this movie would make me a star, and he may as well beat the town to the punch. Michael Douglas was not. Sharon Stone became just as big a star and Michael lost out on the chance to be generous.

WITHIN A FEW DAYS I was on a plane to Los Angeles to meet with Arthur and Warren. The meeting was set for the Beverly Wilshire Hotel, where Warren had lived for years in the penthouse suite. It is a plush but cozy place in the midst of Beverly Hills. Walk across the street and you are on Rodeo Drive. Virtually every major fashion, jewelry, and perfume designer has a shop within a few square blocks. There would come a time, relatively quickly, that I would feel at ease here. I was not there on this day.

It was evening, just past sunset, when I was finally to read with Warren. I sat in the room, more than a little nervous. Arthur was there, and he gave me a quick smile and a thumbs-up, which helped. The scene we started with was the opening one, when Bonnie first meets Clyde. I'm standing, looking out a window, with no clothes on, and I see this guy trying to hot-wire my mama's car. And I say, "Boy, what you doing with my mama's car?" knowing full well what he's doing, and in that moment challenging him sexually—note the no clothes—and very interested in somebody who will try to steal a car in broad daylight. Bonnie throws on a light frock and races down the stairs. Shot with the camera looking up at her from the bottom of the stairs, the image that lingers is one of long, bare legs clambering down the steps; the dress, providing the barest of cover, is all aflutter in the rush of it. And that's the first moment.

In that moment, I was really, as Kazan says, home free. I understood this role. I understood this kind of hunger, this kind of desperation, this kind of need. I wanted to get out of the South, and I wanted to go places. Bonnie wanted this, a piece of this danger, so she can escape the tedium of being poor in West Texas during the Depression. She's a southern girl who wants to go places too. And that's what Bonnie is promised in the first moment of this film. I played that moment like a house on fire and never looked back.

Warren had very specific ideas about the film. He was nobody's fool, Warren Beatty. Nor is he still. After our meeting he and Arthur talked, and I don't know all that was said. I do know that at one point Arthur said, "Either she does it or I don't do it." He really went out on a limb for me. Warren was already one of the most sought-after young leading men in town, and my first film had yet to be seen in a single theater. In the end, Warren agreed with Arthur.

Not long after I came back from London in the eighties, I was flying to the West Coast and Warren was on the flight. I was either in business class or the back of first. Warren came back and sat with me the whole trip. That's a guy with a lot of class. He gave up six hours of his life to talk to me because I was in a vulnerable place. That really stunned me, because who wants to spend six hours with a former leading lady. I was very grateful. I can't say enough good about Warren Beatty—both for the time I spent with him making Bonnie and Clyde, and the times I've seen him since and the way he's treated me. He's a gentleman, a cunning businessman, a great film star, and a very worthwhile person.

Now Arthur is one of those really smart, intellectually gifted directors, very much in the Kazan school of directing. He knows writers. He knows about screenplays. He knows how to deal with actors, how to let the talent breathe and develop a role. I learned, often quite painfully, that a lot of directors haven't the faintest idea how to nurture the talent. But Arthur knew. A great director helps you do better than you ever thought you could, and Arthur was a great director. That's why he let me work through my anguish in the middle of that field. He believed in me and knew I would get beyond my anxiety, my uncertainty, and give him the Bonnie he wanted.

As a director, Arthur Penn was as much philosopher as artist. I would often watch him from a distance, as he surveyed the landscape—a cigar perpetually in hand, horn-rimmed glasses perched on his nose, soaking everything in. He wanted to portray Bonnie and Clyde as the outlaws they were, but not without looking at the ways in which they were connected to, and created by, the times in which they were living. And he didn't want to cheat the violence, make it easier to watch. The violence in *Bonnie and Clyde* is a reminder of the depth of rage and the emptiness of revenge. A gun battle is not clean; the wounds should not be easy to look at. Death, violent death, is ugly—and Arthur was never one to shy away from that sort of imagery.

To both Arthur and Warren, Bonnie and Clyde were more than small-time bank robbers. There was a mythological quality to the Barrow gang that they wanted to explore. The film was set in 1933—Dust Bowl times—when the people, mostly farmers, had been ground down to nothing. Many were losing their farms to bank foreclosures. They were people who saw no way to struggle against the institutions and the forces that were taking away their land and their homes.

I looked at photos that had been taken around that time. What I saw were faces lined by years of working a farm. That life digs deep grooves in a face, and the young quickly look old. There was a bitter resignation staring back at me. Only the children smile, and even that was a rare sight. I didn't research this role in the way that I did roles before and after. Just as Barbara Loden had said of Maggie in *After the Fall*, that it was a character she weaned, that was Bonnie for me. She was my soulmate. She was my baby.

What I wasn't prepared for was how much the mythology of these two characters still lived in the small Texas towns where most of the movie was shot and where Bonnie and Clyde once roamed. One day, we were filming a robbery scene in Point Blank. Now, Point Blank is not much more than a bump in the road. Its dusty main street and handful of aging frame houses don't even merit a mention on maps anymore, if they ever did. The two or three storefronts are the same ones that were put up back in the early 1900s, before the town hit hard times. As the scene was set up, Clyde and his brother, Buck, who was played by Gene Hackman, and I go into the bank, guns drawn. As Buck and I start emptying money from the drawers, Clyde notices a farmer standing in front of one of the teller windows and asks if the money in front of him is his. When he says yes, Clyde tells him to keep it.

The thing about Bonnie and Clyde is they were against the banks. There's the all-important scene earlier in the film where Clyde's teaching me to shoot in front of a run-down farmhouse. A bedraggled family drives up in a broken-down *Grapes of Wrath* Model A Ford. They tell us it's their place, they've just come to see it one last time. The bank took it. And Clyde shoots out the window and then offers the gun to the man, and he takes the gun and shoots out all the other windows. The man smiles and gets back in the car. Then Warren introduces us. He says, "My name's Clyde Barrow and this here is Miss Bonnie Parker." Then I say, "We rob banks." It was about us going after the institutions that had taken away the livelihoods of these very poor people during the Depression.

When we took a break from shooting the bank robbery scene, I wandered over to the honey wagon to grab one of the half-dozen Cokes I would drink each day to keep from wilting. One of the extras in the scene, a woman who looked to be in her late thirties, told me in a hushed voice that this was just exactly as she remembered it. She had been a child of four and in that very bank on the day that the Barrow gang had robbed it. Another told me of the way her parents would set aside a few pennies each day so that they could buy the morning paper to see where the gang's run from the law had taken Bonnie and Clyde next. They themselves might not be able to escape, but they could ride along with the Barrow gang. For these folks, the Barrows' exploits had long ago become the stuff of fiction and fantasy, a serialized novel that rode right through the dust and the heat and the desperation of their lives.

In many of the little towns we shot in, the set would become a sort of Bonnie and Clyde reunion; people would pack a lunch, round up the kids, and come for the day. Many who came to watch or who found a way to be a small part of this film had not just read about the Barrow gang, they knew the real flesh-and-blood members of it. They had gone to the same schools, sung hymns together at church on Sunday, tracked them through county after county. Some were actual relations. It was as if we had stepped into a tide-pool of memories. Old stories were dredged up and told again, rumors were rehashed, scrapbooks pulled out—Bonnie and Clyde, Buck and Blanche and C.W. were in the air, and we were all slipping back in time.

ALTHOUGH WE WERE LOOKING for a certain authenticity, we knew these were characters who lived in legends and myths. To create that sense of proportion, there were elements that had to be glamorized.

One of my favorite shots taken by Curtis Hansen when I was in Texas filming Bonnie and Clyde. © 1967 Warner Bros.-Seven Arts and Tatira-Hiller Productions

A quiet moment, but Clyde and Bonnie's bloody end is fast approaching.

My hair was very blond and many shades lighter than in either *The Happening* or *Hurry Sundown*, worn almost straight and just to my shoulders. The real Bonnie Parker's was brown. She usually wore her hair parted in the middle, pulled back tight away from her face and tucked up under her beret. She had a hard look to her. This Bonnie that we were shaping was juicier, softer, sexier. And I was finally liberated from that damn push-up bra that I hated. Bonnie was lithe and lissome, like I've always wanted to be, and often was in my life and in my work. Bonnie was a creature who wanted freedom, and a bra just didn't fit. That she wasn't wearing any underwear in the opening scene belonged to the sexuality of the woman.

SOMEWHERE BETWEEN *The Happening* and *Hurry Sundown*, I began to believe that I was going to be able to make a career of film acting. There were actresses whose work I loved, and I wanted to find a way to have some fun adding little details here and there that were sort of my personal homage to their work. In *Bonnie*, I found an ideal spot to do something like Joanne Woodward had done in *The Long, Hot Summer*. There's a scene where Joanne is walking down the street, swinging her bag back and forth in a southern, sassy kind of way. Just after Clyde and I have met, the two of us are walking down the street, and Bonnie's pretending to be knowledgeable. I'm swinging my purse the same way Joanne did. Bonnie's walk has a sort of slow sensuality about it, flirtatious, she's coming on to him. But the little purse twirling around gives you a sense of this sweet southern girl, swinging her bag from side to side. It was touching and showed vulnerability, and it added to the illusion. It was like the cherry on the sundae.

When I played in *Hurry Sundown*, and my character comes back from the store, I have her reach inside the grocery bag and grab something and eat it. That was a little like a scene in *Hud*, where Patricia Neal and Paul Newman are in the car and she eats an orange and Fig Newtons right out of the grocery bag. It was so earthy and sexy and I loved it. These were some of my little inside homages to the actresses I loved. Those little idiosyncratic things that they would do. The way Joanne swung her little pocketbook, and the way Pat Neal took some food in her hand and ate it right out of the grocery bag.

AFTER I GOT the role of Bonnie, Arthur and I started talking about what she might wear. I thought jeans, maybe, pants of some sort since they were robbing banks and making quick getaways. But Warren and Arthur wanted to put her in dresses, great costumes that would give her style. They had decided to give Theadora Van Runkle, who was a young sketch artist with a great eye, a shot at designing the costumes. Soon after I learned that I had gotten the role, I met Theadora, who was to affect my own sense of style and become a good friend during these fast times. Until I met Theadora, clothes, and getting to a certain look, creating an effect, had just been part of the job. She taught me just how much fun it can be.

I liked Theadora immediately. She was smart, funny, a very independent spirit, and a genius when it came to clothing design. Thea loved vintage clothes anyway and was excited by the possibilities of dressing the Barrow gang. The look for Bonnie was smack out of the thirties, but glamorized and very beautiful. Great cuts and a very up-market version of the thirties clothes, with period detailing like fagoting, for example, where you pull away certain threads of the fabric so that you're left with an intricate, lacy-like detail. She did this wonderful Norfolk jacket, I recall. All great, even that first poor little dress that I wore with Clyde was great. They all were cut on a bias and they swung. And this time I didn't get my toe thumped.

The Bonnie look became the rage because women saw it and felt they could pull it off. It was glamorized, but real. The maxi replaced the mini of the sixties because of this movie. The clothing had the kind of classic lines that caught the imagination of European designers as well. When I was in Paris, the night after the premiere, a box full of berets was delivered to my room in the Hotel George V. They were from a small village near Lourdes in the French Pyrenees, where the traditional French berets are made. After the release of *Bonnie and Clyde*, demand had pushed production from 5,000 to 12,000 berets a week, and they wanted to thank me. For the next few years much of what I wore onscreen, and sometimes off-, was designed by Theadora.

Theadora and I were to collaborate on clothing for any number of my roles over the years—some were more stunning, others more daring. But none would so turn fashion on its ear. Within a year of *Bonnie and Clyde's* release in theaters, I would be on the cover of *Newsweek*, *Look*, and *Life*, among others, always in an outfit that evoked the young, yellow-haired gun moll whose destiny was sealed when she met a handsome armed robber with dreams of fortune and fame.

Me at two.
My Daddy, John MacDowell Dunaway.
My mother, Grace April Smith.
My Olma, Maggie Lena Fears Smith.

A Leon High School cheerleader in Tallahassee.

Miss University of Florida runner-up in 1959.

When I was a Tallahassee teen.

Kathleen Stanton reprised in the TV production of Hogan's Goat. Luigi Pelletieri

Bonnie Parker, the role that would establish my film career and earn me my first Oscar nomination. © 1967 Warner Bros.-Seven Arts and Tatira Hiller Productions

*Thea and me getting ready for a Bon-
nie Academy Awards night.*

*My newsboy cap—a favorite of fashion
photographers.*

Setside on Thomas Crown. Three photos:
Jerry Schatzberg

My mother and me.
My dearest Olma.
Jerry Schatzberg

Thomas Crown's *legendary kiss
with Steve McQueen.* Copyright ©
1968 United Artists Corp.

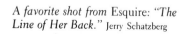

A favorite shot from Esquire: *"The
Line of Her Back."* Jerry Schatzberg

Milton Greene's photograph of me, taken after Bonnie and Clyde. © 1968/1995 The Milton H. Greene Archive

Opposite below: My beloved Duchesse Brisée—the broken duchess—with the Liam tapestry worked by me.

300 Central Park West, my home for nearly twenty years. Ezra Stoller © ESTO

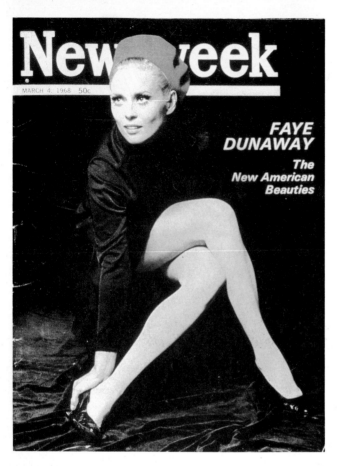

Bonnie *and I made the cover of* Newsweek. Jerry Schatzberg.

With my dear friend, Elia Kazan, during the filming of The Arrangement.
© 1969 WarnerBros.-Seven Arts, Inc.

With Marcello on the set of
The Lovers.

*Marcello and I found Italy
was truly a place for lovers.*
Two photos: © Douglas Kirkland

Peter Wolf and me, newly wed in 1974.

I played Blanche in the twenty-
fifth-anniversary production of
Tennessee's Streetcar Named
Desire in Los Angeles in 1973.
C. T. G. Ahmanson Photo Collection.

Me and Tennessee; we met in
1973 and were friends ever
after.

Evelyn Mulwray in Chinatown, *the role for which I would earn my second Oscar nomination.* © 1995 by Paramount Pictures

Diana Christensen, the ruthless programming executive in Network, *a role friends encouraged me not to take.* © 1976 Metro-Goldwyn-Mayer, Inc., and United Artists Corp.

Backstage on Academy Awards night with Louise Fletcher, who presented the Oscar to me as Best Actress for Network. © American Academy of Motion Picture Arts and Sciences.

With Network *screenwriter Paddy Chayefsky on Oscar night. He was part of our Oscar sweep.*

Jon Peters, who produced Laura Mars, *flew to New York to personally color my hair for the film.* Jerry Schatzberg

A favorite baby picture Terry O'Neill snapped of our son Liam and me.

My angel-faced toddler. Two photos: Terry O'Neill

Liam at fourteen.

Liam was my dashing escort to the Emmy Awards in 1994 where I won for my performance in Columbo. © 1994 Craig T. Mathew/ ATAS

A dinner in Milan honoring Georgio Armani, the designer who has been a favorite of mine for years.

My mentor and dear friend playwright William Alfred. Terry O'Neill

At *Cannes International Film Festival* with *Barbet Schroeder and Mickey Rourke for the* Barfly *screening.*

On location for Arizona Dreams *with my good friend and costar Johnny Depp.*
© 1991 Constellation–UGC–Hachette Premiere

WE WERE WORKING with a tight budget from the beginning, and the cast stayed in Dallas at the North Park Motor Inn, a modest place, then drove each day out to the locations. On weekends, we would rehearse the pages that had been rewritten during the week. There were some weeks when we got new pages every day. Robert Towne was usually around working on the script, which originally had been written by Robert Benton and David Newman.

Anytime I feel hungry to hear good dialogue, I know I can look at a film that Bob has had a hand in writing and find it. I remember watching *The Firm*, which Towne wrote, and a line near the end where Jeanne Tripplehorn says, "I've loved you all my life. Even before we met. Part of it wasn't even you, it was just a promise of you." Good screen dialogue is shorthand, but it's poignant and poetic. It's incisive and yet you cannot use too many words because an image is worth a lot more than any amount of words on the screen. That's what makes it a particular kind of art and it's something that I just love. Screenwriters are forced to be very economical, and yet create these images that will stay and will pierce your heart. Bob Towne could always do that.

An early draft of the script had Clyde, Bonnie, and C.W. in a love triangle. Bonnie was a nymphomaniac, Clyde was a homosexual, and C.W. was in the middle of it all. It was a subplot that had the potential to overtake the rest of the story as it stood. As the script evolved, that piece of the story largely disappeared. There are brief scenes that survived that hint at what might have been more than just a boss-and-sidekick relationship between C.W. and Clyde. During one, the gang is passing time in a roadside motel, and C.W. and Buck are playing checkers, with Clyde showing C.W. how to play. There is a familiar intimacy between the two men that speaks of something deeper.

Bonnie was very sophisticated sexually and Clyde wasn't. He had probably never made love with a girl. What Warren and Arthur wanted to say, and what I really got into and really wanted to say as well, is that it's not all wine and roses in relationships. In movies, it's boy meets girl, and they live happily ever after. But we were trying to do something new and modern with this relationship, which was to say, "Look, the guy is practically impotent," which also happens to have been the truth. It was quite radical to talk about at the time, because God forbid any American man would be considered impotent. Good God. That's more a European notion, that you are able to go into those areas of vulnerability in human beings as they actually exist in life. So we were dealing with the truth, but we were also trying to deal with the truth of human relationships, the human condition. What really goes on between two people.

There is a very famous scene in which we're in bed trying to make love with guns everywhere, and at one point you think we might make it. Our heads are in frame, Clyde is hesitant, and my head leaves the frame. I go down his body, so it's quite clear what Bonnie's doing. The camera stays on his face, tense and fearful of failure, until finally he wrenches away in this agonizing movement. In that same motion, I quickly pull back toward the end of the bed and hold on for dear life to the iron bedstand. Bonnie's trying to go to whatever length she needs to go to connect with this man sexually, because she loves him. But in that moment, she's been rejected. That was a direct homage really to *The Lovers*, with Jeanne Moreau. Later in the film, when I put the cigar in my mouth, I put it in the middle, not the side, because that's how Moreau had done it in *The Lovers*. It's very sexual. Moreau was one of my great idols because she had this incredible oblique sensuality.

Bonnie and Clyde couldn't make it together, but deep within them their desire to connect sexually and emotionally with another person is what this movie's talking about. The movie was groundbreaking in many, many ways. And that scene was beautiful. Later in the film, there is a scene where the wind tumbles the newspaper—a cinematic convention that I'm fond of—after they have indeed finally connected, and made love. It reminded me of those old movies with shots of a calendar, where the pages fill the whole screen and they ripple off each other indicating the passage of time. Those are very important little conventions. But if Bonnie and Clyde could have had a happy, successful, serene sexual life together, they probably wouldn't have gone on killing people and robbing banks. It was a great, classic movie that I'm very grateful to have been a part of.

Once the movie was released, people embraced this very sexually conflicted antihero. Here was a leading man very unlike the sort audiences were used to seeing. Clyde didn't even have the typical bad-boy machismo you'd expect from a small-time bank robber. Instead his bravado was tentative, unsteady. He often had the look of a shy boy, vulnerable, unsure of himself, even awkward. It was a remarkable performance by Warren. *Bonnie and Clyde* came a few years after *Splendor in the Grass* had assured him a spot as one of the country's favorite sex symbols. Some gossip columnists, I'm convinced, stayed in business by writing about sightings of Warren with one beautiful woman after another. Yet in Clyde, he was playing a character whose sexual prowess was called into question, and he portrayed that with great sensitivity and a purity that made Warren as Clyde completely believable.

Though Clyde may have been a stretch for Warren, with Bonnie I was, as I've said, home free. One of my favorite moments in the film is about two-thirds of the way in. Bonnie's very edgy, doing her nails, and the gang is horsing around, and she yelps because they've aggravated her. Everyone but Clyde leaves. Bonnie gets on the bed, very blue, very depressed. Clyde holds her. "Back in the beginning," she says, "I thought we were really goin' somewhere. But this is it, we're just goin', aren't we?" That movie touched the core of my being. Never have I felt so close to a character as I felt to Bonnie. She was a yearning, edgy, ambitious southern girl who wanted to get out of wherever she was. I knew everything about wanting to get out, and the getting out doesn't come easy. But with Bonnie there was a real tragic irony. She got out only to see that she was heading nowhere and that the end was death. That gorgeous scene on the sand dunes of Texas was just unbelievable, because that's where she realized it. It needed to be a scene full of portent.

I called Andreas Voutsinas, who was still an acting coach in New York, to talk about how I wanted to play it. What I was looking for was a way to create a visual image that would speak to all the emotions and fear that she is feeling. And this is what we worked out. My hair is pulled back in a tortoiseshell clasp. It was rigged to look closed, but it was really open so that it could fall out of my hair easily. I had decided to wear a long necklace that I could give my mother when I got scared that this was the last time I would see her. When she starts to leave over the dunes, I start getting nervous and I take off the necklace to give it to her. As I take the necklace off, the clasp catches on the chain and it falls out of my hair, and my hair falls free. It's at that point that you realize, I'm losing my mother. The necklace that I give my mother is a way of giving her myself. It's a way of not separating from her. To give her something to connect us. As she starts to move away from me, that's the moment of loss.

I've struggled with that personally all my life, and still do. Bonnie doesn't want to lose her mother. This was an effective thing to do, with the clasp coming undone. It made the hair fly in a desperate kind of way. The vision you're left with was of loss. Near the end of the scene Clyde says to her, "You know, Mama, we thought we'd come and just settle down and live right next door to you. What would you think of that?" And she says, "You try to live near me, Clyde Barrow, you won't live long." To me she says, "Bye, honey." And I am left with my hair streaming and this kind of stricken look on my face. It's the old thing of the actress who knows more than the character. It's a good moment. All my life is undone.

Just a few scenes earlier, I had taken off from Clyde and the gang, angry and upset, and raced through the cornfields wanting to see my mother. It's a long shot, and as we were shooting it the light changed. A cloud passed in front of the sun and for a few moments threw a shadow across my face. A lesser director would have yelled cut and considered the scene ruined. But Arthur kept it. Because it was like from God. That was foreshadowing. Because Bonnie knew everything was tightening to the point where they had nowhere to go but death. It happened only once, the change in light, but Arthur used it at the beginning of the scene in the cornfield and again at the end.

There was a real kind of fierceness I'd seen in Bonnie that I recognized in myself as well. You look at photos of her and see it in the glint of her eyes, the set of her jaw. It takes a fierceness in life to get ahead. I already knew that. Bonnie was Tennessee Williams, *Cat on a Hot Tin Roof* time. She knew the only way to get what she wanted was through her own sheer force of will. She was driven by her own desire. I know that territory—you do whatever it takes. Bonnie wanted out desperately. She wanted to be something special, something out of the ordinary.

After a rough go at the beginning, I was pretty close to where I wanted to be with Bonnie. You go to another country, a distant place within yourself. I've come offstage many times just knocked out with what I've discovered about my feelings, because I've had to go so deeply into them to play the role. Arthur once said of me that he had never seen such a complicated, torn, intelligent, ambitious girl. He said he always felt in working with me that my talent was crying out for expression and that I myself was crying out for fame. "What drives her to that, what motivates her, I don't know," he said. He had only to look as far as Bonnie to find the answer.

EVERY FILM I do teaches me something. In Texas, I learned a lot from Warren. There are many ways in which we are alike, some that worked to help us through the filming of *Bonnie and Clyde,* others that made it harder. Both of us are perfectionists; we want to get it right and neither of us is quick to compromise for anything less. Just where and how one finds perfection in a performance, however, is a point we diverged on. Warren will do thirty takes without thinking about it twice. Sometimes you need to do that. But by and large, I'm at my best on the third or the fourth. It's given me a chance to get into it. I can go to the thirtieth take, but I find I get pretty stale after the fifth or sixth.

There is a scene that comes early in the movie, soon after we've met. Clyde has just robbed a small store. We're in a stolen car and careening out of town. Now this is more excitement than Bonnie ever imagined, and she is covering Clyde with kisses. It's distracting enough that the car runs right off the road. The scene sets up their romantic tangles and is a critical one. When the car stops and Clyde pulls away from my embrace, telling me "I ain't no lover-boy," I'm ready to wound, and I do: "Your advertising's just dandy—folks would never guess you don't have a thing to sell."

Warren is supposed to bump his head in his hurry to escape from Bonnie and that car. And he did. We did thirty-eight takes of that particular scene. Each time his head hit the door with an audible smack on the way out. By the time Arthur yelled "Cut!" for the thirty-eighth and final time, I'm not sure which of us was in more pain—but Warren thrives on going the limit.

This was a very physical film for all of us, and I didn't want to walk away from the tough stuff. I did all my own stunts. As we moved through October the weather was beginning to turn cold. On the day we began shooting the scene where Clyde and I have been shot for the first time, and we're wading through a river with C.W., trying to escape, a cold front came moving through. In all, we shot over three days' worth of scenes that required us to stand in and slosh through that water.

I stood for hours at a time in some of the coldest, filthiest water

I had ever seen and willed myself not to turn blue. I couldn't let my body shiver, either, except between takes, or the camera might pick that up. There are scenes like this that are awful for a while, but you just concentrate on whether your acting is good. We were all bounced around a lot by the shoot-outs and chase scenes, though I loved driving those cars.

The cast that Arthur and Warren had assembled was remarkable in its abilities. There was no weak link in the chain, and it was great to be in that kind of community of talent. Warren always said about Gene Hackman's performance that it was the most authentic in the movie. I thought Estelle too had that kind of authenticity. Estelle Parsons, who played Buck's wife, Blanche, eventually won an Oscar as Best Supporting Actress for her performance. We all, in fact, really inhabited our characters.

This cast was built from largely unknown or little-known actors. It was Gene Wilder's first film. He was just so funny as the undertaker, and in it you can see the kind of whimsy he would bring to characters over the years. The scene where we've stolen Gene's car and he and Evans Evans, who plays his fiancée, set out to catch us is a classic. We see Gene's bravado and fear run head-on into each other. Michael J. Pollard, a serious stage actor, was a darling, comic original, and as C.W., he was truly the innocent of the group. And if he hadn't been there, I wouldn't have had anybody to do Lenny Bruce routines with, so personally I adored him. C.W. turned out to be a telling counterpoint to Blanche, whose constant whine was really a testament to the fact that she knew very well what devilment we were up to. For C.W., though, Bonnie and Clyde were like mythic heroes, like gods. They could do no wrong and they would never be caught. He bought the myth.

There is a line in Gene Hackman's final scene that I liked a lot. He's collapsed after wandering around blindly on his hands and knees, his head half gone from a shotgun blast, and says, "Clyde, Clyde, the dog got my shoes." Bob Towne's work again. Shoes, if you don't have your shoes, you can't walk anywhere. With that line, you knew that Buck knew, even through the pain, that he was at the end of the road.

The final scene was very complex, because of the difficulty of the effects. Bonnie and Clyde are ambushed and have a barrage of bullets coming at them for fifteen minutes. My whole body and costume had to be made up in layers. I still know the exact position of at least three places on my face where I take bullets—my upper left cheek near my nose, the middle of my right cheek, and my forehead, just left of center. The makeup—which took hours—I remember well. There was a black center where each bullet hole was, and around that was painted a little red rim. On top of that they put wax, which they covered with makeup. Then attached to the wax was a squib and a tiny wire, not much bigger than a strand of hair so that it was virtually invisible.

During the scene, each of the squibs would be detonated. They're little dynamite charges, and when detonated they explode like little bombs. When they had finished with me, there were dozens of wires coming from my body and my face. Up close I looked like an escapee from a mad scientist's laboratory.

For that final scene, the question became how would I react to the bullets that would be hitting me? Bill Alfred always told me, invent from the facts. The facts would be that each bullet hits you with a little impact that throws you back. If you have all those bullets hitting you, you would have a heck of a lot of impacts. Your body would be jerking back all the time. What I evolved was a Saint Vitus' dance, Bonnie's dance of death.

Then it became a question of creating a final image that was indelible. The door had been shot open so my body could fall. The effect I wanted was a kind of flayed body rather than just crumpling out on the ground in a heap. I had my leg tied to the gearshift, so it would look as if it had gotten lodged there. That way I couldn't fall all the way out of the car and the physical image created was very dramatic. It released, as the Greeks put it, the pity and fear of the audience, because they see this girl they've come to know shot to ribbons.

The way they shot it, I do look like I'm caught in an eerie dance. I die, still behind the wheel, the top half of my body fallen to the side, my head resting near the running board, one arm caught on the steering wheel, the other limply over my head, with my hair brushing the grass below.

At one point I looked at Arthur, all these wires hanging from my face, the cameras set to roll, and said, "You know, me face is me fortune." Arthur was quick and tough and he shot back, "You're always broke, aren't you?" I mock cringed. He won that round.

For all the hours and technicians and rehearsals it took to orchestrate that scene and get it right, and for all the angry reactions it drew over the violence, it is the look that passes between Warren and me just as the shooting begins that I think is the most powerful. It is a look that says volumes—they know with absolute certainty that they will die, it's good-bye. For me, the moment is still remarkable for the gentleness of it in the face of the relentless violence. It was a look of love.

After we finished filming in Texas, I was off to Hollywood to do the final postproduction work on *Bonnie and Clyde*. This time instead of having an audition at the Beverly Wilshire, I was staying there. Room 300, an irony since my address in New York was 300 as well. I had a view of the boulevard below and the hills rising in the distance. Each day I'd be driven over to the old Warner Bros. back lot. There is something so magical about studio back lots. Warner's, which was over the hills and in the concrete flatlands of Burbank, had so many legends attached to it. I would walk along and feel the ghosts and the whole history of the town.

Here I was, a new film actress, knowing, as I would pass by a building, or wander into a soundstage, this is where Henry Fonda and Bette Davis made *Jezebel*. Over here, Bogart and Bacall filmed a portion of *Key Largo*; over there, where Joan Crawford created her Oscar-winning performance as *Mildred Pierce*, her knitting always close by on the set. It felt like hallowed ground. They had come before me, and I would follow in the tradition, adding my own footnotes to the history here.

It's a little world and you feel a real sense of belonging. You have the commissary, where you can sit down and rub shoulders with other actors taking a break from a day's filming. You can talk shop, and I loved that. I would sometimes slip inside a soundstage, those huge cavernous buildings, and watch other films being shot. I had a bungalow, which was really a small office, and a trailer, which was essentially equipped for me to live in and work out of during this part of the production.

A back lot is a whole little world. That's what you do when you make a movie, really, you make up your own world. You create it here and there, on location, on the back lot, on a soundstage. When I'm working well, I like to think I'm doing God's work. I'm trying to promote love between people. I feel I'm called to this work. I feel almost nunlike about it at times. But the irony of trying to create a world within a world is not lost on me. As if the world you've been given isn't good enough. Sometimes it seems that man has made a mess of the world we've been given, but I like to think God is there when we set about trying to create a film.

In this town, I guess, the ultimate repetition happens. You get a chance—a real shot—to make it come out right this time, because you get to decide the ending. You hold the choice in your hands—whether to repeat the patterns of the past because that is what you know, or make it turn out differently, because you have the capacity to change. In acting, creating this world, we're trying to illuminate the human condition, at its best and at its worst, when it turns out right and when it turns out horribly wrong.

One night I was back at the Beverly Wilshire Hotel looking at this picture that Curtis Hansen had taken of me while we were filming *Bonnie and Clyde* in Texas. It was a shot on the beach, just over the dunes where I last see my mother. It was a beautiful shot, with my blond hair streaming behind me.

A picture like that is sometimes like watching rushes—it gives you a sense of who you are. And at this moment, I needed it. I was lying on the bed feeling terribly depressed. Then looking at that picture, I began getting a bit less depressed. It was in an ad in the trades that read "CMA Congratulates Faye Dunaway." I remember feeling that I did have an identity, because there I was.

WARREN WAS then and still is one of the most interesting actors and figures in Hollywood. He was so involved in everything related to that movie, when he wasn't in front of the camera, he was on the phone getting something hashed out with the studio, or working through new scenes with Bob Towne, or talking things over with Arthur. Though Warren never stopped respecting Arthur's right as director to make the final artistic decisions, it was very much Warren's movie. On *Bonnie and Clyde*, the movie was Warren's mistress. There was no time in his days for anything else. I don't think he slept. There wasn't a detail that didn't warrant his attention. He taught me a lot about producing.

In a scene just before the final shoot-out, Clyde and Bonnie are coming back from the store and Warren wanted them to be eating peaches. There was a very specific dramatic reason for it. Early in the movie Clyde says to Buck, "Gee, what do you think of her?" Here's this impotent guy with a great-looking woman. Buck looks out again at her and says, teasing, "She's a peach." It was that male camaraderie thing, assuming that Clyde is this great big old stud. And of course he's not.

Later the script has Bonnie eating a peach moments before she's gunned to death. Now that's great. Just before she reaches for that peach, she's playing with these little figurines that are so perfect they have their own little fingernails, and she really loves that. Here's this little southern girl, and you really see it there. Then she starts to eat a peach and guess what happens? She gets mowed down by all these people. That's great screenwriting. That's the kind of singular little thing that's dramatic, poignant, poetic. Your heart breaks for it.

When Warren told the propman we had to have peaches, he came back after a while with apples. Peaches are a summer crop, he tried to explain to Warren. That wouldn't do. Warren gave him twenty-four hours to find peaches somewhere in the world and have them shipped in. But there are times when all the money in the world won't make something happen. And though I know that at this point the price of the peaches would have come out of Warren's own pocket, there were still no peaches to be found.

Pears, we used pears, but they couldn't have the same emotional impact. Maybe nobody else noticed, but Warren noticed it and I noticed it. That's what makes an artist, and that's what makes someone who is going to make a difference, who's able to push something through. There were a million more details, just like that one, that he kept pushing to get as close to perfect as he could. Everything mattered.

With this film, Warren really became the first in a new wave of producer/director/actor power combinations. It didn't come easy. He brought the script to Warner Bros., but the only way he would do the film was if he got to produce it. That was the only way the studio could get the project, and Warren was a big star, so they agreed. I once asked Warren if he was the first actor/producer, momentarily forgetting those early people like Charlie Chaplin and Mary Pickford, who were indeed actor/producers. He said, "No, I wasn't the first one, but I was the best one." That's Warren for you. Snappy, very capable.

Years later I was on a transatlantic flight with Bob Towne and we talked about all manner of things, including *Bonnie and Clyde*. Bob said to me, "You'd have to be crazy if you were a studio executive, and Warren Beatty was producing, not to do it." Because Warren stops at nothing. He's a great, great producer. He and Sam Spiegel were great friends and he learned from Sam.

THE STORY I love best about Warren happened after I was back in New York and Warren was trying to push the studio to release *Bonnie and Clyde*. The executives at Warner Bros. didn't have high hopes for the film and they were dragging their heels. Warren and Jack Warner argued about it, didn't come to an agreement, but Warren refused to give up, literally. One day, he lay on the middle of the floor and said, "Sell me the picture." *Bonnie and Clyde* cost about $4 million to make back in 1966. Even though Warren had put in some of his own money, there was at least $2 million he would have to come up with. They didn't believe him, didn't believe he could come up with the money, but they weren't sure.

Warren said, "Sell me the picture. I'll be in your office six o'clock tonight with a check. Sell it to me." Then he got up and left. It was a ruse and it worked. They're businessmen, these studio guys, so they immediately said, "Who's shown it to Fox? They must want it. What're we gonna do?" It was Warren's chutzpah, that he said, "Hey, sell me the picture." They didn't sell him the picture, but Warren did get them to finally release the movie.

I watched him as an actor take control of his own destiny. Since then we've seen others do that. That's why almost every actor or actress who's big now is producing and has their own company. But it was an important lesson I learned from Warren, that if you have a vision, the only way to protect it is to fight body and soul, to go to the mat time and again. You have to deal with all your wits and everything that you are. It's to go through brick walls. It's intense determination. It's what I learned at my mother's knee and it's what I'm still practicing. It's what I saw Warren, another southerner, do.

I've done it with TNT and *Cold Sassy Tree*. If you can find the material, then you're not at the mercy of whatever scripts are coming to you. You are able to put it all together and choose the best editor, the best composer, the best coproducer, the best everything. Then you get them all together and you fight like banshees to get this movie made great and wonderful. You work together as a team. That's what you try to do, get material that you're passionate about making, then put a top team together. That's how we did *Cold Sassy*. And that's how Warren did *Bonnie and Clyde*.

THE TIME OF YEAR in which a studio releases a film has a lot to do with its success or failure. It's always been about when a particular film can find its audience. The fall is when the more serious movies are released, which *Bonnie and Clyde* was. An adventure film and the *Terminator* kind of films come out in the summer because that's when kids are on holiday. In the fall and the later holiday cycle, you're more interested in grittier, interesting, real films because life is starting up again in a serious way after the summer. Warren wanted the film to be released closer to the holiday cycle—around Thanksgiving and Christmas.

But this battle he didn't win. Warners released *Bonnie and Clyde* at the tail end of the summer on August 13, 1967, in two B-circuit theaters in New York, the Forum and the Murray Hill. The next week it opened in a single theater in Los Angeles, the Vogue. A city or two were added each week. The studio, which didn't have much faith in the film, was surprised that it made money. The film was actually making very good money. By the eighth week of its release, the movie was the number-three film in the country in what it was bringing in at the box office. Still, Warners was putting almost no money into publicizing it.

Warren would personally check in every market that *Bonnie and Clyde* was playing to see what publicity was being done for the film. He flew city to city giving interviews himself to help the film along. Most of the time, he would fight for Warner Bros. to do more. Most of the time, they did. I often wonder what kind of life *Bonnie and Clyde* would have had if Warren had not cared so much.

TIME WOULD TURN *Bonnie and Clyde* into a sensation, but it had a terrible ride with the critics early on. At one point, critics were critiquing each other's reviews. It all began with Bosley Crowther, *The New York Times* film critic, who thoroughly disliked the film. A "cheap piece of bald-faced slapstick that treats the hideous depredations of that sleazy, moronic pair as though they were as full of fun and frolic as the jazz-age cut-ups in *Thoroughly Modern Millie*," he wrote after seeing it at the Montreal Film Festival.

The Village Voice's Andrew Sarris characterized the review, and the subsequent stories Crowther continued to write about the film, as a "personal vendetta . . . a Crowther crusade that makes the 100 Years War look like a border incident."

About that time, Pauline Kael, who was then writing for *The New Republic*, composed a 9,000-word essay on *Bonnie and Clyde* and sent it off to *The New Yorker*. It began: "How do you make a good movie in this country and not get jumped on? *Bonnie and Clyde* is the most exciting American movie since *The Manchurian Candidate*. The audience is alive to it." Roughly 8,800 words later she took final aim at the charge of gratuitous violence that had been levied by so many against the film. "Maybe it's because *Bonnie and Clyde*, by making us care about the robber lovers, has put the sting back into death." After that essay, she would join *The New Yorker* and become perhaps the most distinctive and influential voice in all of film criticism.

One of the more remarkable events to come out of the critical skirmishes that surrounded *Bonnie and Clyde* came about the last week in August. Joseph Morgenstern, who was writing for *Newsweek* at the time, completely reversed himself. His first review wrote off the film as "a squalid shoot-'em-up for the moron trade." A week later, in what must still remain a largely unprecedented turn of affairs, Morgenstern retracted his initial analysis with what amounted to a public apology: "I am sorry to say I consider that review grossly unfair and regrettably inaccurate. I am sorrier to say I wrote it." *Time* magazine too would backtrack. It panned the movie in August, then made it the cover story in December.

Some speculated that it was the reality of the violence that Arthur had managed to capture that so many found offensive and unsettling. It's sex in England and violence over here. We love and hate our violence—it's an American thing—and in England I think the violence isn't as much a problem as the sex, because they are so repressed. Yet Arthur served up violence that was anything but pretty. He didn't sanitize it for the public. It was raw and rough around the edges, and the camera lingered over it. The final scene is played out in slow, bloody slow motion.

You never really know when you're making a movie whether

what you are doing will be embraced or vilified. You are in a world apart, and until that world collides with the real one, you simply don't know. It felt good, what we were doing in *Bonnie and Clyde*. The moments felt right. The performances from the entire cast were incredibly strong. The movie would go on to receive ten Academy Award nominations and win two. Financially it was one of the most successful movies of the year. Its content sparked a debate on violence that went on for nearly a year, and it continues to be referred to as a seminal film on contemporary violence.

What *Bonnie and Clyde* represented for me was something quite apart from all of that, for this was the movie that would separate me from the ranks of other working actresses. It put me firmly in the ranks of actresses that would do work that was art. There are those who elevate the craft of acting to the art of acting, and now I would be among them. I was the golden girl at that time. One of those women who was going to be nominated year after year for an Oscar and would win at least one. The movie established the quality of my work. *Bonnie and Clyde* would also turn me into a star.

SEVEN

I T'S ALMOST CHRISTMAS, 1967, and the London streets are crowded with people. Jerry Schatzberg and I have taken the day to walk the city, and we are slowly wandering down King's Road. In the swinging sixties, it is everything they said it would be and more. The counterculture is in full swing, and the British mod look, that wonderfully sharp English look, is happening.

I had been so busy working—and work is the ethos for me—that I had never even checked London out in the sixties. I remember going to Alvaro's on King's Road and having lunch, and the excitement of being at the "in-in" place. The photographers were there and the models were there. Michael Caine, Terence Stamp, Julie Christie, *tout le monde* of London were there for that Saturday lunch, as always.

We would go shopping at Biba, go to the flea markets. And Ossie Clark, he used to say, in the most outrageous English accent, "Uh-oo, heh-luh-oo, dah-ling, I've gott s'm syoopuh snake-skin shuhts." That was all the rage then, snakeskin jackets and shirts and boots. Soon those very shops were to have the midis which Theadora and I would single-handedly have brought in with Bonnie.

Along Carnaby Street, the shop windows were already filled with mannequins draped with designs inspired by the film. A fashion photographer snapped a dozen shots of me walking along the street. I was wearing a dark midi skirt, a belted sweater, and a beret. A few days later a photo showed up in a story about how the Bonnie look was all the rage. No one, including the photographer, made the connection that I was Bonnie, though it had only been a day or so earlier, at the invitation of the city, that I had flipped the switch on Carnaby Street, turning it into a Christmas wonderland of lights.

Bonnie and Clyde was a hit in Britain. No one could remember when an American film had had such an impact. Tidbits about the movie and the cast made their way into the newspapers on a near daily basis. A few days before I was scheduled to make the trip there, a reporter for one of the London papers called for an interview. He said, "Faye, London's yours." "Good." I laughed. "I'll take it." Crowds and critics alike embraced the movie from the beginning. When it opened on September 7 at the Warner Theatre in Leicester Square, there were hundreds of people waiting at the box office. Ticket sales hit a thirty-five-year high.

Through all of this, I was beginning to get a sense of my own distinction. My name was suddenly mentioned everywhere, in gossip columns, in the fashion pages. One day, I was said to be the top contender for a film I'd never heard of. The next, I was set to headline in an upcoming Broadway production with someone I'd never met. A gossamer web of fantasy was being spun around me, and it was like cotton candy, a sugary sweet confection.

There was the reality as well, top directors calling who wanted me for their next film. There was a certain potency to all of this. I knew that for now at least, I was no longer the seeker, but the one who was being sought. Hollywood is a powerful seducer. It does a good job of hiding the dark side just beyond the glare of the lights. But my work was going well, and though I was still struggling personally to feel better about myself, the scripts were piling up. I could pick and choose.

FROM THE TIME I was at my father's knee, really, I was looking for Gatsby. I think the women in this nation do look for Gatsby—unilaterally. We are taught as girls to look for the man to solve things for us. Hopefully we have grown past that. But at twenty-five, I felt that a man would complete my life, and Jerry was the first in a long line of men after Michael O'Brien that I would hope could fix my life for me. There were millions of photographers vying to photograph me then. The breakup with Michael was still fresh, and kept that way since Michael continued to call and drop by on occasion.

Jerry and I had set a date to have dinner at Elaine's, already well known as a celebrity hangout, a place where deals were made. On the night we were to meet, before I left, I got a call from a friend who was trying to find Michael. I tried calling all his friends, tried everything to track him down, all with no success. I finally left, and went to meet Jerry. Michael was found the next morning. He had killed himself sometime during the night. The irony that I had my first date with Jerry the same night Michael died has never been lost on me.

JERRY WAS ONE of the *haut monde* of New York and one of the hip guys around. He was one of the investors in Ondine, a club that had caught the imagination of New York's café society. It was packed wall-to-wall most nights, and though the music ranged more to pop, it was beginning to book the emerging rock groups and performers like The Rolling Stones, Jimi Hendrix, and Bob Dylan. Jerry was convinced that the future for these clubs was in rock 'n' roll.

Ondine was on Fifty-ninth Street just under the Queensboro Bridge. Tied as it was by its name to the folklore of the sea, Ondine was a cocktail lounge masquerading as a ship, with portholes and nets, and the dark wood of a cabin hold. It was strange decor for a disco, but it worked. Jerry always said it was the content that mattered. The music was right, the people were right. Ondine came to be in the wake of the wild success of the Peppermint Lounge, at a time when it seemed as if all of New York was going out. Because Jerry had photographed so many of the new musicians, they would stop by Ondine when they were in town.

By then, Bob Dylan was my favorite recording artist. The biting satire once again spoke to my own internal revolutions: "She aches just like a woman, but she breaks just like a little girl." I kept tapes of his music with me, carting them along as I would move from location to location for each new movie. While I loved the music, Jerry knew the musicians; it gave us a connection that bridged the fifteen-year difference in our ages. He was settled and secure at the same time he was on the cutting edge of things, very much the man-about-town. He was not chased by the demons that had driven Michael over the edge, and that drew me to him. He seemed to offer comfort, safety. Jerry was to be a ballast in my life, a bit of stability within the whirlwind.

Over our first dinner, Jerry began to tell me about a movie project he was working on. At the time, he was among a handful of very elite magazine photographers, but he was looking to stretch his creativity and wanted to move into film as a director. The script he was developing was loosely based on the life of Anne St. Marie, a top fashion model in the fifties, one of the models Jerry photographed most often.

The story follows the life of this young model, Lou Andreas-Sand in the film, who is a very sensitive, talented woman struggling to be at the top of this very competitive field of hers, who only values the way she looks, and she longs to make enough money to escape the business she believed was slowly destroying her soul. What she longs for is a place by the sea where she can spend her days painting and writing poetry.

This character was just so heartbreaking. "You know I've worked all my life to come to the day when I could be on my own and do my painting and my poetry and live by the ocean. And now I have it and I hate it. I just hate it," she says. To reach the heights and still find no peace, I was so touched by the tragedy of that. Lou Andreas-Sand fascinated me, and just as Bonnie had mirrored my beginnings, I wondered if I would find happiness as illusive as Lou did.

Over the next few years, Jerry and I would collaborate on and ultimately film *Puzzle of a Downfall Child*. Though it would never draw the attention and acclaim of other films I would do over the years, it was a beautiful film. The script, by Carole Eastman, who had written *Five Easy Pieces* some years earlier, was one of the most textured, incredibly detailed scripts I've ever read, and it really revealed the soul of a remarkable woman, and that is why it remains one of my favorites.

A REPORTER once asked me during my first year of making movies, when my career was white-hot, what I would do with all the money I would make and how the money would change me. Would I buy jewelry, clothes, travel to distant places; what would capture my fancy? I said then that I would take the money I made and buy a place in New York and make myself a home of it. I don't think he ever believed me, but that is exactly what I did, the very first thing I did with the money from my expanding career. The child who had spent years being bounced from one house or apartment to another, living in broken-down places where I dreaded bringing friends, wanted very much to put down roots.

I found a wonderful old apartment on Central Park West, 300 Central Park West to be precise. It needed a lot of work but it had good bones, ceilings that towered above you, huge windows that looked out on a panorama of the park on one side and the Hudson River on the other. I wanted to completely rebuild it, to something that was very pared down and modern in design. There were accents of black and green, the colors of Le Corbusier. But it was white that dominated—my beautiful pure white—always my favorite color. After a while yellows and melon colors moved in. And during my time in England, I began to really dive into the vividness of color. But at this time in my life I wanted white—pure, undemanding, sleek, smooth, uncomplicated, clean. That's the environment I wanted to live in. I wanted something that was elegant, yet simple, perhaps to balance the complexity that I found in the rest of my life.

Central Park West was my own private cocoon, twenty stories above the city, where I could retreat and feel completely safe. I would wake in the morning to see this enormous reservoir below, blue and glistening and sparkling in the sunshine, through the panorama of my windows. In the park below I could see the people jogging around the reservoir, looking like little ants. At about five o'clock every day, the sun would turn the buildings across the park on Fifth Avenue pink. At the darkest of times, these vistas would be there for me like a touchstone. This place was the one constant in my life for more than twenty years and I loved it dearly. I would return from two or three months on location, or from travels that would take me away for weeks at a time, and no matter how harried or tired I might be, I would always make my way to the windows, and drink in my view of the city, day or night, and know I was home.

MAKING MOVIES does something to the normal cadence of life. You live in a sort of split reality. I had leading roles in three films in 1966, but by the end of the year none had been released. While the industry was beginning to be aware of my work, the public had yet to see me in a movie. By the time a film makes it into theaters, it feels like ancient history; you've gone on to other things.

Early in 1967, the first two films I had appeared in, *The Happening* and *Hurry Sundown*, were finally released. I did not make it to the premiere of *Hurry Sundown*, which came out in February of that year. Otto Preminger and I were still at legal odds and neither of us was willing to give any ground. *Variety* gave *Hurry Sundown* a rave review, calling it "an outstanding, tasteful but hard-hitting and handsomely produced film about racial conflict," noting that I earned my star billing. But generally the critics hated the movie, taking Otto to task for the film's length—nearly two and a half hours—its clichés, and its melodrama.

Rex Reed's assessment was typical: "Critic Wilfrid Sheed wrote recently that no film is ever so bad that you can't find some virtue in it. He must not have seen *Hurry Sundown*." Sheed himself had said of the movie, "To criticize it would be like tripping a dwarf." Though I was not happy with Otto, I thought the reviews were overly harsh. Whether it was the film's political content, with its strong statement on race and class, or Otto's interpretation, or the reviews, audiences didn't like it much better, and *Hurry Sundown* was very quickly out of theaters and soon forgotten. My mother loved the film, and my character. I'm sure she saw traces of her life in it.

The Happening had its premiere in late March 1967. Appropriately enough, it was in Palm Springs during Spring Break, when the normally quiet desert town is filled to overflowing with college students intent on participating in what is essentially a week-long drunk. I was due in Mexico in early April for the beginning of my fourth film, *The Extraordinary Seaman*, but I wanted to actually attend a premiere of one of my movies, so I booked a flight to Palm Springs.

After a while, the hotel rooms filled with flowers, baskets of fruit, and cards of congratulations; the limo ride to the theater; the red carpet; the party after; the reviews the next day all fade into one long blur. One premiere is very like the next and the next. But this was all still very new to me and I savored it.

The screening went well, with the audience applauding wildly at the end, though I was quickly to learn that was the nature of premieres—you are among friends. Kirk Douglas and his wife hosted the party after and it was as jammed with people as the streets outside, though the tone of it was much more sedate. Since Palm Springs is within striking distance from Los Angeles, there were a lot of celebrities and movie executives who made the trip over. All in all it was a pretty great night.

The evening went much more smoothly than it had a week earlier when the movie was screened at the Directors Guild in Los Angeles. Elliot Silverstein had always wanted *The Happening* to make a social statement, to stand as a film that was more than an entertaining caper.

When the screening ended, the audience walked out to find the words "This picture is a lie" spray-painted on the wood-paneled walls in the Guild's foyer. Exactly which point of view—the establishment's or antiestablishment's—had proved so offensive to the graffiti critic no one ever learned. He or she got away scot-free.

While you never want some fanatic damaging property or in any way causing harm, you do look to have people react in a visceral way to your work. Some controversy generally helps a film, particularly if it means the movie will become a part of the public debate on an issue, as would soon happen with *Bonnie and Clyde* and violence. Little did any of us know that that black scrawl would be one of the most impassioned reactions we would ever get to *The Happening*. I got good notices in the press, and the film turned out to be a modest success, but it fell far below the commercial hopes that Sam Spiegel had for it.

Though Sam remained a good friend over the years and a solid sounding board when I needed one, and gave me an open invitation to use the *Malahne* anytime I wanted, we would never do another film together. My six-picture deal with Otto ended in a lawsuit; my five-picture deal with Sam ended in a treasured friendship. And there you have the two faces of Hollywood.

IN APRIL OF 1967, I began work on *The Extraordinary Seaman* costarring David Niven. There were a couple of other old hands at acting—the legendary Mickey Rooney, and comedian Jack Carter. Another young actor, who had already established himself on the stage, Alan Alda, was also in the cast, the romantic lead opposite me in his film debut. The director was John Frankenheimer, who had been the creative force behind a number of exceptional films, including *Seconds*, *The Manchurian Candidate*, and *Birdman of Alcatraz*. Generally his films had been dark moody pieces, character studies, or thrillers. With *Seaman*, Frankenheimer wanted to try his hand at comedy.

We all set out for the wilds of Mexico and I do mean wilds. After a frustrating try at using the Philippines, the location that John had finally chosen lay about halfway between Mexico City and the tip of the Yucatán Peninsula. A tiny tropical outpost on the Gulf shore, Coatzacoalcos had little in the way of even the basic necessities. It had taken four huge tractor trailers to transport film equipment down in the weeks before the rest of us showed up. Coatzacoalcos had the feel of a jungle, which John wanted, and a river that ran to the ocean, landscape that was critical to the plot.

There are two images of Coatzacoalcos that stay with me above all others. The cockroaches, which were huge—three inches long on average—would move in herds so thick that the ground would look like it was alive. And the ocelots, sleek beautiful yellow cats with dark spots, which were jungle cats that had been tamed, as much as you can tame anything that is wild, and kept like pets by the people there. When the village people heard that I found the cats quite beautiful, several attempted to give me their own ocelots as a gift. It was generous—these were people who had very little to give—and I didn't know how to tell them no without hurting their feelings. Thankfully U.S. Customs laws intervened, prohibiting me from accepting and transporting ocelots back to the States.

We spent our days either on location or in the tiny hotel, where the cast literally took over the lobby. Being stuck in your room waiting out the nearly daily tropical downpours could drive anyone to the brink of madness. John and his wife, Evans Evans, whom I knew from our days on *Bonnie and Clyde*, tried to bring a little civilization to the nights there. They would have elegant dinners, with deliciously prepared food, and fine wines that John had flown in; those who were among the ones lucky enough to get a dinner invitation would all sit around being entertained by David Niven. He was a wonderful raconteur and would tell us tales of old Hollywood, all the behind-the-scenes intrigues that make it such a rich, if often distasteful, culture.

As soon as David was finished with his scenes each day, he would head to the nearest Mexican bar and start on the margaritas, ordering a pitcher of them, and then I would come and meet him there. He sort of took me under his wing platonically and we chatted on and on. He told all these stories about his days in Hollywood with Errol Flynn. David told me one story about the actor Eddie Albert, who had an affair with one of the mogul's wives. The mogul came to New York and saw him in a play and said, "Gee whiz, you're just such a great, great actor. I want you to come out to Hollywood. I want to give you a contract." And he did, he came out, and the story was he didn't work for seven years. The mogul kept him sitting by the pool in Hollywood. That was the mogul's way of getting back at him for having an affair with his wife.

David also told me something that has stayed with me. This was my fourth film, and I would soon go on to do *The Thomas Crown Affair,* and while *Bonnie and Clyde* had been a big success, I wasn't feeling all that self-confident. David told me that each time he made a movie, when it was over, he always felt as if he would never work again. That staggered me. Here was a man who had starred in more than thirty films by the time I met him. He moved with equal facility between comedy and drama, from *Wuthering Heights* and *The Guns of Navarone* to *Prisoner of Zenda* and *The Pink Panther.* And yet he could never rest easy with his success. I would soon find, like David, that success is no easy bedfellow.

Some years later, I visited David and his wife, Hjördis, in the south of France. He had a villa at St.-Jean-Cap-Ferrat. It was Charlie Chaplin's old villa, where the floors were made from marble because it was cheaper than wood. It was the most lovely, beautiful house that he and his wife had. They went and got these wonderful sea urchins, *oursins* in French, right out of the ocean for us. They were round spiky things and you cracked them open and inside was this orange, delicious meat. The first time I'd ever had them is when I went to see David in the south of France.

THOUGH THE NIGHTS were reserved for long conversations about art and politics and Hollywood, by day it was back to the jungle, a "tropical paradise" I think they billed it. It was closer to primitive. Horses would wander riderless through the streets, and chickens would squawk and scratch in front of the lean-tos made of scraps of tin, with palm leaves for roofs, that housed half of the population. There was an oil refinery on the edge of Coatzacoalcos that belched soot into the air day and night, though there was no evidence that any of the profits from the refinery made it back to the people, who seemed universally poor.

But the beach was still pristine, for the most part, and with the right camera angles the steel framework of the refinery was obscured by the dense tangle of trees and plants. And so we set about creating our fiction, which blocked out the harsher realities. I sometimes felt like a camera lens, looking for the right angles to obscure some of the poverty that bumped up against us in Coatzacoalcos. Though you know that you cannot cure the ills of the world, and that it is work that has brought you to this place, that does not make the poverty any easier to witness.

Seaman was a story built around David Niven's character, a half-mad officer in the British navy, now lost somewhere in the Philippines in the midst of World War II. His boat, the HMS *Curmudgeon* (this was not a subtle satire), is stuck on a sandbar. In its glory days it was a gunboat with David, Lieutenant Commander Finchhaven, at its helm. Recent times have turned it into a supply ship, but Finchhaven is long lost in the memories of his battle days.

Mickey, Alan, and Jack are three new recruits who have managed to get lost during a lifeboat exercise and now find themselves drifting through the fog until they too land on the sandbar. The commander manages to enlist their aid in getting his boat seaworthy once again.

Enter Jennifer Winslow, my character. Once again I was "the girl." This time I own a plantation and wield a mean shotgun, which means when the boat leaves, I intend to be on it. And then the story gets complicated. Jack Carter used to explain the film as "World War Two with tacos." All of us spent hours in either water or mud. I was supposed to be fetching, but I felt more like a drowned rat most of the time.

In one particular scene, David was to fall off the ship's mast and into the water below. We had, at this point in the story, put out to sea, though in reality we were in calm Gulf waters. Nevertheless, David was nervous. He kept arguing with John that the waters might be shark-infested, and he wanted a stunt double to do the dive. John kept reassuring him that these were warm, tropical waters, while sharks like the cold.

Finally David agreed to it and made his fall off the boat. A few minutes later, just as they were pulling him back aboard, a dorsal fin appeared slicing through the water near the boat. David screamed "Sharks!" in John's direction. John quickly yelled back "Dolphins!" I don't think anyone ever determined which it was, but David didn't do another take. He was never coaxed back into the ocean and was never convinced it was just Flipper circling the spot where he'd fallen into the drink.

THE FILMING—which was supposed to be wrapped up in ten weeks—went on much longer, largely due to the rains that would drive us indoors. Jerry flew in for a visit, which helped make it seem a little less bleak, at least for a few days. He took some photos of me at the beach, fashion shots; I was wearing a long dress, the kind of jersey that clings to the skin, and a floppy hat. I had loved the design of the dress so that I had one in white and another in black. A few years later, when we were filming *Puzzle of a Downfall Child,* he chose one of those photos to use as part of the portfolio of shots of the film's leading lady. By then, for us, it was a reminder of happier times.

We were beginning to talk seriously of marriage. It was not a neat and tidy affair. Though Jerry had been separated from his wife for some years, they had not yet divorced. He had two sons that were teenagers then, and we wanted to make sure that whatever happened between us did not hurt the boys. But I am a true romantic, and when I am in love, I am completely in love. I knew we would find a way to work everything out.

Jerry left Mexico—he was always on to a new assignment somewhere around the globe—and I concentrated on doing what I could to give this character a bit more substance. One afternoon while we were all in the lobby waiting out an afternoon storm, watching as the streets turned into mud, I got a call with an offer to do *The Thomas Crown Affair* with Steve McQueen. It was a great coup—a wonderful part, a starring role, an incredible leading man—but I could barely filter all that through the haze of pain.

I had an abscessed tooth and it was getting worse. Over a day or so it had gone from dull ache to constant throb, with an occasional lightning bolt of pain shooting through my jaw. But I was not about to trust the local dentist, though the hotel proprietor assured me, through a gap-toothed smile, that he was "very excellent." The rest of the cast and crew had a round of daiquiris to toast my good fortune. I smiled, hoisted a glass of water, took another aspirin, and put a compress of ice on my cheek to keep it from swelling.

David, whose character turns out to be a ghost at the end of the film, was finished before the rest of us and like a ghost, quickly disappeared from Coatzacoalcos. Absolutely no one blamed him, though I think those of us who remained behind were all beset with more than a touch of envy. Before I left the Mexican shore, I had a postcard from him, sent from his home in the south of France. "Here I am, having my wine and sun." It was so like David that I couldn't help but laugh as I prepared to spend another day sitting out a downpour, then standing in a river of mud.

YOU NEVER set out to make a bad film; you make choices based on what's offered you, and the talent attached to those projects—in this case, John Frankenheimer, David Niven—and you throw the dice. Nevertheless, *The Extraordinary Seaman* was a disaster. The studio was livid at the results. John's idea had been to use actual World War II footage intercut with the footage we had shot, to give the film a kind of authenticity. He was a brilliant man and, in most of what he had done in his career, a brilliant director. This film just didn't work.

The movie was promoted, and screened for critics and theater owners a number of times. With each showing, the reaction grew more dismal, a confirmation of the executives' worst fears. The last time the studio made a run at releasing it was in 1969, more than two years after production had been completed.

As far as I know, *The Extraordinary Seaman* never had a real theatrical run. I'm not sure I ever saw a finished print of the film myself. Like Lieutenant Finchhaven, in the end, the movie disappeared into thin air, the ultimate Hollywood illusion.

MY LIFE was becoming increasingly intertwined with Jerry's by then. Jerry was shooting photos of anyone who was hot. All the top magazines, from *Vogue*, *Glamour*, and *Esquire* to *Newsweek*, *Look*, and *Life*, were using him. The Beatles, Mick Jagger, Bob Dylan, all the new rock groups, as well as all the top fashion models, were his subjects. Sort of the American David Bailey, he was. There was a whole clique of them—Richard Avedon and Irving Penn here, and a whole English contingent, Bailey and Terry Donovan, who was a great friend of Jerry's. It was a sexy profession, but many of them tend to be detached and controlling. That wasn't as much true of Jerry. I think he was detached out of extreme sensitivity.

Though I was initially drawn to his *savoir faire*, his being on the cutting edge of what was happening, which I always found attractive, I also respected Jerry's work, another important piece of the emotional equation for me. Perhaps it is because my own work is so important to me that I relate to that in someone else. But he had a real gentleness to him that also made him very dear.

Jerry was a striking-looking man, with sharply chiseled features set off by a sensual mouth and lots of curly black hair. He wore tinted glasses, which helped keep everyone—even me—at something of a distance. In his own way, Jerry insulated and protected himself, in part, I think, because when you really got down to it, he was shy. But he had made that shyness, that sensitivity, work for him on a professional level. It's what I call the "artist man," someone who has that creative side to them, that is always what I need. Someone who relates to the poetry of life, who helps create it.

He had a wonderful studio down on Twenty-sixth and Park Avenue, and I would occasionally camp there when my apartment was being redone. It was not as much the artist's retreat as it was a microcosm of what was going on in the sixties. On any day you could walk in and there would be some star from the music or fashion world, and a cadre of people with them, with Jerry directing the flow of the action—the lights shifting, scenes changing, clothes tried on and discarded as he worked to create the image that had begun to take shape in his mind.

In a sense, when you're involved with a photographer, it is never just the two of you, because the camera is nearly always there to capture some unexpected moment, or an image that is shaded in some unique way by the changes in the light. Jerry was always taking shots of me, just some crazy candid shots, but a lot that would end up on the cover of one magazine or another. The camera, in a very subconscious way, is what I felt most comfortable with. Everything to me, even now, is work. Then, certainly, my life was filled with lots and lots of work.

When you are in front of the camera, motion picture or still, it is really about you and the lens. That lens is no longer an inanimate object there in front of you, but a living thing. Somehow there is a real sexual connection with that lens, and I don't quite know why. With Jerry, at first, it was very much about a new romance, and he was coming up with some great shots, and they had a great deal of sensuality to them.

It all begins with a concept, and there is fun in the coming up with it, always trying for something different. In a way, Jerry was to be the one who documented the Bonnie era, with fashion spreads and cover shots. One of my favorites was the *Newsweek* cover. Me, all black, black, black, white legs, high-heel black shoes, and a red beret. It was one of the great shots taken of me.

Creating that image, all black and white with just the splash of red from the beret, was very much the way Jerry went about photography. He was a stylist, but there was art to it as well. Jerry's work had more of an edge to it; there was an energy to his shots that I didn't see as much in some of the other photographers of the time. The requests started to pour in for the Bonnie look from all sorts of magazines. We were together, and I would rather have worked with him than anyone else then, and so Jerry would take the shots.

JERRY WAS REALLY my first big-time boyfriend, quite successful in his own right. He was sort of laid-back, a little bit too cool, actually. I remember lying in the bed one drowsy Sunday morning and he was sitting in a black Eames chair by the window, the light streaming in behind him. And I was complaining that he was not open enough and accessible enough to me, that I never knew if he loved me. Sounds like a hopeless female, now. But I did have those feelings. Jerry would find a way to stay above all of those roiling emotions.

I was not an easy person either, and was lost as to how to make a relationship into a good one, having no models from my childhood to draw upon. While my career was beginning to provide me with enough money to overcome some of the poverty I felt growing up, I still struggled with the emotional neediness that stayed with me, that lingered on.

It was a time in my life when I was about to meet a lot of successful men; they were there in all the places that I was starting to move. And it was nice, a relief really, to have someone who was as successful as I was. I was far more comfortable in a relationship if we were both financially independent of one another. Emotional dependence was more than enough to contend with.

As I look back on it now, my relationship with Jerry foreshadowed the shape of things to come. Love and life, for me, always seem at odds. The childhood rhythms move in on me again—two years in a place, then word that we would be leaving, the wrenching good-byes, then on to something else. You learn early on not to care too deeply; it makes the leaving easier. You come to expect it, prepare for it, steel against the pain. And so I did.

The first year, in the first blush of romance, it was just terribly important to me to keep the man. Too many times, I felt I spent the first year of a relationship doing everything, giving everything. I was the perfect partner, charming, entertaining, beautiful, successful. Nipping at my heels, like wild dogs chasing me in the night, was always that great fear of losing. It was the legacy of my father and his leaving that I was forever trying to change. That's the Gatsby dream—dance hard enough and fast enough and you will make him stay.

The second year, I was looking around for the next place I would go. The intention was to leave before he did. That's so sad, because he wasn't even leaving. But I never wanted to be without a bridge to get me from one safe place to another. So in order to leave one relationship, I'd have to have another one to go to. And, in truth, I was restless as well. I've always wanted more, and different, and new. It is the strange dichotomy of my soul.

For much of my life I was very frightened to be alone, terrified really. I once rented a wonderful house in Malibu where I could walk out a door and on to the beach, or sit on a deck and see the ocean. It had a chocolate brown velvet chaise in the sunroom that I could lie on and see the ocean. I remember looking forward to just settling down in the chaise, with a book, or nothing at all, and watching the tide come in. The design was open, windows everywhere. It was a house with no dark corners. Yet at day's end, my first there, when everyone had left, and my assistant, the last to go, had just pulled away, I stood inside and began shaking. The only thing I could manage was to dial my assistant, again and again, until I reached her and convinced her to come back. It was the only way I was able to sleep that night, knowing there was someone else, another human being, in the house with me.

I've come a long way from that chocolate brown chaise and the young actress who stood trembling in the silence of an empty house. Today I am most at peace in solitude. Though my comfort in that isolation sometimes worries me, the stillness that I find there is what has helped me heal. In the quiet, I can finally face the pain of my past, sort through the anger, find where my own responsibility lies, and then forgive, mend broken fences, and move on. It took me many miles over some very rough terrain to get there. And I am grateful every day that there were others before me who cleared the path I now walk.

EIGHT

THE DRESS IS BACKLESS, a diaphanous chiffon—my favorite color of beige with just a hint of pink. It is short, easily a foot above my knees, tight around my waist, with loose folds below. The top is really an elegant turn on the halter, the ends of it long, tied round my neck then falling down the front of the dress. The design leaves my shoulders and arms bare. A breathtaking antique cameo brooch pinned to the front looks to be the only thing that keeps it all from falling in a heap at my feet. There is a fire crackling in the hearth, the brandy is warm, and Steve McQueen and I are warmer still. We are about to play chess.

I'm standing by the table, slowly studying the chessboard, when Steve asks, "Do you play?" I look at him, hold his glance. "Try me." And so begins the most famous scene in *The Thomas Crown Affair*, which we were filming in June of 1967. For the next five minutes, as Thomas Crown and Vicki Anderson, we play, move by measured move. Not a word, not one, is said.

The first move is Steve's. It is the last time he is truly in control of this game. Two more moves. I'm gaining ground. Steve reacts with the briefest smile. He moves a piece and I counter. He looks at the board, adjusts his tie, shifts in his chair, and moves again. I'm studying the board, and as I do, I slowly run my hand up and down my arm, then just under the edge of the halter. Steve blinks, then pulls his eyes away and back to the board. My hand is resting now on the back of the couch next to the table. He drops his arm down on the couch as well and our fingers touch. It might as well have been a hot stove. He pulls back. Play goes on. I put my hand on a bishop, and idly caress it as I contemplate my move. Steve bites his lower lip. I run my finger slowly across mine. I'm thinking. Knees bump, we both shift in our chairs. "Check." It's my line.

It is still, I think, one of the most erotic scenes you will find in a movie, though I am fully, if scantily, clad, and Steve is about as trussed up as one can be, with a three-piece suit and tie, the vest buttoned tight from top to bottom. We barely touch each other, the merest brush of one hand against another, separated by a chessboard for the duration. The script was deceptively cool about it. A couple of sentences of narrative that basically boiled down to one phrase, dropped in there by the writer, Alan Trustman: "chess with sex."

The director, Norman Jewison, fell in love with the line and knew from the beginning that he wanted to take his time with the scene, take everyone to the edge of the cliff right along with him. There was no way Norman was going to cheat this one. The board was set up, and the moves followed an 1899 game played in Vienna by chess masters Walthoffen and Zeissi. He believed the authenticity of the competition would add to the heat, the intensity of the scene. Norman always said "You make a movie, not a script," and that was certainly the case with the chess scene.

It took three days to shoot that scene, and a full day to shoot the minute that follows. The kiss. With a final glance at the board, Steve stands, pulls me roughly to him, and growls, "Let's play something else." It begins with the briefest of touches, his lips barely pressing mine. Then we both move in on each other in what was meant to be the longest, most passionate, most sensual, most erotic kiss in the world. And I'm told, it was. The camera starts spinning around us, as if we are wildly spinning. Then we become a thousand prisms of light, a starburst of colors, as the kiss goes on and on.

A few hours into shooting the scene, every time Norman would yell "Cut!" Steve would laugh and yell "Chap Stick!" Humor is about the only way to get through one of those high-intensity scenes. Every man I've ever met since then, if we talk long enough, has mentioned the chess scene to me. And every man I've known since then who has been in love with me has loved that movie. It's the sensuality as well as the sexuality of it, the tease of it, that they liked. The chess scene and the kiss were deemed steamy enough that it earned the movie a "mature audiences" rating.

WHAT A RICH STORY this was. After a brief stopover in New York to recover from Coatzacoalcos and a visit to the dentist, I had set off for Boston to begin filming *Thomas Crown*. It had the kind of meat that I have always been drawn to. Vicki Anderson was an audacious woman who stopped at nothing. A risk-taker she was, always one jump ahead of everyone else. She was smarter than any of the boys, classier than any of the girls. Someone who outfoxes the fox, only to fall in love with her prey.

The story was cleverly written by Alan Trustman, a Boston attorney who said he got bored writing legal briefs and decided to try his hand at screenwriting. *The Thomas Crown Affair* was the result. It was a classic caper, a form popular in the seventies, but one that you rarely see anymore. The central formula is a fast-paced mix of romance, comedy, and mystery with a twist of film noir—and like a good martini, stirred, not shaken.

In its way, the film is an examination of the idea that success and money don't necessarily bring satisfaction and love, a theme that has seemed to work its way into a lot of my films. Thomas Crown, Steve's character, is the prototype of absolute success—wealthy, smart, funny, with a collection of intelligent friends and lovers around him. But at the core of it, Thomas Crown is bored. You get a sense of just how bored when he keeps upping the bet on an impossible shot during a golf game, and seems completely unfazed by losing. It is the risk that now provides the adrenaline rush, not the winning, though it is clear that winning is what he usually does.

In search of that feeling of outwitting everyone, Crown sets about planning and executing the perfect bank heist. None of the seven gunmen involved in the robbery know each other, and they don't know who he is either. It is a scenario not unlike the one that writer-director Quentin Tarantino would use more than two decades later for his remarkable first film, *Reservoir Dogs*. The robbers meet one time, at the bank, then never see one another again. In *Thomas Crown*, it's a complete success; only one bystander gets hurt, no one dies. The take is $1.2 million in cash, unmarked bills. The injured parties represent the heart of the American corporate establishment, banks and insurance companies. The cops have reached a dead end when the insurance company brings in a specialist, Vicki Anderson.

That the chief investigator on the case was a woman turned the traditional notion of the detective story on its ear. The world of cops and sleuths was almost exclusively male. And this was no ordinary gumshoe either; more like a female James Bond, complete with designer dress. Vicki is beautiful, cool, intelligent, and without question the classic example of "the best man for the job is a woman."

One of the most interesting conceits of the story is that very soon after she and Crown have met, she tells him she's quite sure he is her man. And she always gets her man. Most movies would have threaded that question throughout the film, or at best hinted that Crown was the likely suspect. But in *Thomas Crown*, the audience is in on the secret from the beginning. It becomes a question not of whodunit, but only of whether or not she can prove it. Sometimes it's a good idea to let the audience know more than the character. They become a player in the drama, Vicki's partner in solving the crime. It increases dramatic tension and gives the audience more of a stake in what's going to happen. In the script, Trustman quickly got the whodunit issues out of the way. The payoff for the audience comes in guessing when Crown will figure out what they already know.

Vicki's dilemma was, at the time, a newly emerging phenomenon for women: How does one do all of this in a man's world and not sacrifice one's emotional and personal life in the process? When *Thomas Crown* was released in 1968, the issue was taking on a new resonance as women were increasingly trying to make their way in the world as professionals. Women like Gloria Steinem, who was to become a friend, were reshaping the definition of what it was to be a woman. In my own way, I was adding a voice to the debate, because the characters I played tended to be these kind of women, who were struggling to define themselves.

With Bonnie and with Lou, my character in *Hurry Sundown*, the river of my own experience coincided with theirs, like tributaries feeding into the same stream. They are like children, these characters, a part of you. Lou was so like my mother—that was the emotional territory I mined—and I knew from my own experiences the forces that were driving Bonnie. The river I swam in was that of a southern girl who wanted to get out of the South and live a fuller, more interesting life. Bonnie had a level of frustration at the slowness and lack of opportunity that she found in the place where she had grown up. And that was very much me. I had a real hunger to live in the world and make my way in some way that meant something to me.

But from the minute the star system kicked in—and it did after my third picture—I began to play these urban, sophisticated, neurotic women. I didn't decide, "I'm going to be different." I did want the unconventional, but those roles kind of attached themselves to me. It was a mutual attraction. Somehow the part was written and it was on an edge, just like good art always is. And something of the hunger and desperation and power and talent inside me drew these parts to me. These roles were offered to me before they were offered to anybody else working at the time.

I was that image—usually it was the blond, strong, convention-flaunting, groundbreaking woman. Vicki was really the first in what would become something of the archetypal character for me—a woman pushing the envelope. These were women who found out who they were, who expressed who they were, and who were able to function as complete human beings, the way men do in the world. From Vicki would come Diana Christensen in *Network*, and later Laura Mars and others. That I didn't take the typical roles that were there for actresses, where the women are more traditional, feminine, and de-mure, was one part me and one part the star machine.

Those groundbreaking roles came to me with a great deal of regularity. I was awfully good at acting them, but they weren't neces-sarily me. The irony is that these roles created my career, gave me the chance to strut my stuff, to accomplish what I wanted to accomplish in my work, to win the Oscar. And yet with Vicki, this transmutation, the change, the journey away from who I am, began. All these women were dressed to the nines, while I yearn to dress in the simplest clothes now, and I do. But it's been a long journey getting there. I dress in khakis and white shirts and that's about all I wear anymore. But back then, it was all about how you looked, what your hair looked like, what your makeup looked like, and I bought into that illusion in far too great a way.

That's the trick. How do you keep ahold of who you are—the innocence, the sweetness, the vulnerability, the southernness in me—and still forge ahead, still break new ground, still make a difference in the world? For a time, I wanted not to be the little Dorothy Faye from the South. I wanted to be Vicki Anderson, who comes in and who is able to play the game, the guys' game, by their rules and outwit them at it. I've always vacillated between flinging myself headlong into the glamour and razzamatazz of work and wanting a simpler, quieter, closer, more loving connection with a few people in my life.

I've spent a lifetime really zigzagging between the two: work for two years, then a relationship for two years. It repeats that sort of army brat rhythm of life that I grew up with, a life forever on the move. I don't think it's change that I wanted so much, I think I was driven by fear. I learned early on that relationships and connection with people mean pain, and it's not a good thing. I think I've run from that connection because it always spelled pain to me before. Constantly making movies offered me a new place to go, a way to move on to something else, a reason to say good-bye.

WITH THOMAS CROWN, the motor revved, the clutch went in, the gears shifted, the brake was off, foot on the accelerator, fasten your seatbelts, "Look out, honey!" And the transmogrification began. It was a process that I was to fling myself headlong into, and to flee with equal and alarming impulse and power, as I did years later when I spent nearly a decade in England. I wanted it, and I got there, only to find myself manipulated in the eye of the hurricane—not happy, not connected, either spiritually or to the people around me. I was at the mercy of this hurricane and yet still doing what I wanted to do—which was good work. I have never stopped loving the process of acting. But this trip, this ride on the back of fame, which was really to shift into high gear with Thomas Crown, was to take me far from myself . . . very far indeed.

IN THOMAS CROWN, Vicki was trying to break the notion of what a woman's place in the world was all about. Her problems were not easy ones. She is clearly successful, with a track record of getting the bad guy. It is just as clear that the local detective, Eddie Malone, played by Paul Burke, resents this high-priced hired gun, who he learns very quickly can run circles around him intellectually. But he disapproves of her as much for her ruthlessness as for her intrusion into what he believes should be a man's world.

Vicki is at the top of her game and never intends to face the complication of falling in love, certainly not with the man she's looking to see locked up. But eventually she wants it all—love and success—and for a while lets herself believe that maybe it might be possible. But when she is finally forced to choose, Vicki is not willing to sacrifice who she is, the world she has built for herself against all odds, for love. It has taken her too long to get to the top of her field to throw it all away. In the end, Vicki gets her man, but in the winning, she loses her chance to love.

When the production company tried to get cooperation from the Federal Bureau of Investigation in filming this, the request was turned down, largely because, according to their memos on the request, Vicki makes both the FBI and the local detectives look foolish. Apparently no outsider—and particularly a woman—could be allowed to crack a case, even in the movies.

THIS WAS the first time I had been back in Boston since I had graduated from college and headed off to New York to make my way in the world. Good-bye, Franklin Square. Hello, Ritz-Carlton. It was a luscious place, very refined, and they made, without doubt, the best club sandwiches in the world. I think I ate one almost every night. A triple-decker affair, chicken instead of turkey, with their homemade mayonnaise.

The film used more than ninety locations in and around Boston, from Beacon Hill to South End, and not one of them took me back to the Boston I had known as a college student. There were no side trips to the Somerset Cocktail Lounge or the Kenmore Coffee Shop. It was upper-crust, blue-blood Boston this time around, and I loved it. Even the air felt rich, and the work itself felt rich with possibilities.

With Steve McQueen as my costar, it was really my first time to play opposite someone who was a great big old movie star, and that's exactly what Steve was. He was one of the best-loved actors around, one whose talent more than equaled his sizable commercial appeal. Steve I loved. He was darling. He was daunting. Steve McQueen was an absolute professional, and he knew what was necessary technically to achieve his performance every time he got in front of the camera.

Steve was all sinewy and tough, but at the same time he had such a vulnerability. He definitely had archaic notions about women. If he said it once to me, he said it a million times, "A good woman can take a bum from the streets and turn him into a king." He believed a good woman was terribly important in a man's life. But the notion of putting a woman on a pedestal like that made me shiver. I've been put on pedestals by some of the men in my life, and it's a very dangerous place to be—you can fall off all too easily.

Steve had so much charisma and he seemed to trigger those nurturing instincts in women. He was a chauvinist—legendary in that he was—but a chivalrous one to me. There was a strange dynamic between us. We had both grown up on the wrong side of the tracks, but by the time I got to *Thomas Crown*, I'd shaken off anything that might hint of that. I could walk into the art auction or the polo club with absolute confidence. I could order from a menu in flawless French. I knew good wines from bad. My clothes, which Theadora created, all looked as if I had just stepped off a Paris runway, and I moved in them like I had been shopping Fifth Avenue all of my life.

Steve, on the other hand, never stopped feeling he was a delinquent and any day he'd be found out. He worked for weeks until he mastered life in a suit. And in *Thomas Crown*, the look was a good part of it. I had twenty-nine different costume changes, thirty-one if you count the towels in the sauna scene. But the giant bath sheet was as simple as it got. Most were elaborate outfits that went from head to toe with everything in between meticulously thought out.

Steve was wearing $3,000 suits for the first time in his life. The Phi Beta Kappa key that hung on his vest he always said should have been a hubcap. It took him a while to get the kind of fluid movement of someone who is not merely comfortable, but demands that sort of tailoring. But by the time production began, he had it down beautifully. I loved the way he pulled his vest down, with a swift tug at the bottom, after I've just beaten him at chess. That tug said this was a character who was in control—but maybe not quite; well put together, not easily surprised—but he just had been. I got to constantly surprise him, which was a lot of the fun of this role.

The difference in how our lives had transformed us meant that Steve and I were never completely comfortable with one another. I'd flown out to Hollywood to meet Steve before production began. We talked about the film, how each of us viewed it, then later we had dinner at his house, with his wife, Neile, and their children. Then during the filming in Boston, Jerry came to visit a couple of times, and once again, we had dinner with Steve and his family. But I don't think Steve ever truly relaxed around me, nor I him.

It's very rarified air you're moving in, and strange things happen when two movie stars meet. You might meet in the most ordinary of circumstances—with spouses over dinner. But nothing ever feels quite that ordinary, because through the casual conversation you know the next day you're going to be in front of a camera, locked in a sexually saturated embrace. There is something that is surreal about the interconnections you make with other stars in these situations. It may be for only the short time you are making a film, but for that time you have a highly charged emotional and physical link to this other person. And even over dinner, that is not something you forget.

Steve, friends said, didn't know how to deal with someone like me, who was intelligent and not inclined to the old male-female games that he knew how to win. For my part, I saw him as such an icon. That shade of distance between us ended up working very well in creating the relationship between Vicki and Crown. That's what they call chemistry, when the unspoken, underlying realities of the actors—as people—connect with an intensity that then flows back into their characters. Steve and I really had it in spades. Even in the scene that finds us lounging on the deck of his half-constructed beach house, there was still a hint of tension, as if they both knew any moment they might need to begin their intellectual sparring again.

I GOT VERY INTO the style of things for this movie. Norman wanted a sixties look, but high-end, not hippie. As I worked on the character, the audacity, the courage, the fearlessness evolved as real qualities in her. And I knew the sexuality and the sensuality were going to be a big part of this movie. I've been accused of being a clotheshorse—and this movie contributed to that—but clothes evolve from who the character is. The boldness of the woman creates the look. It was the age of the mini, just as it was starting to happen. I said to Thea, "Let's go very short, this woman doesn't do anything by half measures." And Thea said, "Fine, let's do." And the micro-mini was born.

It was the era of Twiggy and Liza Minnelli. Everyone was beginning to do the very long nails and the emphasized eyelashes underneath, as I was in this film. I would put two rows of false eyelashes on top, and on the bottom I'd put a row of individual lashes that had to be glued on one lash at a time.

Steve, who was such a dyed-in-the-wool man with very specific ideas about a woman's place, was talking to me about my nails once

My grand entrance in The Thomas Crown Affair. *The Thomas Crown Affair* © 1968 United Artists Corp.

and said, "I think they're too long, Faye, don't you think . . . ," and my script happened to be open. The page was scribbled on all over, no white space left, full of notes on the character and the subtext of the lines. He just looked at the page, then at me, and walked away. He never liked the nails, but he told me a few days later that he could see it wasn't a frivolous choice I'd made. Those nails meant something.

In later years, Steve would say again and again that *Thomas Crown* was his favorite movie and that I was the best actress he had ever worked with. And Steve stood in the top ranks of leading men of all time. He was so cool and such a great star.

As a DIRECTOR, Norman Jewison was an absolute love. If he liked the way a scene was going, it was not unusual for him to come over and grab Steve and me in a great bear hug. He was just coming off a tremendous run of success with *The Russians Are Coming, The Russians Are Coming* and *In the Heat of the Night*, which would go on to win an Oscar for Best Picture in 1967 and earn Norman a nomination as Best Director. He was this wonderfully tall Canadian, who looked like Julius Caesar in a polo shirt and jeans, with strands of sandy curls on his forehead.

Bonnie and Clyde was beginning to kick up dust about violence then, and one day Norman started telling me about the first time he crossed the border to come to this country. The sight, he said, was eerie: a line of cops, all with their black leather holsters and guns. In Canada they carry billy clubs. He told me it was the first time in his life he'd seen police carrying guns.

That he was smart went without saying, but Norman was very kind, very loving, and very warm as well. One night, for instance, he threw a clambake, with lobster, for all of us, cast and crew alike, on the beach. He had surrounded himself with talented young people whose ideas he would solicit. Some directors are not that willing to create a shared vision. For example, the editor on the film, Hal Ashby, would go on to become one of the industry's top directors. It seemed like it would take a lot to be at odds with Norman. And there was a lightness about him, his touch, that made him perfect for *Thomas Crown*.

That is not to say the set was completely without tension, or complications. Haskell Wexler was director of photography on the movie. As he and Norman had designed it, not only would we be using real locations, quite often we would be acting out our parts within some real-life situations. In other words, they didn't shut down and rope off sections of Boston to shoot a scene; life would go on and Haskell shot us within it. One of the bank robbery scenes was shot in a real bank, on a real day, with real customers about. No one tried to intervene. But reality sometimes has its price. Filming for a scene at the police station had to be halted one afternoon when some of the officers, who were acting as extras in the movie, had to leave to go investigate a crime a few blocks away. Ironically, it was a bank robbery.

By *Thomas Crown*, Haskell was already well known as a brilliant cinematographer with a remarkable eye. He had won an Oscar for his work on *Who's Afraid of Virginia Woolf?* in 1966, where he had been Mike Nichols' director of photography. He would hide cameras everywhere, camouflaging them so that the camera position never forced a scene to unfold in a specific way. For the scene with the kiss, he did what is called a 360-degree camera move, with the camera circling us time and time again, I seem to recall at an ever increasing speed. The camera became a character in the kiss. The way Wexler shot it had a great part in making the kiss memorable.

Like most cinematographers, Haskell's favorite time to shoot was what we call the magic hour, which is really only about fifteen minutes. It is that moment each day when the light is in transition. It comes just before sunset when the sun is completely red, and as the sun sinks beneath the horizon, it turns the sky pink. The texture and the way the light plays off everything is distinct, and distinctly beautiful. We spent an afternoon at a lovely stretch of beach near Provincetown, setting up the shot and then waiting for just the right light to shoot a scene with Steve and me in the poppy red dune buggy speeding along in the sand.

Finally the light was perfect and everyone was called. Just then Steve, who loved working on cars about as much as he loved acting, took off in the dune buggy, which he had helped build. Steve went on, skidding this way and that, looking as if he might roll it at any moment. Norman and Haskell started having a tense discussion. The light was fading. Steve was still off in the dune buggy, way down the beach, very much out of earshot and ignoring the rest of us.

Steve finally turned the dune buggy around and headed back toward us. He roared to a stop, hopped out the side, and said, "What are you waiting for?" If Norman was the kind of director given to screaming, this would have been the moment for it.

It was a classic standoff, the kind that happens so often between leading actors and directors. In these moments, a director can lose control of the entire movie if he's not careful. At the same time, he can irrevocably damage his relationship with the actor. Norman was wise. He did neither. He took off down the beach for a walk by himself, his hands jammed in his pockets, a cigar clenched in his teeth. He must have walked a good half hour or more. When he got back to the set, he had a white feather, donated by one of the seagulls that constantly circled the beach and the water beyond.

Norman devised this absolutely crazy story that the feather had special powers and whoever had the feather would be the director that day. So he handed the white feather to Steve and said, "You be the director for a while, then we'll give it to Faye, and then I'll take it back." Steve looked at him for a minute, then started laughing, and took the feather and stuck it in Norman's cap. It was exactly the way to handle Steve, who would have fought to the death if Norman had decided to assert his authority as director rather than trying to make peace. There were no more disputes about who was in charge here.

That settled, I climbed into the dune buggy next to Steve and got ready for the ride of a lifetime. Steve was both an expert driver and a fearless one. The car was low-slung, with two huge back tires, very flat, to give it some stability. But when you hit the top of a dune and you're suddenly airborne, the tires don't feel like they're going to do you much good. The sand doesn't give you any traction either, so just a little turn of the steering wheel can send the car into a fast tailspin.

I dug my heels into the floorboard and hung on for dear life. It was terrifying, yet at the same time it was terrific fun, all the thrills and chills of a ride on a roller coaster, which I love. I've since taken my son to ride the dunes, a great hit with a twelve-year-old boy, though it was a tamer version of this wild ride. I was convinced any number of times that Steve was going to roll the buggy. There was one shot that Norman really wanted. He told Steve to race the buggy as fast as he could just to the water's edge, and only when the front tires hit the water was Steve to turn. "It'll make a great shot," said Norman.

If you've ever seen a car hydroplane on a patch of water, it's an amazing image, a huge piece of machinery just skimming effortlessly along. You won't see that, however, in *Thomas Crown*. Steve and I were in the buggy, headed straight for the ocean, top speed, and he's flooring it. The wind is whipping around us; the engine, I swear, is howling; and it looks to be about three seconds before we're destined to hit the water's edge. Steve starts trying to turn the steering wheel. It jams. He's pulling hard now, but it's not moving. There is no margin for error here, and the buggy is up to about 60 mph, hurtling straight toward the ocean.

If this were a movie, about now everything would slow down. I'd have time to contemplate the chances of just getting wet versus getting crushed and trapped under the car. Unfortunately, this is not, at the moment, a movie. And nothing, nothing slows down. If anything, I think the car picked up speed. Before I realized it, we were about twenty feet into the water. The force of the ocean, and the brakes, before they were flooded, finally stopped the car.

Steve and I are very, very wet, and I've swallowed a mouthful of saltwater, but otherwise, we're fine. We get out, drenched, and start sloshing our way back to the beach. I give Steve a smile and a thumbs-up across the waves. He grins and yells that he's going to give me a Purple Heart. When I get to the beach, I collapse on the sand, laughing and shivering. But I'm secretly relieved when I hear that the saltwater has ruined the engine and that the dune buggy will have to be completely rebuilt before it can be driven again.

WHILE IT MAY BE the chess scene that stays with most people, there are other moments in the movie that I am more fond of. Vicki's entrance is great. I walk seemingly for miles in close-up, with dark glasses and a big hat and a slight smile. You don't know who this woman is or what she's up to. But you know it's going to be something pretty spectacular. And I liked very much the earlier scenes with Paul Burke, when I've just been brought on the case and I'm working out who master-minded the heist. Then when I solve the riddle, realizing that the thief is Thomas Crown, it becomes about finding out who he is. I liked the discovery of it all. They were very active scenes, ones that give you a real sense of what Vicki Anderson is all about, how her mind works.

Near the end of the film, once again I put in an homage to an actress I admired, this time to Eleonora Duse, and the scene Shaw wrote so eloquently about in her *Magda* performance, where she sits nervously twisting her wedding band, subconsciously expressing her fear that her marriage might be over. In the movie, Crown has just pulled off a second heist, to prove he can do it and to see if my love for him is great enough that I will take his side in all of this.

I have made my choice, and I'm sitting in a car in the cemetery where the money will be dropped and where we are supposed to meet. But I am with the detectives, who are working the case, and the cemetery is surrounded by police, ready to pick him up. The drop has been made, the money is sitting there, and we're waiting for him to show up. Everyone is nervous, convinced he won't show. As I argue that he will, I know he will, I take the long chain I decided to wear around my neck and idly begin to twist one end around the finger of my left hand—the wedding-ring finger. The scene goes on, the tension rises, and the chain twists tighter around my finger, subconsciously expressing the fear as Duse did—that it's over.

I'm particularly fond of the last scene in the movie. We've been waiting now for a while and just as we are about to give up, Crown's Rolls-Royce turns into the cemetery and makes its way toward us. Everyone jumps and runs to the car, as a startled Western Union boy rolls down the window, a telegram in hand, and says, "Vicki Anderson?" As I open it and begin to read, Steve's voice comes over, saying, "Left early." Then we cut to a shot of Steve sitting in a first-class seat on a jet, on his way to some place that I'll never go.

"Please come with the money . . . or you keep the car. All my love, Thomas." I walk a few steps, tearing the telegram in pieces. Just then a plane flies overhead and I toss the torn pieces in the air, as if it were a handful of confetti. As the pieces fall around me, a single tear starts falling down my cheek. I planned all that and I loved it. I thought it was a great final moment for the character. It blended the irony and the mock frivolity of flinging the confetti in the air, a way of saying, "Thanks for the party." Only the tear concedes her loss. He is the love of her life, but when the choice must be made, she refuses to give up all that she has built for herself. The traditional decision was always that the woman gives up everything and becomes the wife, the mother. And that's all wonderful. But the struggle that Gloria Steinem talked about, and what these roles were trying to say, and what I was trying to solve in my own life, is how do you have both of those things? Which you can do. But it's very hard. Ultimately Vicki chose her self.

ABOUT MIDWAY through shooting *Thomas Crown*, Jerry was launching a new disco in Greenwich Village. He and the other investors in Ondine had had a falling out, and so he'd found other partners for a new place, Salvation. It replaced an old nightclub, and the architect had taken the dance floor, dug down a few more feet, and turned it into more of a deep pit. It would have been perfect for moshing, if we had been that adventurous then. The stage was on one side of the dance floor; the other side rose, arena-like, a step at a time, with each platform scattered with cushions for people to lounge on, and long, low tables, painted in bright, psychedelic colors, for drinks.

Opening night, Jerry had booked Jimi Hendrix, who had become one of Jerry's friends as he traveled through the music world with his camera. The place was packed by the time I showed up. It was just before *Bonnie and Clyde* hit so I was able to slip in completely unnoticed and surprise Jerry. Not long after, on Halloween night of that year, after the movie was the talk of the town, there were people outside Salvation waiting to see me arrive for the huge party Jerry was throwing. It wasn't anything on the scale of what I would experience a few months later in Paris, but it was a taste of things to come. And I liked the taste of it. I told someone that night my attitude about Hollywood: "They used to be able to take you and make you into their creation. They could bend you and make you into whoever they thought you should be. Well, they can't do that to me."

By *Thomas Crown*, with all the talk surrounding my performance as Bonnie, I felt like an actress on the Oscar road. Late one night while I was still shooting *Thomas Crown*, Warren Beatty called me. They had just screened *Bonnie and Clyde* in Los Angeles. "Everybody wants you," he said, "and so do I." It was a pretty alluring thing to say. I knew he meant it as a compliment, not a flirtation, because there never was an affair. I never fooled around with any of these above-the-title guys, because I felt they were too dangerous for me. They were often womanizers of the first order. They were affectionate womanizers, but womanizers they were. And I knew that meant inevitable parting. No way would I ever think of a long relationship where I would remake the pain of my past and my parents' divorcing with a man like Warren or, later, Jack Nicholson. Though I adored their friendship, I never wanted it to progress beyond that, because I knew it would have been a relationship doomed to failure. I don't know how the rest of the women did it, but I wasn't about to let myself in for that kind of heartbreak.

Then too, I wasn't a little starlet, some brainless beauty, and I didn't ever want to give anyone a chance to draw that conclusion. I knew what I wanted to do and I did it. It had to do with a growing belief in myself and what I could accomplish. I really did believe in myself, more than I have at many other times in my life. But I was just at the beginning of my prime then, one success building off another. Nobody could really cross me. I could call my own shots and make my own choices, and I was okay. I don't feel it often, that sense that everything is okay, that there's not danger lurking around the corner. But I did then.

•

THERE IS SOMETHING about this business, that once you are an insider, you are adopted into this particular family of man. Perhaps it is because fame puts such a distance between you and the rest of the world, it is easier to move within an insulated environment where fame has touched all the others too. In a way, it is a great equalizer. You had to be something out of the ordinary to get in, but once inside, you're a bit like everyone else. And you have the business as an immediate common bond, a ready cadre of people as obsessed about the process as you are.

It was in this way that I had met Richard Harris. He was crazy and wonderful all at the same time, and became an immediate friend. Richard by then was legendary for his work in the theater in Britain, and American audiences were getting to know him through his more recent work in film. Those who saw him in *This Sporting Life* could not fail to be affected by this dark drama of the British working class. He had first seen me in a workshop performance during my Lincoln Center days and had told me he thought I had a rare talent.

We spent a good deal of time together off and on during the sixties. And we talked about many things, one of which was the idea of doing *Hamlet* together, first on the London stage, then on film, with me playing Ophelia to his prince. Richard said if he was going to do the film, he wanted me to be a part of it. Richard was a classical actor; he had become very dear to me and I really did want to work with him, it just never happened. And when we began talking of doing *Hamlet*, I was missing the stage. It demands of you a clarity and continuity of performance that you don't find anywhere else, forcing you to use and develop all those emotional muscles needed for good acting.

I had been working pretty much nonstop for a lifetime, it seemed. Five movies in two years had taken most of my time. I don't think I had spent a full week in my new apartment, though I had had it more than a year. So when I got a call from Richard to come to the London premiere of *Camelot*, where we would also have a chance to discuss the possibility of our doing a play, I jumped at the idea. Jerry wanted to make another trip to Britain anyway, so we headed out in late October to visit a potential prince and meet a lord and a lady too.

Camelot was set to premiere in the Warner Theatre, where *Bonnie and Clyde* had opened a few months earlier. Princess Margaret and Lord Snowdon were to be the royal guests of honor at the King Arthur and the Knights of the Round Table Ball afterward. With British royalty, and members of the country's royal theater family as well, Richard and his costar Vanessa Redgrave, the premiere was to be a world-class event.

The fashion press was enchanted with the outfit I wore. The dress was tight, a plunging neckline and the barest mini. Over that, I wore a loose midi-coat, of the same brown satin, its edges trimmed with a thick row of ostrich feathers. I would be named to the Best Dressed list at the end of the year and appear in roughly two dozen different fashion spreads in magazines around the world within the next few months. Europe was to embrace me as a star far more quickly and more enduringly than my own country. My French friends have said to me, "You never have to do anything else in your life for us to love you forever."

Quite different from Hollywood, I found, where it's all about today. That is both the charm and the bane of this country. People seem to be unable to relate to and appreciate a body of work. It's all about what's going on *now*; there is no awareness of history, of what created now. Memories are terribly short in America—it's a young country, adolescent.

As 1967 DREW to a close, I was exhilarated, but I was also exhausted. I wanted very much to just escape it all for a while. I took Jerry home for Thanksgiving to meet my mother and family, not quite knowing what to expect. But they hit it off famously, and it was a remarkably trouble-free holiday. My mother had remarried a few years earlier to a good and decent man, Jim Hartshorn. They were now living in Columbia, South Carolina.

In January, the Academy Awards announced its nominees for 1967, with my name on the list. It was an extraordinary feeling to be so new at filmmaking and receive that sort of critical acclaim from my peers. I felt very grateful to my colleagues in the industry and thrilled that *Bonnie and Clyde*, which had had such a rough ride at the outset, was getting so much attention. Warren managed to convince Warner Bros. to rerelease the film based on the strength of the nominations, something that was unheard of in those days.

Jerry and I headed to Paris that February for the *Bonnie and Clyde* premiere, with plans for an extended vacation. Ismail Merchant was interested in talking to us about being involved with *Puzzle of a Downfall Child* as a producer. The script was still being revised and there was no studio backing yet, so we were in the market for one. Ismail was in Bombay where the film *The Guru* was being made, with Michael York and Rita Tushingham, and he invited us to come meet with him there. So after Paris, we decided to spend some time in India.

Why Air India decided to surprise me, I'll never know. But as in all things, timing is everything, and after an exhausting round of screenings, parties, and interviews in Paris, I was not really in the mood for a surprise. But there was no other word for it—well, perhaps shock might do—when I walked out the door of the plane in Bombay and looked at the tarmac below. There was a sea of faces all turned to watch me, a welcoming party that the airline had organized. At their center, a howdah being held by four boys who looked to be just teenagers was there to transport me from the airplane to the arrival area. My feet were not to touch the ground. Young girls, their dark eyes wide above the white veils of their saris, were holding baskets of flower petals to cover the pathway the howdah would follow; others were carrying rose water to sprinkle along the way.

It was truly royal treatment, and I smiled and tried to be gracious as the boys knelt down in front of me so I could climb into the seat. Suddenly I was up, shoulder high, the litter swaying as they carried me along, the petals fluttering around me like snow. There were cheers, and I waved as the procession slowly moved along, secretly thanking whatever gods looked over the Bombay airport that they hadn't been able to locate an elephant.

We visited the *Guru* set briefly, resolved nothing more with Ismail than that we would talk again—a common malaise in Hollywood—then set out to see Bombay. It is impossible to walk through the city and not be overwhelmed by the poverty. What seemed remarkable to me at the time was the kind of kinetic energy of the people as they made their way from home to market. We would meander through the open bazaars for hours—that was the only speed possible, as the crush of bodies kept everything at a languid pace.

In the shops, I found and bought lots of silver and Indian jewelry. One piece was an antique necklace that I fell in love with. Long strands of silver had been intertwined to form the chain, which held a hand-tooled silver bell, tarnished from years of wear. I bought a number of saris, the cloth dyed in patterns and colors unchanged for centuries, from vendors along the street, ancient, toothless women who laughed and clucked at me.

The poverty, though, was overwhelming; the streets were lined with the poor. We traveled north from Bombay to Jaipur, then finally to Delhi by way of Agra, through this constant stream of people. Starting, stopping, starting, then stopping again. Our car horn never stopped beeping the entire journey. All this poverty in contrast to the splendor of the palace of the Taj Mahal. And in Jaipur, we saw the palace of the Maharajah of Jaipur, which was absolutely phenomenal; encrusted jewels in walls, and mirrors everywhere.

Moscow was our next stop. I wanted to go to Russia because of Mrs. Khrushchev's face. I just saw this peasant woman and it reminded me of my Olma. And I was curious to find out who these Russian people were. We'd arranged for a driver and a guide to meet us at the airport. Our plan was to stay a week in Moscow, then fly to St. Petersburg (known as Leningrad at that time) for a few days before heading back to the States. It was March, but the city was still frozen, and I disappeared inside fur coats and hats.

We were probably crazy to even consider the visit. The Cold War was heating up again around the subject of Vietnam, and I carried a certain paranoia about the country that had for so long been an enemy of my own. It took us hours to get through the Moscow airport. Uniformed men searched our luggage, taking out every single piece of clothing, unfolding it, looking in every bag. I'm convinced they thought that I was concealing contraband of some sort in my cosmetics bag, which was stuffed with the tools of my trade. Most of my jewelry was confiscated, with no explanation. Though they said I would be able to retrieve it on our way out, I never expected to see it again. The decisions were unilateral. There was no room for discussion. The Russians definitely had "Love it or leave it" down long before it ever entered our vocabulary.

We finally got our baggage back and found the car that was to take us to town. The ticket agent had told us our guides would meet us at the car, so we were not surprised to find three people in the car when we got in. Their English was fairly primitive; of course that was far better than my Russian, which was limited to what I could manage using the Russian-English dictionary I kept stuffed in the pocket of my coat. But they were jovial sorts, with hearty laughs, gladly answering all of our questions. About halfway to town, though, Jerry and I started glancing at each other. These three were not just jovial, they were dead drunk. After a few more questions, which they dutifully answered, we discovered they were not our guides, just three Russians looking to hitch a ride to town. I think I relaxed a little after that. The government might be intimidating, but the people were warm and friendly.

The hotel we'd been booked into was the Hotel Russia, a huge, dreary place that boasted five thousand rooms. We finally did connect with our guide, who turned out to be not nearly as much fun as our trio of hitchhikers. He had the sour scowl that I envisioned that most of the KGB wore. Moscow is a beautiful city filled with contradictions and contrast. There were no easy answers even then. The graceful architecture from ancient times bumped up against the newest buildings, which had been stripped bare of any aesthetic. It was a cold city; the faces of the people were, for the most part, closed and careful in public. When we were with our guide, we could not approach any of the Russian people without making them very anxious, which only fed my theory of our guide's KGB connections.

There was a Georgian restaurant we went to that was quite interesting, but some of our best times were the hours we spent in the clubs. They had theater clubs, cinema clubs, journalism clubs—all of these clubs in which they could get things from the West that most Russians never saw. We went to the cinema club and found they loved Stanley Kramer, which is why *Oklahoma Crude* did so well over there later on. They were able to get movies that the rest of the people couldn't. The clubs were really for the Russian elite, but what a strange contradiction in terms that the elite had to go underground to experience these forbidden pieces of Western culture.

MOSCOW HAD BEEN a world apart, but the trip to St. Petersburg was completely surreal. We had wanted to visit the Hermitage Museum, which had the famous collection of modern French paintings— Monet, Matisse, Gauguin, Degas—and much of Fabergé's work in enamel, and the famous Fabergé eggs, which he had done when he was the court jeweler for the czar. We took off one morning on Aeroflot, and settled in for the flight, which was a little more than two hours. It was a clear day, and through the window we could see the sign on the side of the airport—MOCKBA—receding along with the Moscow skyline. The flight was completely uneventful. No voices came over the intercom, not the stewardesses', nor the pilot's. We made the trip in silence. We were descending when Jerry looked out the window and grabbed my arm. "Faye, it looks exactly like Moscow." When we touched down, we could see the sign, MOCKBA, once again. "Maybe it means 'airport,' " I said. And when we discovered that Mockba (Moskva in our alphabet) is Russian for Moscow, not airport, our paranoia reached a new high.

After we landed, just as the passengers were to get off the plane, we were told that bad weather had forced the plane to turn back. I was relieved that we weren't in some sort of Alice-in-Wonderland maze where every city was called Mockva, but then disappointed when I realized we would not get to St. Petersburg. Russia in those years could make you feel ill at ease pretty quickly. There was always the train to St. Petersburg, but somehow, after the flight, it didn't seem worth the risk.

On the day we left, when we walked into the waiting room at the airport terminal, we saw about fifty East German soldiers sitting there watching television. I looked at the set to see if I could figure out what they were watching. It was the Battle of Stalingrad. It must have been horrendous for them to sit there watching that bitter defeat. These were young Germans, hardly more than boys, who would face a lifetime of the Nazi legacy. I wondered how their history would frame their lives.

I left Russia with all my jewelry returned to me and with an added appreciation for the kind of freedom that I was born into. While I did not always agree with my government, about Vietnam in particular then, at least I could rail against it without fear of retribution. Freedom was very much on my mind after this trip in other ways as well. I was increasingly restless in my relationship with Jerry. He was a good and kind man, but I was beginning to worry that I had committed to marriage too soon. That side of me that pines for a longtime companion was losing ground to the side that wanted to focus once again on a career, with no distractions.

My relationship with Jerry was too comfortable, too easy really. I was edgy, and I started to think about breaking it off. There was a chance that *Puzzle* might be ready to film by the summer, and in my mind, I think I was delaying any separation until we had finished the movie. It was something that I knew Jerry cared about deeply—it was a chance for him to direct—and I was now critical to getting backing for the project.

The fortieth Academy Awards were scheduled to take place April 8, not long after I returned from Russia. Four days before the ceremony, Dr. Martin Luther King, Jr., was assassinated at a Memphis hotel. His funeral was scheduled for April 9. Word came quickly to Academy president Gregory Peck that at least five people scheduled to appear on the show—Sidney Poitier, Louis Armstrong, Diahann Carroll, Sammy Davis, Jr., and Rod Steiger—would not do so if it went on as scheduled a day before Dr. King's funeral. In response the Academy postponed the event for two days and canceled the Governor's Ball afterward.

Theadora, who always did wonderful creations, designed my Oscar dress. The inspiration for my look for the evening was the way Botticelli's model, Simonetta Vespucci, looked in his painting *Birth of Venus*. My hair was pale blond and pulled straight back, with a chignon at the nape of my neck. Thea chose black satin for the dress and designed it with a dropped waist. It was short in the front with a slight train in back, and these wonderful black silk flowers rimming the collar that rose like a fan behind me, and then went all the way down the front and down the train of the dress—calla lilies, roses, all kinds of different flowers.

I remember to this day, it was Lily Fonda, who was then one of the great cutter-fitters at Western Costume, who handled the fitting. She did all my clothes through *Chinatown* and *Network*. Lily would tell me stories about Marlene Dietrich, how she would stand there for hours for a fitting, endlessly and completely patient. That was a different era, when stars were pampered and petted by the studios so that they would feel like great, exotic creatures. And I was lucky enough to be on the tail end of it.

It is difficult, once you've been nominated, not to want to win—and I was no exception. I would have loved to have ended that night with a gold statue in my hand for my performance in *Bonnie and Clyde*. But I can honestly say I would have been shocked. Though Dame Edith Evans, who had starred in *The Whisperers*, and I were rumored to be front-runners, at that point in my career, I simply didn't believe it was possible the Oscar would be mine. Apart from her early win with *Morning Glory*, Katharine Hepburn, after eight nominations for Best Actress, but no Oscars, for her work in such films as *The African Queen, Suddenly, Last Summer*, and *Long Day's Journey into Night*, finally was accorded her due.

Though Hepburn won the Oscar for her performance in *Guess Who's Coming to Dinner*, it was really her body of work that the Academy members were recognizing that night. This is how the Oscar often works. People rarely win for their first performance. It is usually after being nominated twice, three times—if then. I was not to win until my third nomination. On that night in 1968, I was disappointed not to have won, but it was an important night for me. I was a young actress, and I knew there were other roles for me to play. What surprised me was the deluge of telegrams I received the day after. The funniest was from a New York chum. It read, "Bonnie, you wuz robbed!"

NINE

I T IS NOT YET DAWN and Marcello Mastroianni and I are up in the eagles' nest. That is the name the workmen have given to the suite of rooms they are building for us at the very top of Marcello's villa in Lucca, Italy, just north of Pisa. Marcello is hours from waking, but sleep eludes me. I love these rooms, with their windows looking out over the red-tiled roofs below and the rolling hills of the Tuscan countryside just beyond the city's walls. You can almost see forever. The sunrise here is the most beautiful I have seen anywhere, ripe and golden, and it will warm you even on a winter's day.

Marcello and I have been together, deeply in love, a year now. We have found that our passion for houses is a shared one, and the house in Lucca is our current project. We build it as we build our relationship, with much love and laughter and affection. But it is not always easy between us; that is what has robbed me of sleep. I want to marry and have children and grow old with this man. Marcello tells me that is what he wants too. We even have names for these children we dream of, Luca and Clare, a boy and a girl. But what I have come to believe is that Marcello wants it all—to keep his wife, from whom he has kept a dignified distance for years now, and still not lose me.

He thinks of divorce each time I accept a role that takes me away from him. He calls, he flies to me to tell me that I am what he loves, that he only feels whole when we are together. But once we are together again, his conviction slips away because he does not believe I will ever truly leave him. I fear he will talk of it forever, and one day I will awaken, old and without a child or a marriage. And that, I think, in the stillness of this morning, is more than I can bear.

We met early in 1968 with the idea of costarring in the film adaptation of an Italian play, *The Lovers*. I had seen Marcello in Federico Fellini's *8½* and found in his performance a purity and truth that is exceedingly rare. In my mind, he was and remains truly one of the greatest actors of our time. If I decided to take the part, it would mean giving up a starring role in *Paint Your Wagon* with Clint Eastwood and Lee Marvin, but I thought this might be my only chance to work with Marcello, and I had to at least give the project serious consideration.

I admit, when we first met, I was a bit starstruck. And Marcello, he was gorgeous. I thought it a shame that the great Italian painters were of another time; his face, framed by his very dark hair, had the kind of beauty and nuance that would have made a wonderful subject. He wore a black sweater that night with a scarf around his neck, and looked very dashing. He was charming, funny, and had an electricity to him that made him a very compelling man.

Vittorio De Sica was set to direct the film. De Sica, one of the most distinctive voices in the neorealism movement in Italy, had received much acclaim for his film *The Bicycle Thief*. It was an emotional story of an unemployed laborer whose chances of employment are dashed when his bicycle is stolen, and it won an Academy Award as Best Foreign Film in 1949. De Sica cast it completely with people he found on the street. None had acted before, and it gave the film a raw, almost documentary quality that was quite exquisite. He said his aim was to de-romanticize cinema, to strip it bare.

I wasn't sure why De Sica wanted to do a more conventional drama now, but he and Marcello and I had dinner together in New York to discuss the possibility of working together on *The Lovers*. We must have looked like something out of a Fellini film, with the patchwork of languages and gestures we used to try to talk about the movie. I was fluent in French and could speak a little Italian. Marcello understood a good bit of French and could speak the barest of English. And De Sica could speak a few words of English, which he laced with Italian flourishes that made the language sound very musical and always dramatic.

The story, I thought, had possibilities, but the script was in miserable shape. I was to be an American fashion designer with only a few weeks to live who escapes to Italy in search of some final moments of love. Marcello is an Italian engineer whom I had chanced to meet in an airport years ago. I call him and we spend my last days together. Dealing with mortality, particularly when you know exactly what you have left to you, I thought would make for a character that I could really dig into. The strange contradiction of how we humans go about living intrigued me, how often we fail to make the most of life until we see the end before us. As Emily in Thornton Wilder's *Our Town* says, "Do any of us ever live life while we live it—every, every moment?" After exacting a promise that Marcello and De Sica would work on the script, I agreed.

In May, I left for Cortina d'Ampezzo, where we were to shoot the film. Marcello and I kept our distance for quite some time. We were working hard and I was navigating my relationship with De Sica, who seemed to be far more comfortable working with the non-professionals he found on the street—as he had in *The Bicycle Thief*—than he was with actors who knew their craft, as both Marcello and I did. De Sica was a brilliant director. But his tendency, perhaps because of the language problem, was to show me how to do something rather than to work with me from the ground up, which was the way I was used to working.

When I was filming *The Arrangement* a few months later, I received a photo someone had snapped on location in Italy. Kazan, who was directing the film, looked at the photo and said, "You see there, Faye, Vittorio's telling you to do something and you're not listening to him at all." I laughed and said, "No, Gadg, I'm not, because he was saying, 'My darling, Faye, you must do this like this.' " He would stand there making these funny faces to demonstrate what he was looking for. I'd watch, trying to appear completely engrossed, but thinking all the while, I'm not going to listen to him because if I listen to him, I'm going to imitate what he's doing. I'm going to make a face here instead of feel a feeling.

It's precarious, the creative process. We're like blotting papers, we actors. I soak up what's around, and it's very hard to shake it once it's come in. When I am open, vulnerable, *in* the creative process, I am defenseless. So I try to guard that creative process, keep it inside, locked away, safe, mine. And from a well of safety comes my work: pure, unadulterated, original. That is the goal. So I shield my soul, as it were, from imitating gestures. De Sica would act out the moment for me, which had the effect of dictating my performance. I had to block it out, because if I were to mimic it, the moment would not be true. With non-pros, maybe he had to do that. But line readings and indicating—"do it this way"—should be done with professionals only as a last resort.

I might not always have listened to him, but I adored De Sica, he was such a character. He loved to gamble and was rather notorious for it, especially for the huge losses he would pile up. When producers wanted to get him for a film, they would go to the gaming tables and search him out. He was well known and never hard to find. There they would wait until he was losing, then slip the contract onto the table and a pen into his hand, and say, "Sign here." And he would. And another game would be played, and another film would be made.

Vittorio's life was a complicated one. He had two families that he loved, one with his first wife, and another with the woman who would become his second wife. And he lived with them both. He would get up in the morning, shower, dress, then open the bedroom door and say, "Good morning, my children." He'd sit down and have breakfast, then go out the door, ostensibly to work, with a "Good-bye, my children." Out one door, then in the back door of another house. "Hello, my children," he'd say, and sit down to another breakfast. All this before he began his workday. This was his routine for twenty or more years, morning and night, breakfast and dinner. I only met wife number two.

This story was told with a great deal of affection by the people in Italy. It was just a true example of how Italians—and Marcello was no exception—so often have these dual lives, because divorce was not permitted. That rule of course didn't stop people from falling out of love with someone and in love with someone else. So you have these double lives being lived. It was something I came to know only too well.

A REPORTER on the set of *The Lovers* asked me how I felt about playing a love scene with someone like Marcello. He was a film idol, and certainly in Italy thought of as the kind of leading man that women were immediately smitten with. I remember telling him that you're always a little in love with the other actor when you play those scenes. And that is when I fell in love with Marcello, in a scene early in the movie when the two of us have our first romantic encounter.

It was a passionate moment. He takes me in his arms and we are

A Place for Lovers: *the film where Marcello Mastroianni and I met and fell in love.*
© Douglas Kirkland

kissing, and suddenly neither of us was acting anymore. I had vowed early in my career to avoid set romances. So often, once the film is over, so is the romance. It's too easy to give yourself over to the emotion of the scene that has brought you together. And when the scene is gone, when the play ends, the emotion so often dies with it. I had seen it happen to others and I didn't want that to happen to me, and so I resisted being swept away. But with Marcello, I broke that rule.

There's is a moment in the film when I challenge Marcello to steal something for me, as a bizarre test of love. He does, quickly stuffing the item into my coat pockets. At the climax of the scene, Marcello is to grab me and pull at my pockets to prove to the crowd that has gathered around us that I am the thief, not he. We had done a number of takes, with Marcello suddenly pulling at my pockets, and me jumping back, startled and surprised.

De Sica was clearly frustrated; he was not getting what he wanted.

Suddenly he strides over to me, roughly grabs my coat pockets, and I scream, startled by it all. "The problem here," said De Sica as he walked back to the camera, "is that when Marcello does it, you like it. And you," he said, turning to Marcello, and shaking his head, "you are too gentle with this one." The next take De Sica got what he wanted.

I am always attracted to an artist, a soulmate. As an actor, Marcello was remarkable and unique. He still is. He used to say, "I never prepare . . . but I prepare." He always kept it in that sort of balance, so that he never really said, "What am I doing here?" But the ideas were always there, floating around. It made his acting very fluid, effortless in its look, because he never pinned down exactly what he was going to do until he did it. Marcello was the king of Italy. He had such a powerful presence on screen; he was the matinee idol everyone knew and loved. It was all very alluring, but beyond all of that, Marcello was fun to be with. He could take any story and turn it into a tale that would leave you laughing. Oh, we laughed so much, Marcello and I.

Cortina didn't help; it was so very beautiful, snow-covered still when we arrived, this tiny town in the shadow of the Italian Alps. In the evenings, we would dine on wonderful Italian food and talk and laugh. There was the shipboard aura of a set, that sense of adventure and of being in a cocoon together. I loved being with him, watching him.

For months, I had been drifting in my relationship with Jerry, and though we hadn't talked about it, I believe he sensed we were growing apart. I cared about him very much, but I knew that I couldn't commit to a lifetime any longer. Jerry had come to see me in Cortina, and the days had been filled with tense silences and hollow laughter. He got word while he was there that his divorce was final, which meant that nothing stood in the way of our getting married now. When we finally talked, he was to fly out to an assignment in London the next day.

I remember he was sitting in a chair in my hotel suite, and I was sitting behind the desk, just across from him. I could see the rugged and unforgiving beauty of the Dolomite mountains through the window behind him. It was too beautiful to be so sad, and it all felt a bit unreal, but I knew it was over between us, and said so. We talked for a while, until there was nothing more to say. I told Jerry that nothing would keep me from doing *Puzzle of a Downfall Child*, that I still believed in the film and wanted to do it with him.

On June 6, Jerry left Cortina for London. It stays in my mind because a few hours after he had gone, the radio stations broke in with a news bulletin. Robert Kennedy had been killed while he was campaigning in California. We had been filming on one of the slopes when we got the news. Vittorio shut down the set for the rest of the day, and I went back to my room in the hotel to try to deal with the enormity of what had happened—John Kennedy, Martin Luther King, Jr., and now Bobby. I cried a great deal over Bobby Kennedy's death, as I had before over President Kennedy's and Reverend King's. I loved all of those men. King's recordings I still listen to to this day, admiring the orator that he was, the great human being that he was.

What was this assassination saying to me about my country? I felt such grief in my heart, in my soul, about the violence. I thought that day, What is going on in my country? And I grieved at the loss of those magical brothers.

The news of Bobby Kennedy's death just uncorked a lot of those thoughts that day. I thought about what was going on in the sixties, campus unrest, big city riots. I had been on an express train since I graduated from college, and that derailed any kind of social activism. I had gotten to the top of the mountain—my own eagles' nest—where I could say, "Here I can live and here I can be free and here I can have a degree of luxury and a degree of creative liberty." But it wasn't so simple, I was learning, standing on top of the mountain, and it certainly didn't mean I was free from the havoc this sort of violence wreaked on the nation's psyche, my psyche as well.

But it seemed that these deaths, this violence, all tied into the value system in this country, which was, for the most part, the almighty dollar. And power, of course. In the East, there is a coterie, a small group of people that I really love. It's Robert Coles, and it's William Alfred, Peter Wolf. It's Boston and Cambridge and Harvard— where education happens at the highest levels for me. And New York. It is there, with these friends, that I have become more socially and politically aware. And I hope to be more so as my life goes on.

At the time, I was trying to find a measure of personal happiness with this Italian man, with my work, with doing something meaningful that relates to who women are in our society. The identity of a *woman*—not just me, but all women.

On that day, with all of these thoughts swirling through my mind, with tears in my eyes, I went downstairs and finally found some of the crew, who had gathered in the hotel bar. We talked of America and of the violence there. They asked if I was afraid, living as I did in New York City. I cannot say that I never felt fear as I walked the city streets, often late at night, but you have to own the world you live in. You cannot retreat from it. The harsh reality now, as then, is that violence exists. Pretend it does not, and you'll never change it.

Mine was a country that was riddled by violence then, and is now, still. I fled to Europe, to the lovely seasoned history of England and France and Italy. To the age of these countries. There was a vigor in America, a vigor that spawned the violence, but it also spawned an energy of thought that I missed when I was in Europe.

RELEASED IN 1969, A *Place for Lovers*, as it came to be called, was a film that turned out to be an artistic disappointment to both Marcello and me. Though when I next saw De Sica in the spring of 1972 when he won the Best Foreign Film Oscar for *The Garden of the Finzi-Continis*, he argued otherwise. "You see, Faye," he said, "we were ahead of our time." The previous year *Love Story* had been a huge hit and had received a Best Picture nomination. De Sica was convinced we had told the story of love in the face of death too soon.

Shooting in Italy was so beautiful. We used the Villa Maser, an incredibly grand, muted-yellow Palladian estate as one of our locations. Eleonora Duse had lived in Treviso very near the villa. She had a simple lodge-ish kind of house in town not far from the townhouse where Gabriele D'Annunzio—the Italian writer—lived. He had brought a whole facade from Holland and put it on the front of his townhouse. They're crazy, the Italians. He was the man who stole, and broke, Duse's heart. She was desperately in love with him, but he left her. When Duse died outside the stage door of a theater in Pittsburgh, she was broken-hearted.

Shaw's essays on Duse and Sarah Bernhardt, in which he compared their performances, had such an impact on me. Duse's performances were so alive and so real, very much what we call Method acting. Sarah Bernhardt, considered one of the great stage actresses of that time, was representational; she would pretend to feel. Duse *experienced* the role. It was the kind of performance that drew the audience in. You were caught up in the rapture of watching her go through an experience right there onstage in front of you. For a time I adopted Duse's style of eyebrows, and used to make mine look like hers. Duse's brows went up at the beginning and then on, in a wavy sort of way. It gave her face a comic-tragic quality that I liked very much.

The set in Cortina folded, and Marcello and I set out to see if we could build a life together. It was the beginning of a very European romance. There were lazy spring nights where we would hire a gondola and spend the evening on the Grand Canal of Venice, talking, sipping wine, and watching as the thirteenth-century palazzi that line the waterway slipped slowly by.

We spent a summer on his sailboat, cruising the Mediterranean with his crazy Italian crew, who each time they would come within a hair of crashing into the rocks would throw their hands up and say "*Ma, il destino,*" as if it was their destiny to crash. We only laughed at their disasters, although once Marcello did look at me and say, "You know, baby, it's very serious. The sea, you cannot joke about the sea."

That summer we sailed to Corsica as well. The days were long and we would linger over sumptuous lunches. We'd sit on the deck, a light breeze cooling us, and dine alfresco—mozzarella, basil, and tomato drizzled in olive oil; fresh parmesan and even fresher pasta. Marcello and I made side trips to Lucca, where work on the villa was constant, and visits to friends in Rome. Marcello's friends became mine, and Federico Fellini, one of his closest, took me under his wing. Federico and I had many a long lunch together, where the pasta would be steaming hot and smothered in rich sauces, and the talk would be of Marcello and movies.

We went to Rome where Vittorio Gassman, another prominent Italian actor, threw a party to introduce me to the city. He had a huge villa on the Appian Way, just outside the ancient city, and the party went on for days. Gassman had been married for a time to Shelley Winters and was a master at throwing an old-fashioned Roman orgy that would make a Hollywood party pale in comparison.

There were bands, and elaborate pantomimes and parodies were staged. There were tables, heavy with trays of exquisite food that were constantly replenished, and Vittorio had an endless supply of expensive champagne, smashing the bottles each time one was emptied. It seemed that everyone who traveled in Italian social, film, and political circles was there, along with a fair number of celebrities from the U.S. as well. Marcello and I were there together, but not really together. We were keeping our relationship under tight wraps, and this was one of those bashes where news was sure to travel fast.

I love Italy still. But as much time as I have spent living there, there was much of it I never saw. Marcello wasn't much of a sightseer, so I never really had a chance to explore Venice, or visit the Sistine Chapel, or see any of the great works of art that fill the churches and museums of Italy. I would have to say I have never really been to Florence, though I've been through it hundreds of times in a Ferrari. It's strange that I didn't have the independence I now have to just go on my own. We were inseparable, really. If I were with Marcello now, I would certainly be going off to Florence without him, I can tell you.

But it was a great pity that I was so young that all I did was stay with him. I wish now that I had taken more time with it. But our life was all about being secret. We were like spies in love, slipping into this villa or that, a friend's apartment there, always avoiding the paparazzi, who followed Marcello's every move. I would fly into the airport with a wig on, a brown wig, because the paparazzi in Italy are awful and unrelenting. At the beginning it had an allure to it, but that quickly wore thin and I came to hate it in the end.

I was never at ease being the other woman. I knew the pain the other women in my father's life had caused my mother. My brother and I were silent witnesses to it all, the snapshots randomly removed from a photo album when he returned from the war, the unexplained absences. Marcello had a daughter, Barbara, and as much as I loved this man, I never wanted her to be hurt by this, as I had been all those years ago. But I thought Marcello and I were different, that we might have something together.

It was such a young time and my head was really turned around. But I was basically doing what I hated with a man that I loved. Marcello and his wife, Flora, had lived separate lives for years before I became a part of the picture. By the time I met Marcello he had a wife and a mistress, who had been with him for years, and a succession of romances on the side. A relationship with me meant that he would have to give up all of that. And for a time he did.

I sometimes felt like Ingrid Bergman when she came to Italy with director Roberto Rossellini. They called her "La grande inconnue," the one who knows nothing, and I sometimes felt like that. You come there, in love with a man who is married to someone else, not fully realizing that you are up against centuries of men who have marriages and mistresses. It is a place where wives manage never to lose the man to the mistress. Ingrid and I were interlopers in this very established, strict, rigid Catholic culture. We come in and expect to take their men away. It didn't happen for me, and I was to grow too bored with the game to wait for it.

BEFORE I LEFT for Cortina, I had a call from Kazan asking me to take the role of Gwen in *The Arrangement*. They were going to be shooting the film in New York in the fall. I don't suppose there is anything that I wouldn't have done for Kazan; he gave me my start in this business. But it was not easy to say yes either.

The film was based on his best-selling book, a novel, though really a very thinly disguised autobiography. The character he wanted me to play, Gwen, was in reality Barbara Loden, who had been his lover, then his wife. I knew Gadg, and I knew Barbara from working with her at Lincoln Center. It was her performance in *After the Fall* that had kept me mesmerized on the catwalks for hours not that many years ago.

Kazan asked me to take the role because I was hot box office at that time. I could sell tickets. But it was unjust that I was playing a role that Barbara should have played. She was married to Kazan, and she was the character. Kazan said years later that she never forgave him for not standing up to Hollywood and giving her the role. Though I had a lot of misgivings about accepting the part, Kazan called me personally and asked me to do it, and I couldn't turn him down.

I loved the character, though. Gwen had an edge to her; she's someone who doesn't take anything from anybody, or if she does, she is wise about it. As Kazan said in the book, "she had a built-in bullshit detector." The line that says it all comes about halfway through the film, when Gwen tells her lover, "The fucking I'm getting is not worth the fucking I'm getting." There was no lying, no pretense, and no sham to Gwen.

In *The Arrangement*, the lead character, Eddie, is an advertising man, not a movie director, but then Kazan was very cunning because both were in the business of manipulating emotions. It was very much the story of a guy who sells out, which some people accused Kazan of doing during the black-list days. Gwen is the younger woman he falls for, and Deborah Kerr played the long-suffering wife. The film takes you through Eddie's examination of his life.

The movie was an important one for Gadg, the sequel to *America, America*. For one scene, Gadg got permission to reconstruct then burn down a house on Parsons Point at the foot of Little Neck Bay that had been demolished only a few months earlier. It was a period of time when I was very, very pale; my hair was ash blond. It had to do with my wanting to escape my fame, I think; to be so pale as to be invisible, really. I was finding it hard to take all this scrutiny and all this attention. It's not really something I like.

I want love, but not all that attention. There is a great misconception, I think, that people in the public eye somehow love all the attention. Maybe some people do just love it, but I hated it. Deep down I hated it. And that's why I got a reputation of being cold, because I pulled so far back from it. I felt very tentative and very sensitive to all that. That's the irony, you see. The very stuff that makes us great artists is what makes us terribly sensitive and terribly vulnerable. When you get to be a big star, you have to go out there and be hard-boiled. You have to say, "Oh, that's okay. I don't care if you look at me," or overhear, "Oh, she didn't look as good as she did yesterday." I have very mixed feelings about fame. I really wanted, even then, to live much more simply.

IT FELT VERY STRANGE to suddenly be playing this woman that I had known and admired and emulated all these years. Though the setting of the film was not the movie industry, there was no mistaking the fact that Gwen had been modeled after Barbara. She had this wonderful, sardonic humor that Kazan gave to Gwen. And having been there in the Lincoln Center days, I knew much of their story firsthand. There were times when it did feel like déjà vu.

Marlon Brando was to play the Kazan character, Eddie. But he withdrew from the role after Robert Kennedy's death to spend more time involved in social causes. Kirk Douglas knew the role was suddenly available and contacted Kazan. These things happen, and though I would have loved to have played it with Brando, Kirk was, in a funny way, very right for the role. The ragman's son knew about selling. For all his bluster and bravado, Eddie is a weak man who dreams of greatness but hasn't the gumption to really try for it. Gwen becomes his conscience, unwilling to forgive him for all those concessions.

Kirk's acting style was a lot like Kirk, sort of brash and very straight-ahead, which was also a lot like Kazan. Kirk was really a generation before me. I really thought of him as Spartacus, the kind of actor who starred in those epics, someone who was so much larger than life. That size worked with the character Kazan had designed. Eddie was supposed to be a metaphor for success, burning up with energy, thrashing through it all. He is a man caught in the web of his various arrangements, with his wife, his mistress, his job, his unfulfilled dreams, and his very vacant life, but barreling through it nonetheless. Eddie was a character who needed to look and feel rock-solid, which provided a stark contrast when he began deconstructing along the way—and Kirk, if he is anything, is rock-solid.

Kirk was very pragmatic in his approach to acting, and a bit of that philosophy ended up rubbing off on me. We had one scene where Eddie and Gwen have gone to the ocean for the day. The beach is deserted and we're like teenagers, youth recaptured, chasing each other around the rocks, into the water, a puppy-love scene. But for much of it, I'm to be topless, though there are to be no shots of me from the front. To make sure, there are these tiny little things—I guess technically they are pasties—that you can use to cover yourself. Though it's not much, it is a little reassurance that if something turns up on film, with the pasties there, those frames won't get used.

I walked onto the beach and took off my robe to get ready for the scene. Kirk looked at me, set that formidable jaw of his, and in what sounded like the voice of Spartacus roared, "What the hell is this? Faye, it's just gonna get in the way." It was not just a play; he really hated it for some reason, the contrivance of it. Kirk tried to convince me that it was infantile, and that these things were far too tiny to save me from any indignity anyway. I thought about it, and decided he was probably right. And off they came. Nothing was revealed in the final film anyway.

Working with Kazan was like coming home. It was great. If you had by chance forgotten how much fun the process of moviemaking can be, Kazan was there to remind you that this was a high time, this

The infamous beach scene with Kirk Douglas, my costar in The Arrangement. © 1969
Warner Bros.-Seven Arts Inc.

business, something to savor. We knew each other's rhythms and
styles. I knew what he wanted, he knew what I was capable of. He
would throw you right to the lion's den, put you right inside the
character. One day I showed up and Kazan sent me off. "Go decorate
Gwen's apartment, Faye." Not all directors would have. But Kazan
wanted me to figure her out and create her environment. So off I went.
This is what makes Elia Kazan the granddaddy of them all when it
comes to directors working with actors, because he knows our process.

I'm trained to go in there and tell you what this woman would
have on her bedside table. But so often in movies they don't go to that
detail. In the sitcom I did for CBS years later, *It Had to Be You,* there
was no connection at all between the character and the environment.
Nobody wanted to show me the set. Nobody even wanted to discuss the
set. I had to work extra-hard to help create an environment for that
character. Too often in my career I've found that people just look at
you as if you're an interloper when you go and try to be part of the set.

But Kazan wanted his actors involved; you were never an interloper in his world. With Kazan, and Lumet, and other great actor's directors, it was all of a piece and you were a part of it.

I figured Gwen had to like Billie Holiday, because Billie Holiday was the original, pure honest integrity. I found a Billie Holiday poster that I liked. Then I made a cartoon caption for it—"Take a bath, man, don't explain"—and put it above her head. I remembered the line from one of her albums, a three-record set where Billie Holiday did the narration. At one point she said, "I got married again. This time to Willie McKay. He came in one night with lipstick on his collar and started explaining, explaining. Take a bath, man, I said. Don't explain. And the more I thought about it, it turned from an ugly scene to a sad song." I liked the honesty of it; it felt right for Gwen. The poster went up on one wall of Gwen's apartment. It is something I've kept to this day.

Marcello flew in while we were shooting and spent a few days with me in New York. He fell in love with my Central Park apartment, and we set about mapping out a redecorating scheme. Always the egalitarian, I demanded that we split the cost right down the middle. When he couldn't get away to see me, we would burn up the transatlantic phone lines for hours, plotting where and when we would meet next. My focus was more with Marcello than the work then, my own dicey arrangement.

NOT LONG AFTER I finished filming *The Arrangement*, Marcello took a role in a John Boorman film, *Leo the Last*, that would keep him on location in London for several months, beginning in early 1969. Marcello took a flat for us to live in, in beautiful, exclusive Eaton Square. It was very English, lots of chintz and down. We were there three months and at the end of that time, we found a mews house, which we did up mostly with things from Italy, Italian leather, all very modern.

Suddenly we were both living an expatriate life. This kept us out of Italy, and it was easier for me to get lost in the London crowds. Very few people knew I was there. It was a very different life for me. I had spent most of my years working at one thing or another. For the first time, I came close to dropping out so that I could spend all of my time with Marcello. I almost disappeared into the relationship. A business manager of mine once said that I was a chameleon with the men in my life. Whatever they were, or wanted me to be, I became. If he liked me to dress in a certain way, I would dress in that way. I did things his way, rather than mine.

The reality was that my identity was more caught up in my work than my life. The work is what sustained me for years at a time. It mattered to me above all. Still does, pretty much.

But with Marcello, I didn't need the acting as much. There were choice roles that came my way during those years, but I turned down most of them to spend time with Marcello. And despite protests from my agents, I was too much in love to regret it.

For a while, London was idyllic. Theadora Van Runkle and her boyfriend, Bruce, came over to work on a movie and we would hang out together. Here I was living the life of Sadie, the married lady, and thought it enchanting. Thea couldn't quite believe it. Marcello would go to the set during the day. I'd be busy working on things at home. Reading scripts and deciding what was worth leaving all this for. Then I'd get dressed for dinner. We'd meet and often go to the Guinea, a wonderful London pub, and have a scotch and water, then salad, followed by these wonderful grilled lamb chops and baked potatoes. Meals that were delicious and worth lingering over.

Some nights we stayed in and I learned from Marcello's assistant/chauffeur/chef how to cook pasta. Though Marcello was skeptical at first, I became a great pasta maker. Sometimes, Thea and I would spend the day antiquing. Other times we'd cook up huge, savory stews in the afternoon. We'd French the vegetables, round turnips, oval carrots, and it was such fun. I was very much in the role of the actor's wife, and found it a part I was surprisingly comfortable with.

It was really an intense affair, quite strong, and it worked on every level, which is why I held on so long believing that we could make this into something permanent. One day, I was in the kitchen and called to Thea, "Where are you?" I finally found her in my bedroom, standing there in this hushed kind of silence. It was a very English bedroom, puffy, warm, very beautiful and very cozy. "Whatever are you doing?" I asked. "Just feeling it," she said, "feeling the love that is in this room." For Marcello and me, it was a time of great love, great passion, and great affection.

•

Dusty Hoffman comes clean in Little Big Man *with a little help from me.* MGM

I HAD TURNED DOWN a number of roles, when Arthur Penn called me about working with him again. It was a cameo, and I did it as a favor to Arthur—a few weeks' work and a lot of fun. The movie, *Little Big Man*, was to star Dustin Hoffman. I had known Dusty for years—we had both been starving actors trying to find work in New York theater in the early sixties—but we had never worked together. His big break, *The Graduate*, had come in the same year as mine had with *Bonnie and Clyde*. We would talk occasionally about how success was affecting our lives, our relationships.

It was going to be a picture of gigantic proportions, shooting for months on end in four states in this country, including the Little Big Horn battlefield, and one spot in Canada. The story is really all Dusty as Jack Crabb, a 121-year-old Cheyenne. We follow his life for decades as he moves between the world of the white man and the Indians. The movie was designed to succeed or fail based on Dusty's performance; his character was in virtually every scene.

My character was named Mrs. Pendrake. Early in the movie, she and her husband, Reverend Pendrake, take Jack Crabb in. But Mrs. Pendrake soon finds herself interested in far more than saving his soul. Mrs. Pendrake resurfaces in a brothel during the second half of the film, the reverend by now long gone. But there was a sweetness to both sides of her, preacher's wife and prostitute, that I really liked.

Dusty and I had a great time together on that film. One day we were shooting a scene; it was his close-up and I was off-camera. Sometime later he told me I was one of the best actresses he'd worked with. Coming from Dusty, that meant a lot to me. He was already without question a great actor. I loved working with him.

We shot in Billings, Montana, and Nevada City, Nevada, while I was with the production. Thankfully I missed Calgary, where they went for snow. The temperatures suddenly hit new highs there, the snow melted, and the production was delayed at least a week. At one point I heard they were negotiating with a medicine man who was promising he could deliver a blanket of new snow for a hundred dollars. Arthur was always an inventive director when it came to getting what he wanted.

One of my favorite scenes in the movie was the bath scene. It was so like a scene Penn had shot in *Bonnie and Clyde* but never used. I'm convinced Arthur had liked the idea and simply tucked it away, certain that there would be a right time and a right place for a scene like that. It was an old tub, filled with bubbles, and Dusty is there dutifully letting me, Mrs. Pendrake, give him a bath. It's a funny scene because he is clearly very distracted by her closeness and this ritual of washing, and she's getting quite turned on by the process as well. She sings an old hymn, "Bringing in the Sheaves," but it doesn't manage to make the moment any less sexually charged.

Later in the film, she meets Jack again. By now she's living a life of prostitution and she's miserable. She tries to explain to Jack this journey of hers from preacher's wife to the backroom trade that she now finds herself engaged in. "When it's not sinful, Jack," she tells him, "it's not much fun." When it's a job, she hates it. I loved the poignancy of that line. The final moment of that character had a sweet, funny poignancy.

Dusty was always searching for a way to make each take fresh. He wanted to make the performance different and unique every time. Everyone develops their own way of getting that freshness, but his, I think, goes down as one of the most entertaining. He had grown up in Los Angeles and knew the local radio ads all by heart. Earl Scheib's was his favorite, maybe because he had gone to high school with Scheib's son Al. Dusty would get just the right nasal sound and promise, as Earl had done for years, that "I'll paint any car, any color for $29.95 . . . guaranteed." When the assistant director called "Rolling," before Arthur said "Action," Dusty, to keep himself loose, would go into these ads, rattling off their corny, hard-sell spiels—you hear it on the printed takes. And then on "Action," he'd go from unabashed commercialism to high art, moving right into the heart of Jack Crabb. It was an amazing thing to watch.

I WAS SPENDING more and more time in Europe with Marcello. But in October of 1969, I returned to New York to begin filming *Puzzle of a Downfall Child* with Jerry. Relationships between directors and actors are tricky enough, but here we were former lovers, once engaged to be married. Since Jerry was directing for the first time as well, that added its own layer of pressure. I knew how much Jerry wanted to do a movie, his movie. He'd had great success as a still photographer, but he wanted to become a film director very, very much. This was the next logical artistic step for him. For both of us, though, the weeks we spent working on *Puzzle* were a little like tap-dancing on eggshells.

Puzzle was such a labor of love for him. When Jerry had photographed Anne St. Marie, he had come to know the story behind the face. She was incredibly beautiful, very elegant, extremely thin, with dark hair pulled back and fifties-style makeup, which tended toward the dramatic. But beyond that her life was a complex and moving one, with all the intrigue and emotion you need to build a good dramatic story. Jerry had spent hours talking to her about her life. Most of the writers' fees—and this was a script that would go through many hands—he paid for out of his own pocket. For my part, I took on the role without getting paid for it.

Lou Andreas-Sand, the character in the script, was a character I loved and wanted to play. As with Bonnie, Lou was someone I understood. The film attempted to look at what happens to these women

Puzzle of a Downfall Child, *Jerry Schatzberg's directing debut and one of my favorite roles.* Copyright © by Universal City Studios, Inc. Courtesy of MCA Publishing Rights, a Division of MCA Inc.

who are so dependent on their physical appearance, who are too old at thirty and find themselves discarded by an industry they helped sustain. The money—even though for Lou it was substantial—was never enough to offset the tragedy of knowing that her cachet was in what she looked like, not who she was. As it happens, modeling is quite an artful thing. It is not easy to be a great model. Lou worked very hard at it, was very good at it, and yet it fed on her insecurity, her neurosis.

If you stripped it down to the bare essentials, *Puzzle* was yet another examination of the American Dream. You are brought up to believe that if you want something badly enough, and you work hard enough, you'll get it. The implication is that when you get there, you'll be very happy, but that's not necessarily so. In fact it is rarely so. It's having an emotional connection that makes you happy, loving yourself and others. Lou touched something in me because I was on a treadmill that was not unlike hers—achieving, achieving. This isn't good? I'll change, I'll do this instead.

There was such a sadness to it all, to work a lifetime to make that one little dream a reality, to be safe from the photographers and the agents she feels are destroying her, only to get there and find she hates it. What do you do when your dream turns out to be a nightmare? The story had personal reverberations for me, but my decision to go on with the project had to do with art as well; that character and her struggle was a beautiful, true thing.

The script was so rich, and it is always such a treat to work on material like that. You can drown in it and it is real, more than real; it is art. There are sometimes small things that make a character indelible in my mind. With Lou, she had a very specific way of talking; she never used contractions. But the thread running through *Puzzle* was her real struggle with sanity. At one point she tried to argue there was no problem because it was "all in her mind," which of course was precisely the problem.

We shot around New York and on Fire Island. At one point I'm to hold a falcon. Now I'm not easily frightened by animals, but there is something about the look of a falcon that never lets you forget its lethal nature. It is a fearsome bird. Though there were always handlers nearby, once I slipped on the leather glove and took the falcon on my arm, I had to be able to control it. Though they aren't large, there's a weight to them.

When I pulled off the bird's hood, I could feel its talons tighten on my arm as it got ready to lift itself into the air. There is both beauty and a sense of peril in that wildness, but it makes you feel very much alive. Richard Harris always said he sensed a wildness in me. "Faye, love," he would tell me, "just run the length of your wildness. Live whatever is in you."

JERRY AND I had good days and bad days during filming. In one scene, Lou has come up with a list of photographers that she refuses to work for. The list is on her dressing table, and she adds new names to it along the way each time someone offends her, and scratches others off when they make amends. On one particularly rough day, after Marcello had flown into New York to see me, we happened to be shooting that scene.

At the time, I felt that the way Jerry wanted to play the scene was really not right. We had discussed it and were still at odds over it. I picked up a pen and added Jerry's name to the list of photographers my character was refusing to work with and put it back down on the table. He saw it, scratched through it, then put it back on the table in front of me. I wrote his name in again. This time, it remained. It is in the film today, that list, with Jerry's name on it.

Though there were a few tough moments, we had more good days than bad. It was wonderful to watch Jerry. I have a real vision of his face as he smoked a cigarette by the camera, and it was very nice. You could see the carefulness of this man who was doing his first movie. And he was lucky. He had in me a hot box-office name, he had an excellent screenwriter in Carole Eastman, and he'd been given the money to do a movie, not a chance given to many people. He handled it all with a great deal of grace. But it was quite sad, too, because we were no longer together.

Puzzle was never a big financial success, but it was very well regarded by many in the industry and really launched Jerry as a film director. He went on to have a directing career that included *The Panic in Needle Park* with Al Pacino; *Scarecrow*, starring Pacino and Gene Hackman; and *Honeysuckle Rose*, with Willie Nelson. Though both of us went on to have much bigger successes, *Puzzle* remains one of my favorite films by an old friend who is also one of my favorite directors.

TEN

ROME ON CHRISTMAS EVE is unlike any other place in the world. Late into the night the city feels far from slumber as families make their way down the ancient stone streets to Midnight Mass. It becomes a city lit by thousands of candles and filled with the sound of bells. Tonight the air is crisp and clear and I look up into a night sky of stars. Both Marcello and I are in Rome for Christmas in 1969, but we are not together. He is with his family and I am with the director Marco Ferreri, his wife, and some other friends. Ferreri has done many films with Marcello, and I have come to know him well.

Marcello and I exchanged our presents a day ago, but tonight, when I am once again alone, it feels a hollow fraud. Christmas, holidays, these will never be days that we can share. I did not live with him in his life the way he lived. There were so many doors that would forever be closed to me, so many places I could never go.

But I was just not going to be blue on Christmas Eve. I got dressed up to the nines, with white satin trousers and a white cashmere sweater. I wanted to look wonderful. Marco smiled when he saw me, kissed me on both cheeks, and said, "I like the way you look tonight, Faye." He knew what I was doing, that I was refusing to give into the whole embarrassment of being without Marcello on Christmas Eve, the sadness of it, really. That night everything changed for me. What I wanted to think was wonderful and special was tragically ordinary. I was the other woman and I hated it.

Marcello and I always managed to talk around the difficulties between us. We would spin wonderful fantasies of how our life would be. We were very much in love. Sometimes Marcello and I talked about his leaving his wife and us marrying, and ultimately there was a final confrontation. It happened in Milan the next spring, when he was filming another movie. Since we were in Italy, I had to stay in hiding, as usual. My room in Milan became like a prison. It was in this terrible Euro modern building—stark, cold, without either beauty or charm.

I don't remember now the film he was shooting. I only know that I could never be on the set, because it might cause difficulties for him. There was always the chance that word would leak to the international press, who followed him relentlessly. This life in the shadows was feeling very shabby and sad to me. But then Marcello would walk in, with his soft, gentle smile, and a funny story about something crazy that had happened during the day. And I would almost forget the long hours alone. Almost.

One evening I finally told Marcello that I could not live any longer on talk and dreams; I really wanted a child, and for us to be together. If he loved me as he said he did, then I wanted him to divorce his wife and to be with me. It was not the first time we had talked of this, but never had Marcello reacted in such a negative way. "You knew this was my life when you met me. You knew I was married," he said. It was as if I alone had created this relationship, and the problems that came along with it. I knew that was not so. I did not argue; there was no point to it. He would never get a divorce, and we would never marry. There would be no Luca, no Clare for us.

Not long afterward, I was in Rome having lunch with Fellini, just the two of us, and we were talking about Marcello and me. "Federico, I don't think I can take this much longer," I told him, my eyes filling with tears. He said, "I know. He's going to lose you, and that is going to make him very, very unhappy." Federico knew Marcello well. He had told Marcello again and again that he should leave everything and go to me. Never had he seen Marcello like he was when we were together. But Federico knew the ending long before Marcello and I had reached it.

Marcello tried to act like the argument in Milan had never happened. We both loved Rome, and he found an exquisite old baroque apartment for us on the Piazza di Spagna that he said would give me the taste and the soul of Rome. It was also the piazza to which ex-patriates had gravitated for years. The house that Keats died in was on the edge of the piazza, and not far from its center, on a small side street, Henry James and the Brownings had lived. Marcello brought on one of his favorite architects to redesign it for us.

I was guilty of holding on to the fantasy as well. My apartment on Central Park West was still in the midst of being renovated for us too. Art, sculpture, clothing, furniture, all the trappings of our shared life and many of our favorite pieces had been shipped to New York. He knew my passion for houses and perhaps he thought that would help bind me to him. And Marcello often said he was an architect *manqué*. We were, I guess, somewhat the same, with our pretending as if we would last forever.

One day I was having lunch with Nadia Lacoste. She was one of those savvy French women, very smart about the world, a publicist who looked after Princess Grace. I kept turning over in my mind the idea of marrying Marcello, whether to continue to try to find a way with him. "Make the decision with your head, not your heart," she told me. I just looked at her, because with Marcello, it had nothing to do with my head and everything to do with my heart. But I wish now I had paid more attention to my mind rather than my emotions. Too often I followed my heart, and it took me away from this business that I love. Rarely did it end in the happiness I kept searching for.

As 1970 MOVED from spring to summer, my agent called to tell me about a project that was to be filmed in Spain. He had been keeping an eye out for productions being shot in Europe, since I was spending so much time there. I got the script for *Doc* and decided as soon as I was about halfway through reading it that it would be my next project.

Doc, which was New York Post columnist Pete Hamill's first screenplay, was a revisionist view of Doc Holliday, Wyatt Earp, and Kate Elder and the gunfight at the OK Corral. Hamill was the first to examine the relationship between Holliday and Earp; history hinted that they were sometime lovers. I would play Katie, and decided to wear a gold tooth. I loved it.

The West—cowboys, marshals, and gunfights at high noon—has long been a favorite subject of Hollywood. It is one of the few purely American landscapes that can be used as a backdrop for the classic battle between good and evil. The script by Hamill tried for a realism that left you feeling the grit of days on the trail without the benefit of a bath.

The language was as raw and harsh as he envisioned the life of Wyatt, Doc, and Kate to have truly been. Even the legendary gunfight at the OK Corral, which was enough grist for Leon Uris to turn into an entire script for director John Sturges in the late fifties, was going to be reduced to twenty-three seconds. It doesn't take that long, Hamill reasoned, to gun down a man.

Production was scheduled to begin in Almería, a town that sits at the foot of Spain just across the Mediterranean from Algeria. We were all due there in late August, with hopes that we would escape most of the brutal heat of summer on the Spanish plains. The weather did not cooperate. There were days on end when the temperature rose above 100 degrees, which meant that all of us were pretty rank and realistic without much help from makeup.

For Frank Perry, the director, it was the first movie he'd done that was not written by his wife, Eleanor. They were in the midst of a painful breakup, which would end their long collaboration. I think Frank, who had such a sensitive yet strong hand in his earlier films, *David and Lisa* and *Diary of a Mad Housewife* among them, was a bit adrift at the time.

Frank wanted very much for this film to be a powerful statement about the real West, to take the characters beyond the cardboard gunslinger and dancehall girl that filled so many Westerns. But he was clearly at a loss without Eleanor, and you could sense his vulnerability.

The desert, before *Doc* rolled into town, was like a blank canvas. It could be anything. Frank had Tombstone built on a seven-acre basin just outside Almería. It was rough but beautiful terrain, with a range of mountains ringing the dust bowl where we were to spend the next two months. More than eighty buildings, from a saloon to a church, were constructed by the crew. Not just false fronts, either, but three-dimensional buildings so that we could shoot inside. Once the town was built, the final touch was to transform the desert floor itself. For days, the crew would take hoses and spray the sand with water, then push the wagons over the mud again and again to dig real ruts in the newly laid-out roads.

I had a wardrobe that consisted almost solely of dusty gingham dresses. Only one fancy dancehall dress with petticoats and sequins for this Kate Elder. Frank envisioned my Kate as far more bedraggled, the way she might really look if she did, as legend has it, entertain as many

A gold-toothed, grinning Kate Elder in Doc *on location in Spain.*

as thirty customers a night. My gold tooth was fitted so that I could slip it over my left eyetooth. I quickly found it was easier to smile than scowl with my gold addition, and that seemed to lift my spirits. The boots I was to wear for most of my scenes had been carefully caked with mud from the streets of our Spanish Tombstone.

I hadn't been long in Almería when I began to realize how much I had missed working. *Doc* was the first movie I'd been involved in that year, and it was nearly September. We all had great hopes for *Doc*, and Frank had put together a really good cast, with Stacy Keach as Doc Holliday and Harris Yulin as Wyatt Earp. Suddenly I was with American actors of the Dusty Hoffman ilk.

Stacy and Harris decided Hamill was taking liberties with an important genre—the Western—and a mythology distinctly American. The two were very serious actors, very earnest about the work. They came to the conclusion that the idea of a homosexual liaison between them would never play. They saw it as yet another cheap shot to these Western heroes, who had no way of fighting back. It was sort of an inappropriately intellectual comment too, to say that Wyatt Earp and Doc Holliday were homosexuals. It was too far outside America's romance with the mythology of the wild West for audiences to accept. Stacy and Harris set about dismantling the script, a page at a time, a day at a time.

But somehow what sounded, in the wee hours of the morning, like it would work never quite panned out as well the next day. And Frank would agree on a new concept, a new version of the scene, and shoot it; invariably, in the rushes the next night, the scene would fall flat. Then Frank would leave the rushes sullen and angry, blaming Stacy and Harris, and refuse to speak to them for a while. It went on like that for the whole movie.

The three of us, Stacy, Harris, and I, were almost inseparable. We talked about work all the time—between scenes, between takes, in the evenings. We talked about acting and how you could get in there, inside it all. To this day, I would take that above almost everything. I just love it, the whole investigation of it. I love it much more than a quiet night in front of the television or the fire. I love it much more than a wonderful trip to Paris. I love it much more than walking on a beach with a man. I love it more than anything.

One of the first scenes Stacy and I have together set the tone for the film. Doc has just won me in a card game and we've gone upstairs to my room. He looks me over and says, "You're just about the filthiest woman I've seen since I left Baltimore, and that's twelve years ago." To which Kate replies, "Why, you mean-faced, flat-assed pigsticker, you don't exactly smell like no field of roses." And we were just flirting.

Doc was an extremely physical movie. Before it ends there are food fights, fistfights, catfights, and of course, gunfights. At one point, I am running half-naked down the stairs away from another customer, when Doc picks me up, slings me over his shoulder, and carries me back upstairs. Near the end of the movie, I find Doc in an opium den. I'm to take an old kerosene lantern and hurl it against the wall next to him. It ultimately sets the entire building on fire. Since the flames were real, Frank wanted to get it in one take if possible. I was really nervous. They had pumped a lot of smoke into the opium den for effect. Smoke always makes my eyes burn, and it can sear your lungs if you take a deep breath. But what was driving me crazy was that it was so thick I could barely see the path I was to take out of the room.

No matter how careful everyone is, when you're filming that kind of scene, there is always the chance that something can go wrong. The flames started slowly then began to build as the burlap curtains caught fire. Stacy and I stumbled toward the doorway. It's what we were supposed to do, but between the smoke and the fire, both very real, it became a mix of what you've rehearsed and a numb knot of fear in your stomach that something could go wrong. As we cleared the smoke- and flame-filled building, Frank was dancing toward us. "Fantastic. Absolutely fantastic. One take. It's in the can. You okay?" It was; both Stacy and I survived to film another day.

It was so hot, and we spent so many hours in clothes that would be drenched in sweat, but I had more fun on *Doc*. Hedy Sontag and Fred Dennis, Hedy and Freddy, good friends from New York, were in the film. We would hang out together, along with Stacy, Harris, and Denver John Collins, who was Judy Collins' brother. Judy and Stacy were seeing each other then, and she made a sojourn to Almería during the production to see them both.

In Spain, the National Fiesta travels the country for months, and the main event is the bullfights. It came to Almería in August every year, before traveling to other nearby villages and towns. Legend has it that August is the most dangerous time for matadors; the injuries come more often and are more severe. The crowds swell and the arenas are packed.

I saw my first bullfight on a Sunday afternoon, and it was unlike anything I had ever encountered. I'm mindful of the cruelty to the animals in this spectacle and I know that the odds are weighed against them with the picadors plunging their pics into the shoulder of the bull early in the game. Nonetheless, it is an ancient ritual, fighting the bull, that has a mythic power that had always entranced me then and still does now. I am not an aficionado in the sense of Hemingway, but the power of the struggle, the life-and-death dance between a man and an animal, and the skill and grace with which the matador fights the bull still intrigue me. Barbet Schroder used to say that he learned everything he knows about directing from the corrida, the bullfight.

That fall we saw a fighter named Paco Camino. Camino was a classicist and the crowd loved him. He was like Mozart and Beethoven in one tight, compact body. Camino was so pure. He would move on the floor of the ring with the grace of a dancer and the arrogance of a god, the red muleta cutting through the air to set the rhythm of the fight. He would create such crescendos, the murmur of the crowd rising and falling with him. It was like a concerto, very classical.

El Cordobes, the other great star of the time, was like Mick Jagger and The Rolling Stones. He would go up and make faces at the bull, he would hit him on the nose, he was outrageous. The bullfighters we saw were among the best of that time and yet, even with the best, the stakes are so high, where one wrong move can spell the end, and every moment of action is charged, drenched with intensity.

After the bullfights, we would go to roadside cafes, rustic, simple places, and drink sangria, and talk of the dance of death we had just witnessed. They were the kind of places that Hemingway and Fitz-gerald would frequent when they were in Spain, places that were rich with local flavor, from the food to the people to the wine. The nights would be cool, and we'd sit for hours talking, serenaded by the mar-iachis and their songs of love and loss.

HARRIS YULIN was much like my father, very distant, very removed. So of course he intrigued me. This emotional unavailability really hit at the heart of all my past history. I think that the structure of society for so many years left American women thinking so little of themselves that we came to expect the men in our lives to keep themselves at an emotional distance. That sets up a cycle of resentment and anger that is almost impossible to break.

But at first, it was not so difficult between Harris and me. There was a lot of charisma about him. And there is also an energy field that exists on a movie set. You're suddenly all dressed up, transported to a different time and place, you have a gun on, and you're making a movie together. It's all very sexy, very successful stuff you're engaged in, which I'm sure I found attractive too, being a girl who likes success.

Harris was a very talented actor as well, knew the craft, and was very serious about his work. He had studied acting at UCLA with Jeff Corey before going to New York. Once he got there, he had acted on stage in *The Entertainer* and *The Rehearsal*, and directed the Terrence McNally play *Cuba, Si* at New York's Theatre de Lys. By the time he got the role in *Doc*, Harris was already on his way to becoming a character actor of substance.

When I met Harris, I had just lived through two years with Marcello, and there was still no sign that we were going to move on from this backstreet affair. I was sick and tired of it. The work was the foundation of my connection to Harris; I could spend hours talking with him about the process, get completely immersed in it. I stopped taking Marcello's calls. And as soon as he noticed what was happening, that something was wrong, he called more urgently, and then he flew to Spain.

Hedy and Fred Dennis, my New York friends who were in Spain working on *Doc*, had met Marcello when he'd come to visit me in New York. When Marcello showed up in Almería, they befriended him again, keeping him company while I was working. But by then, Harris and I had fallen in love.

IT ALL CAME APART on a Sunday. Marcello was staying at the Agua Dulce Hotel near Almería. I met him there and told him again that it was over. He said he would leave his wife, we would marry. It was too late. For me it had already ended. But Marcello wouldn't accept that our romance was over; he didn't understand how I could love him one day and end it the next. He never saw that the agony I felt had overcome the love. At the same time, I can't say it was all Marcello's fault. I was the one who decided to leave, and in the end it was he, not me, who was destroyed by our parting.

We talked for hours, saying the same things again and again. I didn't want to fight with Marcello; in my mind there was nothing to fight about. He would go back to his wife, I was sure, and I would take back my life. Sometimes love really isn't enough, and it was just too late. I finally walked out of his suite, slipped into one of the phone booths in the lobby, closed the door, and sank down into the seat. I was so very tired.

IN DECEMBER, soon after *Doc* finished filming, I was due in Los Angeles for the premiere of *Puzzle of a Downfall Child*. Paul Newman and Joanne Woodward were throwing a party for me at the Directors

Guild to celebrate. *Puzzle* was one of a handful of films that Paul and his partner John Foreman would produce.

I was worried that the party might be ruined. Both Marcello and Harris were in L.A. But if Marcello had come to the West Coast with the idea of seeing me, he must have thought better of it. Our paths never crossed.

The party turned out to be a big success. Jack Nicholson was there, Rita Hayworth stopped by, and I was completely taken by surprise when Marlon Brando walked in. After so many months in Europe, that night I felt like I was truly ready to come back home.

When we came back to the country after *Doc*, Harris was living on West End Avenue and had a relationship he had to extricate himself from. I lived on Central Park West. We were committed to each other and wanted to see if we could make it work. I was ready to settle in with Harris, but I had committed to do a film that was going to shoot in Paris in January of 1971. Originally called *The House Under the Trees*, it was a thriller with the renowned French director, René Clément. Ironically, it was written by Sidney Buchman and Frank Perry's estranged wife, Eleanor. So I went from one Perry production to another.

I went back to Europe for three months to make this movie. It was not a happy time for me, although Francophile that I am, I adored being in Paris. By the time the film finished, I was completely fluent in French. Every night I would call Harris. He was there, but not as there as I would have liked. He was the closest to my father in that way, so that I was never quite sure of the depth of his commitment to me. It was made worse by the distance. Ironically, I had gone from one unsure situation to another. Marcello was physically and socially unavailable, and Harris was emotionally unavailable. I kept going to unavailable men.

Frank Langella, a former Lincoln Center compatriot, who had wowed the critics on Broadway in the play *A Cry of Players* with Anne Bancroft, was my costar. He had just starred in one of Frank and Eleanor's most successful collaborations, *The Diary of a Mad Housewife*, and gotten very good notices. At a lean 6'4", Frank was a tall drink of water. He had dark hair and brooding brown eyes. He turned thirty-one and I turned thirty that January, just as we went into production.

One of the few things that redeemed that time for me was the chance to work with René. He was one of the most widely respected postwar directors in France and had won two Oscars for his earlier films, *The Walls of Malapaga* and *Forbidden Games*.

René had loved films from childhood. He would tell stories of how this passion began. When he was only twelve, he nearly burned his house down with a "projector" made out of a paraffin lamp to show the "films" he had made. Finally his parents broke down and bought him a projector for his sixteenth birthday, and he would spend hours each day watching Charlie Chaplin shorts and trying to figure out how it was done.

He was an extraordinarily handsome man, nearing sixty when we shot this film, with silvery hair that he combed straight back. He almost always smoked a pipe, and somehow managed to look as irrepressibly fresh at midnight as he did at six in the morning.

Where Frank Perry had struggled with a script in flux and a couple of actors who were a bit like wild horses, René had a very firm hand. He had come up through the trenches of the industry and knew how to do everything. Long before he directed his first film, René had worked as a cinematographer, all the while experimenting with light and lenses, forever pushing the medium, never afraid to ask more of it. That was one of the reasons I had wanted to work with René: he understood the camera and knew how to use it in ways not many directors did.

This was a time when my French really helped. René hated using an interpreter, and for any cast members who couldn't speak French, he would usually try to mime what he wanted from them. You could read his level of frustration in the expansiveness of the mime; it was a case where bigger was not better. That René could be a bit of a tyrant was no secret, but he loved the fact that I could speak his language, and I was gaining enough of a command of the process that I suffered very little on this film.

I liked very much that my character, like Kate Elder in *Doc*, was more real and less glamorous. In the film, the characters Frank Langella and I play are expatriates living in Paris with our two children. He's been an industrial spy and when he tries to duck out of the game, the children are kidnapped and held as a trump card. With my children's lives at stake I am on the edge of insanity. It was the first time

I had played someone's mother, and the scenes I had with the children were a double-edged sword. They reminded me of how much I wanted to have a child, and at the same time I wondered if I would ever find the right man to marry and have children with.

The House Under the Trees was renamed *The Deadly Trap* and was picked to close the Cannes International Film Festival May 28, 1971, which automatically conferred upon the film a certain prestige. That was less than five months after the first day of shooting, a remarkably compressed production and postproduction schedule. I don't know whether it hurt the film that it was so rushed, but in the end, the story didn't quite hang together as well as it should have.

Ultimately, it was much ~~more well~~ *better* received in Europe than in the States, where it was released a year later. Though I was well-known in my own country, at times I have found more acclaim in the international markets—France, Britain, Japan. Europe, in particular, has always seemed to understand me, sometimes more than my own country.

As soon as we wrapped up production on *The Deadly Trap* in France, I went back to New York and began the process of really separating myself from Marcello. Marcello stepped up his campaign to get me back and sent me a wonderful sculpture by an American artist living in Rome, Beverly Pepper. I didn't accept it because I felt that would have been opening the door again to him. I had to get on with my life and try to find a relationship with Harris. And there was the matter of finishing my apartment. The redesign Marcello and I had begun was not completed. For almost a year before Marcello had first seen the apartment, I had carried a magazine featuring Charles Gwathmey's work around with me, because I loved his work. He was an up-and-coming architect, but scarcely well known. I was the first to use him for a private apartment. Now he has really become the darling of people in my business, doing homes for Dusty Hoffman, and an apartment in New York for David Geffen, and for many others as well.

I found Charles before he was trendy. A disciple of the great French architect Le Corbusier, Charles was one of the foremost practicing contemporary architects around. He'd done a house on Long Island that caught my eye. Caught *House & Garden*'s attention too. And now he's quite famous. His work had a softness to it; he did a lot of curves that I thought were sculptural and beautiful, and yet it had a density to it as well. It was modern without being linear and angular.

When Marcello and I were together, we had taken over the rest of the floor and gutted the rooms. Charles took out walls, adjusted the heights of the ceilings, thickened the walls to create window seats, and changed the size of the windows, making them much larger and more dramatic. They became like living murals of the city, framed against the wall of the living and dining areas. The art was primarily two pieces, a painting in the central hall by Leah Rhodes—large geometric shapes in black and white and orange against the white canvas of a wall—and a wall hanging by Richard Lindner in the living area. And there were private terraces on either side of the apartment that I could use, as well as a tiny terrace off my bedroom, the perfect place to have a cup of coffee in the morning and read the paper.

The floors throughout the apartment were a blue-black slate, the walls a creamy white. Everything that could be built in was, to keep an open feeling. In the living room, a twenty-foot sofa was set into one wall, then covered with black leather cushions, which Marcello had brought over from Italy. The dining area, which was a part of the living room, had a pedestal table, with a huge round slab of polished black slate.

My private rooms were my favorite. The bedroom was smallish and Charles rebuilt it so that it was almost in the shape of a modified triangle; the bed was surrounded by bookshelves and views of Central Park. Off the bedroom was a huge dressing room wrapped with floor-to-ceiling closets that had wonderful built-in compartments, in dozens of shapes and sizes. In the third room of the suite, Gwathmey created a bath/sitting room. Le Corbusier had done a classic chaise, which Charles had brought for the apartment. We put it up against the wall in the bathroom and drew a profile of it on the wall. From that, Gwathmey created a white mosaic-tile chaise, the width of a double bed, with a sunlamp above it. There was a sauna too.

Outside the bedroom suite was the huge living room; guest room, later to be my son's room; kitchen; and library. I had a restaurant stove installed in the kitchen so I could prepare anything from a poached egg to a five-course gourmet dinner. What pleased me so when it was finally finished was that you could walk into any room and feel a sense of peace and serenity. It was spare, simple, contemporary, but never cold. There were times, after spending months away on far-flung locations, that I would come home to 300 and not leave the apartment for days at a time. There I could regain some sense of balance, sort through my life yet again. It was about as perfect a place as I could have imagined, even without Marcello.

MARCELLO ONCE SAID that our meeting was too late in his life; if only he'd met me when he was thirty. But he was married at thirty, just as he was married at forty when we met, so I think it was just a game he would play with himself, trying to make our ending come out differently. In most ways, ours was a wonderful relationship, a glorious affair—very alive and passionate and fun. In many ways, it was a once-in-a-lifetime liaison with a fabulous man, and I wish to this day it had worked out and that I was spending time in Lucca. Maybe now I might be able to go and truly enjoy the beauty of Rome and of Florence, be less attached to the man in my life. I'm older and wiser. And then again, maybe it would not have worked out even if he had said "I'm leaving Flora" a year sooner.

Fellini called me a few months after our breakup to tell me how destroyed Marcello was. But he did not tell me to go to Marcello, he said it was Marcello who should come to me. It was a messy breakup. Marcello even thought maybe it was because he had shaved his head half-bald when he came to see me in Almería—he was playing Caesar, and with his typical boldness had decided he would shave his head, which was a great idea—but that had nothing to do with my not loving him anymore. He cried. He called me. His daughter even called on her father's behalf at one point to beseech me to rethink this. But it was too late. It was not to be.

THERE WERE THOSE who said Marcello was weak. He would even levy that charge at himself. He smoked too much, drank too much, ate too much, and loved too much. He agonized that with me he was always hesitating—not in loving me, in that he held nothing back—but in making a commitment, afraid of how life might resolve itself if he left Flora. It was the first time his marriage was truly threatened, and despite his love for me, he was still very much a Catholic and could not imagine divorce. I thought he was a remarkable man. I wish he could have left Flora, that he could have moved on and made his commitment to me. But in terms of how Marcello lived life and who he was as a man, the decisions he made, the chances he took—the force and power and strength that I saw during my two years with him were anything but weak.

There are days when I look back on those years with Marcello and have moments of real regret. There is that one piece of me that thinks that had we married, we might be married still. It was one of our fantasies, that we would grow old together. He thought we would be like Spencer Tracy and Katharine Hepburn, a love kept secret for a lifetime. Private and only belonging to the two of us.

Very late one night, years later, I was thinking of Marcello and how we had left each other so bitterly. I put in a call to him with the idea that maybe we might still have a chance to be friends. "Ciao, Marcello," I said when he came to the phone. "I thought we might talk." There was a long silence, then he said very quietly, "But why?" Perhaps it was for the best. But as I slowly put the phone back in its cradle, I wondered.

ELEVEN

THE WEATHERMAN has just announced that it is 24 degrees outside and dropping, and he is predicting rain. I'm on a sheep ranch thirty miles outside of Stockton, California, that has been transformed into Oklahoma, circa 1910, for the film *Oklahoma Crude*. Wooden oil derricks that have been put up by the crew dot the landscape, but otherwise I look out onto an expanse of low, rolling hills, virtually treeless, with nothing to provide any shelter from the cold wind that has begun to pick up, though it's still early fall in 1972.

Underneath the thin cotton dress, my costume for this particular scene, I'm wearing a wet suit. It makes movement something less than fluid, but there is no other way to survive the hours we will be spending in the cold. In spite of the extra socks I've put on under my steel-toed lace-ups, my feet are going numb.

Next to me, out of sight, is a cup of ice. There's no worry that it will melt in this weather. Each time before I say my lines, I pop a few cubes in my mouth—it helps keep my breath cool, so that when I speak, there won't be little puffs of mist in front of my face, something that would not escape the camera's eye. It's been a challenge trying to look hot in freezing weather, but that's what we're trying for, since the entire film is supposed to take place during a dry scorcher of an Oklahoma summer.

THE DIRECTOR, Stanley Kramer, chose this Stockton location after searching Oklahoma, New Mexico, Arizona, and Texas for the right look and finding it cluttered with telephone wires and electrical lines that destroy the authenticity of that time period. Stanley is someone to whom the integrity of the piece, down to the last detail, is of extreme importance. He has built his career on projects that carry a message of social responsibility. *On the Beach, Inherit the Wind, Judgment at Nuremberg, Guess Who's Coming to Dinner*—what a legacy of prodding audiences to think he has brought with him.

Oklahoma Crude is an ambitious project. In the film, Stanley wants to explore the fight of the little guy, or in this case the little gal, against the emerging oil conglomerates. He was fascinated by the stories he had found of the women who had helped settle and survive the West then, long before women's liberation would even be the germ of an idea.

In Lena, my character, you have a woman who is caught between her ambition and her femininity. When the film opens, she is as tough as nails, a shoot-first-and-ask-questions-later woman. It is what she has found necessary to survive in the oil fields. Along the way, she slowly opens herself up to her estranged father, played by John Mills, and a lover, George C. Scott. I understood that dilemma well, the conflict between ambition and love, the fear of trusting someone else with your love.

One of the offshoots of playing Lena was this amazing burst of energy I got the longer I was with the character. It was absolutely physically impossible for this woman to have done all the things that she did. But somehow she did it, just dug down and found the resources deep within her. A week or so into production, I found myself waking up in the morning literally saturated with all this energy. It has happened with all the characters I have cared about; somewhere in you, in your genes, in your cells, the character begins moving in on you. You become them and they become you.

THE CREW spent weeks turning back the clock, and Stanley was in heaven. He had five thousand acres to play with. They removed any evidence that a sheep farm had ever existed here. Newer fences were pulled down and older ones put up. The propman somehow managed to find old, horse-drawn freight wagons, a 1903 steam engine, a Mack truck only a few years older, and a 1910 Chevy. After that, Stanley's requests for Model Ts were a piece of cake.

The locals assured us that the weather would likely be mild and predictably clear through the fall. Stockton, it seems, was known for its stable climate, something that you look for anytime you're shooting on

George C. Scott helped me bring in an oil well in Oklahoma Crude. Copyright © 1973 Columbia Pictures Industries

location. Surprise is rarely something a filmmaker wants, but surprise is what we were handed. After we began production in late September of 1972, the weather broke season averages almost on a daily basis. There was heat, cold, fog, and rain.

One week the set was closed to outsiders because it was so hot and dry the Forest Service feared any random spark would set the place ablaze. Two weeks later the temperature dropped into the fifties, and the wind was so stiff that clouds would blow through a scene changing the light three or four times, which plays havoc with every take. Fog shut us down completely for two days, and that was a financial nightmare for the producers to have a huge crew and an expensive cast sitting on their hands for two days. The only thing we were spared was snow. And earthquakes.

The weather complicated a lot of the scenes, but then there were some scenes that did not need the weather to provide complications. At the climax of the movie, I finally bring in an oil well, and Stanley wanted to recreate a gigantic gusher. It took ten consecutive days of filming, working from dawn to dusk, fifty thousand gallons of something that looked—and felt—like rich black crude oil, that we were periodically covered with, and four cameras rolling all the time to get it. In the final cut of the movie, the scene, which had cost a half million dollars, was ten minutes long. But it looked like the real thing.

GEORGE HAD MARRIED the actress Trish Van Devere only a few days before we began production, so he was back at the trailer with her or off to the house they'd rented anytime he was not needed on the set. Mills was there with his wife as well, the novelist Mary Hayley Bell. They were warm and funny and helped keep the downtime in Stockton from being unrelentingly boring. And I found a nice house in Stockton that I had rented for the duration of the movie.

Each day, George would come in to see the rushes, two big dogs on a leash beside him. When he walked in, there was an invisible wall around him. It gave new meaning to the word "boundary." He walked into those rushes, he sat down with his wife and his dogs, he watched the screen, and he left again. That was it.

It was the first time I had worked with George, and I don't think I've ever run across another actor quite like him in the way he came at a role. It was as if he came to the set each day with his part in a briefcase. To conjure up the character, all he had to do was pop open the case, pull out the part, act the scene, then pack it all away again at the end of the day. It was just there. Never a false move. I loved George and loved watching him work. His acting in *Dr. Strangelove* and *The Hustler* are two of my favorite performances put on film by any actor.

Both George and John Mills did some very funny things with their characters. I wanted to as well, but Stanley said he knew from his years of directing, and from his experience with Tracy and Hepburn, that one character has to be the fulcrum. He had decided it had to be Lena.

Once I did play it a little lighter. It was a scene in which I slide down on my chair, and in this particular take, I'm literally sliding out of frame. Everyone in the screening was laughing and on the sound track you heard Stanley's distinctive voice: "Cut." At that moment, I could have throttled him. He could at least have said "cut" later so he had the option to use the bloody moment. I think it would have been a better film if he had allowed me to play Lena a little looser. I was not happy about this. I thought the whole notion of this one, single, little woman bringing in a big oil well was outrageous to the point it should be funny. Though I didn't always agree with him, Stanley was a director who respected his actors. He was this great, craggy American director, who had an inherent kindness and goodness to him, in the way he ran a set and in the way he worked with all of us. He was *the director*. It was his choice, his movie, and as my friend Jack Nicholson would say when we were filming *Chinatown*, my job was to help the man make the movie.

MY HAIR, which I'd let go back to its natural milk-chocolate brown, had gotten very long by *Oklahoma Crude*, and I'd piled it up on my head in curls like the Gibson girls of the 1890s. My wardrobe, all nine pieces of it, was a far cry from that in *Thomas Crown*. Every piece of it had been created as though ordered from the pages of Sears and Levi Strauss & Co. catalogues from the early 1900s. Denim overalls, cotton long johns, I think they figured the entire tab for the clothes would have come to something under twenty-five dollars. And then there was one pretty flowered dress at the end.

This role was where I wanted to be. Lena was tough, an ambitious woman who was not going to bow to the male establishment. Very real this woman was, and that's the direction I wanted to head my career in. I had come to a time in my life when I wanted to reconnect with my roots. I wanted to strip away the veneer of glamour that had attached itself to me and remind everyone that there was more to me and my talent than the slick, sophisticated, urban woman roles I seemed to be offered more and more. I could get dirt under my fingernails and handle a rifle and not look as if I had been transplanted from the Upper East Side.

The playwright Harold Pinter once said he tended to "get quite exhausted being this Harold Pinter fellow . . . Harold Pinter sits on my back." I knew exactly what he meant. You have this other persona, shaped by the expression of your work, and if you're not careful it will overtake you.

THE FILM was a modest success when it was released a year later. Ironically the Soviet Union was the country that embraced *Oklahoma*

Crude. Stanley was invited to show it during the Eighth Moscow International Film Festival in the summer of 1973. It shared the Gold Medal with an entry from Soviet Lithuania, *That Sweet Word Liberty*, and a Bulgarian film, *Love.* You knew it was definitely not a traditional film awards show when they handed out the Best Anti-Fascist film award and another for the Best Anti-Imperialist film.

One Russian reviewer writing in the *Red Star*, the Defense Ministry's newspaper, said the film deserved the Gold Medal because "two persons win a moral victory over the despotism of business and force," which is an assessment I think most of us involved in making *Oklahoma Crude* would have agreed with.

MY TRANSITION from blonde back to brunette in *Oklahoma Crude* began with the time I spent with Harris Yulin. It was what my friend Ara Gallant used to call the liberated seventies, sort of an evolving hippiedom. Harris and I were together. We hung out, talked about acting. I stopped wearing makeup except when I had to for work. I wore my hair in a ponytail. And I shocked people when a photo of me turned up with my underarms unshaven.

It was not merely a cosmetic change I was searching for, but a personal one as well. I wanted to go back to the theater, to stretch and redefine those muscles that acting on the stage requires. I wanted to reconnect with and get closer to the things that brought me to this business. After *The Deadly Trap* wrapped in the spring of 1971, theater was where I decided to focus my attention.

That year, PBS wanted to include a production of *Hogan's Goat* in its Theater in America series. WNET in New York was set to produce it. Bill Alfred called and wanted me to play Kathleen Stanton once again, and I was happy that he had thought of me for it. It was the role that had given me my success. This time I was playing Kathleen to Robert Foxworth's Mattie, with George Rose as the evil mayor and the Emmy-winning Glenn Jordan directing.

Though it was early in his career, Glenn already had a clear understanding of the quirks and nuances of television as its own distinct medium. He had directed a beautiful version of Clifford Odets' *Paradise Lost* for WNET the year before. Though the underlying purpose of the *Hogan's Goat* project was to recreate a theater experience on television, Glenn understood that one has to slip into a different place to achieve that. You can't just set up a static camera, as if it were the audience, and let the actors move in front of it.

It was wonderful to get to know Kathleen Stanton again. I was coming to the character now with a decade of experience, both in acting and in life. This Kathleen Stanton had a maturity that I could never have given the earlier off-Broadway character. It was not that one was better than the other, it was more that the life you give the character is always shaded by your own, and mine was painted in far different colors by 1971.

I am grateful to the production for the link it gave me once again to Bill Alfred. We had lost touch in the onrush of my career. And then he had his own substantial obligations with his Harvard classes. He has now retired, but taught English there for forty years and is famous for his Middle English course. His Chaucer lectures are renowned, as are his Lear lectures, and his playwriting seminars. I still meet people in Hollywood and New York who were students of Bill Alfred. In my relationship with Harris, I had already taken a step back into the deep pool of the theater, and the process. With Bill, it became an ongoing dialogue of what is good and pure in the language. We were like explorers in a cavern, always looking to see what we would find around the next literary bend.

And Bill was forever looking out for me. Not long after *Hogan's Goat* finished shooting, I was going through a really rough time in my life. We had long talks about how one deals with adversity, what it takes to travel that road. Bill gave me a beautiful rosary, a Franciscan Crown, to help get me through that troubled time. I have kept it close to me to this day, more than twenty years now. It has been with me in triumph and despair, joy and sorrow, and all of life's daily struggles in between.

Early on, Bill Alfred gave me as a motto "Silence, Exile, and Cunning," from James Joyce's *Portrait of the Artist as a Young Man*. I took it as my motto then and still hold fast to it today. I have given it to my friend Johnny Depp too, and we both live by it. It's meant to be the credo of an actor. It's the only way you can survive. Silence, exile, and cunning.

Keeping boundaries intact in this very public life, though, is far from easy. I give myself away all the time—to the men in my life, to the people, to the agents, to the producers, so that I have nothing left.

Sometimes you have these moments—I saw them with George, and with Jack, and I had one with Roman Polanski—where you just have to guard yourself because you know people will just rip you apart. They'll tear you to pieces if you don't hold yourself back from them.

That's what Bill was trying to tell me. Don't say it all, don't say too much, don't say anything. Don't let the bastards get you down, that's what we say, laughingly. How can we win through? How can I do what I need to do and weather what they're trying to get me to do?

Bill has sent angels around me a lot of times too, I'm sure of it. We used to joke and call my guardian angel George. Once we took a picture at Christmas, and when I had the film developed, in the background just behind me, there was the name George. Whenever I've reached a low point in my life, I know I can count on Bill to send along George and his battalions of angels.

THAT SUMMER I agreed to do a small summer theater production of *Candida* back east. I would have the lead and Harris would direct. I began to reinvestigate acting, to live, eat, and breathe it once again. *Candida*, however, was not the play to choose to reignite my passion for the theater. It was the most boring role ever, because she has all the answers. Everyone comes to Candida and she's never in peril, never in crisis, never in a dramatic situation. I didn't enjoy it at all.

Candida was about as far from my emotional life at that time as I could imagine. If the character had been created for a farce, perhaps I could have managed to find some emotional context. But I could never reconcile how Candida could have such wisdom, when her life was so modulated. If you have never truly found yourself in jeopardy, how can you know the depths of fear?

Perhaps she felt so alien to me because my relationship with Harris was fulfilling in many ways, but uncomfortable. There was something that never did quite work between us. But instead of giving up on it, I set about trying to make it right. He became like a riddle I was determined to solve. He did remind me of my father. He was emotionally unavailable, in my opinion. I think it was my way of trying to work through this problem with my father. To be freed of the compulsion to be attracted to unavailable men.

There was always a nervous tension to our time together. He was the polar opposite of Marcello, who had that wonderful Italian ebullience. Harris was dark and brooding, where Marcello had been full of life and light. It was a painful relationship with Harris and doomed to failure.

THE YEAR was not an easy one. I was getting offers, but couldn't decide which project I wanted to do next. There was a script based on a D. H. Lawrence novel, *The Plumed Serpent,* in which I would costar with Omar Sharif with Christopher Miles directing, that looked promising. The story was set in Mexico, and would be filmed there as well, a psychosexual saga of a British woman who becomes involved with the remnants of an Aztec tribe and their ancient rituals.

Christopher, the brother of the actress Sarah Miles, had a real feel for D. H. Lawrence already. His first film, *The Virgin and the Gypsy,* had been based on the Lawrence work. And I was talking to Joe Papp about a summer Shakespeare in the Park production, playing Rosalind in *As You Like It* as well. But all that was still months away.

There came an offer to star in a movie for television for ABC with Richard Chamberlain. *The Woman I Love* was the story of England's King Edward VIII, who gave up the throne to marry the twice-divorced American, Wallis Simpson. I liked the script and the character, and I was also interested in working with Dick. He was a big success on television, our own Dr. Kildare, and on the stage both here and in Britain. I wanted to be able to move between the various mediums with ease. Each demanded something different from you.

Doing this TV movie would also mean reaching a mass audience, one that I had not spent too much time in front of recently. Neither *The Deadly Trap* nor *Doc,* both released in 1971, had generated much attention, either critically or financially. *The Woman I Love* was scheduled to be shot in early 1972 in Los Angeles with Paul Wendkos directing, and I would be able to finish it with time to spare before the next project got under way.

Wallis was another character I enjoyed playing. I spent hours poring over everything that had been written about this woman and Edward. There were at least eight books—and then days more spent reading her memoirs. But I felt I knew her before I had read the first line. She had an early life of genteel poverty. Though it was in Baltimore, it was very much like the life of the old southern aristocracy, many of whom had lost their money, but never their dignity. She had spent time in Shanghai and that added a layer of reserve. And her marriages had ended unhappily. This was a woman who had been in the crucible and grown stronger for it.

Then she met Edward, and found herself in the romance of a lifetime. He was soon to be King of England, the world's most eligible bachelor, and he was absolutely and completely in love with her. In reading through old papers and correspondence, you get a picture of this woman, for the first time truly in love with someone, but knowing their love will destroy him. Though she tells him to forget her, and keep his right to the throne, she had her own ambitions too. I'm not sure she would have offered to give him up, if there had been a chance that he would have left her.

I was very unused to the pace of television. A few days of rehearsal, a couple of weeks of filming, pack up the bags, and good-bye. You barely had time to know the character, much less the other actors. I rented a house in Malibu while we were filming and spent long hours walking on the beach, longer hours on the phone. Harris had stayed in New York. The final day of shooting was January 14, 1972, my thirty-first birthday. I spent most of it alone.

It was almost a year before the movie made it to television. The date was delayed in part by the Duke, who was quite upset that such a production would be undertaken while both he and Wally were alive. His lawyers wanted to see the film before it was aired. I don't know how that was resolved, though when the movie finally aired in December it was not long after the Duke's death. And though we were faithful to the historical record, in this case much of it created by the Duke and Duchess of Windsor themselves, in deference to the family *The Woman I Love* was never shown in England.

NEW YORK was frozen when I returned in the dead of winter. February is generally a hard month; the city has been cold for too long. You can feel it in the people walking past you on the street; they are tired of it, edgy, waiting for the first thaw to send the last ugly gray bits of snow melting into some storm drain. Even the trees in Central Park look like brittle old men whose bones ache from the cold.

Harris had moved into my apartment, but spending more time together was doing nothing to cure the ills of our relationship. Another problem began festering. I was much more in demand than he, and where my options were broad, his were narrow. I passed on some projects so that we could work in the theater together or just be together.

I just needed more than he could give. Maybe I needed too much, maybe I was just too frightened. But in this, I think it was something inside of him, as well as me, that ultimately defeated us. Some difficulty really opening himself up and committing. In the end, he left me. Some days I wondered if he had ever really been there at all or if I had merely dreamed it.

For the first time in a long while, I was alone, and I went through a great deal of pain at this reliving of being left by a man. It would be some time before I would come to like being alone. I did some analysis to try to work through his leaving, but the best therapy for me was going back to work. In a way, Harris's leaving was such a relief. This tortuous time had ended.

SALVATION CAME in the form of a Harold Pinter play. I agreed in April to commit to a three-month run in Los Angeles, though I worried that with a May 25 opening, there was little time to rehearse. Pinter had long been one of my favorite playwrights, and I would often pick up his plays to read late at night, just to listen to the sound of it. A copy of a Pinter play, Fitzgerald's *The Great Gatsby*, and my current book, are generally on my nightstand.

Pinter is very spare in his writing, nothing is unnecessary, but you can spend hours within the few words he gives you, digging around for meaning. He has this ability to put you in a place where you're saying, "What is *really* going on?" *Old Times* was very much in that tradition, with the audience never sure of what was real, and those of us performing the play having to struggle early on to find our way through it.

The closest Pinter comes to explaining himself in *Old Times* is in the middle of the first act. My character, Anna, has come from Sicily to the English countryside to visit an old friend and roommate and meet her husband, though as with all of Pinter, nothing is ever that simple. But they are talking of things past when Anna says, "There are some things one remembers even though they may never have happened."

Old Times is just like that. You try to sort through the conversation between these three and figure out what is real, what is remembered, and what may have never happened. The Center Theatre

My West Coast stage debut in 1972 as Anna in Harold Pinter's Old Times. C.T.G. Ahmanson Photo Collection.

Group, the resident company at the Mark Taper Forum in Los Angeles, was going to stage *Old Times*. It was the most recent of his plays; written in the winter of 1970–71, it premiered in London performed by the Royal Shakespeare Company in June of 1971.

The play had a stunning run in New York, where it had gotten five Tonys, including Best Play. But this was to be the first West Coast staging, and my first time to perform on stage in the West as well. They had signed on Jeff Bleckner to direct it. Jeff was just off a very successful run of David Rabe's *Sticks and Bones*, which earned him a Tony nomination. Santo Loquasto, who had designed the sets for *Sticks and Bones*, was going to do the designs. And I convinced them to get Thea Van Runkle to do the costume design.

Verna Bloom, who had been on Broadway and was newly getting attention in film with her role opposite Peter Fonda in *The Hired Hand*, was cast as Kate, the friend I've come to visit. And W. B. Brydon, who had worked primarily on stage in Canada, was cast as Kate's husband, Deeley. By late spring, I headed to Los Angeles to begin rehearsal.

I rented a little place in Malibu and went about working Harris out of my system. Each night I would come home to that empty place and make my way from room to room, looking under each bed and checking each closet. But as I took on the ghosts of that house, I got stronger. By the time I flew to Stockton for *Oklahoma Crude* the next fall, the memory of that relationship had gone from sharp pain to dull ache.

Jeff had seen the play in London and though he liked it, he had found it cold and without passion. He wanted to see if we could find something more visceral underneath. Just before we began rehearsals, I suggested we contact Pinter to come and work through the play with us, a notion everyone scoffed at. They said he wouldn't come. But the play had the flavor of Europe, and the cast, even in New York, had always been British. We would be the first to give it an American translation.

Pinter had given few clues in the play itself. His only stage directions are pauses and silences, something that actors and directors through the years have spent hours trying to decipher. "What do you think he means?" "We have to wait a beat of twenty here." He doesn't characterize what the actors have to say. He's unique in this. Most playwrights bend over backward telling you how to play a line. Pinter gives you the respect that you'll be able to figure that out. He doesn't tell you how to do anything. But he does indicate where there is a pause and where there is a silence. He indicates the rhythm of the piece.

Pinter once said in an interview that a pause happens when one character says something that the other characters are unable to respond to. They are struck dumb, as it were. And a pause ends when the other characters have recovered sufficiently to speak again. A silence is the same as a pause, but more so. It lasts longer and is harder for the characters to recover from.

There is a single stage direction in *Old Times*, beyond the pauses and silences. At one point Pinter has Anna respond "coldly," otherwise he leaves it to you to interpret his play. I stared at that direction and I played it in every conceivable way that one could. One night I played it almost dead. Years later when I finally met Harold, over lunch I asked him two things about *Old Times* that I had been storing up. First, I wanted to know if he would have come to Los Angeles to work through the play with us. He said, "I would have loved that." Then I said, "I've been waiting for years to ask you, what did you mean by 'coldly'?" He sat there for a moment, a quizzical look on his face. "You know, in *Old Times*, you wrote, Anna said 'coldly,' " I prodded. Finally he laughed. "I haven't the faintest idea."

I found myself very much in agreement with Pinter on the whole topic of memory, though. He said when he looks back at times in his life, there are just a few images that remain, not complete memories. Memories, he said, were a burden, and if we held on to all of them, we would explode. To survive, there are all sorts of memories that we must discard along the way. I wondered if I could find a way to discard more of the memories that did carry with them such a burden for me, sometimes more than I could bear. And there are other times when I wish I had not discarded so much; there are moments, lost long ago to me, that I ache to recapture.

I LOVED performing *Old Times*, because each night it was endless. You could say all sorts of subtextual things. This roommate who has come back to visit, does she really want the life of her old roommate? Or was she the older version of that young woman she remembers? Were they roommates or both the same woman? Or were they lovers? as the husband in his bewilderment accuses. There were questions you could endlessly ask about the play. Jeff once said it was hard to understand, harder still to try to talk about it. In that, we agreed; the difference is I never tired of the investigation.

There was a night very early in the run of the play that is indelibly stamped in my mind. We had finished the first act and the lights had gone to black. The audience was absolutely silent and still. It was overpowering. That is really where you want them to be. Pinter has brought you to a point where everything you thought you understood up to then has been undermined. You are suddenly lost in a world of tangled memories and suppressed emotions. You don't clearly know who any of these three characters really is anymore. And you don't know when any of this is happening. Pinter seems to have traveled back in time to make the past present.

The three of us are standing up there in the darkness, in the silence, and I'm thinking, Wow, we did it. You could feel the audience's involvement. It was palpable. You could almost touch it. You could hear them thinking, you really could. There was something happening out there; we had connected with the audience in a very profound way. Suddenly, Brydon began clapping. He was nervous at the stirred feeling and that the audience wasn't responding in a conventional way. I don't know what exactly was going through his head. What I do know is that there was a mystery in that moment and he had broken it. No, destroyed it.

Later I flew at him. "Don't you ever do that again!" I said, more "coldly" than I had delivered the Pinter line. "Don't you ever tell an audience what to think, ever!" I was really angry. It was such a manipulative thing for him to have done, to interrupt that moment for the audience, for the actors. This is what we had built to, this is what we were trying to create, a moment of real, true, silent—yes, silent—connection between performer and audience. And he had been fearful about the connection and he had sought to dispell it. And that's irreverent. His clapping left the audience confused, wondering if somehow their reaction was wrong. The play ran from May into July and never again did Brydon applaud himself.

Old Times affected me in a lot of very complex ways. The play itself reminded me during a difficult point in my life that there are a million facets to life. There is never just one answer. Professionally, if I hadn't taken that step to go back to the stage, in a serious way, I think I would have suffered for it.

Ultimately, I find the stage much more challenging than film. It's a much bigger job and much harder to do. There is no second take, no one to yell "Cut." You never forget when you're bad on stage. On the other hand, it's very hard to be good. The audience waits for you, like a silent monster. And it demands that you use all your technique. Being on the stage is like training for a marathon; not one of your emotional muscles is left alone. When you finish a stage run, you can do anything.

As tough as it is to do it well, I've always loved the theater best. To me, acting on the stage is an experience, not an imitation of an experience. The theater has always been my home. Clifford Odets sums up the mystery and the wonder and the magic of the theater when he has Georgie in *The Country Girl* say, "Nothing is quite so mysterious and silent as a dark theater . . . a night without stars . . ."

TWELVE

I^{T'S} EDGING TOWARD midnight and the crowd at the Fillmore
is in a frenzy, following the J. Geils Band's lead singer, Peter Wolf, as
if he were a pied piper, twisting, turning, sliding across the stage, the
microphone cord coiling like a snake behind him. He looks to me to
be half rock 'n' roller, half mystic. It is certain that he has cast a spell
over the hundreds of screaming fans that have locked into his rhythm.
As I stand in the crush of people, wet from the heat and the sweat, my
own and that of those pressed around me, I think he must be a dark
prince, this swaying man with his seductive voice.

Rail thin and all in black—skintight pants, dancing shoes, and a
coat that hugs his body—once he takes the stage, you cannot look
away. He has the face of an apostle, all bones and hollows above his
dark beard. Hidden behind his dark aviator shades are velvet eyes that
you can drift in forever. His voice, though, is what locks its grip on
you, as he weaves in and out of music and a smoky rap, telling tales
of passion and pain. The blood of every important recording artist—of
blues, jazz, rock—runs through the veins of his music.

I've come to San Francisco in September of 1972 with Bryn
Bryndenthal, who works with *Rolling Stone* magazine, during a break
in filming *Oklahoma Crude*. We met on the film and she is a great fan
of the J. Geils Band, a Boston rock group that has lately taken the
country by storm. Their live album *Full House* had just been released,
and their tour that year was building more steam with each city they
hit. When Bryn found that they were to play in San Francisco, a short
plane ride from Stockton, she insisted that I come see them with her.

Stockton has more of an airstrip than an airport, and it was the

234

first time I'd taken a Piper Cub. It was a tiny plane, just four seats, and the pilot was in one of them. We were getting ready to take off, and I looked over at this very young pilot, who looked much younger than me, as he took out the airplane's manual and started going over the pages that dealt with how to get the plane up in the air. My heart stopped. "Wait a minute!" I said. "We're not moving from here until I know what you're doing." It turned out that it was a procedure required of all the pilots of these small planes, and even after a million flights it was part of the routine to do it. Later, I would hop on a Cub to fly from New York to the Hamptons without a second thought, but I don't think I relaxed this first time until we touched down in San Francisco.

Bryn knew the band well and we got there early enough to stop by the hotel, which was one of those rock 'n' roll hotels like the Tropicana on Sunset Boulevard, a real slice of Americana, with very much an on-the-road feel to it. I ended up in Peter's room, waiting for Bryn or something. One of those "I'm in the lobby," "Come on up" kind of things. The land of rock 'n' roll. You know it's groupie time. We started talking about nothing consequential, just small things. I ordered a club sandwich, which I always do, and a diet Coke. I was trying to untangle these necklaces of mine that were strung with a thousand hearts, which had somehow become a mess on the trip from Stockton. So I'm sitting in Peter's room at the table across from him and our hearts are literally in my hands.

The necklaces, about eight in all, were ones Marcello had given me, all these tiny hearts in a huge tangle lying on the table in front of me, with Peter just across the way. It was slow work getting them straight again, and the sound of the hearts hitting against each other was our background music. We talked for a long time; it was easy and comfortable. He got ready for the show and I finally got my necklace in order. That's how we first got to know each other—simple and nice.

Though I had seen bands play at the clubs in New York, and had every one of Bob Dylan's albums, a rock concert was something new for me. While everybody else was seeing rock concerts in the sixties, I'd been out working. The experience was really liberating. This was one crowd I could disappear into pretty easily. The concerts, certainly Peter's, were raw and intoxicating, as if you were reaching back and touching something more primitive and visceral and pure. Bryn and I had backstage passes and made our way there after the band, sweat-soaked from their nearly three hours onstage, finally closed down the house for the night.

I am glad that I first met Peter in the quiet before the storm of the stage, that our relationship began in stillness, not frenzy. Because there is so much gentle kindness in him; he's really a man of quiet contemplation and intellect. Having seen that other side, you understand better the dazzling kinetic energy he has onstage.

We sort of circled each other, feeling a connection but wary of it at the same time. But from the beginning, it was a connection that seemed to come without all the anxiety that had traveled with too many of the other men in my life. It was an encounter so casual, so simple, that it could easily have been a first and a last time. I left that night not even thinking of whether or not I would ever see Peter Wolf again.

At that moment, I wasn't looking to fall in love. If anything, I was looking to make sure I didn't. I wanted to focus very clearly on the work, with no distractions, no more tangled heartbreaks. And there wasn't much time to think about a relationship. Peter's band was on tour, which meant he was on the road for weeks still, and I was due back in Stockton the next day. As I left, I turned round to give him a wave good-bye, and saw those serious eyes of his studying my departure, the slightest grin tugging at one corner of his mouth.

IT WAS ABOUT that time that I got an offer from the Center Theatre Group at the Ahmanson Theatre in Los Angeles, the sister to the Mark Taper Forum. It came while I was still shooting *Oklahoma Crude*. The Ahmanson was going to put on the twenty-fifth anniversary production of Tennessee Williams' A *Streetcar Named Desire*, and the Pulitzer Prize–winning playwright was going to be involved in the production. It was quite a coup for the theater, having beaten out attempts by both the Kennedy Center in Washington and Lincoln Center in New York to get the playwright involved in their revival of the play.

Tennessee had made it known that he wanted James Bridges, a talented young director who was getting a lot of attention for his work on the movie *The Paper Chase*, to direct the play. Tennessee had recently met Jim and been impressed with his instincts, and he didn't seem inclined to accept anyone else. Fortunately Jim was excited by the prospect of taking on such a legendary work, particularly knowing that Tennessee would be collaborating. Though I had not met Tennessee, I was told I was his first choice to play Blanche. He and Fitzgerald were among my favorite authors. I knew just how true the texture and the angst they gave to this place where I grew up really was.

Rehearsals would have to begin in mid-February so that the play could premiere on Tennessee's birthday, March 26, with the playwright in attendance. It was an extraordinary play, populated with characters I had seen growing up. I knew the psychology, the smell and the feel of the place he had written about, and I wanted very much to do it. No southern woman had played the title role. Vivien Leigh and Jessica Tandy had played it, Leigh in Kazan's movie and Tandy on Broadway, and they were both English. Leigh had won an Oscar and Tandy had won a Tony. But it was important to me that a southern woman should play the most southern of heroines in Tennessee's masterpiece. To my ear, the English accent turned southern was not authentic.

As much as I wanted to play Blanche, there were a couple of other projects that had my attention as well. There was a chance to play Daisy in the film version of *The Great Gatsby*. Francis Ford Coppola had written the screenplay, and Robert Redford was to play Gatsby. I flew down to Los Angeles to do a screen test for the role. What I didn't know at the time was that the director, Jack Clayton, wanted Mia Farrow to play Daisy and had all but promised it to her. But there were executives at Paramount who wanted him to at least consider me.

Beating out the director's casting choice is one of those hurdles that is almost impossible to clear. But it's doubly hard if you're completely unaware of the intrigues going on behind the scenes, which I was. I would never have agreed to the test if I had known that the director had his mind made up otherwise going in.

In February, I was scheduled to be in Mexico filming *The Plumed Serpent*, but I couldn't bear to say no to Blanche. I stalled for weeks, seeing if there was any flexibility in the movie's shooting schedule. As it happened, the schedule turned out not to be a problem. Money was. The producers ran into some financial snags that would delay filming a bit, and Omar Sharif, who was to costar, had other commitments and decided to pull out of the project. That threw everything into limbo, and I quickly signed on to do *Streetcar*.

I had been booked into the Château Marmont, a well-known old

Hollywood hotel, for the duration of the play. What the Marmont gave you, beyond apartments with kitchens and an efficient staff that would see to whatever you needed, was anonymity. You could disappear inside the corridors and be sure of being left alone. Old friends might be staying down the hall, but unless you bumped into them, you would never know. The staff would screen every phone call with exceptional care. When you stay long enough in the public eye, you learn to treasure privacy, and the Marmont assured that.

That is even more important when you're in a play, since you do little else. You sleep, you get up, you have a light day. About four o'clock in the afternoon, the play starts to move in on you. With film, you go home and it's all done. It's not like you've got to go back to it the next night. A play is always hanging over you, consuming so much of you. Emotional reserves become critical, since you know you'll have to be able to reach deep inside yourself to build that performance anew through every one of those nights.

LIKE MOST everything else in Los Angeles, the Ahmanson was a relatively new theater, just seven years old when we did *Streetcar*. When we began rehearsals, Jim Bridges said he wanted to try to return, as much as possible, to Tennessee's original vision for the play. He had unearthed an early version of the play that included Tennessee's first ideas on stage direction.

Over the summer, he had traveled to New Orleans to meet with Tennessee, to see the neighborhood firsthand, and to track down the streetcar itself. I went back to the South as well, to soak up some of the feel of the place, to unlock old memories. I stayed in Tallahassee for a few days and drove out to see all the old plantations that were not far from where I had lived in high school.

Years later, like Bridges, I would make the pilgrimage to New Orleans to find the streetcar. By then, it was in a graveyard for old, abandoned streetcars. And I wandered through it, picking my way through the weeds, and looking for the name *Desire* that I knew would be painted on the front of the car. I thought it was regrettable, but probably fitting, that the streetcar named *Desire* was encrusted with grime and decaying in this forgotten place.

Jim Bridges was the sort of director who trusts his actors. He was a lovely man. A director, he said, had a place, but it was never to overtake the rest of us. Instead, he wanted to get the best people he could find, then create an atmosphere where they could relax, experiment, and let their character grow. It's a wonderful philosophy, but one that only works perfectly when all the actors eventually come to the same point with their characters, so that everyone is living in the same universe. On *Streetcar*, that didn't always happen.

Jon Voight had been cast as Stanley. He had starred in *Midnight Cowboy*, which had gotten him an Oscar nomination, and had some stage experience, including a role in the Broadway production of *The Sound of Music*. But he was facing a very tough task. Brando had really retired the part of Stanley Kowalski, first on the stage and then again on film. The film had forever etched Stanley Kowalski in everyone's minds. Turning in a better performance than Marlon's had proven to be close to impossible for all the actors who had tried in the years since the movie was released in 1951. The only other real option for an actor was to try to go at Stanley in a different way. It was a high-risk strategy, but the one that Jon decided to take.

Jon could talk ad infinitum about Stanley; he was very articulate but always, I felt, trying to bend things toward his own ends. In this case, it was a character shift that would have made Stanley less of a monster and Blanche less of a victim. Since *Streetcar* is built around Blanche's slow unraveling, if you tamper with the fundamental motivation for that character, you tamper with the entire play.

Streetcar opens with Blanche already somewhat unhinged, having come to her sister, Stella, Stanley's wife, to visit and sort out her life. Her brave front is a thin veneer for the psychological turmoil going on inside. The turning point, the moment that pushes Blanche over the edge, comes when Stanley and Blanche are alone in the dingy apartment on a hot, muggy night and he rapes her.

Jon wanted me to play Blanche as more of a seductress in that scene. In his interpretation, it is Blanche that would make the advances, teasing him, drawing him into the moment. Essentially he argued quite forcefully for Blanche to consciously cause the rape. While I love analyzing each character, and the dynamics between my character and the others, at some point the character really is mine to understand and define.

I had spent too many hours with Blanche, getting inside her head and her heart, to buy Jon's scenario. I don't think she did want Stanley to rape her. I don't think she wanted him to take her to bed at all. She uses those wiles because that's what southern women—all women to some degree, but certainly southern women—were taught to use in order to survive and to be a woman and to get their way: "Oh, I'm just a little woman."

That's the very sort of thing that I've tried to fight against in all my work. Jon took it to mean that Blanche wanted him to rape her because she was flirting with him. She wasn't. She was trying to survive with this man who was an animal, who would kill her as soon as look at her. He was attracted by her and knew that he wanted to conquer her in a very masculine way as well. It finally breaks her. She is conquered by him. She is broken. She's flung onto the bed and she's violated and that's what makes her go crazy. But how could the woman ever have consciously wanted to be violated? What arrogance, the man saying that any woman would want to be raped.

This was not an argument that began and ended in one day. Jon kept raising the idea. In my mind, Vivien Leigh's portrayal of Blanche in the film had been very much like that of a prostitute. I wanted to give some class and nobility to this southern woman. She had lived a tough life and I wanted her to have dignity in the face of her madness. Bill Alfred and I worked on the character to give her that, and I wasn't going to let it get stripped away for what I thought was an all-too-common male convention that "no" really means "yes."

There was a line in the original play that had been cut during various revisions that I wanted to put back in. Blanche says "Men don't see women unless they are in bed with them. They don't admit their existence except when they're lovemaking." That said everything about Blanche to me. She had set her sights high and did not want to exist like Stella, as a mere appendage of a man. The entire play was such a sensitive exploration of the misconceptions we have about men and women, the male machismo cast against the coquette. I didn't want that damaged.

By the time the play opened, Jon and I had reached a detente. In the end, I played it as I had wanted, with Blanche not inciting the rape and in fact fighting a desperate struggle to prevent it. Except for our difference about the rape scene, we had few disagreements about the tone of the play. Jon was a really fine actor, and you always gain from working with those who are good at this craft. He was very much into getting to the truth of things, and was tireless in rehearsals. I ended up liking his performance quite a lot and thought he took an unfair beating from the critics, who really could not get beyond Brando's performance to see what Jon had brought to his. His Stanley was more boyish, more human, and in the end, a bit more easy for the audience to forgive.

It was a fun performance for me, but hard, very draining. At the height of the madness each night, I would go from standing straight up to falling to my knees, in one swift move. The audience would invariably be startled by the force of it, the crack of knees hitting the stage. We fashioned padding for my knees, but I still would have to soak them each night to keep them from being bruised and swollen. It's a moment I'm very proud of. It was something of a Michael Chekhov psychological gesture, because Blanche was really trying to get saved during the entire play. Blanche had emotionally deconstructed at that point, and with that crash, she had physically done the same.

My old friend Thea Van Runkle did the costumes and gave Blanche a wardrobe that ran parallel to her various emotional states in a really extraordinary way. Throughout it, Thea used very fragile materials for Blanche. Always draped softly, there was nothing severe in the clothing, and, like the character, it seemed to have moods. When I would move, the dresses would almost float around me, and when I would stop, they would cling. At one point in the play Blanche says, "Soft people have got to shimmer and glow—they've got to put on soft colors, the colors of butterfly wings." Thea covered me in butterfly wings, flimsy pastels that were exactly what this woman, with all her illusions and her fragile psyche, should wear. For the final costume, Thea put me in colors of the Madonna, a pale blue dress with a red cape, somehow also resonant of the crucifixion—as Blanche's aspiring toward something finer and better in life was crucified in her.

I don't spend that much time reading reviews of the plays and movies I've done. Even the good ones will drive you crazy, because the highest praise invariably comes with some caveat or another. But a line from one of the reviews of *Streetcar* stays with me. The critic wrote that he believed my Blanche had very likely been a good teacher. I liked that very much. It made me feel that the reality and dignity I had worked so hard to give this woman had come through.

The other review that I cared about was Tennessee's. The party after the premiere was at the Sovereign restaurant in the Union Bank building not far from the theater in downtown L.A. It was the event of the season in Hollywood. Johnny Carson was there, Henry and Shirlee Fonda, Charlton and Lydia Heston, Jack Lemmon, Bob and Rosemarie Stack. It was one of those incredible nights that you know will stay with you a lifetime.

Tennessee was already there, surrounded by people, when I walked in. I had scrubbed all the stage makeup off my face and put on just enough powder to get by. I felt good about the performance—but then, you never really know. When I walked into the room, Tennessee immediately spotted me, broke free of the crowd around him, and literally danced all the way across the room. He was hard to miss, wearing a brown satin Yves Saint Laurent suit and waving his white panama at me.

He grabbed my hand and started racing around the room, from one group to another, saying I *was* Blanche. He told me later that he thought I was brave and adorable and reminded him of a precocious child, and that my performance ranked with the very best. It was high praise indeed coming from him. That was the beginning of a friendship, and whenever we were in the same town, we would always break bread together and talk of another project that we would do some day.

WHILE I WAS DOING *Streetcar*, the producer Pierre Spengler called and said he wanted to talk to me about a remake of the Alexandre Dumas novel *The Three Musketeers*. The story had been translated to film any number of times, most brilliantly in 1921 with Douglas Fairbanks starring. But the last time it had been done well was in 1948 with Gene Kelly, Lana Turner as Lady de Winter, the role they wanted me for, June Allyson, Van Heflin, and a long list of other good actors capped off by a wicked performance by Vincent Price as the infamous Cardinal Richelieu.

The director for our remake was to be Richard Lester, an exceptionally funny Brit who had managed to create a stunning film starring the Beatles, *A Hard Day's Night*. He had taken their music and a fairly thin plot and woven it into a wonderful fantasy that captured the bizarre side of London in the sixties and the manic energy of the Beatles too. What should have been completely popcorn had an intellect that Lester was clearly responsible for.

The cast they were trying to put together for the film was a high-octane one, including Michael York, Oliver Reed, Raquel Welch, Geraldine Chaplin, and Dick Chamberlain, with Charlton Heston as the cardinal. I decided it would be a great treat to work with such a wide range of actors and to take on a parody, something lighter, with more comedy to it than I had previously done.

I read every single page of my contract, which was not something I often did. But I was at a point in my life where I was trying to reclaim a lot of the handling of my affairs from business managers and the like. And with *Musketeers*, I just had a feeling that something was afoot. Peter Wolf and I had reconnected and were seeing each other on occasion, and he happened to be with me at the Marmont when the contract was delivered. He was quite astonished that I wanted to read it all and left me alone to plow through it. Still I didn't catch it. In fact none of those of us starring in the film did, nor did any of our multiple agents and attorneys. It managed to commit us all to do two movies instead of one. For one salary.

It was nearly a year before any of us discovered what had happened. The first time we screened the completed film, there, during the closing credits, was a trailer for the sequel, starring me, Michael York, Charlton Heston, and the list went on. It was to be fashioned from extra footage, I learned later. There was an immediate outcry from the actors that we had been taken advantage of. No one had agreed to the idea of filming two movies for the price of one.

Fortunately for us, they needed the musketeers themselves back for a few days more of shooting to fill in some of the gaps they had discovered in patching together *The Four Musketeers*. That, I believe, and the threat of lawsuits from a dozen or more major actors, is the only reason any of us got an additional sum for our efforts.

There are, unfortunately, episodes like this and others one hears about in my business, such as the David Begelman scandal written about in the book *Indecent Proposal*. All too often you find yourself up against these kinds of characters or facing moments like these that make you aware that show business really is a kind of a racket. When I speak to my friends who live in the East, who live honorable lives, I realize that. For someone to outrageously cheat and connive in this way was at first unbelievable to me. You think that you're working in a profession that has some nobility, attempting to achieve art, when in truth, on the other end of the spectrum are some of the most greedy people. All they care about is living off and using the actors and anybody else they can. Yes, art and commerce. It's the *demi monde,* the shadowy world, where there isn't all that much honor. And I forget that sometimes.

THE TIMING, for me, was going to be a tight squeeze. *The Three Musketeers* was going to begin production in Spain in early May, and *Streetcar* was going to have its final performance April 28. I really would have liked more time to recover from the demands of eight performances a week, and to prepare for my role as Milady, but it was a huge cast with so many big names that scheduling had become a nightmare. They couldn't afford to delay an hour much less a few days.

I flew out of Los Angeles on the twenty-ninth and breezed through New York. There I dropped just about everything I owned at the laundry, and tried to catch up on all the things that had fallen into limbo while I was doing *Streetcar.* I carried the script with me everywhere I went, which was very shortly to fittings for the elaborate wardrobe I was to wear, and then I was off to Spain. There was no room to breathe. Even less once I was trussed up in the corsets I wore throughout the production. They were no more forgiving than they had been three centuries ago.

Filming in Toledo, a little south of Madrid, began in late May. The crew had turned the town into seventeenth-century Paris. We would move from town to town, turning back the clock three hundred years, then move on once again. In the village of Salamanca, the wine cellar in an ancient castle was turned into a Parisian cabaret. The castle itself was used for a number of scenes, and even the local church was overrun by the movie crew for a few days of filming. By the time we moved on to another location, the local magistrate said he had collected enough in fees to feed even the poorest in the town for an entire year.

In all, there were more than fifty locations and a hundred different sets used to re-create all the pomp and ceremony, as well as the village life of that time. It took a huge crew, about two hundred, to coordinate all of this. With the actors and crew staying for a few days, then packing up and moving on, *The Three Musketeers* started to take on the look and feel of a Gypsy camp.

For the first month, all the sets were closed to outsiders. The European press corps, which always followed movie productions closely, was banned, and they were outraged. But the producers had become increasingly nervous as several other film companies announced that they would be making their own version of the Dumas classic. By the time we had gathered in Spain, there were two Italian versions being shot, one French version, and an animated film in the works as well.

I ALREADY KNEW that Spain had the capacity to get quite hot, after the August sizzle that had settled in during the filming of *Doc*. It was even worse inland, where we were, than along the Mediterranean, and we were expecting to shoot through the summer. Given that, May was generally one of the mildest months in that part of Europe. You could be relatively assured that you would not be hit with one late blast of winter, and the temperatures were generally much cooler than the hot furnace of August. But that year Spain turned hot early, and stayed hot.

My costumes, designed by Yvonne Blake, really were replicas of the kind of court dresses you would see in France in the seventeenth century. They were exquisite and matched the period down to the last details. That meant pantaloons, hoops, corsets, and hose. And that was just the first layer. Most of the dresses were very formal, with long sleeve, low necklines, and heavy floor-length skirts. Those that were sleeveless were to be worn with gloves that buttoned to the elbow.

The dresses themselves had stays, to make sure the waist looked tiny and the bust looked huge. In these clothes, even Chuck Heston would have had cleavage. After I had spent a week in a corset, someone in the crew handed me a photocopied article that was making the rounds on the set. It detailed how autopsies on the corpses of women in the upper classes during the period often showed bodies that were completely distorted, with the rib cage compressed so much that their hearts and other organs had been completely relocated. I didn't doubt it for a moment.

The final pieces of my wardrobe included jewelry, in particular an elaborate cross, and about a dozen different wigs, piled high with curls in the elaborate coifs the costume designer created for Milady from accurate period portraits. Though they tried to keep us as cool as possible, between the heat and the lights it was difficult. We must have gone through pounds of talc keeping everyone looking crisp and dry. On the day we shot the induction of D'Artagnan into the Musketeers, with the entire royal court in attendance, the temperature soared to 122 degrees and we were outside, filming on the patio of the Aranjuez Palace. There were moments the set looked like a commercial for bottled water. Each time Lester would yell "Cut!" we would all grab a few bottles of water and down them in a single gulp. The heat was withering, but we stopped for nothing.

That included a series of accidents and injuries on the set. With all the battle scenes and small duels, it was a very physical film. Michael York, who played D'Artagnan, nearly lost an eye in one duel and had his leg slashed in another. Oliver Reed was nursing an infection on his wrist that he got when he was pierced by a sword. Frank Finlay, who played the blustering Porthos, was slammed in the face with a two-by-four in a laundry fight and burned in another scene. Christopher Lee, who was Rochefort, sprained his left knee in one duel and pulled a muscle in his shoulder in another. Daily, it seemed, we were adding to the list of walking wounded.

Raquel Welch, who played Constance, the film's heroine and D'Artagnan's love, and I have a horrendous row in the film, complete with hair pulling and a great deal of pushing and shoving, all choreographed so that our scene would make a boxing match look civil. The battle royal begins when Milady tries to carry off a necklace, the prize that everyone is after at some point in the film. I'm supposed to brush by and literally remove it from around Raquel's neck. I wanted to play it a bit like Dietrich had done the barroom brawl in *Destry Rides Again*, where everything looked out of control and wild.

Both Raquel and I had been working with trainers to make the fight as physical and brutal as Lester wanted, without either of us sustaining any injuries. Everyone was particularly sensitive to it since so many actors on *Musketeers* had come away from these fight scenes hurt. It was going well until we reached a point in the scene where I'm supposed to push against Raquel. We had rehearsed this without any difficulty. But this time, just as I pushed, she lost her footing and fell, spraining her wrist. I felt awful and it was little consolation to me that the injury was a minor one. Though you are always trying for reality in your performance—and with these physical scenes there is always a risk—you never want that sort of reality to intrude.

It was all made worse by rumors in the press of a feud between Raquel and me, which simply did not exist. We had very few scenes together and for the short time we were on location together, there was no friction between us. But the press seems to feed on conflict, and if they can't find it, they sometimes create it. So there were reports of the two of us not wanting to work together, which was absurd. While Raquel and I did not have the kind of relationship where we would hang out together between scenes, we did have one thing in common: we were professionals and there was a job at hand, which we both did to the best of our abilities.

Oliver Reed, as Athos, was one of the central characters that I found myself playing against in the film. Where Milady is icy, Athos is smoldering. Oliver was a huge flirt and just a lot of fun, someone who helped keep it light on the set. We had a great time playing off each other in those scenes. We played it like a poker game, each of us upping the ante. I'd get more icy, he'd smolder more. If you see the film, you would think that we could not spend two seconds in the same room without attacking each other. But Oliver was a great and funny friend, and a terrific actor to work with—one of those people who reminds you of the fun this business can be.

LESTER'S DIRECTING STYLE was unlike anything I had ever seen. Instead of shooting some of the shots from a distance, then doing close-ups separately, he kept three cameras rolling at all times to get the coverage he needed all at once. There was never a time when you thought the camera was on someone else. It might be, but there was sure to be another one or two trained on you. You had to be there every moment in every scene you were in. But I found Lester to be a brilliant director, with all the reserve and the dry wit of the British. And he had a decisive nature, which kept what could have been a horribly unwieldly production under control.

David Watkin, who wielded the all-powerful camera, was a hilariously funny guy, but like the corsets and stays, at times he could be a pain. He was a groundbreaking cinematographer in the field and very much on the leading edge of those who were beginning to use indirect lighting, bounce lighting we call it. He would shine the lights onto a white Styrofoam card, and the light would bounce off it, which created a nice ambiance, not quite as good as candlelight, but soft. But it didn't help the actors. Simply put, it makes you look awful, unlike being lit from the front, which blows out almost all of the imperfections and makes you look beautiful. Most actors learn relatively quickly what they need to know about lighting. It can help you or hurt you.

But Watkin was brilliant, and equally eccentric. He hated Spain and missed England and his lover dreadfully. Fairly early in the production, Watkin took to sitting in the hallway. They would call to him to come and get a reading for the light inside the room. But he'd stay in the hallway, and just call back a reading. Somehow he would be on the mark each time in gauging just the right amount of light for the spot where you were actually going to be shot. He was just that good. Though bounce lighting was in fashion at the time, I thought it made everybody flat, and didn't illuminate the eyes, which is what you need to see. People's eyes.

Lester was shooting so much film that the production ran nearly five months, through the summer and into the fall. Of course I guess that's to be expected if you're trying to get enough for two films instead of one, though he pleaded innocence at the end of it. The story was that when Lester got to editing it, he had shot so much that rather than edit it down to one film and lose so many elements of the story and the performances, he just chopped it in half. I suppose anything is possible, but the wording in the contract that gave them the option to do that up front made it hard for those of us who had worked on the film—rather, films—to swallow the explanation.

While we were in Spain, Peter Wolf came to visit me. I remember him dashing out to go swimming in the Mediterranean, and he stepped right on one of those sea urchins, like the ones I had eaten in David Niven's house on the Riviera. Except Peter had stepped on the outside, on the spines, of the *oursin*, and they pierced his foot. He was laid up for a really long time—his gentle, Piscean feet.

Peter had an idea for an album cover he wanted to have done while we were in Europe. As soon as I finished shooting *Musketeers*, we were to go together to Paris where the artist, Antonio, was going to paint my eyes and my lips for the new J. Geils album. It is sometimes strange how life is filled with unexpected interludes that in retrospect feel surreal; the stopoff in Paris was one of them.

I remember sitting in Antonio's studio while he was painting me, and in one of the other rooms was a young model, who had just come to Paris for the first time. She was a tall, lanky blonde from Texas named Jerry Hall, who would go on to meet and marry Mick Jagger. Out the window I could see an old man watching his television set. I never saw him move; he just sat there transfixed by the screen. Antonio noticed and said, "That's Jean-Paul Sartre." I thought back to Sartre's play *No Exit* that had marked my departure from Lincoln Center. But it had also marked a breakthrough in my work with Andreas Voutsinas. When I first felt I knew what I was doing as an artist. How far I had come since then.

ABOUT MIDWAY through the production of *Musketeers*, a lot of late-night calls started coming from Jack Nicholson to the hotel in Madrid where I was staying. He had a project he was involved in and wanted to make sure I kept my options open until I got an offer on the part. Some of the executives at the studio wanted Jane Fonda, but Jack was lobbying hard for me.

It surprised me a bit, since I didn't know Jack well. We had met on occasion at various parties and premieres, but what we really knew of each other was the work. I had a firm offer to do another movie and though I wanted to work with Jack, I couldn't find a reason to wait for the executives at Paramount to make up their minds. But Jack is a master at winning you over.

The last time Jack and I spoke, I remember sitting in the hotel room in front of an ancient wooden writing desk. I kept running my hand over the surface, which had been scarred and pitted by others through the years, who had, like me, sat in front of it pondering and plotting their future. We talked for a very long time, far into the night, with Jack trying to explain what this movie was about and why I should do it. I finally said, "Jack, why should I wait for something that might not be real?" He told me, "Dunaway, it's real, and it's worth waiting for."

The movie was to be called *Chinatown*.

THIRTEEN

JACK NICHOLSON is staring at me, his face in a barely contained rage. When Jack is angry, he gets very quiet. He is very quiet now, the words barely able to escape his lips as he tells me he doesn't want to hear another lie. I'm shaken by the sense of menace that is in the air. I stumble over my words as I try to explain. Smack. My left cheek is stinging and there is a faint red mark left by his fingers. Smack. The force of the blow across my right cheek wrenches my neck. It has caught me off guard. I lose my footing and raise my arms to ward off the other blows I know will follow. Smack. Again and again he hits me. Within minutes I'm in a crying, crumpled heap on the couch.

"Cut," says Roman Polanski. "I think we should do it again." Roman has a wicked grin on his face as he instructs the crew to get ready for another take. He is enjoying this moment far too much. It's mid-October, 1973. Jack and I had worked on this scene between Jake Gittes and Evelyn Mulwray for hours. It is a pivotal one in *Chinatown*, when the central mystery of the movie is revealed. We kept trying to stage each of the blows so that it would look as if I had really been slapped again and again. Each time he asks me a question and I answer with what he believes is a lie, another blow comes. But there are always a few seconds lost at one point or another, the natural hesitation that comes when one person is trying to get as close as possible to physical contact and the other is trying to react as if the blow has really been landed.

Finally I said to Jack, "Look, you're just going to have to hit me. There's no other way. We'll never get it perfectly with all those slaps. There will always be one that will be off." Jack looked at me, "You sure, Dread?" I shook my head yes. With permission granted, Jack hauled off and slapped me. It was real and it hurt like hell, but it was great. The scene turned out to be wonderful, and there is not a moment in it that looks false.

Chinatown was one of the three films I did that would be judged as classics. It would stand alongside *Bonnie and Clyde* and later *Network*, all great films that I am blessed to have had a hand in creating. I worked with Roman Polanski, an auteur filmmaker of the first order from Europe. Roman had survived the Nazi concentration camps. He has had a complicated connection to women for much of his career, with taste that ran to young, malleable girls. And that's not what I was. Ours was a personality clash from the beginning.

On the other hand, I could never have asked for a dearer friend to me or more loving person than Jack. Jack Nicholson is one of the most distinguished actors in the pantheon of great leading men— Cagney, Bogart, Cooper. And there is something really gorgeous about Jack. He's a true original, a crackerjack thinker, an innovator, and crazy like a fox.

We would hang out in Jack's trailer, while they were lighting for a scene, and Jack and I would discuss our roles. We would commiserate. He is one of those people who has the capacity to be a really good friend, the best, and that is what we have, a really good friendship.

On Sundays the whole Nicholson pack would pile into his Rolls-Royce—Lou Adler, Carol Kane, whom everyone called Whitey, Anjelica Huston, Harry Dean Stanton, and Ara Gallant, the great hairdresser from New York, who had come to do a few streaks in my hair for *Chinatown*. We'd usually end up at El Cholo, this wonderful hacienda-style restaurant, a favorite of Jack's, just west of downtown. It is ancient by L.A. standards and has the best authentic Mexican food in the city, nachos and guacamole that no one does better. We'd sit there and while away the afternoon eating and talking, sharing a pitcher of their margaritas, also legendary, with Jack holding forth on work, life, politics, sports, Lakers games, everything. I also went to Lakers games with Jack, and to rock 'n' roll concerts. James Taylor was a favorite.

I tried to avoid any sort of romantic entanglements with my leading men and only twice broke that rule. Though there was a chance one moment early on that Jack and I might get involved, I was with Peter and Jack had just started seeing Anjelica, and it was one of those things best left alone. I was wary anyway of hanging out with Nicholson or Warren Beatty in that way. I was uncomfortable with the fact that they were such fast travelers—admitted womanizers, really. It was one of those things Jack and I talked about in our trailer tête-à-têtes. He was bemused that he and Warren, at different points in their lives, often ended up with the same woman. It didn't make him happy.

FROM THE BEGINNING, Jack took on *Chinatown* like a personal project. Robert Towne, who had written the screenplay and whom I knew from his work on the *Bonnie and Clyde* script, was one of his closest friends and had written Gittes with Jack in mind. *Chinatown*, Jack would say, was a state of mind—anything could happen. It would become the catch phrase for all of us on the film. He told me he sensed that quality in me, those times that he called me in Spain to talk about the project. Kazan had said I walked in a cloud of conflict—you never knew what I would do next, and there was always a certain intrigue. Jack believed those qualities were essential to make Evelyn Mulwray work as a character.

What I had to try to create, from the inside out, was a character who had some mystery to her certainly, but something just a bit unpredictable as well. As Jack saw it, it would rest on Evelyn to convince the audience that they were in a place where the conventional rules of logic did not apply. *Chinatown* had to feel like a different world. Jack told me long before I saw the script that it was one of the greatest roles for a woman he had ever seen, and he was right, though I was in the script for surprisingly few pages. I loved Evelyn Mulwray; I *was* Evelyn Mulwray. She is what she seems and she is nothing that she seems, all at the same time. If you start at that point, the lack of logic begins to make sense.

A detective story in the Raymond Chandler style, the plot itself was a complex one, with all of the elements of great human drama—greed, lust, lies, incest, power, jealousy, murder, and money. I don't think Towne left any major vices out. At the fulcrum of the story, two things were at risk: the water supply of Los Angeles, and Evelyn Mulwray. It is a story that begins with death and deception and ends the same way. It's the murder mystery genre, and Chandler was the biggest

With my pal Jack Nicholson in Chinatown. © 1995 by Paramount Pictures

writer of it. He wrote a lot of great characters, almost stock characters, as did Dashiell Hammett. And one of those stock characters was the woman who is incredibly alluring, but less than innocent. Mary Astor played such a character in Hammett's *The Maltese Falcon*, and I played Evelyn Mulwray in that tradition.

But the playing of it was fascinating because it was like a mosaic. I had to construct each of Evelyn's reactions so that the audience would think at that moment that I was guilty. And yet when they remember that moment at the end, they would realize my reaction was not because I was guilty, but because of the truth. That was the first thing I had to work out, how Evelyn could always seem guilty when she is the least guilty of all the characters, how to convey that her reactions come from the pain of her past.

Like the Fitzgerald heroines, Evelyn Mulwray's voice was full of money. That's what the voice had to be. You often don't make a conscious decision. I noticed the voice one day when I was watching the rushes and thought, Oh, interesting voice. Good choice. But in reality, I didn't make the choice, it just happened; the voice evolved as the character did.

What happens between Evelyn and Jake was anything but a conventional love story, and I liked that as well. At first she finds him an inconvenience and dismissable. But over time, she comes to regard him as quite a rare man. And by the end of the film, she has probably fallen a bit in love with him. But Evelyn is a woman who has been so scarred by her past, she really can't let down her guard long enough to truly fall in love.

John Huston played the villain, Noah Cross, a powerful man whose money holds many in a vise. Cross is the master puppeteer behind all the intrigues, but the source of his power is the water supply. It was a neat touch by Robert Towne, I thought, to call him Noah. Cross is also, as Jack finally discovers, both my father and the father of my child, having raped me when I was fifteen.

Huston was perfect for the role. He was a powerful-looking man, though he was already suffering from emphysema when *Chinatown* was made. Huston would come into parties and everyone would stand out of respect for the legendary filmmaker. Then in the lowest, huskiest voice, he would say, "Oh, my dear . . . no, no, no, don't rise," as if he were quieting his subjects.

He had such social grace and elegance, every time I saw him. But Deborah Kerr told me once that she had done a film with him where she had to stand in leach-ridden water for hours, and he wouldn't let her come out between takes. There was that sadistic side to him, and though I never saw it, I always sensed it was there.

Throughout the film, Huston mispronounced the name Gittes. Jack's character was Jake Gittes, two syllables, "Git-tes." But from the first time he said it, Huston called him "Gits." "Mr. Gits." That was Huston's invention. Jack couldn't get him to say his name right and it used to really get under his skin. Which was of course exactly what the character Noah Cross was always trying to do to Jake, keep him off-center.

I watched Huston's scenes when I could. It was long a practice of mine to be out of my trailer and on the set as much as possible, because that is where you learn this business. I came away from those scenes most often convinced that Huston just didn't understand how to pronounce the man's name; that's how good he was. But once, in a flash of his eye, I saw that he knew it, knew exactly what he was doing.

A FEW DAYS into filming, Roman decided he wanted to cut Jake's nose. He liked the metaphor of a nosy private detective getting his nose slashed. And he wanted to do it personally, as his cameo in the picture. It was a nasty cut, with Roman putting the tip of the knife into Jack's nostril and ripping through it. That scene remains one of the most awful and grotesque in *Chinatown*.

The special-effects man created a knife with a hinged tip that would give at the least amount of pressure, with a tube of blood hidden on one side of it. But there was always the fear that somehow that hinge would catch, and you can see it in Jack's eyes, despite the fact he checked the knife in Roman's hand before every take to make sure he was holding it right.

From that point on, Jack progressed through the film with huge gauze bandages and white adhesive tape, and then ugly black stitches and a nasty scar. In a scene that comes shortly after his nose has been slashed and I've been called by some farmers to retrieve him, I have to try to clean the wound. The damage to Jack's nose looked so real and so horrible, it was easy to forget that if I pressed the alcohol-saturated cotton ball to his nose it wouldn't really hurt.

There are few people that I have loved working with as much as Jack. He was just a dreamboat, a real gent. He is smart, he's an intellectual, he's articulate. He and Brando were cut from the same cloth. He's sanguine; Jack plays for high stakes. As an actor, he's there in the moment and there's always humor running through his work; a real kind of almost Lenny Bruce-ian hipness. He makes up his own words, as Marlon has all his career, and he's a true American original. Picasso once said about Gary Cooper that he had *La vrai élégance américain*. And you know, Jack's got that. He's not as tall as Coop, and that's what Picasso was referring to, that bony Abe Lincoln sort of elegance. But Jack has reinvented the true American elegance. He is in the stream with Brando. He's the next in line. I think he's emulated Brando quite a lot, as we all have—men or women.

Jack's a sexy man, he's an amusing man, he's always got a twinkle in his eye. We all know that smile of Jack's, that real kind of knowing, intelligent, joking flirtation in his eyes. Ironically and sadistically, Roman had in one fell swoop handicapped Jack's race to become a leading man. The role in *Chinatown*, Gittes, was the first time he had played a romantic lead, which he knew and he fought for. He had come from that young, Roger Corman group of actors. Then he made a big mark when he played George Hanson in *Easy Rider*.

Once Jack and I were having one of our heart-to-hearts. I was talking about Polanski and how I was having a real difficult time getting the performance to the level of aliveness that it had to have, because I felt like Roman was thwarting me and not supporting me. And he turned to me and said, "You think you've got troubles, Dread? You realize this is the first time I'm playing a leading man, and I'm spending three-quarters of the movie with a bandage covering half my face?" He gave me that famous Jack Nicholson look through the darkness of the trailer, and the irony of the situation was not lost on either one of us.

LIVING IN LOS ANGELES now, I pass by the Eastern Star Home all the time. It is in Brentwood, on Sunset Boulevard as it edges toward the ocean, and was one of the locations we used. Each time I pass that building, *Chinatown* memories wash right over me, even that undrivable yellow Packard. Driving the Packard was like trying to move a giant steamer—there was a little finesse to it, but more brute strength. It was worlds away from the cars I had driven in *Bonnie and Clyde*, which were as smooth as silk to maneuver.

In *Bonnie*, one scene I'll never forget had Warren jumping on the running board of the car, and just as he jumps, I had to gun the engine and speed off. It was quite a dangerous move and took a lot of guts on Warren's part, but we did the scene time and again and I managed to pull it off perfectly every time. At one point he leaned in and said, "You've got a lot of class." It remains one of my most cherished compliments.

Like Bonnie, Evelyn had a very distinctive style about her. The clothes designed by Anthea Sylbert were wonderful, a 1930s look, very upscale. Whether I was meeting someone or I had just come in from riding, I looked carefully put together. I did very, very thin eyebrows for Evelyn, another trademark of the times.

FROM THE FIRST DAY, this was a production filled with ragged edges. Roman was back in Los Angeles for the first time since his wife, actress Sharon Tate, had been murdered by the Manson family in their house above Benedict Canyon. He was nervous and twitchy throughout the film. *Chinatown* was very important to Roman. He had not had a hit since *Rosemary's Baby,* and on that he had gone over budget; the studio was watching him like a hawk.

Before *Chinatown*, I had met Roman only once in passing at a party in Rome. He agreed with Jack that I was right for the role of Evelyn. But from the moment I stepped on the set, I felt he was not happy with me. I found him to be a very odd man and I got strange vibes every time I was around him. It was very difficult to pin down exactly what it was, but I was clearly not his cup of tea, ever. Nor he mine.

Roman was very much an autocrat, always forcing things. It ranged from the physical to the mental. He was very domineering and abrasive and made it clear he wanted to manipulate the performance. That approach has never succeeded with me. At that moment in my life, I lacked the maturity to take a beat, count to ten, and say, "Well, that's who the man is, let me see what I can do here." In part, it was just bad timing. The movie-star mill had begun to really grind me down by *Chinatown*, and I was vulnerable because of it.

Roman too had his own problems with women. He always hung out with very young girls. Young girls are not threatening, young girls don't have ideas, they're not independent, and I was all of those. I was a pretty considerable actress by that time, as well, with strong opinions about my work. Those differences set the stage for a clash.

I should have been able to recognize Roman for what he was and not let that interrupt my work process. I failed abysmally at it on this movie, and I've lived to bitterly regret it. There isn't a single shark of a reporter to this day who doesn't try to make the episode in *Chinatown* a defining one in my life. No one talks about my work with Kazan, Lumet, Pollack, Jewison, McQueen, Nicholson, Chayefsky, all the great experiences I've had. But my falling out with Roman, I am always asked to explain.

The friction between us began from the start. During the makeup test, Lee Harman, who was my makeup man, had finished, and Roman came by to check it. He wasn't happy; he wanted me paler than I already was, though my skin is extremely pale to begin with. Instead of explaining what he wanted, he just started striding around, saying "No, no, no, I want it like this," as he grabbed the powder and began covering my face with it. The effect was awful, but his methods were worse. I came away from that encounter thinking that he was a bully. Now I think what he did to me throughout the film bordered on sexual harassment.

I was very serious about my work; I knew Evelyn Mulwray was a great role and I hated being constricted. What Roman did was give you the results. Directors in what I think of as the Kazan school will never give you the results, or only as a last resort. But Roman was into line readings—he would read, you were to mimic. He would do the same with gestures. "Do this. Do that." Most good directors will not try to paste on things that are not organic to the performance. What I do in a scene has to be organic, it has to come from me. What Kazan will do, if he's not getting what he wants, is try to correct the source of the gesture. "What are you thinking here?" "Are you scared of him now?"

You can't say to a flower, "Be red now." The flower grows from a tiny seed, and it becomes what it is, which happens to be red. Acting is all about how I find the truth of the moment. How I become red, if that's what is called for. Only then do you have a chance to make something that's truly heart-stopping, because it comes from deep within. But Roman never would work that deeply. It wasn't part of his training, I suppose. But for me, it is what the craft of acting is all about.

The first scene we shot, I was late to the set, not by much but late nevertheless. There was a lot to getting the hair and the costume right, particularly the first day; that is when you are really stepping into the character for the first time. But Roman was very exasperated with me. In the scene, a woman, played by Diane Ladd posing as Evelyn Mulwray, had hired Jake in an attempt to frame my husband. The news of it has hit the papers and I've come to Jake's office to confront him with the fact that we have never met. There is a brooch at my neck, and it's a focal point, because as you look at my face, the brooch catches the eye. I realized almost immediately that it was awry, and asked for a moment to let the dresser straighten it.

But Roman insisted that it not be touched. I thought it cruel of him, and unnecessary. It would have taken but a second to fix that brooch. Pollack, or Lumet, and certainly Kazan would have said, "Okay, let's get it right." And only then would they shoot. Roman, though, had to exert his control over me and the scene. There was a streak of perversity in Polanski. He had tragedy in his life. It began early on in the concentration camp, which was probably the root of it. And he was small in stature, so I'm sure that he suffered as a child for that as well. But I found him needlessly sarcastic, needlessly cruel.

There is another scene in the film, where Jack turns to leave and I gasp and my hand flies to my throat—the gesture of an elegant, sensitive woman, a lady well-born. "Oh, that was wonderful," Roman said, "just like my mother." That, I believe, was the first and last time he said anything I did during the entire production was good. I was trying to give a good performance—that's all I've ever tried to do. If Roman was pleased, I was happy. But he was never pleased. By the time we had our notorious confrontation—it is one Roman loves to talk about—there was a lot of bad blood between us.

WE WERE FILMING that day in the Brown Derby restaurant, a Hollywood fixture for years with its clientele of power brokers in the film industry. Evelyn and Jake have met to talk, with Jake determined to unravel the mess. His concern at the moment is to find out who framed him and who murdered Evelyn's husband; he's convinced that the same person is behind both. She simply wants him to drop the entire matter.

Evelyn's hair was marcelled, deep waves very close to the head. The hair had to be immaculate, reminiscent of the old screen goddesses like Carole Lombard. It's a style that had to be set with a very strong setting lotion so that it would hold the tight ridges of the marcel wave. The camera was on me. I vaguely knew someone sprayed my hair, but I was immersed in the scene. I wasn't in the habit of watching everything the hairdresser did. I was intent on the moment. Suddenly, Roman was very close to me, pulling a hair out of my head. And I was horrified. He did not ask. He didn't bother to tell me, as most directors would have done, that he thought there was a stray hair that the camera was picking up.

Whether there was or was not a hair, though, was not the issue in my mind. It was a sadistic act. It came at the end of a very long litany of things that Roman had done, mentally and emotionally, to me— not to Jack, not to anyone else who was around. With me, Roman was always barreling through and stomping on delicate areas. When you're in character, you're in a very vulnerable place. Directors know that. I was playing a woman who had been raped by her own father. She was a woman always on guard, to make sure that no one would ever rape her again. It was the subtext of all her relationships.

Roman dropped the hair he had jerked out, his mouth curled into

A marcel is done w/ a hot iron.

a smirk, and he began to walk away. I was furious. "Don't you dare ever do that sort of thing to me again!" I told him. "Don't even touch me, much less pull a hair out of my head." It was not the hair, it was the incessant cruelty that I felt, the constant sarcasm, the never-ending need to humiliate me. I felt the time had come to draw a line that Roman would never dare cross again.

I left the set and went back to my trailer. I was not going to do another scene until I had aired my grievance with Bob Evans, the producer, and had assurances from Bob, Roman, and everyone else in a position of power on the film that this sort of incident would never happen again. I always felt Roman was treading on me, that he never accorded me any respect. And I deserved respect—I had earned it by that point in my career, and I was due it as a human being.

WE ALL ENDED up in Bob's office over at Paramount. It was an awful thing, filled with anger and acrimony. Roman should never have done what he did. Of all the movies I've worked on, of all the directors I've worked with, there are only two directors that I haven't gotten along with—Otto Preminger and Roman Polanski.

A great deal was made of it by Roman and by the press. They're often such piranhas, the third estate, and they feed off negativity. It's said the need to build people up to the level of star status is equaled only by the need to tear them down again. And I've certainly found this to be true in this particular incident. It has hounded me over the years and still to this day is like a story told wrong in a parlor game, whispered round from one person to the next, only to be completely exaggerated at the end. I'm always asked about it, because journalists seem to want to see actors in uncomfortable positions. It's a very sick business.

And yet the confrontation with Roman follows me, and is largely responsible for a label I dislike—"difficult." Another way to say it is "perfectionist," you know. God is in the details. I do want to get it right. The fact is a man can be difficult and people applaud him for trying to do a superior job. People say, "Well, gosh, he's got a lot of guts. He's a real man." And a woman can try to get it right and she's "a pain in the ass." It's in my nature to do really good jobs, and I would never have been successful if I hadn't.

•

I WAS NOT the only one on the set to have a row with Polanski. He really lost it a couple of times with Jack. One day, everyone around Jack happened to be laughing when Roman walked up. He started scolding Jack in none-too-polite terms.

Jack didn't say a word, just stared down at Roman while he went on and on about the jokes. "You are not helping me make this movie, Jack," he said. Jack paused a beat, looked at Roman, and said in a very measured tone, "Roman, if there's one thing I'm trying to do, it's to help you make this movie." And I flicked my eyes over to him, I had heard him. That's all I had ever done with all the directors I'd ever worked with—you just want to have a good movie. And yet I knew that I wasn't pulling it off in this movie, because the man made me feel so awful. He hurt me so with his inability to work with me as artists working together, as colleagues. So I looked at Jack and thought, Yep, he's right. I clocked it mentally. And I've never forgotten it, because that is the main obligation—more than anything, really—you have to help the man make the movie. And it was a lesson I learned from Jack that day.

THERE DID COME a time when Roman pushed it too far with Jack. Jack is a huge fan of the Los Angeles Lakers basketball team, and when they are playing, he tries to be there. If he's on location, he's got a TV set rigged up, whether he's in L.A. or Antarctica. Anytime you're shooting scenes, there is a lot of downtime. On this day, the Lakers were playing, and Jack would run back to his trailer in between setups to watch the game.

Roman was having trouble getting what he wanted, and though it wasn't Jack's fault, it was increasing Roman's frustration level each time Jack headed back toward his trailer. At some point, Roman decided he was going to put an end to it. And just as when he had pulled my hair, the idea of talking to the actor about the problem never occurred to him. Instead, Roman went into a rage, picked up a bat, and charged into Jack's trailer swinging at the TV set. He smashed the set to pieces then stalked out.

Jack, who had been just a few feet from the TV, was incensed. He stormed out of his trailer, got in his car, and headed home. That shut the production down for the day. Roman apparently left about the same time, and somehow the two of them ended up next to each other at a stoplight. Jack turned to Roman and told him what he thought of his heritage, but by then Roman had cooled off, having expended all his anger on the television set, and he just laughed. That broke the ice between them and was the only thing that saved Roman from another trip to Bob Evans' office.

Years later, Bob Towne and I happened to be on the same transatlantic flight and we got to talking about *Chinatown* and Roman. His fights with Roman were legendary as well. Bob said that the difference between the two of them was that he learned something from his fights with Roman, but he didn't think Roman learned anything. If the same situation occurred again, Roman would react in exactly the same way. Bob would not. Roman was a great filmmaker. He was talented, skilled, and smart. But something made him come unhinged too easily, and when it did, Roman was out of control.

THE FINAL scene in *Chinatown* was designed for maximum impact. Other than when Jack's nose is slashed, it is the only other scene in the movie that is bloody. It is set in Chinatown, the first time anyone in the movie has set foot in the area, at about four in the morning. Evelyn is trying to escape with her daughter to keep her away from her father, who is increasingly interested in finding the girl, who's just turned fifteen.

As we drive away in the Packard convertible, I ignore the police shouts to halt. Finally one man shoots, and the bullet enters the back of my head and exits through my eye. A very gory-looking appliance was to be designed so that my eye would look as if it had exploded. But as the day for shooting the sequence drew near, Roman realized he had forgotten to place the order for the appliance. "It doesn't matter," he said, "we'll just shoot you through the head."

But it did matter. In the relationship between Evelyn and Noah Cross, Towne had created an examination of a contemporary, feminized version of Sophocles' *Oedipus the King*. Ending the scene with her eye destroyed had not been a random choice. Towne had meant for the film to say something about the price of what one sees, using the image to create another layer of understanding that an audience could lock into.

"No, Roman," I said, "we have to have the Oedipal reference. If Lee can do it somehow in this short time, will you let us?" Roman said

"Yes," with a glint in his eye. I'm sure he thought we'd never be able to come up with something in time. Lee Harman had his moments of genius; *Chinatown* was definitely one of them. He went to work trying to build the wound onto my face as fast as he could. He took a rubber appliance that he'd used for the nose of Kim Darby's double in *True Grit* as a base on which to build the wound. When he had finished, it looked as if a bullet had just come out of my eye.

It took six hours to create the wound, but it was done before I had been called for the scene. So we beat the odds on that one. In the final cut of the film, I come through the frame, and my eye, now a bloody, gaping mess, shows for a brief moment. Lee had done a masterful job, just the right amount of gore.

The next day we were all looking at rushes and I was thinking how good the eye looked, when it struck me—the lights in Chinatown were on. All along the street, the houses were lit up like it was early evening, which it was when we shot the scene. But the illusion we were trying for is Chinatown at four in the morning, dark and still. No one in Roman's production team had looked up and noticed the lights were on. That entire day's shooting was a loss. We had to do the whole thing again. But then, that was Chinatown, as directed by Roman Polanski, where nothing happens as you expect it to.

EARLY ON there was a disagreement between Towne and Roman over the ending. Roman wanted Evelyn to die. Towne had originally written it with Noah Cross dying and Evelyn surviving. Polanski finally won that point, and the ending was changed. The film was about damaged lives, the kind that no one really survives. Cross's death would have been too neat and tidy after such a messy, corrupt life. And there was a great tragedy to Evelyn's death, just as she is escaping.

As it was, when *Chinatown* wrapped, we all thought that something special had been created. But you still never know whether or not the public will take to it. When *Chinatown* opened the following June, it did create a sensation. It's always nice when the audiences and critics alike both embrace a film.

It was a milestone of sorts for most of us who worked on the film. Jake Gittes would become the first in a very long line of wonderful romantic leads for Jack. Evelyn Mulwray would stand alongside Bonnie Parker as one of my best performances. Bob Evans would build on the success of *Chinatown* to become one of the top film producers in the industry. And Robert Towne would become one of the most sought-after scriptwriters ever.

Chinatown was nominated for eleven Academy Awards, including Best Picture. It brought me my second Best Actress nomination. The night of the Oscars, Peter and I and Jack and Anjelica were sitting a few rows behind Bob Evans at the Dorothy Chandler Pavilion. We all wanted the award, but we fancied that we were being pretty cool. And we were teasing Bob because from where we sat we could see the wet collar of his silk tuxedo shirt. He cared so much for the film, that's why he was drenched. *The Godfather, Part II* won Best Picture that year, with the film's director, Francis Ford Coppola, picking up the Oscar for his work as well. In my category, Ellen Burstyn won for *Alice Doesn't Live Here Anymore,* for her portrait of a young widow. Only Robert Towne won an Oscar for his efforts on *Chinatown.* We were all very disappointed, but that's Hollywood.

In the end, we could take solace in having been part of a film that would become a classic. And though it was largely overlooked by the Academy, *Chinatown* was recognized by just about every other industry group, from the Golden Globe Awards to both the National and New York Film Critics. It is still one of the handful of films that I am most proud of. Jack was right, *Chinatown* was definitely worth waiting for.

FOURTEEN

ONE OF MY FAVORITE fairy tales is the Grimm brothers' story of Rapunzel. As a child, I would read it again and again. The resourcefulness of Rapunzel always appealed to me, for whatever the obstacle might be, she would overcome it. When she was finally locked away in a castle tower, she still found a way to meet her true love. Her hair grew long and thick, and each night, she would let it down the castle wall, so that her prince could climb to meet her.

This was a fairy tale princess with more than just beauty. Rapunzel had guts and moxie and an absolute belief in herself. And I understood, when I was quite young, the realities of being trapped by your circumstances and what it took to get beyond them. My love of that childhood story was one of a thousand things I told Peter. We talked about anything and everything, and Peter remembers it all still. Peter was the first love I had where there were no secrets, no subterfuges. I had never felt closer to anyone in my life. He was rock-solid and always there for me, a very emotionally connected man.

That did not mean it was always easy for us. We were both very much in the public eye, under the kind of scrutiny that destroys many relationships. His band was very popular and almost constantly on tour. I had a lot of projects going as well. We would catch a few days together whenever we could. But there were weeks when we could not see each other. Rumors would surface in the gossip columns that we were breaking up, or back together. How the papers came up with the information I'll never understand, since it was so rarely based in any reality. But that didn't make it any easier.

Peter and I had had a long stretch apart in 1973, when I finally got a break in filming and managed to catch up with the band on the road. We hadn't time to talk before the show, and I slipped out into the crowd to watch him. It was one of my secret pleasures. Peter was onstage and absolutely on fire. There was a current, white-hot, running between Peter and the crowd that night. His mood became theirs.

The air felt potent, manic, crazy, like we were all careening toward the edge of the world. Peter made you feel as if there would never be another night quite like this one. His hair was a mass of wet black strands that would slap against his cheeks like whiplashes every time he moved. His black aviator shades seemed to catch the spotlights at every turn, shooting the beams of light back into the crowd like a mini-laser show.

Before Peter started his life as the lead singer for J. Geils, he had been a crazy late-night DJ. As the nights would push into morning, he would spin out these long, spontaneous, rhythmic raps, a sort of rock poetry on whatever he happened to be thinking about. With his intellect, which was extraordinary, a genius-level IQ, he was always thinking of something, forever turning ideas over in his mind. He grew quite famous for it, these raps of his. People started calling it his "woofuh goofuh" rap. Other DJs tried to copy it, but it was so much an invention of Peter's unique mind that it made copying it virtually impossible.

I had heard him take off on these riffs when we were just having fun, goofing around—woofing, goofing. But now Peter was playing with the crowd. The current changed, shifted; he started telling them about the next song the band was going to play. Leaning into this moving, heaving mass of people, dropping his voice way down low, very intimate, he began to explain:

> *Now hold on. This song has a little intro to it.*
> *It ain't supposed to be sad,*
> *Though you might feel it that way.*
> *It's a song about desperation.*
> *Every now and then we do get desperate.*
> *This is a song about L-O-V-E.*
> *And if you abuse it, you're gonna lose it and if*
> *You lose it, you're gonna abuse it and if you abuse it*
> *You ain't gonna be able to choose it, 'cause*
> *You ain't gonna have it further on down the line.*

Peter had barely taken a breath; he was like a locomotive, picking up speed. The audience was absolutely enthralled and I was listening to every word. As the story unfolds, the guy is alone, and nothing works to distract him from thinking about the girl he has lost. Television, radio, books, nothing works. So he decides to go see his girl and tell her what's on his mind:

> Well she opens up the door and you just kind of
> Walk up to her and you say, baby . . .
> You look waaay up in her green mascara and say
> Oh my darlin',
> You know her and me was at the party as friends.
> Do not believe what they say.
> That's only gossip they're telling you down at the Wisecracker Lounge.
> Darlin', take your big curls
> And you squeeze them down, Ratumba.
> What's the name of that chick
> With the long blond hair?

The crowd screamed "Rapunzel, Rapunzel!"

> Say hey, Rapunzel, hey Raputa
> Raputa, dabuta
> Raputa, dabuta
> Send me down your long hair and let me climb
> The ladder of your love.
>
> Love comes once, and when it comes
> You have to grab it fast
> Because sometimes the love you grab
> Ain't gonna last, and I believe
> I musta, I believe I musta,
> I believe I musta got lost . . .

The song is called "Musta Got Lost," and it's about love and commitment. Forever after, the crowds would scream for the rap Peter did that night. They happened to be taping the concert for a live album, which was good, because the rap had been completely spontaneous. He had to go back and listen to the record to learn it, so he could use it again. It is the song of his I still love the best, because in the midst of thousands of screaming fans, Peter found a way to talk to only me.

WE WERE TRYING to find our way in this relationship as 1974 began. It was a hectic year in my life between work and trying to balance that with a personal life, a real one. Peter and I had been together for nearly two years now and for once I wanted to break the cycle of my past relationships that seemed to always end after two years. I had spent a lifetime, from that first new army base, moving on, always moving on. I wanted to believe that things can change, that people can change. Peter and I began to talk more often of marriage. I was just turning thirty-three and he was twenty-eight that year, though I didn't know his age at the time.

The age difference was noticed. In this country, it is always noticed when an older woman, even just a year older, is involved with a younger man. It is one of the sillinesses of society—if a woman is any older than a man, much is made of it. Needless to say, much is not made of an older man marrying a younger woman. But with Peter, I felt we were, in a sense, starting fresh. Both Jerry Schatzberg and Marcello Mastroianni had lived a full life before they met me, complete with marriages and wives and children.

Peter had been in love before, had suffered through the loss of that love, and was wary of caring that much again. But even with that, he did not come to our relationship with volumes of experience and decades spent in building a life with someone else. He taught me that age is such a useless barometer of maturity anyway. What one's life is all about is what matters, and Peter's was about all the right things.

That spring I was back in New York to star in Arthur Miller's *After the Fall*. The project had been in the works for years and after going through a series of hands, it looked as if the only way it might get made was through a special on television. It was staged as a play, not adapted for film, which made it far less complicated and expensive to put on.

We were going to film it at the old Globe Theater, with Christopher Plummer taking on the role Jason Robards had done all those years ago at Lincoln Center. I was to play Maggie, the role that Barbara Loden had played so beautifully with Jason. Gil Cates, one of the top directors working in television then, was directing the play, which his company was also producing.

Having the chance at playing the role of Maggie was really like a dream come true for me. Watching Barbara's performance in the play had become a kind of gold standard in my mind against which I measured my work and that of others. Barbara always arrived at a real purity of emotion. In all the times I saw her perform, she never pretended to have a feeling that she didn't have. While I had learned from watching Barbara in the role, I never wanted to duplicate her performance. In time, I found Maggie for myself.

As with Bonnie, I knew the territory well. This was a woman who never felt good enough. Maggie was a completely wounded soul, a girl who had grown up on the wrong side of the tracks. There was a wonderful man in her life, who belonged to another woman, and she felt the shame of her affair. He was an intellectual, well-bred, everything that she wasn't. This was another play that I used to read into the tape recorder at night: "A suicide kills two people, Maggie—that's what it's for." What a profound sadness she felt. I was never that lost, but I knew enough of the experience that I could extend myself into it.

The play aired in December 1974 on NBC and was given top reviews, which pleased me. I had wanted our performances to do justice to the play for Arthur Miller, whom I had liked from the moment I first heard him read *After the Fall*. He had shouldered more than a fair share of criticism for this play, because many people felt that he was to blame in letting Marilyn down, and in the play, was excusing all of his own culpability. I think Jason may have felt that. But I didn't.

But I thought Miller was right. He did talk in the play about how he, as an intellectual, held back from a woman who desperately needed a lot of emotional reassurance. But I thought it was true and I didn't agree with the detractors. I also thought Miller was accurate in the way he drew the workings of her mind, how he rooted it in her earlier pain with her mother and her own fears, and how that evolved. Being one of those women myself, someone with complicated origins who then became a movie star and prey to all of the male shenanigans in that business, I understood all that. And I understood something of the complications that can come up when you're a woman trying to do something original and good in the business. Again, I think Miller drew that well, and he takes you through how all of that stuff together, mixed with the alcohol in Monroe's case, really contributed to and caused her death.

I wanted to do Maggie well too as a quiet tribute to Barbara, and what she had meant to me. My aim was to strip Maggie down to some pure essence, to expose the most essential ingredients of this woman. The reviews of my performance led me to believe that I might have. One critic said he found Maggie so unlike some of the high-gloss, polished, and refined characters I had come to be known for, and that there was a great deal of power in the simplicity I brought to the role. Another wrote, "that waif Faye Dunaway, part child of nature, part ruined saint, alternately bewitched and harrowed us." I thought it apt that someone would see in Maggie that particular dichotomy—part child and part ruined saint.

THE THREE MUSKETEERS had a brief showing around Christmas of 1973 to qualify for Oscar consideration, but the film hit most theaters around the country the next March. Though I had a good time in the film and had found Richard Lester a really brilliant man who had a great deal of finesse in working with actors, I don't think I quite expected the way the critics and the public would embrace the film. Most were charmed by the farce of *Musketeers*. I turned out to be the villainess everyone loved to hate, and the movie quickly became a hit at the box office.

That March the Harvard Drama Club named me their Hasty Pudding Woman of the Year. I always loved going to Boston because it gave me a chance to spend some time with Bill Alfred. And it was great fun riding along like a parade queen, perched up on the back of a convertible, waving to the crowds on the way to the awards. The drama club traditionally puts on a skit before you're given your little brass pudding pot—for me it was titled "Keep Your Pantheon." It was suitably raunchy, as always, done in drag, and very, very funny.

How could I not love a group that had dubbed me "The most explosive package of beautiful talent to have hit the stage and screen in years"? But underneath it all there was a very good feeling, with that recognition coming from others who care as much as you do about the dramatic form. This was a young, intelligent, and cynical bunch, and I was really pleased they had thought to honor me.

It was as if 1974 was the year the country decided to recognize me. Besides the Hasty Pudding award, Robert Redford and I were chosen as America's favorite screen stars, and the theater owners picked me and Jack Lemmon as their stars of the year. All this was before *Chinatown* was released in June. It took me a little by surprise. Though I had been in eight movies, the last big hit I had starred in, *The Thomas*

Crown Affair, was in 1968. I was not, however, about to argue with the polls, and if anything felt grateful that the fans remembered me in this way. *Rolling Stone* capped it all off by naming me their favorite Groupie of the Year because of my relationship with Peter.

IN MAY, I began filming *The Towering Inferno*. It was a huge disaster film, producer Irwin Allen's attempt to repeat the success he'd had a few years earlier with *The Poseidon Adventure*. But what set *The Towering Inferno* apart was that it marked one of the first times that a single talent agency had put together such an intricate package of producers, directors, and stars. My agents, Freddie Fields and David Begelman, were among the masterminds, if not *the* masterminds, of the deal on this one.

The premise for the film came from a couple of best-selling novels that dealt with the human drama that was bound to unfold if one of these new glass high-rises went up in flames. The character I played, Susan, is the wife of the tower's architect. It was a decent role, but the characters didn't really have a chance to be very complicated, because the real star of the film was the fire. But Susan had a few nice moments, and besides, most of my scenes were love scenes with Paul Newman, who played my husband, Doug.

The nicest moment was my first one in the movie, when Doug comes into his office after being away on a trip. I'm hidden at first, engulfed by his chair. What begins as a welcome-home kiss turns into a sweet seduction scene. Newman was great to work with—one of the single sexiest men in movies. I loved him. And I love his wife, Joanne Woodward. I had long emulated Joanne. I thought Paul and I were really good together, and our scenes were fun.

My character was the editor of a fashion magazine. The conflict the plot presented Susan was becoming a common one for me as well. She has just this day gotten a big promotion, while Doug has only now decided he wants to retreat from the city altogether. They are facing the career-versus-relationship dilemma for the first time, just as the fire breaks out. The movie ends with both Susan and Doug surviving, but what may happen to their marriage and what choices they will make was lost along the way, another victim of the fire.

The cast was filled with big names. Beyond Newman, Steve McQueen was also in the film, along with William Holden, Jennifer Jones, Robert Wagner, and Fred Astaire, who surprised everyone by getting an Oscar nomination for his turn as a charming old con artist who becomes gallant in the face of disaster. In an unusual move, Warner Bros. and Twentieth Century–Fox had teamed up to do one movie rather than go head-to-head with competing high-rise disaster films, which they both had in the works initially.

The real power behind *The Towering Inferno* was Irwin Allen, who convinced Fox and Warner to work together. On a more practical level, his action sequences, which showcased the fire and various means of fighting it, had a larger role than most of the actors. They built nearly sixty sets to re-create the deadly spread of the blaze. By the time the filming ended, almost all of them had been reduced to little more than charred rubble.

Irwin had a vision of what the movie should be and he exerted it throughout production. When it came to a choice between giving more screen time to the smoke and fire, or to the actors, the fire nearly always won out. He directed the action sequences himself and shared a directing credit with John Guillermin, who handled the actors. Though John directed the scenes I was in, you could feel the hot breath of Irwin on his neck at all times.

Irwin's iron-clad control over the project was brought home to me in a very pointed way one day when I had some disagreement over a payment he was supposed to make, and I asked Freddie Fields to take care of it. Freddie promised he would talk to Irwin. Later that day I walked into Irwin's office and asked if he had talked to Freddie yet. "Sure, I've talked to him five times today already," said Irwin, but not about my disagreement, he told me. I realized that this was Freddie's package and Irwin was a much more important client than me, because he was a producer, and Freddie stood to make a lot more money off him. A package means the agent gets 10 percent of the entire budget of the film, so that's a lot more than 10 percent of my salary. Art and commerce. Commerce and art. The actors and actresses are really pawns in the game of the Hollywood agents. We are their little chessmen. We are the power, and yet they manipulate us, or try to, so that they can control us.

I remembered then that I had fought with the agents about taking this part in the first place. But they had argued it would be good for my career, and there was the fact that Paul and Steve were both going to be in it. But at the end of the day, it was the star machine at it again, grinding up anyone who got in the way.

It is a weird, insidious business. The producers use the agents.

The agents use the actors. The press uses the actors. Actors are always left to stand in the center of the storm, having to defend themselves and their humanity in order to get the job done. I went to Freddie that day thinking he would defend me—such naïveté, even at that point in my career. It was business. Nothing personal.

IT'S NOT THAT *The Towering Inferno* was a terrible film to be a part of. But it was also not the sort of film that I think any of us felt would ever add a great deal to the body of our work. There are films that I have made that did much worse at the box office, yet had characters with such promise. This was not one of them; mine was not a character that demanded you understand her. But then with the way the film was designed, no one really had a chance to know any of the characters anyway.

Even Steve and Paul, who fought the blaze each in their own way throughout the film, were not given roles that had many intellectual or emotional layers. When it came right down to it, I was involved in the film because my agents really wanted the value of my name added to the project, I didn't have another film that conflicted with the shooting schedule, and Paul and Steve were going to be a part of it.

As the production ground on and on, I started thinking about escaping everything. I wasn't at all sure anymore that the career was worth what I was giving up in terms of happiness. I also wanted to make a real go of trying to have a personal life with Peter. I had rented a house in Malibu for the summer I was scheduled to be on location in Los Angeles for the film, and Peter and I would take long walks on the beach, watching the sun set and discussing our future.

Marriage wasn't exactly an institution that the rock 'n' roll world embraced in those days. Both of us worried whether or not a marriage could hold two careers that, by their very nature, meant we would spend long periods of time away from each other. There was no blueprint out there for us to follow. And Peter wasn't sure he was ready for that sort of commitment anyway. He would always tease me that it all had to do with the sign he was born under. He was a Pisces; as he said, "slippery when wet."

But I very much wanted marriage and to have a child, to create the kind of family life I never had. I was thirty-three and knew I could not wait forever. And in my heart, I wanted my child to have a father who was there, really there for him or her, and a mother and a father who truly loved each other. I did not want my child to have a father like mine, who was distant, and then gone completely from my life.

I HAD VISITED Frank Barcelona and his wife, June, often with Peter. Frank was really the godfather of rock 'n' rollers and had helped guide many careers. He had an estate in Ossining, about an hour from New York City. Frank's place, while not a mansion, was a very hypnotic house on the Hudson River. We would talk late into the night about all kinds of things, and Frank would tell the most wonderful stories. I've know two great raconteurs in my life, who could tell stories that had you hanging onto every word—one was David Niven, the other Frank Barcelona. Frank was a great friend of ours.

I was still shooting *Inferno* and Peter was back east. The idea of marriage was becoming more and more real. We both seemed to be going in that direction. Peter finally went up to see Frank about it. That was the turning point in our decision to get married. Frank and Peter talked all weekend and when Peter flew back to L.A., we went to the courthouse to get a marriage license. I'll never forget the clerk who took down all the information. He had spent more than a few years sorting through the lives of couples who end up in Los Angeles with the notion of getting married. Whether you were a star or an ordinary citizen, the details were usually about the same. He hinted that he could read people pretty well, but Peter and I surprised him. "I can't believe this is the first marriage for the two of you," he said. "Don't see that too often in Hollywood."

That August, the temperatures soared. It made evenings along the Malibu beach wonderful. Each night, hot air would hit the cold blanket of the ocean and send fog rolling toward the shore. Peter and I would set out on our nightly walks and disappear into a cloudy mist. Everything felt very cool and silent. It was wonderful being with him and feeling cut off from the rest of the world, in our own silent place. I wanted to spend the rest of my life like that.

The band was in turmoil, with the sort of *East of Eden* dynamic that often begins to play itself out when people are thrown so closely together. Peter was worried that it all might crumble, that I might be picking the wrong guy to marry. I told him it didn't matter to me what happened with the band, I believed in him, he was what I loved, not the image of who he was.

On the sixth, we decided we had thought about marriage from every side of it, we should just do it. The next morning I called my mother and told her I was getting married. We found a judge in Beverly Hills who would marry us. His name was also Wolf, Judge Leonard Wolf, which I took to be a very good sign. Just before noon, Peter, in a yellow linen suit, black silk shirt, and a long scarf, married Dorothy Faye Dunaway in Judge Wolf's chambers.

I was wearing a dress that looked like summer in the South, a pale peach jersey and chiffon dress that was as soft as the wind. My hair was very simple, brown, my natural curls barely brushed out. I carried a bouquet of long-stemmed roses and carnations. Lee Harman and Susan Germaine, my makeup man and hairdresser, helped me get ready. We really wanted it to be so private, and it happened so quickly, that we didn't call any friends beforehand. The four of us celebrated with lunch at Scandia afterward, though I can't for the life of me remember what we ate. I was so happy I could have eaten a hamburger as easily as paté.

There were a few more scenes for me to shoot on *Inferno*, so we postponed the idea of a honeymoon, deciding instead that I should plan to go with Peter when the band toured Europe in a month or so. We'd turn that into an extended celebration of our wedding. The one thing we knew was that neither of us wanted to set up house anywhere near Hollywood. Peter had gone to school in Boston and lived there, as did his band. I had friends there and had long loved the city. Boston seemed to make sense as the place for us to put down roots. We decided to keep my apartment in New York as well, so there would be a base for us there too.

Just a few days after we married, with *Inferno* finally finished, Peter and I got ready to leave Los Angeles. I had a few loose ends I wanted to take care of though. I was scheduled to go to Morocco very soon for the film *The Wind and the Lion*, in which I was to costar with Sean Connery. It was a role that had a lot of potential. A feisty American widow in Tangier is kidnapped and held hostage by a sheik, who Sean was to play. And I was very interested in working with the legendary Mr. Connery.

But at the time, I was coming off two years of intense work, going from movie to stage production, to movie, to television production, to the stage, and back to film again. I was exhausted from the constant and intense pressure of the work. As much as I loved acting, I needed a break. And I did not want to begin this marriage with me in Morocco for months on end and Peter on the road with the band.

I called Herb Jaffe, the producer, and begged off the project. Emotionally, I was tapped out. Candice Bergen signed on for the part, and I concentrated on my new role as the wife of Peter Wolf. As the plane took off from Los Angeles, with Peter beside me and our future stretching out in front of us, it felt like the weight of Hollywood just lifted off my shoulders. I felt freer than I had in years.

THE FIRST ORDER, once we touched down in Boston, was to visit Bill Alfred, to get his blessing on this marriage and introduce him to Peter— the two men I loved most in the world, except for my brother. We had a cab drop us off in front of Bill's house. It's a beautiful old Victorian, at the end of Athens Street, "like the Greek city," as he tells cabbies.

We stood outside calling to him, laughing and waving, pointing at our wedding rings and shouting, "We did it, we did it!" I felt like a girl again, caught in that first blush of love. Bill looked out the window and saw us. I was wearing a big straw hat with my hair piled up underneath it, and Peter had his arm round my waist. Bill got a bit misty watching us. "I've never seen you look so happy," he told me. I have never felt so happy, thought I. We really were so happy, we had a sense of the infinite promise of life.

When we first married, Peter was very busy with the demands of the band, which was really on a roll and still caught up in a lot of internal turmoil. I collared Bill to help me scour Boston for a place for Peter and me to make a home. For a long while, it seemed all I would find would be what Bill would call "bankers' houses." "You can't have that, Faye," he would tell me. "You need an artist's house." He was right. The bankers' houses were uniformly dreary and ordinary. I finally found an apartment in the Prudential Center that seemed right for this time when Peter was on the road a lot and I was often away working as well. It seemed ideal to make a cozy nest, and I set about redecorating it.

I spent ages working with Dick Franklin, the carpenter, doing a massive record cabinet for Peter's extensive collection. It was very well thought out, but it took forever to get it right. I adored that little apartment and still do. The apartment was cozy, warm; we had a beautiful, large Oriental rug in the living room with strong, lapis colors of blue. There was a very soft down sofa that was quite beautiful. And paintings that we had begun to gather. Religious art that I bought for

Peter for every birthday or Christmas occasion—he loved it and we collected it. He was a painter and had studied first at the High School of Music and Art, then the Boston Museum School of Fine Arts.

I began to grow lots of flowers in the apartment. It seems I had a green thumb—everything flourished. This apartment was the perfect counterpoint to the New York place, which was clean, stripped-down, and pure. But the cozy look of Boston, and the pure bachelor contemporary feel of New York—that's how we lived. Our lives settled into a rhythm. Peter was touring and I was reading scripts, when I was not on the road with him. Bill and I had gotten in the habit of meeting in the late afternoon a few times a week. We'd have a perfect dry martini at six and spend the early evening hours discussing a play, or a book one of us was reading, a new author we had found, an old author we had rediscovered. When Peter was in town, our pleasures were simple ones. We went to movies, or to dinner, and we saw Bill frequently. It was a very happy time for me.

The band was taking a lot of Peter's attention; on that front it was a very turbulent time for him. But in our home, between us, there was a certain peacefulness. I thought of those times not long ago when I was watching an old Hitchcock movie, *Dial M for Murder*. It is my current favorite movie of all, and I love the set better than anything. Every element in the apartment is in perfect balance and harmony with the others.

But in this one scene, Ray Milland is talking to this fellow whom he wants to hire to kill his wife. Milland tells him about following his wife one day and watching her as she visits an old school chum. He watched the two of them through the window, his wife and this other man. He was making spaghetti on an old gas ring. The next line I loved so much, I wrote it down and kept it: "They didn't say much; they just looked very natural together. That's probably how you can tell when people are in love."

That was Peter and me. We were there for each other, without an effort. We were like two warriors standing shoulder to shoulder. That's how we used to think of ourselves. There was no ego clash between us, though we were both always ambitious. If he needed something, I would help him with it. And if I needed something, he would help me with it. For the two of us, life was always about, "Okay, how do we do this?" It was never about, "Why aren't you doing this?" With Peter, I never had to wonder if he loved me, he simply did.

FIFTEEN

WATERGATE. Such disillusionment, such an attack on the faith that so many of us had in our country, our government. It was as if the Nixon White House had undertaken a scorch-and-burn policy when it came to the country's collective psyche. Like the rest of the world, I had watched the congressional hearings with emotions that ranged between anger and profound sadness. Whatever innocence we might have had left as a nation had surely been lost.

Though I had vowed to take a break for a while after Peter and I married, one day I got a script delivered to me from Sydney Pollack. Sydney, who was going to direct the film, wanted me to at least read it and see what I thought. That night I curled up in bed, picked up the script, and began reading *Three Days of the Condor*. The story that unfolded as I read seemed to capture the mood of the country in the aftermath of Watergate. It gave us a good guy who actually found a way to fight back against the things Watergate had taught us to fear most in our government officials—excessive paranoia and unquestioned power.

Robert Redford was to star in the film in the role of a CIA analyst who unwittingly uncovers a secret intelligence ring within the agency, a discovery which proves a very dangerous one indeed. The role I was being asked to consider was that of a young woman, Kathy, whom Redford takes hostage in his desperate run to escape those who are out to assassinate him.

It was a solid story, a thriller with a conscience that looked as if it could be quite popular as well. And Pollack, I believed, was absolutely the right director for a project like this one. To my mind he had distinguished himself by choosing films along the way that made a strong social statement. Though he was probably best known at the time for *They Shoot Horses, Don't They?* and the romantic film *The Way We Were*, with Redford and Barbra Streisand, I had been an early fan after seeing *The Slender Thread*, a drama starring Anne Bancroft that dealt with suicide. It didn't get a lot of attention, but it was done with a great deal of sensitivity and insight.

I was more than intrigued with the prospect of working with Robert Redford. He has this really extraordinary presence on-screen, and I had hoped for some time that there would be a film that would be right for the two of us. You always look for those opportunities that will allow you to work with someone like that, to both have the experience and to see what you can learn from it.

Though I was well-established by then, I was still a bit intimidated at the idea of being in a film with him, particularly since he and Sydney had worked together on three earlier films. They would be old pals and I would be the newcomer. Nevertheless, I was close to saying yes if it wouldn't mean much of a separation from Peter.

When my agents told me the movie was going to be filmed on location in New York there seemed to be no reason not to do it. I could stay in the New York apartment during the week and fly to Boston on weekends. And it would be easy enough for Peter to shuttle between the two cities on occasion too. I felt very lucky. For once I was going to be able to have my cake and eat it too.

WE WERE SCHEDULED to start filming in early November of 1974. The film itself was supposed to take place in the dead of winter. Sydney wanted everything to feel barren and cold. Redford always said it was because Sydney was melancholy by nature. But it made sense for the movie as well. Sydney wanted nothing to soften the world that is left to Joe Turner, Redford's character. For once, the trees in the city still had their leaves, and Sydney brought in a conservationist to help the crew defoliate them on the streets we were using.

Redford and I started going to Sydney's townhouse a few weeks before the production got under way to work on the script by Lorenzo Semple, Jr., which was undergoing a rewrite by David Rayfiel to sharpen the dialogue. We would sit there and read the lines and talk about the characters, and it was great fun working with those guys. The joke was that Redford would keep saying, "Give me some funnier lines,

Faye's got all the funny lines." It wasn't true, I didn't get all of them, but they did make me quippy and funny, using humor to deal with the fear.

Through the rewrite, Kathy developed into more of a character, with a few more layers to her that Sydney actually took time to explore in the film. The idea of being a hostage—which is the point at which she enters the film—who becomes a lover was a risk. The love scene had to be integrated into the plot in a way that didn't derail the tension that has been built around Turner's need to stay on the run.

Along the way Sydney decided it would create a certain harmony if she was a photographer in the Diane Arbus tradition. He wanted to draw a portrait of this woman as being a very lonely, isolated girl. Maybe a bit fearful. And those were areas that I have, but that hadn't been part of my palette in terms of the movies I had done. Sydney saw that and thought we could draw that out. I was able to be home free again in terms of playing that kind of thing.

My apartment in the film was lined with wonderful black-and-white photos that were barren and empty of people. While on the surface the photos said something about the emptiness of Kathy's life, it was just as much a window on the world that Turner would ultimately find himself in—solitary, a man without a home.

Rayfiel worked on the script throughout most of the production. We would get new pages often every day and he would work through the weekend as well. In the end, all his efforts paid off in creating a much better film, smarter, with more twists and turns. I still count it among those films of mine that I really like. And it had a kind of *Casablanca* resonance, of political intrigue and star-crossed love, that a surprising number of people really responded to.

WHEN IT CAME to Bob and me, we just never hung out. Redford was intellectual, I think, very preoccupied with the business and with other projects and with the world. He wasn't one of those people like Jack that I just felt immediately in sync with. But I felt the movie pairing really worked. As Robert and Faye, we just didn't get to be as close as Jack and I did.

It was rough, though, getting to the point we needed to in those first scenes I had with Redford. Our encounter starts with my kidnapping. We essentially meet when Turner sticks a gun in my ribs and forces me into my car. When we get back to my apartment, what occurs between us is not that easy to pull off. Turner has a handgun and I must seem convinced he's going to rape me or worse. He's not really a bad guy, but if he relaxes his guard any, even with me, he could be killed.

Now I'm sorry, but the idea of being kidnapped and ravaged by Robert Redford was anything but frightening. And Turner's character was very much like Redford's—serious, kind, down-to-earth, and very good-looking. Redford has such gentle eyes, it's just very, very hard for him to look menacing. And the wire-rimmed glasses they had him wear to fit the character, who was a CIA bookworm, made him look more sensitive and vulnerable than ever.

Nevertheless, terror is what was called for. And Sydney needed some close-ups of me that would show real fear in my eyes. For the rest of our scenes to work, the relationship needed to start from that point of distrust and terror. Bob was off-camera, playing the part of evil kidnapper, and it was my job to look duly fearful.

Every time Bob would lunge at me, it would take every ounce of control on my part not to dissolve into giggles. For some reason my

Held hostage by Robert Redford in Three Days of the Condor, *a great assignment.*
© 1995 by Paramount Pictures

mind locked onto the idea of "rape and Redford" and pronounced it inconceivable. I really couldn't, for the life of me, imagine it. Finally Sydney could see that it wasn't working and he sent Redford to his trailer. The cameras were rolling, I was in position, and suddenly Sydney lunged at me, growling "I AM GOING TO GET YOU!" I'm tied up at this point, unable to get away or move much at all, but Sydney kept moving toward me, his eyes glaring at me as he went on detailing all the horrible things he was going to do to me, and let me tell you, Sydney has an inventive mind. He is also a great actor, and he scared the hell out of me. Sydney kept the camera rolling and he was relentless.

For that performance by Sydney Pollack, I will forever be grateful. It was a great performance, for which he got no credit. In the end, the scene played really well. Thank you, Sydney.

I STILL THINK the love scene in *Condor* is one of the most quietly beautiful of any I've been in. Because of the way Sydney would begin with one image and let it dissolve into another, you never knew quite what you were seeing for the first few seconds.

What would begin as the rise and fall of a naked back would fade into the empty street in front of a park bench in one of the photos on the wall; the curve of a knee would emerge as a handrail, caught in another photo in silhouette against the sky. The colors he used were so muted, it went from cold to warm, from abstract to concrete, as if we might be the people who had left only moments before the photos were snapped, leaving the scene colorless and empty without us.

The subject of the film drew attention from the outset. Former CIA director Richard Helms stopped by the set one day, which was more than a little surreal. And most days would bring crowds to the locations to see if they could get a glimpse of us. I liked working with Redford, though he was at times difficult to connect with, and his mind was often on other things. He was in the midst of trying to work out the snags on his next film, *All the President's Men,* and there were distractions from his Sundance venture in Utah. When he wasn't in front of a camera, he was on the phone.

AFTER CONDOR WRAPPED, I went back to Boston to work at having a relationship. For nearly a year, I didn't take on any new projects and tried to disappear into some sort of normal life. Even without me, my public image took on a life of its own, thanks to Roman Polanski. He took great pains in every interview he did about *Chinatown*—which was getting a lot of attention at the time, with its slew of Academy Award nominations—to talk about our fight. I was getting hounded by the press for my reaction to what he was saying, and I decided to stay out of it rather than get into a battle of "he said, she said" in the press. It all seemed very distasteful to me, particularly since there was so much about *Chinatown* that was worth talking about.

Spending time with Peter was the only thing that helped keep me grounded. We built our own reality and to a great extent, Peter became a buffer between me and the rest of the world. He kept me safe. I needed that very much because the other reality, the one being created in the press, was spinning out of control.

What was really going on in my life during that time was a wonderful romance with this terrific guy I had married. Peter would program music for me, spend hours putting together tracks of musicians he loved, then playing it for me. I already loved jazz and rock 'n' roll, but Peter introduced me to so many blues singers. We would spend hours listening to music and talking about it; he used to call it the "College of Musical Knowledge." Peter knew entire histories of hundreds of individual songs—who wrote it, who had influenced that person, when it was recorded, and any number of other details.

Peter is really a wonderfully talented painter as well. Though he put aside his painting for years, we would wander through museums and talk of art. And Peter would sing to me. Our love and our life would find its way into some of the lyrics of the songs he would write. If he came home late, he always brought me dinner. It was, for me, a magical time.

I spent a lot of time on tour with him that year and found I really liked the whole gypsy feel of it. Taking a plane to a new city every few days, checking into a hotel, and then going over to watch the band set up for a gig. We'd go to sleep very late after they had played, but still get up early the next day for coffee over a Formica-topped table at whatever local diner might be handy. One thing Peter and I had in common is that we were early risers, and no matter how intense the day, he never needed more than a few hours sleep.

One of my favorite trips with Peter was one we took to Dallas. We had been out late the night before, and I had forgotten that I was going to mend his pants. These were not just any pants, but the ones he wore onstage, so they had to be fixed. He was getting ready to take off the next morning when he realized the pants still needed to be hemmed. "Okay, no problem," I said, taking the pants, getting out a needle and thread. I sat in the middle of the bed, still in my nightgown, hemming those pants.

The cab came, he had a plane to catch. I wasn't through. "Don't worry," I said, grabbing a coat and pulling it over my nightgown, and carrying the pants, and a needle and thread. I hemmed all the way to the airport, but still wasn't finished. So I marched in with Peter, still in the trench coat I'd grabbed, his pants in one hand, a needle and thread in the other, and bought a ticket. I finished hemming those pants somewhere over Kentucky.

When we touched down in Dallas, Peter and the pants stayed in Texas. I kissed him good-bye and headed back to Boston, still in my nightgown and trench coat. He says to this day, those are the best-hemmed pants he's ever had. The pants, in fact, are now completely worn out. But the hem is still there. We had on occasion this kind of joyful madness.

Though I'm not sure I can trace it back to Peter and his infamous pants, I do love needlework and took up needlepoint with a passion. The piece I am most proud of is one that I started not long after my son was born and finally finished years later. It's the face of a beautiful, brown-haired boy, the face of an angel, Liam. Though he's now a teenager getting quite grown up, and with a photographer for a father there are pictures of him everywhere, one of the first things I see when I wake up each morning is that pillow, with that child's face, filled with innocence and surrounded by brown curls.

AFTER NEARLY A YEAR of turning down projects, I got a script that was based on a true story, one of the many tragic ones we have due to the Nazi regime in Germany, that I wanted to find a way to do. *Voyage of the Damned* was the story of 937 Jews who booked passage for Cuba on the SS *St. Louis* in 1939. They thought they were escaping Germany, but they were just pawns in a Nazi propaganda game that left the ship at sea, with no country willing to let its passengers disembark. In the end, most of the passengers ended up back in various concentration camps, where more than 600 ultimately died.

It was too horrible to imagine, and yet it was a story that needed to be told, that must be told so that none of us ever forgets the Holocaust. Stuart Rosenberg, who was to direct the film, had a great deal of experience coming in, with such films as *Cool Hand Luke* and *Murder, Inc.* But for Stuart, as I think it was for all of us, *Voyage of the Damned* was much more than just another project.

There was so much meat to the story, though, that I thought had been lost in the script. I took it over to Bill Alfred's house and we worked to see what we could do to my lines. It was too important a subject to be frivolous, and I felt there was not enough depth in the draft I had been given. Unfortunately, I don't think the film ever achieved what it should have. A movie of that voyage should have had the same sort of emotional resonance that Steven Spielberg achieved with *Schindler's List*, or what Stanley Kramer had done with *Ship of Fools*. The elements were all there, the promise of it was there, just never realized.

We began filming in November 1975 in the waters off Barcelona, Spain. Stuart had managed to get use of the MV *Irpinia*, an Italian cruise ship, and had it converted to the SS *St. Louis*. Though you always knew you were making a movie, there were moments that were chilling nevertheless. Coming to the ship that first day and seeing a huge flag with a swastika flying from the stern. Handing over your papers to the ship official and watching as he stamped them with a red "J" before handing them back with disdain. That darkness stayed with all of us through the production.

I was to play Denise Kreisler, the wife of Dr. Egon Kreisler, who has been a consul, a doctor, and a university professor. He was played by Oskar Werner, a talented actor who managed to always look boyish, with his rosy cheeks and longish hair that constantly fell into his eyes. We were far more well off than the other passengers, but then one of the points to be made was that education and economics would not save you from the Nazis.

In the end, I felt they had taken away some of the dignity that this woman deserved, and I wish now I had gone with my instincts and resisted it more forcefully. Too many directors thought it was enough to put me in a glamorous wardrobe. But that is never enough. It's very hard to be so strong in this business, to stand up to everything you need to in order to protect a character that needs protecting. It's sometimes hard to know when you're right, too; you may have a feel for it, but you need to bounce ideas and thoughts off other people. You need people of goodwill around you, ones who don't have a self-interest in the outcome other than what is best for the character, and what is best for you. That's one of the reasons Bill Alfred means so much to me.

What I thought was so compelling about the story was the idea that human life goes on in the face of such incredible loss and disaster. Crisis does not remove or alter one's fundamental human nature. The optimist still has hope, those filled with depression become more so, a marriage in trouble is still troubled. But the script never made enough of it, and the times it did, the larger issues were pushed too far in the background. The delicate balance between the two was something that the film never quite achieved.

Stuart used all of the major actors in the cast to a greater degree than most films ever do. He always wanted our faces in the crowd; that is how it would have been with everyone on the ship together. So unlike with most films, where you are generally only there when the scene features you, we were there all the time. Oskar, Max Von Sydow, who played the ship's remarkably humane captain, Lee Grant, who was nominated by the Academy for Best Supporting Actress, Sam Wanamaker, Malcolm McDowell, Julie Harris, and a dozen others spent virtually every day, all day, on the set. It made for some interesting dynamics on and off the set.

Oskar was very sweet, charming really, but we quickly dubbed him the "octopus," because once evening rolled around and he had a few drinks, those arms and hands of his were everywhere, but platonically placed, always. But he never stopped being sweet, so I think most of us who found ourselves temporarily within reach were more amused than offended.

The cast quickly fell into two camps, Lee's and Maria Schell's, who with Nehemiah Persoff played a middle-aged couple going to meet their daughter, who has already fled to Cuba. Maria's camp took over the left side of the dining room at the Ritz in Barcelona, where most of the cast was staying, and those closest to Lee would go to the right.

I stayed in the Hotel Sophia and tried to keep out of it all. But I was intrigued enough that one night I got Lee Harman, who was still doing my makeup, to go with me to check out the scene. The walls of this dining room were lined with mirrors. What could be better, or worse, than for a whole gaggle of actors to be in a room filled with mirrors? Harman and I had just been seated when Ben Gazzara came over. Ben sat down, lit up a big cigar, and said, "Well, Faye, what are you doing here?" He was talking to me, but not really. His eyes kept drifting right past me to the mirrors on the wall. He was looking at himself in the mirror and then checking out the rest of the room. It was a scene that was being played out through the entire room.

LEE GRANT AND I had a wonderfully emotional scene together. At this point in the film, her husband has attempted suicide and is now in a Cuban hospital, while she remains aboard, and her daughter has only hours ago killed herself, choosing to die in the arms of her lover rather than return to Germany. I find Lee in her cabin, out of her mind with grief, scissors in hand, clumps of hair on the dressing table in front of her.

She's cutting her hair systematically, and on the edge of killing herself. But until I come in the room, Lee is completely mesmerized by that newly discovered destructive aspect of herself. It has her so in its grip that she can't quite see it or feel it. I have to find a way to extract that from her and put it in me. In that scene, I have to become the embodiment of her self-destruction, in order to save her. "You want this done to you? Give me the scissors, I'll cut it for you." Look at it, I had to get her to look at it. It was the only way to pull her back from the edge. "Your heart was flitting like a bluebird in a cage," she said after the scene was finished. In the film I'm pretending to be mean to get her to snap out of it. And my heart is beating so because I'm trying to save her life.

You always hope that something in your films will reach the audience, touch them. I know that there were moments in filming *Voyage of the Damned* that had a profound effect on most of us involved in making the film. Two of the most difficult scenes to film, from an emotional standpoint, were the departure from Hamburg, where all of the passengers had left family as well as the country that they had loved and now lost, and the burials at sea of those who died on the passage to Cuba. The tears you see were real ones.

I HAD BEEN SOUGHT for both *Towering Inferno* and *Voyage of the Damned* partly for my marquee value. Both were relatively small roles, but much of the publicity surrounding the films when they were released was tied to my name. In terms of the price of stardom, those were minor indiscretions. There are times when you find yourself absolutely flayed in magazines, newspapers, and television reports for things you had absolutely no part in—that is when this career reaches its most painful. With the fans, the audience, I've never found a problem. It is this moat of critics and reporters interpreting who I am that I have to cross that can be particularly difficult.

Nevertheless, I have always accepted that, and expected it, as part and parcel of this profession I have chosen. And there are many sides to celebrity that I love; not all are dark. But for my mother, my celebrity had few advantages and ultimately caused her great pain. There had always been a fragile, emotional side to my mother. The hardships she faced with my father, and the constant worry about money both before and after he left, took a toll from which she never really recovered. When *Bonnie and Clyde* hit with such force, and overnight I was featured on magazine covers and in newspaper articles, my mother was so proud. She started a scrapbook and carefully kept everything written about me in it.

At the time, she was working at Fort Jackson in Columbia, South Carolina, where she had moved after my brother, Mac, and I had both left home. She worked in stock control for the base, where she was in charge of requisitioning uniforms. For a time, it was a job she loved.

But as I grew more visible, she found herself the target of rumors and gossip from the other women in the secretarial pool. There would be days when none of the other women would speak to her. She routinely began to get the worst assignments, such as being left to handle the phones at lunch, when the others went out together. Slowly they simply cut her off. She got to the point where she felt like she couldn't say anything about me, because of the envy and resentment that was growing more and more pointed.

For so many years, my mother had loved her work. She was someone who took great pride in excelling at whatever job she might have. It might have been a very humble job, but she always brought dignity to it. That was the way she had raised me, and it was the way she lived her life, to do the best she could. But by the early seventies, as my career continued to keep me in the public eye, the bitterness and envy directed at her by her coworkers began to wear her down. The only place she had a refuge was at home with her husband, Jim, and at her church, where she had a small circle of friends.

Finally, one day she came home and completely collapsed. She couldn't face going back to that office, and didn't know if she could face going on with her life. Though both of her children had become the successes she had raised us to be, it was as if the world was conspiring to deny her any pleasure from it. She sank into a really deep depression that frightened all of us. Jim checked her into a clinic when he felt that nothing he was doing could reach her. Though she emerged from the depression several weeks later, my mother was never the same again. The darkness that she had kept at bay for so many years drew closer and never went completely away.

I felt at such a loss to help. As much as I loved my mother, I couldn't remove the pain she had felt at the hands of others. That was beyond my power, short of walking away from the life I had worked so hard to build. And that is something that would have destroyed her. She told me that whatever else might happen, she did not want the pettiness of those around her to win the day.

As soon as she felt well enough, we began working with an architect, picking out plans for a house just like she had always wanted. That I could give to her, and I hoped the building and decorating would demand enough of her attention that she would begin to heal emotionally. But I decided then, that if I should be lucky enough one day to have a child, I would go to whatever lengths were necessary to keep the awful glare of publicity away. I have chosen this career, but my mother, my brother, and my child did not, and they should not have to suffer for it.

There were those who thought it strange when I dropped out of sight without saying why months before my son was born in 1980. Some questioned why I was unwilling to let anyone but my family and a few close friends know. Others argued against my move to England not long after, where I spent nearly a decade, because of the damage it was likely to do to my career. I would not listen.

No one will ever know what I felt the day I saw the depths of my mother's depression. There was a weariness in her that did not look like it would ever leave. And when I looked into her eyes, all I could see was anguish that went on and on forever. It changed me. When Liam was born, I didn't care what the cost, I was going to protect him. I was determined that he would have time to be a child. Not the child of a star, but just a child, with no labels over his head, and having the liberty to grow up and become the person he was meant to be. Maybe, for him, that would keep the pain away.

SIXTEEN

After Tennessee Williams came to Los Angeles to see the production of *A Streetcar Named Desire* that Jon Voight and I had starred in, he set off on a trip that would take him through the Far East and end in either Italy or Spain, both countries that he loved. His intention, he told me, was to spend more time in Europe. We had stayed in touch as he drifted between one continent and another, and when I landed in Spain in the fall of 1975 to film *Voyage of the Damned*, I found that Tennessee was there. We decided to meet in Madrid. It is one of Europe's most beautiful cities and as projects took me back to it over the years, it had become a favorite of mine.

I think one of the reasons both Tennessee and I loved the region is that for all its Spanish culture, there is a texture to the life that always reminds me of the South. Never have I been to Spain that I didn't at some point think of home, of dirt roads and decorum, dignity in the face of poverty, and the structure of the emotional content of the place so defined as it was by class.

But then it was impossible to be anywhere with Tennessee and not be reminded of the South. He was ever the old southern gentleman with me, treating me like a fragile magnolia blossom that might brown with the least exposure to any harshness. Tennessee might make his bed with men, but he dearly loved the company of women.

It was a crisp sunny day in Madrid, not quite winter, when we met. Tennessee was driving an old Roadmaster whose top we immediately decided must be put down. I wrapped a long scarf round my head and felt like Isadora Duncan, and a little like Zelda Fitzgerald too. Tennessee had taken on the look of Madrid, slipped into it like an old suit. I think he even wore those wonderful dark green glasses, with tortoiseshell frames, like so many of the old Spanish men did. They were always dressed completely in black and would stare at you through those dark green glasses like they were the blind from purgatory. Tennessee had a sort of drowsy, slept-in look about him, a shirt whose color had long been lost in the wash, and a cocky gait to his walk. He was often not well, but on this day, I found Tennessee in top form. We spent the day driving through the streets of the old city, with Tennessee providing a running commentary.

Tennessee was not just a great writer, he was a wonderful companion when he was in the mood to be. Nothing escaped his notice, and in everything, his perspective was unique. Tennessee never just saw things, he *saw* them, and when you were around him, he let you in on the secret. The world always seemed much richer, saturated with meaning, when he was around. He was one person whose love life was more complicated than mine, and we would always commiserate on the difficulties of romantic entanglements.

We spent the day exploring Madrid. Tennessee and I had lunch at Botin's, the most famous restaurant in Madrid for those who loved Hemingway and the corrida. We had the house specialty, suckling pig, burned black and crisp over an open fire, smoky grilled vegetables piled high on the plate, thick crusty loaves of bread, and heavy red wine. It was delicious. The best. Absolute best. We talked for hours and hours about the vise and the vice of southern women, a subject that we both were endlessly fascinated by—Tennessee because he had been so surrounded by them growing up, me because I too had been raised by the same strain of women, and because I was very much bound by the emotional traditions myself, though I fought against it.

Tennessee understood the struggle, the warring within one's soul between having to be strong and proper, and at the same time having an intensity of emotion often pulling you in the opposite direction. Finding a balance between the two was nearly impossible; one side or the other was usually winning out. It is an inner life always at odds with itself. No peace to be found, and Tennessee and I both knew it well in all of its dimensions.

As the day wound down, we made our way again through the streets of Madrid one last time. "Look at that, honey," he said suddenly. "You see those shutters and those windows up there?" It was dusk now and the huge shutters had been pulled shut at one house after another. "There's a dead person behind every one of them," he said, with a grin of his peeking out from under his mustache so that he always looked like he was up to some mischief. I looked up—he was right—and I laughed.

Tennessee and I had visions of putting together either a play or a movie based on one of his short stories. I had been drawn to a story of his called "The Yellow Bird." There was an old recording of Tennessee reading it, and Peter and I would read the story to each other too. "Alma was the daughter of a Protestant minister," the story began. It went on to tell how she came home one day, went upstairs with something in a brown paper bag, and when she came down she had peroxided her hair. Alma walked out the door, got in the car, and drove it right through the garage doors. "I'm gone for good," she calls. "I'm nevah comin' back." I still say those lines all the time. And Peter used to tease me, "She's gone for good, she's never comin' back." They touched the core of that southern girl running, always running, that was inside of me.

Spending time with Tennessee made me eager to throw myself into a really good character study again. At the time, I was looking for a project that would challenge me. The scripts that I had been reading didn't have quite what I was looking for. So the idea of working with this playwright, who had created such powerful women, was a seductive notion. But it was a project that we never did, somehow. And then too, before "The Yellow Bird" had begun to take shape, Paddy Chayefsky called about a role he wanted to talk to me about.

IT WAS IMPOSSIBLE to be an actor in Hollywood and not be awed by the talent of Paddy Chayefsky. Anyone who has studied the craft at all knows the incredible gift it is when the dialogue you are given is something extraordinary. Often you find yourself feeling lucky if a script gives you just a few good lines that you can work with to pull your character out of the muck of blandness and banality. Rarely do you pick up a script and read page after page of brilliant writing, but that is what I found when I began reading the script that Paddy had sent me, *Network*.

The words are always your starting point. If they are there, you have a real chance at making something wonderful happen on-screen or onstage. Paddy is a writer who has consistently given actors that chance. He had brought a remarkable beauty to the lives of ordinary people in *Marty*, which won him an Oscar. In *The Hospital*, for which he won another Oscar, he had given us a view of just how dark his comedy could be. In *Network*, everything came together in an amazing rush of adrenaline, comedy, drama, and the clash of ordinary and not-so-ordinary lives, laced through with Paddy's own social commentary on the demons of our own making.

When I got the script for *Network*, I was happily ensconced again in Boston. I felt Peter and I were growing closer, and with Bill there, the three of us had created a sort of hybrid, extended family that gave me a great deal of emotional comfort. I didn't like to leave that safety net any more than I had to. But I read the script and was hooked.

If nothing else, I wanted to meet with Paddy Chayefsky and find out how he had constructed this woman, Diana Christensen, that he wanted me to play. Diana was a TV baby, almost without a soul. Television was her reference point—it defined her life, just as much as it defined life for her. She didn't choose it, she was raised on it; that is just the totality of who she was. And she was driven, more driven in her career than I was in mine, but I knew what fueled that sort of ambition. There was not a moment in the film, even while she was making love, when her mind was not on her work.

She sums herself up aptly in an early scene when she is having dinner with Max, the man she will become involved with. It is their first meal together, and she is running down the litany of her failed relationships. "It seems," says Diana, "that I'm inept at everything . . . except my work. I'm good at my work. So I confine myself to that. All I want out of life is a 30 share and a 20 rating."

Diana was the incarnation of the kind of insensitivity and doled-out nerve endings that TV produces. To play her as Paddy had written her, Diana was not the kind of character who would engender a drop of sympathy. "Why did you make her a woman?" I was ultimately to ask. "I can't find a thing about her that even remotely makes her sound or feel like a woman." Paddy laughed and shrugged. "I needed a love story."

"What do you mean you needed a love story?" I asked, knowing even as I said it what the answer was: Hollywood would have demanded it. Besides, I knew I wanted this role. What I hoped was that

I could convince Paddy to give Diana a little more humanity, or that I could find a way to let it seep into the character somehow. There was no scene where Paddy had told you what she lost—all that she has given up in her life for the ambition. But Paddy said he would leave it to me to help people find all of that in the way I shaded the character.

Diana was another jewel in the necklace of these articulate, smart career women that I played. I wonder now, what is it about our culture—our writers—that defines these women as heartless? Why couldn't a woman strive, without losing her humanity and womanliness? I don't know why the William Holden character couldn't have been a woman, and the Diana Christensen character have been a man. The protagonist, if she is a woman, if she steps out of the mold, is turned into something larger than life, driven, cold, amoral. And Diana fell right in line with that.

Peter read the script and said I shouldn't do it. Bill read it and tried desperately to talk me out of it. They both thought Diana was too heartless. They worried that people would think badly of me, would confuse the character and the actor, and come to believe I was like that. They were trying to protect me. From *Network* I didn't need protection. A few years later when I was being pushed to do *Mommie Dearest*, I would have given the world to be surrounded by people who would have argued against my doing it.

But *Network* was something quite apart from anything I had seen. I thought it was a seminal work on the power of the medium and the Machiavellian world that controlled it behind the scenes. Diana represented, in my mind, the axis on which it all turned. I knew this was a great role, one of the most important female roles to come along in years. For all her inhumanity and ambition, Diana also represented the price being paid by many women who were trying to dig their way into the top professional ranks. This was the mid-seventies, and if you wanted to succeed as a woman in a man's world, you had to be able to beat them at their own game. Diana, I knew, would end up right in the middle of that debate.

SIDNEY LUMET was going to direct the film, which was another plus, I thought. Lumet had the advantage that some film directors did not: he knew television well, having gotten his start there. Lumet loved movies, but he believed they ought to say something and his usually did. He had made powerful statements in *Serpico* and *Dog Day Afternoon*, which along with *Murder on the Orient Express* he had done just prior to taking on *Network*. It was exciting to think of what Lumet might do with what Paddy had given him.

Lumet was also legendary for being someone who directed with remarkable speed. He nearly always brought in his film days ahead of schedule, which basically put him in a category of one, since rarely does a film end on schedule, much less come in early. Paul Newman used to say Lumet was the only guy he knew who could double-park in front of a brothel—that's how fast he was. *Network* was no exception. We would finish shooting seven days ahead of schedule.

After a few days on the set, I teased Sidney about his seeming to direct on roller skates. He was a blur of movement as he zoomed from one place to another, nudging and prodding, "Sweetie this, this, and that." But there was a method in his madness; Lumet kept up the energy level. And that is so terribly important, because there is always so much waiting around anytime you're making a movie. His energy was something that you couldn't help but absorb just by being around him, and that kept everyone alert and alive through very long hours.

The director always sets the tone. And on this film, so did assistant director Burtt Harris; he was phenomenal. Burtt, whom I worked with again recently, is one of those New York Damon Runyon kind of characters. He invented a kind of lingo that has been emulated since then. "The girl," I think was his. I always remember Burtt's "86 on a girl" meant they were finished with "the girl" for the day. When something is 86'd on a New York diner menu, it means they don't have it anymore. Sometimes he'd say, "Home and mother," which meant I could head for home.

While Sidney was fast, he never cut corners. He just seemed to be able to get it right more quickly than most. In the first scene that Max and Diana have together, we're in his office and through the windows behind us, the RCA Building is visible. We began shooting that scene just at dusk and expected to be there for hours. All the lights in the RCA Building were on in the offices.

Suddenly Sidney started worrying that at some point they would begin to turn off the lights, and by the time we finished shooting the entire building would be dark. That would ruin the background continuity of the scene. An assistant director was dispatched to make sure that didn't happen, while we continued shooting. I don't know whether the assistant director ever got through to RCA or if we were just lucky, because when we finished shooting at midnight, the RCA Building was still ablaze with light.

IN OTHER HANDS, *Network* might well have been a disaster. Lumet really made it work. Then again, I'm not sure anyone else would have taken on the script. It was page after page of nonstop dialogue. Virtually no stage directions, just dialogue and speeches. But Lumet is so New York, very edgy and energized. *Network* demanded that current of electricity be there to keep the audience involved and with you through that much dialogue.

Lumet is an interesting director in that regard. He does not particularly believe that what the audience sees is more important than what they hear, so he is not afraid to let the language carry the piece during the moments and scenes where it makes sense. There are other film directors who act as if the spoken word is beyond the scope of the audience, so it is pared to a minimum, and visuals are a more critical element. There are times, though, when a picture is not worth a thousand words, and *Network* was very much a case of that.

For any film, the cast becomes a central component in the ultimate tone of the movie. Take *Dr. Strangelove*, which is one of my all-time favorites. I cannot imagine what that would have been without Peter Sellers. I do know it would have been a very different film. Lumet was very careful in putting together the cast of *Network*. One of the nicest things Sidney ever said about this cast was when he told someone visiting the set that while there were a lot of stars, the material in *Network* was so demanding, it took great acting and that was far more important to him in casting this film than a pretty face.

When the cast was still being put together, I lobbied to get Robert Mitchum to play Max Schumacher, the role William Holden ultimately took on. I thought Mitchum was a wonderful actor, a swaggering sort of sexy, dangerous guy. And Mitchum definitely had the irascibility so needed in the role. But Lumet said no. He told me he didn't want any one actor to imbalance the movie.

Mitchum is an idiosyncratic kind of guy and he very likely would have been making waves through the production. The same might have happened with Brando, another name that was in the hat, though having now worked with Marlon, I don't think so. But creating a cast that will come together and fit like disparate pieces of a puzzle is critical to the way Sidney works. No tantrums, no bad behavior on Lumet's sets. He doesn't have time for it.

In the end, the casting was so right. William Holden was perfect for his part. He *was* Max Schumacher. Bobby Duvall I had never worked with, but knew from the years I spent in New York at the beginning of my career. He hung out with Dusty Hoffman and all the rest. There are a lot of actors who seem to reach a plateau, even if they are quite wonderful, and never move beyond it. Duvall is an idiosyncratic actor in the tradition of Brando, Nicholson, and Hoffman. He's so authentic, like Hackman really.

He is such an original. Duvall never refers to the character in the third person. For example, speaking about a scene and my character, Diana, I would say, "Well, what's she doing here, Sidney?" Duvall would never say about his character, Frank Hackett, "What's he doing here, Sidney?" He would say, "Well, what am I doing here, Sidney?" or "I don't think I'd do that there." He would never talk about the character as if it were divorced from himself. I remember Bobby Lewis at Lincoln Center taught us that you can only be an artist choosing materials within yourself. And that was in line with what Duvall was doing. It's a subtle thing, but I really like it.

One of the most important things Sidney Lumet does—which I have never known another movie director to do—is that he takes two weeks of rehearsal. Not five days, not one day as most people do. Two entire weeks where he goes to a rehearsal hall with his actors and he tapes out the room, the size of the rooms that will be in the set, exactly as if you were rehearsing a play.

The second week, Sidney brings in the heads of all the major departments—cinematographer, prop master, costumer, everyone. Now we may get on that set in a month's time and we may have a new idea. But it will be based on the foundation laid in that room. You can only have that "Hey, what if I did this?" idea if you've already done the groundwork. If you haven't done that first step, you're saying, "Well, gee, where do I go now? Where's the chair in this room?" So you're way behind the game. Sidney's the only film director I've ever met who knows that, and I've made a lot of very good movies other than with

Sidney. But for working out and for developing the performance, those two full weeks of rehearsal were invaluable.

That is also why Sidney's always finished shooting the film under schedule, because he's so well prepared. He knows where he's going to move his camera. He doesn't have to take ten minutes to say, "Oh, where am I going to move it?" Or tell the crew where he's going to move it. They know as well. All those little shavings off five minutes here and there, maybe twenty-five times a day, and you're much more secure in your work as an actor or as a cinematographer or as a prop master. You do it more quickly and the quality's better, because you've had the preparation time. Sidney's very smart.

BILL HOLDEN was wonderful to work with. He played Max with a crusty elegance and just the right mix of street smarts and schooled intellect. He and I had brushed up against each other briefly in *Towering Inferno*, a movie that had left a bad taste in his mouth. He felt the film had so exploited our names that he wanted to talk to me before we began *Network* so that we could provide a united front in making sure that didn't happen again. But the material and the people behind this movie were worlds away from the clique that had been behind *Inferno*, so that was never a problem.

Bill and Peter Finch, who played Howard Beale, the newsman who slowly disintegrates before a growing number of television viewers, had to create a dynamic between them that would make the two of them feel like very old friends. Though they didn't know each other before *Network*, they became fast friends and the interplay between them on the set began to take on the feel of the characters they were playing. They closed down a few bars in New York during production, some for the movie and some entirely on their own.

I wanted to play Diana as a woman. You could have played her unattractive, you could have played her in trousers, you could have played her any kind of obvious way. But my choice was always to play these women as very feminine, so that you saw it was a woman in power, not an imitation, as Gloria Steinem said, of the last man. Gloria always said that the first woman in power is going to be by definition an imitation of the last man in power, because that's the only role model she's got. My women—Vicki Anderson in *Thomas Crown*, and Diana—I tried to give sexuality and femininity. I was

Talking ratings and relationships with William Holden over dinner in Network. Network
© 1976 Metro-Goldwyn-Mayer Inc. and United Artists Group

Finchey (Peter Finch) and me in Network, *the film that would win both of us Oscars.
We lost Finchey to a heart attack just weeks before the show.*

making a subtle point that you don't have to give that up in order to be powerful.

I told Sidney that I thought she should have long hair; there needed to be something wanton about it, really sexy, foxy. She was a daytime program executive. That's the choice. Just like in the scene where she wore a slinky evening dress when she is introduced to the network affiliates, her watch was a very modern Rolex. The choice of that dress and the design of that dress, white, clinging, and cut very, very low, with the hair, long, loose, but elegant, tells you something about Diana. Theoni Aldredge did the costumes, and she created these great sexy little blouses and skirts for Diana. They were audacious and feminine at the same time.

One of Lumet's good ideas, in one scene, was to give Diana food. She was so thin, a bundle of nervous energy. I was watching something and eating ravenously. We chose a huge hamburger and french fries and heaven knows what. It was a clever directorial touch because it's against convention. Where most women are always watching their diet, Sidney wanted Diana never to do that. It also told you something about how voracious this woman was—she even ate aggressively.

The most difficult scene for me and for Holden, as well, was our "love" scene. Max and Diana have gone to a snow-covered cabin outside of the city, but of course Diana can't really leave any of it behind. She gives him a running analysis of everything that is going on, from the moment she gets in the car. It doesn't stop when they get to the cabin, or when they undress. There is not a second when the dialogue stops. The speed of it parallels the rhythm of their lovemaking, faster, a climax, then slow.

Diana's running dialogue, with its very precise pacing, was incredibly difficult to pull off with any sort of reality. I could not afford to stumble on a single word; it would have killed the momentum of the scene. It was the exact opposite of "sex as chess," five minutes of quiet seduction. Instead I had to gasp and moan while detailing the prospects of a congressional investigation. I was very nervous about being able to pull that scene off, all the words and the pacing of the scene.

People always think of me as being cool and smart and very secure, and I'm not at all. There's that in me that's been carefully hidden, and particularly with Diana, I could never let anyone know how sensitive I was, or how frightened I was to do this. I couldn't let the camera read my fear. Sidney knew the risk I was taking. He said I was trading in all the goodwill I had built up in *Condor* and *Chinatown* to play Diana. I'm not sure I could have done it, taken Diana to the edge, if Sidney had not understood that.

Holden came very close to not doing the love scene. There were long talks about it. He had a strongly held belief that making love was a private thing that should not be exposed by film. As it was constructed, the scene required a great deal of physical and emotional exposure from both of us to make it work. I don't think either of us would have ever agreed to do it if we had not been convinced that the script would not hang together without it. But it was absolutely necessary. And it was, in the final film, a great, great scene. Completely unique, and completely correct for this character that Paddy had created.

Then too, for the scene to work, Diana had to be on top. Paddy had been relentless in driving home each of the points he wanted to make. I'm never at ease in love scenes, and actually feel quite shy about them. But this was a scene I was terrified to do. It seemed so outrageous, and I felt foolish astride Bill and babbling away about ratings in between gasps. It is one thing when the camera is shooting two people in bed, mostly hidden by sheets and blankets, with a shoulder exposed here, a leg there. It is quite another when you know that the camera is spending a lot of time shooting close-ups of your face as you try to enact this incredibly intimate moment.

Even though it was a closed set on those days, it was not easy, and this was the most difficult love scene I had done. Lumet shot that scene in a series of cuts, all very carefully orchestrated. We filmed it a piece at a time, from every angle, and yet in the editing, Lumet was able to make it look continuous and fluid from the minute we get in the car until we finish making love. Actually, it helped that Lumet choreographed the sex sequence. It made it easier for me to break it down into specific bits of action, rather than one long emotional and physical moment.

The only way we all got through it was with a huge measure of good humor. Bill could not make it through a scene without dissolving into laughter at some point along the way. And Lumet was great, he just went zooming about on his invisible roller skates as if this scene was like all the others. It all worked to help relieve the tension both Bill and I felt, and there was tension on that day to spare.

WHETHER IT WAS the love scene or a network meeting, Lumet made everything about it easier because he knew without hesitation when he had what he wanted. He doesn't have that fear that plagues some directors, which makes them believe that the next shot will be the best. Sidney is able to say, "No, this one is it, we've got it." Actors are usually struggling enough as it is, so it is very reassuring if the director isn't.

One of the most powerful scenes in the film is Diana's final one with Max. She is dealing with a ratings drop of monumental proportions, when Max walks into her apartment. The relationship is in a tailspin too. "What do you want me to do?" I ask him. "I just want you to love me, Diana." Suddenly Sidney yelled "Cut." I said, "Wait a minute, Sidney, I have another line." But he said, "No, no, all you need is the look. You looked at him as if he were from Mars. It's perfect."

Everything I had done with the character was building to this point. Hopefully you see in that moment what you've suspected all along, that Diana isn't connected as a woman, doesn't feel like a woman. I got the quintessential expression of it in that moment, in that single look. With just those few seconds on the screen, you knew that she was completely unable to love.

NETWORK was the movie that television loved to hate. When it came out later that year, there was a terrific uproar from the industry that it was too far over the top. At one point, NBC barred Lumet from a screening of one of its TV movies because executives there were so angry with his film's portrayal of television executives. Barbara Walters worried that audiences would take *Network* as truth, not satire. Edwin Newman said, "I don't believe TV producers would do 'anything' to boost ratings." And Walter Cronkite, whose daughter Cathy had a small role in the film, said, "Since the birth of television, all of us have known how we could hype our ratings almost instantly through the methods of the penny press, but you don't see any hint of things like that." I wonder if they would say the same of their industry today.

Much of the fury was directed at two particular elements of the story. One is the reality-based show that Diana puts on. Essentially it's a terrorist attack of the week, and as she saw it, it would blend actual footage with a dramatic segment to set up the story. At the time it seemed outrageous to everyone. Today, it is not unlike many of the reality-based shows on television, like *Rescue 911* or *Cops*, which have proven to be very popular. The conceit of the script was the ultimate Hollywood development deal. We had a radical Communist under contract to the network to work with the terrorist groups in sorting out which criminal activities might have the most dramatic appeal.

The other scene which sent network executives into a rage was the last scene in the movie, which I thought was brilliant and still stands as my favorite scene of all time. Howard Beale, the mad prophet of the airwaves, has turned from asset to liability for the network. This man— who got millions of people to scream out their windows, "I'm mad as hell and I'm not going to take it anymore"—must be gotten rid of. Unfortunately, since the chairman of the board wants him kept on the air, it falls to the programming department to do something.

It's really dark, black comedy, this scene, and so completely funny. Duvall is running the meeting and what we are talking about is murder. That seems to be the only way to dispose of Howard Beale. At one point someone says, "What we're talking about is a capital crime here . . . the network can't be implicated." Sidney's direction was absolutely brilliant, using the frightening power of understatement. He had us play it as if we were discussing whether or not to make a routine programming change in the schedule, not to carry out the murder of a human being. That was the key, though it was very hard to get my psyche to that place where this character that I am playing and acting would deal with murder as something absolutely ordinary and mundane.

But as I thought through the scene, I began to examine my own feelings about television. There is something weird and soulless about TV that this scene seemed to capture. I don't understand all of what happened as we were filming that day, I only know what I felt and what I instinctively knew. And I knew that Diana Christensen didn't even once let it into her mind that it was murder that was on the table, even as she says the words. "The issue," says Duvall, "is should we kill Howard Beale or not." Then I say, in this impassive, pragmatic voice that I still find surreal when I hear it, "I don't see that we have any option, Frank. Let's kill the son of a bitch."

The final line in the film is delivered by the narrator: "This is the story of Howard Beale, the only known instance of a man who was killed because he had lousy ratings." Lin Bolen, the broadcasting executive that Diana Christensen was loosely modeled after, gave some credence to the notion of the power of ratings to determine life and death—literally—when she said after the film was released in 1976 that "the ratings game is at its zenith. The numbers have never meant more than they do this year."

Perhaps no one could have predicted that the ratings game would only get more vicious, though Paddy warned that these were things to come. He was just as dark a prophet in the interviews he gave in the months after the film was released as the Howard Beale character he had created. And the reality of it is, then and now, that though murder is not the actual remedy, program after program is killed each year because of lousy ratings, with little regard for any of those affected, something I would experience at close range years later.

In the end, *Network* touched a raw nerve in the country. Audiences went to the film in great numbers and literally howled with laughter through the whole of it. Thousands upon thousands of people put bumper stickers on their cars with Howard Beale's mantra, "I'm mad as hell and I'm not going to take it anymore." It became a catch phrase for the anger in the country, just as it had in the film. There was a great disillusionment and a growing sense that television was a part of the unraveling of the nation in some strange way that people could not quite fathom or articulate. *Network* was truly art predicting life.

SEVENTEEN

IN THE FORTIES, when Bette Davis was a contract player at Warner Bros., she had come across the story of Aimee Semple McPherson and wanted it for her own. Sister Aimee was an evangelist in Los Angeles in the 1920s whose magnetism drew crowds by the thousands. But at the height of her popularity, Sister Aimee disappeared during an ocean swim only to reappear a month later in Mexico. There had been, she said, a strange kidnapping from which she had finally escaped. But there were rumors of a love affair, and she was taken to court on charges that she had conspired with her mother to concoct this hoax so she could spend the month with a lover.

It was one of those stories that you fall in love with if you're an actress. A strong, charismatic woman, caught in a web of intrigue, perhaps of her own making. There was love, lust, politics, religion, and a domineering mother, all the stuff that makes for great drama, a kind of Greek tragedy set in Southern California. It was easy to understand why Bette had spent so many years trying to convince Warner Bros. to make a film of it with her in the starring role.

THIRTY YEARS LATER in 1976 when Hallmark Hall of Fame picked the Aimee McPherson story for one of their projects, Bette was far too old to be considered for the starring role. When the movie was originally cast, Ann-Margret was slated to be Aimee, with Bette taking on the role of her mother. It was one of the reasons why Bette decided to do the film. The two had gotten along well when they played mother and daughter in 1961 in the Frank Capra film *Pocketful of Miracles*. But Ann-Margret dropped out of the project before anything was really under way.

The producers felt they had to get a strong screen actress to play the title role, otherwise they were in danger of Bette's legendary presence overwhelming the project. When my agent asked if I would be interested in playing Aimee, I decided to consider it. It had been years since I had done television, and the idea of working with Bette was too good to turn down. She was nearing the end of her career and there would not likely be many more chances to do so.

And I very much liked the character. Aimee was a strong, demanding role, one that really was designed to carry the movie. I liked the playing of it a lot—it was a role that tested you. I had to play it so subtly and from a very interior place, so deep inside that you sensed it but you never could say, "Ah, she is guilty, she did do it." Anthony Harvey, who had done such a wonderful job with *The Lion in Winter*, was set to direct it, with filming to begin in Denver in the summer of 1976.

One of the attractions of being involved in a television production is the mass audience. I do quite a lot of television. I thought of it like a free concert, where you work for less money than you normally get, but you reach millions and millions of people, who perhaps become acquainted with you for the first time. Ultimately when NBC aired *The Disappearance of Aimee* in November of 1976, it drew a huge audience. Ironically CBS also did quite well airing *Chinatown* against us.

Problems preceded me to this movie and problems continued as we moved closer to production. By the time I had arrived on the project, Bette was unhappy with the way things were unfolding after Ann-Margret's departure. Then Tony began talking about the possibility of casting Harris Yulin as the district attorney. Harris was, and is, a good character actor. But our relationship had had such an unhappy ending, I wasn't keen on the idea of him playing opposite me, playing a role that would require me to dredge up a lot of those feelings.

Tony thought it would be great, that our past history would create the kind of sparks that he wanted to see fly between the district attorney and Aimee. I was just as determined not to have a painful episode in my life exploited in this way. It got very difficult at one point, with Harris on the phone to me in New York asking how could I say no to his being in the movie. He asked me to reconsider. I said no. I think it was a tawdry impulse of Tony Harvey's to give a very good actor a chance to play a role simply because he could dredge up past pain between us. That's just not cricket. It's not the way you do things.

DENVER WAS SWELTERING that August and we were in period costumes throughout the production. Edith Head had little more than a week to put together the wardrobe, but she didn't cheat the look at all. Though the fabrics were light, there were often several layers to contend with. Since I was a minister, I spent a fair number of days in heavy, full-length church robes.

There was no relief when we moved from church to court. The Denver courtroom, in which many of the scenes take place, was not air-conditioned. You had to walk up two flights of stairs to get to it, which meant you were hot long before you said your first line. When there was enough of a break between scenes, both Bette and I would retreat to the dressing rooms, which mercifully were cooled.

While the story was a compelling one, the script had serious problems. I had listened to hours of recordings made by Sister Aimee, and she had a fervor and a rhythmic cadence to her sermons, which is much of what swept people up. But the script just never captured the flavor of those speeches. I called Bill Alfred back in Boston and told him I needed his help. We worked with her recordings as much as we could, trying to get an authenticity into the dialogue.

Television is always fast, and there's always very little time for preparation. So we had to contend with that. But I was much happier, finally, with the revised speeches, which were at times lifted verbatim from what she had said. Why the writer felt he had to better the original Aimee Semple McPherson sermons, I don't know, but I was happy with how they turned out in the end.

Throughout the production of *The Disappearance of Aimee*, there was a struggle for power. It was palpable and people noticed it. Bette was not content playing a supporting character. While I understood that it must be difficult for her to watch someone else in a role she had wanted for herself for so many years, it is something else again to attempt to refocus the story, particularly one that was already problematic.

From a completely pragmatic point of view, the script told the story of Sister Aimee. Minnie Kennedy, Aimee's mother, was a secondary character in the real-life story, and a secondary character in the script that John McGreevey had given us. Aimee's rise and fall was the central premise; it formed the ballast for the plot from one scene to the next, from beginning to end. If you change that, you are no longer doing the same movie, and you are likely to sink the entire project in the process.

It came to a head one day near the end of production. The last scene had been rewritten by someone else so that it was all about Mama Kennedy. I had just finished reading it when Tony came to me and said, "Bette says, would you please say okay to this because she really loves it." As it was rewritten, 90 percent of the argument would have been Bette's and I would have been left with virtually nothing. And I looked right at him and said, "No. I will give her 50-50—you can give us both an equally strong argument—but I cannot give her 90-10. I'm sorry." When we filmed the scene, the air was electric, or perhaps lethal is more accurate.

IT IS NEVER EASY to be in those kinds of situations where someone is jockeying so hard for more attention. I had great respect for Bette's talent. I wanted very much to be fair, to be generous with this woman who had for so long been an icon in the industry. And I had been in the business long enough to know that given the choice, actors and actresses always want more screen time. But it was Aimee's story and I was Aimee. The burden of carrying the movie was on my shoulders, and it was on my name that they were going to sell it. I could not agree to a 90-10 split in one of the movie's most critical scenes.

You learn early on in this profession not only how to fight, but that you must, it is required. If you fold, if you let yourself bend, you will not make it, truly make it. You have to defend yourself from the assaults of others, just as you have to defend the character you are playing.

I learned the lesson quite early that to survive you have to start with the realization that most of the people you will come across in Hollywood are trying to use you for their own ends. It is a business run off ego. You must be prepared to look out for yourself, because the moment you entrust that to someone else, you'll find yourself used. Not everyone is a villain, certainly. Some people surprise you. But sadly, not very many.

Bette had never been much more than civil to me up to the point of our disagreement, but afterward she became quite cruel. She attacked my professionalism and she attacked me personally. There were charges she hurled in my direction that were simply not true. To one writer she said that I spent my evenings riding the streets of Denver in a limo drinking champagne. I did not. To another she predicted that I would not be alive in five years, saying she was convinced I was on a fast track to an early death. I'm still very much alive.

As I write this nearly two decades later, what I know is that the journey I have taken through life has brought me to a place today where I am happier and more fulfilled than I have ever been. I had watched Bette on the set when she was out there trying to entertain the troops, which she did any time I was off the set. There was a sort of desperation in it.

I also understood well her need for acceptance. It is one of the demons that plagues most of us in this profession, the desire for a performance that is embraced, for fans that reaffirm your place in the constellation of stars. All that, I knew about Bette Davis that summer in Denver. Her spirit never flagged, though her body was beginning to let her down, and I admired her grit even in the face of our discord. Just as her book *The Lonely Life* had given me insight into what my future held as a young actress on the rise, I looked at the anger that flared up in her, turning her cheeks crimson and making her eyes flash, and I realized I wanted to be careful not to let this be my future one day as well. I let it alone and never said a harsh word about her.

I think at some point I became for Bette the symbol of what she could no longer have, of what age had robbed her of. I was not around Bette enough in those twenty-one days on the set to possibly warrant the resentment she harbored against me for so many years. I knew she was ill, and it seemed to have somehow fractured her mind. More than a decade later, she was still publicly on the attack. She went on *The Tonight Show* with Johnny Carson, her final visit there before her death, and held forth on her vast and varied opinions of me, none of them favorable.

A few days later, after a flood of calls from friends of mine telling me about her performance on Carson, I sat there watching a tape of the show. The vitriol of the attack absolutely stunned me. It was cruel, uncalled for, and I was hurt. Some of my advisers tried to talk me into a public counterattack. But though I was hurt, I couldn't muster any anger, only pity.

Watching her, all I could think of was that she seemed like someone caught in a death throe, a final scream against a fate over which no one has control. I was just the target of her blind rage at the one sin Hollywood never forgives in its leading ladies—growing old. But I thought it incredibly sad that this woman, who had given a voice to so many classic roles, in her last TV appearance before her death could find so little to talk about beyond a month-long television production with me. It was as if in some weird way she was railing against herself.

The ultimate irony for me is that despite the acrimony, *The Disappearance of Aimee* turned out to be well received by the audience, and was embraced by the critics as well. I too was pleased with the final result that all of us achieved in *Aimee*. In the end, I gave the character what I had hoped to: mystery and complexity. She was, most probably, a charlatan of the highest order.

I TRIED TO MANAGE something of a normal home life through-out the various productions I was involved in. As it was, I had gone from doing about four films a year to barely two. Peter spent some time in New York with me when I was filming *Network*, and we would have dinner together when we could. One day he brought the whole J. Geils Band to the set, which was fun. Between his career and mine, we couldn't go about making a life together in any conventional sense.

From the time I was in my early twenties, my life had been lived in terms of when I was shooting a movie and when I was not. With Peter, it was more so. When there was a movie, there was nothing but work. When there wasn't, it was a holiday. The closest I came to observing traditional holidays before my son was born was Christmas. My mother and Jim would always come to visit wherever I happened to be, and she would cook a traditional meal of turkey, stuffing, and all the rest of the fixings. Bill Alfred soon became a regular at Christmastime too. And each year I would have my tree, with tinsel put on one strand at a time.

But the intensity of the lives that Peter and I were leading was wearing on the relationship. And then too, we had been together for nearly four years, married two, and I wanted to seriously consider taking off a year to have a child. I was getting ready to celebrate my thirty-sixth birthday, and feeling very much that time was running out for me.

Peter was still very young and just not ready to start a family. For the first time in our relationship, the difference in our ages began to work against us. Having a child was very important to me, as it had been years before I met Peter. He had known that.

For all my life, I had looked to that moment of fulfillment. I can't imagine living my life as a woman and never having a child. It was just one of those experiences not to be missed. I wanted a child with all my heart. Though the timing was just not right for us then—we tried to resolve it but never could—in the years since Peter has become a very good friend to my son.

Our troubles were made all the more painful because with Peter, I felt I had finally resolved one of the other central dilemmas I seemed to always face—focusing on either a man or a movie. Peter was my champion, and has always had a wonderful blend of talent and business savvy. Underneath the songwriter who could write such moving lyrics about love was a street-smart kid from the Bronx. There were never any hidden agendas with Peter, and I could always count on him to tell me his true feelings about any project I was considering. But somehow, time, life, and the world kept wearing away at our relationship.

That spring, I went to the Cannes International Film Festival. Peter did not. The next time he went on tour, I flew up to Canada to spend a few days with him there. We drove out in the country and took a long walk along a melancholy old river bog to try and sort through our problems. "We're wrecking our marriage, we have to stop," I told Peter. He did not disagree. We decided that we would find time to work on the relationship, to handle the problems that were dividing us. I left Canada more hopeful than I had been in months. But as 1976 drew to a close, nothing had been resolved.

NETWORK hit theaters in November of 1976. And while those in television hated it, movie critics loved it. Vincent Canby, writing in *The New York Times*, said of the film that it was "outrageous. It's also brilliantly, cruelly funny, a topical American comedy . . . these wickedly distorted views of the way television looks, sounds and, indeed, is, are the satirist's cardiogram of the hidden heart, not just of television."

You cannot invest too much in what the critics say. They are a peripatetic bunch. Characters you think they will love, they hate;

others you're convinced anyone could understand will confound them completely. And the price of admission to their particular theater is your soul, because that is what you have thrown up there on the screen. Nevertheless, it is nice when a critic actually gets from the performance what you wanted to give. Canby said I took a woman of psychopathic ambition, who was completely devoid of all feeling, and made her touching and funny. That is what I had wanted to give Diana all along, her humanity.

Diana, though, was in for a rough time with some feminist groups, who felt Hollywood had simply found a new way to portray women in a bad light. Deborah Rosenfelt, who was co-chairperson of the Modern Language Association of America's Commission on the Status of Women in the Profession, took great exception to Diana and dubbed her the "Great American Bitch." "The Bitch has moved out of the house and into the corporate structure," she wrote. "Dunaway's character embodies not only the fabled bloodlessness of TV executives, but also the frightening impersonality of the medium itself."

That, of course, is precisely what Paddy had hoped to achieve in that character. While I understood her concern, I was also someone who had been there in the front ranks of my profession trying to push the envelope on the characters I chose. I had consistently played strong women, women who took control of their destiny quite apart from men. And I knew that Paddy had designed *Network* as a parody, a satire, with the extremes that go hand in hand with that. But what I found so rich in irony is that Paddy had thought of the character, given birth to it really, as being a man. Only did man become woman as a concession to commercialism and the need for a romance.

Network did all of the things that studio executives love. It made a great deal of money and it garnered a great number of Academy Award nominations, which translates into a lot more money at the box office. In all, there were ten nominations. Nearly all the major cast members received nominations; only Robert Duvall was overlooked despite an inspired performance. Both William Holden and Peter Finch were nominated in the Best Actor category. Paddy was up for Best Screenplay, Lumet for Best Director, and the film for Best Picture.

For me, it was my third Best Actress nomination. With *Bonnie and Clyde* I had never expected to win—I was too new, had no body of work and no history with the industry. With *Chinatown*, I still didn't really allow myself to seriously hope for an Oscar, though I thought it was another strong performance and certainly worthy of consideration. With *Network*, it began to seem like my time had come. The word on the street was heavily in my favor, the studio had mounted a major publicity campaign to back all the nominees, and I let myself hope that this time it would be so.

IN THE MIDST of all the buzz, *People* magazine assigned photographer Terry O'Neill to do a photo spread on me. One of the shots he wanted to take of me was on the Charles River in Boston. It was early spring, but the river still looked wintery, solitary, and serene with a thinning blanket of ice. Terry kept telling me to move back. He wanted me as far from the river's edge as possible. The ice was getting thinner and thinner. Finally it was little more than a sheer pane—I could sense the river below—and I shouted that if I moved again, the ice would crack.

I should have taken that as an omen, because as it happens I was on thin ice indeed. Instead I looked at Terry and knew that this charming Anglo-Irish cockney, camera in hand, would be the next love of my life.

It is so difficult to unravel the threads of your life and your relationships, to figure out which strand is the one that finally broke. That moment in my life was a very complex time. I wanted a child, and with my marriage breaking up, I wanted very much to find someone I could love and have a family with.

Success too was becoming more of a problem. It has brought me many things, some very wonderful things. The most important thing was freedom to choose the best work available—every possible script was sent to me now. But it never brought me comfort. As much as I wanted success, I ran from it too. You can track much of my career in terms of success, then retreat. I had had some tough times with stardom by the time *Network* came into my life.

The intensity of the experience had been really accelerating since *Chinatown*. *Network* only heightened it. What few boundaries I had set, what lines I had drawn to protect my privacy, began to crumble completely. I had everything and I had nothing. I was invaded by the business; it crept into every corner of my life. Even with my eyes closed, I still felt the glare of the spotlight.

That glare was unbearable to my psyche in ways that I could not begin to articulate at the time. Now I have learned to be strong in the face of it, to walk through the fear. And I've discovered on the other side of fear is freedom, because none of the threats that fear makes you are true.

But then, those inner voices of my past would start in on me: "Who do you think you are? You don't deserve this. You're not good enough." The self-doubt intensified and came very near to destroying me. I had witnessed it at work on my father, and knew that it was part of the legacy he gave to me. It was as if we were born skinless, left to try to survive without any protection in this world. Of all the patterns in my life, this was one of the most devastating.

In 1977, as I stood on the brink of absolute success, the Oscar within my grasp, I was in a fight for my very life.

EIGHTEEN

ARCH 29, 1977, the day of the forty-ninth annual Academy Awards, dawned crystal clear. The winds had swept the air in the Los Angeles basin clean of pollution and you could see the mountains rise in the distance, snow-capped still, wrapping the city like an ermine stole. I want to sleep, to make the rest of the day go more quickly, but it is 5 A.M. and I can't lie in bed another minute.

There is a steady stream of calls, flowers, telegrams—some from friends and family, others from those who are in the business of hedging their bets that you will be the one to win. But with all of that, March 29 is beginning to feel like the longest day in the world to me. I am trying hard not to let the thought of winning an Oscar settle in. The envelope is still sealed, the verdict is still out. Nevertheless, I jot down some thoughts, something to say, just in case.

Nearly twelve hours later, Peter and I are finally making our way along the red carpet laid out in front of the Dorothy Chandler Pavilion in downtown Los Angeles. We move along through a sea teaming with light and life. Flashbulbs are popping, reporters are shouting questions, television crews are everywhere, and the fans are there, some having spent the night in sleeping bags to secure their seats in the bleachers, shouting and waving, calling for autographs.

Inside, the auditorium is cavernous, and we make our way toward the front. One thing a nomination assures you is great seats. One of the hosts this evening is Ellen Burstyn. Since she won the Oscar in the Best Actress category the year I was nominated for *Chinatown*, I can't decide if this is a good sign or bad. Then too, Warren Beatty is another of the hosts for the night, and he was there when I received my first

315

nomination for *Bonnie and Clyde*. Jane Fonda, yet another of the hosts, was the only other actress Paddy and Sidney had considered for the role of Diana in *Network*, the role that has gotten me here tonight. Exactly what that might mean for my chances, I don't know, but the evening feels weighty and full of portent.

For weeks now, everyone I have talked to has been telling me I am sure to win the Oscar for *Network*. But I know by now that in Hollywood, there is no such thing as a sure thing. I was equally proud of my performances in *Chinatown* and *Bonnie and Clyde*. But then sometimes, it is just not your time to win. The other actresses under consideration are Sissy Spacek for *Carrie*, Liv Ullman in *Face to Face*, Talia Shire in *Rocky*, and Marie-Christine Barrault in *Cousin, Cousine*. Liv Ullman has been mentioned most often as the other strong contender.

By the time they finally get to the Best Actress category it is late in the evening, and *Network* has picked up two Oscars, Paddy for his screenplay and Beatrice Straight for Best Supporting Actress as Bill Holden's long-suffering wife. Before the night is over, there will be two more. Peter Finch, who had a heart attack only weeks before the Academy Awards show, won in the Best Actor category, one of the few times an Oscar has been given posthumously. For all of us who knew Finchey, it was an emotional moment when his wife came up to accept his award. And finally I will, this time, win my Oscar.

I will never forget the moment, and the feeling, when I heard my name. Louise Fletcher, who had won the Oscar the year before for her portrayal of Nurse Ratched in *One Flew Over the Cuckoo's Nest*, was the presenter. I sat there stunned for a moment, wanting to make sure that I heard her right. Then Peter hugged me, and everyone sitting near me began to murmur their congratulations, and the reality began to penetrate.

My emotions were an absolute jumble, and to this day the strangest memories stay with me, physical things mostly. I was suddenly sick that I had decided to wear extremely high heels. I was terrified that I might fall. The weight of the Oscar as Louise handed it to me surprised me—it's so much heavier than you expect. You're trying to hold it and think and talk. But then too, it was reassuringly solid, weighty, and I liked the feeling that it was truly an award of substance.

I don't remember much of what I said, except that I had wanted to make a point of thanking "the boys in the backroom." It was a Dietrichian way of thanking the people who helped me on a personal level, my immediate team that helped me prepare for work each day.

It was, without question, one of the most wonderful nights of my life. The Oscar represented the epitome of what I had struggled for and dreamt about since I was a young child. The emotional rush of getting this accolade, the highest one this industry can award you, just hit me like a bomb. It was the symbol of everything I ever thought I wanted as an actress. It was the payoff, the reward for this complete one-track obsession of mine to be great at what I do. For that one moment in time, I felt wonderful. No self-doubts squeezed themselves in to spoil the day.

There was the Governor's Ball after the show, and then a huge party back at the hotel. Peter and his manager, Dee Anthony, had had T-shirts made for me with a giant picture of an Oscar and the words: "All the way with Faye." It was a terrifically sweet thing to do, and I slipped on one of the T-shirts and wore it the rest of the night. It was a wonderful, magical night and I wanted to bottle up the feelings forever. I wanted a night that would never end.

I HAD COME to Hollywood that year feeling a bit the renegade and I would leave feeling like royalty. In years past, I had gone to the show wearing the most elegant, glamorized of looks. This year I had been determined to find something very simple to wear. It was an impulse that was not all bad, but I had yet to find the right balance between losing myself to the Hollywood star machine and establishing the separate identity I wanted to have. I was still looking to recover that softer, warmer Dorothy Faye of my childhood.

I went to Geoffrey Beene and picked out a two-piece black silk design, pants and a top, with long, loose lines—a sort of karate-styled couture—set off by a black-and-white roped belt. My hair had grown quite long, and like the clothes, I decided I wanted to wear it loose and natural. Peter and I had flown to Los Angeles in late March and checked into one of the pink bungalows at the Beverly Hills Hotel on Sunset Boulevard. By Oscar night, the hotel was packed with celebrities. You could not walk down the hall, or into the Polo Lounge or around the pool, without rubbing shoulders with someone in the industry.

It was an incredible time for me. As an actress, I was hot and about to get hotter. Everyone wanted to meet with me about their next project. On one particular day, my agent had five scripts that had arrived from five A-list directors. Those he added to the dozens of scripts that were flowing into his office in the weeks just before the Oscars. The bidding to get me to sign on before the Academy Awards were announced was intense. It was the ultimate poker game. If I won the Oscar, my fee would just about double. Even if I didn't, the studios were still getting a very bankable star. My agents were convinced I would win, and wanted me to wait.

In the days before the awards, Peter and I had dinner with Jon Peters and Barbra Streisand at Barbra's house. Jon had produced two of her recent pictures and now had a project in mind that would be the first he would produce on his own. It was called *Eyes*. He had brought the project to David Begelman, my former agent, who was now in the business of producing movies. Jon had a short list of actresses he was thinking of for the starring role. David looked at the list, pointed to my name, and said, "If you make it with Faye, we'll do it." By the time negotiations were completed, I had the Oscar and my fee had jumped to $1 million, a huge sum for an actress in those days.

PROFESSIONALLY everything was heating up, personally everything was falling apart. Terry O'Neill was in town and got an idea for a photo of me if I won the Oscar. There were dozens of photographers approaching me with ideas, but Terry's was the only one with any originality. Two days before the Academy Awards, I agreed that if I won the Oscar, he could take the shot the next day. The shot was titled "The Morning After," and it quickly became a classic. It shows me poolside at the Beverly Hills Hotel. The place is absolutely deserted. It looks to be just after sunrise, but thankfully it was actually shot much later in the day. I'm in the satin robe, a pale blush color, that I wore for a scene in *Chinatown*. The ECM, for Evelyn Cross Mulwray, that was embroidered in the lapel was redone to read FDW, for Faye Dunaway Wolf, not long after the movie was finished. I have it still.

It is a beautiful, bittersweet shot. I look pensive, weary, but there is a seductive glamour to it, as I lounge there in my pink satin robe and black patent leather sandals with their clear stiletto heels. The front pages of papers with their Oscar headlines lie strewn around my feet.

On the round glass-topped table next to me sits a tray with a cup and a pot of tea, beside an ice-filled glass and a Coke, both untouched. Front and center is the Oscar. The pool stretches out behind me, the water a pale blue; a single row of white chaises, like sentries, line either side. My look is very far away.

In Terry's picture, success is a solitary place to be. In my life, it has been the same. One of Terry's favorite films is *Sweet Smell of Success*. Like the film, what Terry managed to capture in the shot was the emptiness of it all. Or as Peggy Lee sang, "Is that all there is?" We re-created the photo again not long ago for the hotel, to memorialize the picture as part of its restoration and renovation. I love the picture's poignancy as much as its triumph. It's a great picture. It was Terry as an artist pointing out the value of life as opposed to the value of awards, with Peter Finch dead and me sitting there with an almost *dolce vita* kind of decadence. It was Terry up and down that picture, the details and drama of it—his comment on the emptiness of success. Though I struggle with my world, I never agree to a sardonic view of it.

AFTER THE OSCARS, I once again began a mini-retreat from the business to try to figure out my personal life. What had begun as a flirtation between Terry and me on the *People* shoot mushroomed into a serious affair during the week I spent at the Beverly Hills Hotel. It began simply enough, as warm California afternoons would find me poolside. Terry and a colony of his English friends would often be there as well. We would sit for hours on the chaises and talk and laugh. It seemed, at first, that laughter came easily with Terry. I later came to realize that he had some strains of the comedian in him, where comedy covers the pain, and a joke is there to help rescue one from confronting darker emotions.

After the Academy Awards, Peter flew back to Boston without me. Not long after, I moved back to Central Park West. We talked, but then we reached a point where there was nothing left to say. As I look back on my life, I realize this is the one man in my life that I know, to the depths of my heart, never meant me harm. He was and is a mensch—a combination of humanity, great intellect, and deep emotions. We have been through such pain together, but even the end of our marriage did not destroy our bond. He is my friend still, and quite possibly the one true love of my life. Though I doubt that our lives will ever come together again as they did when we first met, when I think of Peter Wolf I always remember the Portuguese proverb: "Never say you will not drink from that glass again."

FALLING IN LOVE was more than complicated with Terry. We both had a great many emotional entanglements that we were far from free of. I was ending my marriage to Peter, and Terry had a wife and two children that he was leaving to be with me. We decided to take a month and spend it together, away from everyone and everything, and see if there was any substance to this relationship, if there was enough there to try to build a life together.

My first project after winning the Oscar was the one Jon Peters had proposed to me only a few days before the Academy Awards. It was soon renamed *Eyes of Laura Mars*. I would get the summer to myself, as shooting was not scheduled to begin until the fall. I also had my sights set on a George Cukor project titled *Vicky*, which was the story of Victoria C. Woodhull, an early feminist and the first woman to run for president in this country, in 1872.

James Toback wrote the script and George was to direct. It remains one of the tragedies of the business that *Vicky* never became a movie. Though another writer was brought in at some point to work on a rewrite, the final draft remains one of the best scripts I have ever read. We were hoping that Cary Grant would costar in it with me. He was a friend of Georges, who owned the rights to the story. But before the final production monies had been put together another Cukor film, *The Blue Bird*, came out and took a beating. *The Blue Bird* was a highly publicized joint effort between the American and Russian film industries, a remake of the 1940s dark fantasy classic of the same name. It had a very expensive and high-profile cast in Elizabeth Taylor, Ava Gardner, Jane Fonda, and Cicely Tyson, among others. But both critically and at the box office, it was a bust. Financing for *Vicky* began to dry up.

It is the nature of the business that for every project you decide to do, there are likely to be other films you have to pass on, and that was the case for me in the months after *Network*. While I was holding out hope that the financing would get sorted out on *Vicky*, I passed on a couple of very strong proposals, especially *Julia*. Jane Fonda, who was involved in developing the project, went on to star as Lillian Hellman.

The role of Julia, Hellman's friend who fought and was finally killed by the Nazis, which Jane had offered to me, was ultimately played by Vanessa Redgrave. The role of Julia won Vanessa an Oscar, and Lillian was one of Jane's strongest performances. Others that I let go of, like *Fun with Dick and Jane*, left me with no regrets.

AUGUST OF 1977, Terry and I flew into Dublin, then rented a car and set out to discover ourselves and the Irish countryside. Terry didn't drive, so I did. We headed out cross-country to Shannon, which sits on the west side of the isle. From there we drove to the Bay of Dingle, the Ring of Kerry, and into Cork where Terry's family is from, and on through Waterford. We walked through crumbling castles, we shared the road with herds of sheep, we stopped in the village pubs along our route for a meal of freshly caught salmon and chips, with a splash of malt vinegar. We always came away happily stuffed from that wonderfully hearty fare, with endless stories on the local lore and a rundown on the town characters. We went to Yeats' Tower, the place where Yeats had lived and worked, and visited that as well.

What a beautiful place Ireland is. I could see why Terry loved it so. The language is musical, the people are universally warm, and the countryside is some of the most beautiful I've seen anywhere in the world. Though everyone says it, Ireland *is* the Emerald Isle, everything is just saturated, drenched in the color. Soft rain wafts in front of you. Then it's gone. And then it's back again. It is a magical place.

Since I was to play a fashion photographer in *Laura Mars*, Terry bought me a beautiful little Leica and began to teach me how to shoot it. He told me to always remember that it is not the camera that takes the photograph, it is you. That changes in a very fundamental way how you think about what you're doing. I got better at it, but never close to the art form that Terry achieved.

His photographs always struck me as very beautiful and serene in style. He is famous for the details in his photos. I remember a shot he did of the rock band The Who that had a million densely packed details in it. He took tons of photos of me, some candid, some with elaborate setups, but regardless there is a certain mood to them that is quite unlike most of the photos that have been taken of me. His photographs always looked like paintings, I thought. The beauty and intensity of color and light are unique to Terry. He was very good at keeping the look natural. He would talk to me in front of the camera to keep me relaxed and simple. Terry would be behind the lens. It becomes a kind of slow duet, very highly charged, the dance of it all. Terry was very quiet, but very intense.

AFTER FOUR LAZY, wonderful weeks in Ireland, I came back to the States and began preparing for *Laura Mars*, which was set to start filming around New York in October. There was a distinct advantage that I never counted on in having Jon Peters as the producer. We decided to do my hair red for the movie. Jon, who had begun his career as a hairdresser to the stars, flew to New York and personally took care of it. It was definitely a unique moment, having my producer doing my hair, but he was great and left me feeling like this was one production where I would be well taken care of.

Tommy Lee Jones, who was relatively unknown at the time, was cast as the police detective/serial killer that I fall in love with. He was an extraordinary actor, with the kind of talent you could sense the moment you met him, and interestingly, had been a student of Bill Alfred's at Harvard. There were layers to this man that you knew he would be slow to give away and a kind of sexual chemistry that you knew would translate wonderfully on film. Tommy Lee took acting very seriously and he went at his role with a kind of ferocious energy that worked to deepen both his character and the tension of the movie.

Like *Network*, *Laura Mars* was an effort to blend entertainment with social commentary. It took aim at the advertising industry and the way images were being used to manipulate the public into relating to certain products. The scenes that Laura creates to sell clothes, perfumes, and furs are both highly erotic and violent. In the late seventies, the images seemed over the top, but if you look at them today, they are not unlike many of the shots that are now used in fashion ads.

Photographer Helmut Newton was originally recruited to create the huge photo montages that we needed as a backdrop for the film, but then Rebecca Blake, another well-known fashion photographer, was brought in. I spent weeks with Rebecca, studying the way she went about her work. She had a stunning style that blended the erotic with something that bordered on sadomasochism and fit precisely with the plot, in which the illusion of death Laura creates ultimately becomes reality.

I came to this project with a ready store of personal experiences about how magazine photographers work. I had logged in more than a few hours in front of the camera for the fashion spreads that began to feature me after *Bonnie and Clyde* and had continued through my career. Then too, two of the most significant relationships in my life were with top-notch still photographers, leaving me to pick up a great deal by sheer osmosis. I tried to fold all that experience into the role of Laura Mars, hoping to reach a level of understanding that went beyond the sophisticated urban professional woman, which was clearly becoming the archetypal character that Hollywood seemed to view as exclusively mine. Such typecasting recognizes a certain level of achievement at the same time it threatens to limit further growth.

Irvin Kershner was directing the film. He had begun his career as a still photographer and knew the world of Laura Mars inside and out. He clearly loved the subject of fashion photography he had been given in this film. It is always a good sign when the director has a very distinct point of view about a movie; it usually means there will be a steady hand guiding the project.

Irvin knew just how to use strong, visceral images to enhance the dilemma of the scene, and when to pull back on the visuals so that the quieter moments could be played out without competing against

Behind the camera for a change in Eyes of Laura Mars.

the intense backdrops used through most of the film. He was to become, over time, one of the directors the industry turns to with suspense-thrillers and action-adventures, handling duties for the second installment in the *Star Wars* trilogy, *The Empire Strikes Back*, in 1980, before going on to James Bond in *Never Say Never Again* and *Robocop 2*.

It was great filming in New York and it became a reunion of sorts for me. We spent a number of days shooting a scene in Columbus Circle. In the film, it is the backdrop I've chosen for a magazine spread that I am shooting. In the scene, I'm orchestrating a complex string of events, which include ordering around any number of very scantily clad models, as well as deciding the precise moment that two cars must be set ablaze. That was enough to ensure a crowd.

At one point Paddy Chayefsky stopped by for a while, and on another occasion Elia Kazan dropped by the location and we had a chance to catch up. There is something very comforting for me about being able to reconnect with those exceptional craftsmen with whom I have been lucky enough to work. It reminds me of my professional roots, and that some of the best aspects of this business can be found in the people you work with.

The climax of the Columbus Circle scene called for me to suddenly stop in the middle of directing the action, appear suddenly confused, and finally make my way away from everyone. What editing would later insert at that point was the flashback I was experiencing of yet another murder taking place. Ironically some of those passing by who had gathered to watch the scene being shot thought there was something wrong with me. For me, the price of being convincing in that scene was having to have my publicist field calls the next day from the tabloids that were tracking reports that I had gone into some sort of catatonic state and then wandered off.

Though the production of *Laura Mars* progressed with few problems, in personal terms the time was a very turbulent one for me. I was talking once again to Peter, who wanted us to give the marriage another shot. Terry was never far away either. On any given day, I was of two minds, being pulled in opposite directions emotionally.

It was a difficult time for Terry as well. He was torn between our growing romance and his wife and children. Over the next several months, he would leave and go back to them several times. And he found America difficult, desperately missing London, where he was based. It was everything you'd expect it to be when a man is leaving his family for another woman. But just when I would think we might not end up together, we would end up together. We would while away the time, with Terry, whose wit is one-part Irish, one-part Cockney, romancing me with funny stories over exquisite dinners. Terry could be clever and witty and absolutely charming. And every time I saw him, charming is exactly what he would be.

WHILE PETER AND I had very separate careers, Terry put aside his photography for a time to manage my career. After considering a number of projects, I finally decided to become involved with what was a very troubled production, the remake of *The Champ*, the story of a washed-up boxer, now working at a racetrack and raising his young son alone, who tries to make another go at the ring. Ryan O'Neal had originally been signed for the lead, but he pulled out when director Franco Zeffirelli passed over O'Neal's son, Griffin, for the role of T.J. in favor of a national sweep for an unknown young actor. It was Franco's first American film, and he was not about to be daunted, even though he did not have a leading man and filming was scheduled to begin in February.

There were serious talks with Robert Redford, but Redford wanted major changes in the script, which would push back filming, and on that Franco was not to be moved. On March 1, Franco still did not have a star, but he started shooting some of the race scenes and background footage. And he had found his young T.J., a newcomer named Ricky Schroeder. Franco would find a way to make this film.

Jon Voight was finally signed as the lead in late March. After reading some scenes with Ricky Schroeder, he said it would be a crime not to let the youngster have a chance at the role. I was signed a month later. Through all of the negotiations, Franco filmed. He would not be stopped.

My role as Annie, ex-wife and estranged mother, was very much a secondary one, with not very many scenes. Once again I was looking for smaller roles, because I was so busy trying to get my private life in order. And the film offered a chance to play the role of a mother, which was emotionally where I wanted to be in my life.

•

I ABSOLUTELY ADORED Franco. He was wonderful to work with. Around him you felt almost a sense of opera, there was so much emotion and drama to everything he did. There was also a kind of passion he brought to his work that never flagged, no matter how long the day. And he was another director who loved actors and took time to try to understand them.

At the time, I was on an emotional roller coaster with Terry. As difficult as it was for him, I was full of guilt and anguish at the idea that he was leaving his wife and two children. He had a daughter who was the same age that I had been when my father left. Neither of us knew what was the best thing to do. Franco was a real friend to me, very loving. He'd tell me to come over to his house, and on weekends he would gather up those of us at loose ends and have us spend Sundays with him. He was someone who sensed the emotional upheaval I was living through, and was there for me, as steady as a rock, without ever prying.

There are those few people who have come along in my life at very troubled times who for a brief moment have extended their friendship in simple ways that truly touched me and that I will never forget. That sensitivity to the human condition is something that Franco brought with him to work every day. He was someone I felt I could trust with my emotions, and let them work freely through the character, which I did.

Franco and I had another shared passion beyond the making of movies. Before he became a filmmaker, he had gotten his degree in architecture from the University of Florence. It was common ground that we both took delight in sharing. But Franco had other ideas in mind when it came to this other love of his. When a film premieres, the ticket sales nearly always benefit a charity. Franco's choice, I think, was one of the most unique.

The benefit premiere for *The Champ* was held in Palm Springs in the spring of 1979, with the proceeds going to help fund the building of a parish church in the nearby town of La Quinta. Franco was not only going to serve as part benefactor, but also as the architect. He based his design on the thirteenth-century chapel in the Convent of St. Damian San Damiano in Assisi, Italy, where St. Francis first took his vow of poverty. Though Franco's is a country filled with beautiful churches, he had a special affection for this particular one, having used it in his film about St. Francis, *Brother Sun, Sister Moon*. Whatever the success of his films in the States, the church would be a lasting gift he could leave people in this country.

I had long been interested in Catholicism, and Franco's passion about building this church rekindled it. Bill Alfred, my mentor and a deeply spiritual man, is also Catholic, and we have talked off and on through the years about spirituality and the nature of religion in one's life. All that had been brought into sharp focus for me in 1977, when Bill had a heart attack. After pacing the hospital corridors for hours, talking to every doctor I could, contacting specialists to make sure they did not allow this good man to die, I realized how little control we truly do have over our destiny. It's not that it was a sudden revelation, but Bill's brush with death reminded me of the fragile nature of life.

In the days I spent at his hospital bedside, life seemed more dear, and God much closer. I began seriously studying Catholicism in the hopes that I could find some measure of peace in my life. The good things in my life that have come to me seemed more often than not to be inextricably bound up with Catholicism. I've always felt the Church calling me and still do. And too, if Terry, who was Catholic, and I should marry, I had visions of a wedding in the chapel of St. Patrick's Cathedral, though deep down I knew it was probably not a realistic dream.

My feelings about the spiritual side of life were often conflicted and unsure. Stormy times, it seems, always brought me to a point of picking up the thread of my conversations with Bill. Usually I left those talks intent on looking more closely at spirituality and the nature of religion in my own life. I knew from watching Bill that it was his anchor, and there were times when I wanted very much to find such an anchor for my own. It would take a few more storms, however, before I would begin to take a serious look at developing a real place for it in my life.

NINETEEN

NO MORE WIRE HANGERS!" Those words remain, even now, an ugly wound on my psyche. But on this day, it's Terry, not me, who's screaming them. Terry O'Neill, my manager, the father of my son, and soon to be my husband, has jumped from his chair and is about two inches from director Frank Perry's face. I've no energy left and have collapsed in a heap on the floor of the closet that has been built on Paramount's Stage 8.

Though the take is over, the tears are still streaming from my eyes, making strange, surreal rivers in the mounds of cold cream that have been smeared on my face. The muscles in my cheeks and around my mouth ache from the contortions I use to transform my own face into that of legendary film star Joan Crawford. But the tears are no act. This character sears my soul. The role is more painful than any I have ever taken on, and it is slowly wearing me down.

Terry, who is one of the film's executive producers, came over to talk to me. "You can't do it anymore, you're being pushed too far," he told me. No one else had stopped it, or shaped it, or done anything to modulate the scene. It was camp that had gone way over the edge, from the white face, to the screaming rage of Crawford, to the child that I must hit with wire hangers. Everything about this production was out of kilter, off-center, and somehow I could never find my way back to some sort of middle ground.

I'll go all the way with something, because that's how I work, that's the nature of the profession. Jack Nicholson always called me a "gossamer grenade," because I would never hang back. He said he knew he could count on me to expose myself down to the core. But if you do that, fling yourself into it, you need a director shaping the performance. You're in the middle of it and you have to trust that someone will keep the entire film in sight, that someone will keep the proportion of it in line. That didn't happen on *Mommie Dearest*. Normally I'm a big girl and I don't need for anybody to take care of me. But somehow it just got the better of me this time. My self-protecting radar was somehow failing me. I just got lost, as Peter said in his song. I didn't have anybody except Terry to help protect me, and it just overpowered me.

There is every attempt at art, and I love the life of an actor in terms of striving for some kind of beauty. But the underbelly of this business will kill you as soon as look at you. It killed Judy Garland, make no mistake. She was a dead woman the minute she started taking uppers and downers and put herself under the control of the moguls. This is an ofttimes immoral world that we work in. And in this movie, I lost myself for a while. They were stronger than I was. I don't think there's any wonder that I fled this country after that movie. That I yearned for, went looking for, and found during the eighties a softer, gentler, more human world. I fell into trouble here.

The film, which was being shot in early 1981, was based on the book by Christina Crawford, Joan's adopted daughter. It went into development soon after the book was published in 1978, nearly three years before I became involved. The Crawford that Christina portrayed in her book was an obsessive and abusive mother, powered by an endless wellspring of rage. The book follows in detail the almost daily psychological and physical torment of Crawford's children, adopted after she suffered a series of miscarriages.

Anne Bancroft had initially been approached for the role, but pulled out because no one could come up with a script that she liked. There were rumors on the street—which I heard in later years—that she had decided against the role because the general sentiment in the industry was that anyone who played Christina's version of Crawford would pay a price for taking on one of Hollywood's great legends. I don't know which of the reasons was the real one, though I suspect it was a blend of both.

What is a sure testament to the difficulty of the project is that by the time the screenplay reached me, four people were credited with the writing of it; one of them was the producer Frank Yablans, director

Frank Perry was another. Christina, who had written an early draft, was off the credits entirely but still involved with the production, which did not bode well for harmony.

All of these behind-the-scenes intrigues over the making of *Mommie Dearest* never made their way to the house in Connecticut that Terry and I had retreated to in 1978. For nearly three years, I had been virtually out of sight. Not since *Eyes of Laura Mars* had I accepted the offer of a leading role. We read the script, carefully considered it, and had long conversations with Frank Yablans and Frank Perry, who assured both me and Terry that they wanted to tell the whole story. Expanding the book's scope, they wanted to create a story of what it was like to be a star in Hollywood, and to have been someone like Joan Crawford. They wanted to show her side of it, and make it a much more balanced story. And based on those assurances from Yablans and Perry, I accepted the role.

The script was structured in a way that meant I would be in almost every scene. The acting demands were extraordinary, and it was clearly a role that would force me to test and stretch my talent once again. It would be far more intense than the films I had occupied myself with since *Laura Mars*, which had for the most part paid me top dollar for supporting roles and left me time for the other interests in my life.

AFTER FILMING ON *The Champ* wrapped in the summer of 1978, Terry and I bought a Mediterranean-style white stucco house just outside Stamford on Long Island Sound and began to remodel it into our dream house. It was on three acres, with enough shoreline of our own to fit a football field or two. There was a tennis court and a swimming pool, and we built an eighteenth-century-style kitchen with two fireplaces and a beamed ceiling. It seemed the perfect place to raise a family.

We were still both in the process of trying to complete separate divorce proceedings, which was proving exceedingly painful. And we wanted to finish the house before we started our family. Though I was still benefiting from the afterglow of the Oscar for *Network* and there were any number of offers coming my way, I passed on most of them, unwilling to put off having a baby any longer.

During the summer of 1979 we opened a small boutique and

gallery in the Los Angeles area, on Santa Monica's Main Street. It was called Dunaway/O'Neill and it expressed our love for art, original fashion, and antiques. The only clothes we carried were those of a young Japanese designer, Yoshie, whose style had captivated me during a trip Terry and I had made to Japan. All the paintings we displayed were by women artists, and then we threw in a selection of French country antiques, simply because we loved them.

In early 1980, I finally accepted a small part in *The First Deadly Sin*, which was set to film in New York and star Frank Sinatra. The movie was the first Frank had done in nearly a decade, and I wanted this opportunity to work with him. And the role was undemanding, to say the least.

I played Frank's dying wife. The script required that I spend two weeks lying in a hospital bed, getting progressively weaker and paler. Never once was I out of the bed. I don't even recall ever sitting up.

As I had on so many projects, I called Bill Alfred. We worked on some nice touches, I thought, though like everything else about this role, my dialogue was very limited. I did manage to get in a mention of my Christmas tree fantasy, a great green pine covered with single strands of icicles. Frank plays a police detective trying to deal with the fact that I'm dying while he tracks a killer and gets ready for retirement. I just get weaker, most of the time drifting off to sleep while he reads to me from a favorite children's book of ours, *Honey Bunch*.

Frank was great. He had a chivalry to him and he still does, I daresay. Mickey Rourke had it too. They were both very kind with me, very debonair. Terry was there on the set the whole time, worried about how it would go, whether Frank was really serious about coming back for this movie. I wasn't on the set except for our scenes, but in those Frank treated me with real respect. It was a terrific two weeks.

One night Frank took us with him to a casino in Atlantic City, where he was truly in his element. We stayed up all night talking to Frank about his life, about what it was like in Hollywood. He told us about Ava Gardner, about how people would just stop in their tracks when she passed and turn around and stare at her, she was just this truly *beautiful* woman. It was one of the most memorable evenings I've ever had—I loved talking to this wonderful artist.

The First Deadly Sin had an interesting history of its own before

I joined the production. It was another project that had been years in coming to the screen. At one point Roman Polanski was going to write the screen adaptation of the best-selling Lawrence Sanders novel, and then direct it with Marlon Brando starring. But in 1977, the movie was put on hold when Roman left the country when legal problems surfaced after he was found to be involved with an underage girl.

Frank's interest quickly helped resurrect the project. After so many years with the project moving along sluggishly, once Frank was in, everything else happened with amazing speed. The movie began casting in January, finished shooting in March, and was released in October. There were high hopes for the film going in, but it turned out not to be the kind of blockbuster return to the big screen for Sinatra the producers had hoped it would be.

As of this writing, however, *First Deadly Sin* remains Frank's last leading role. When I look at the body of his work, and my own experience working with him, it's hard not to hope that there will be one more great role out there for Frank to play. But for me, it was a lovely little part, a chance to work with a legend, who became a friend, and two weeks of work that I thoroughly enjoyed.

AFTER THAT WRAPPED, Terry and I returned once again to the Connecticut house, this time to get ready for the baby. I was supposed to attend the Academy Awards that spring as a presenter, but decided against it. Instead I stayed home and finally got the role I had been wanting for years. Liam Walker Dunaway O'Neill, who made his arrival that summer, was a strong, beautiful baby, with a lusty cry and a ravenous appetite.

Liam was the sweetest, most adorable baby imaginable. He had beautiful blue eyes, wisps of blond hair, and the sweetest disposition I'd ever seen. I remember it from his earliest moments. It's who he is. Since his birth, my life has never been the same. I love that boy with my life. As Bob Coles once said to me, children give you another chance. In my life, Liam certainly has. There is magic in him, and an incredible joy for me in watching him grow. Though having been a parent now for fifteen years, I know it is not always a bed of roses. We have had our difficult moments. But Liam has taught me more about life and love and laughter than anyone.

I used to call Liam my little Charlie Laughton, because he had

My little Charlie Laughton. Terry O'Neill

these great wobbly little cheeks, like the actor. As he's grown up, I've tried to guard against his disillusionment. It has made me happy that even far into his childhood Liam was able to trust, and still trusts in the fundamental goodness of others. Even now as a teenager, when boys are finding their way into manhood and there is pressure to be tough, Liam still feels it deeply if anyone is ever hurt. Looking at him as he has moved from babyhood through childhood and now into young manhood, it heartens me so to find this boy of mine has become such a good, moral young man, taking on the responsibilities that come with age with a great deal of strength, courage, and grace.

Liam's life has been one of both privilege and pain. I know my divorce brought him pain, pain that I know firsthand from my own life. But I also remember that the time leading up to what I knew would be the inevitable divorce was even more painful than the actual

Made up as Eva Perón for the miniseries Evita.

divorce. And I knew that to "stay together for the children" was a big mistake that my parents had made for a while. Had Terry and I stayed together, when the marriage was really over, I think it would have been worse for Liam. I'd like to give him a Utopia where everything is perfect, but I can't. And I won't. I'll fail in many ways as a parent, but hopefully succeed in many ways as well. I try to teach him what is right and what is wrong. I want him never to forget that with privilege goes service, something that can be learned from the Kennedys. I always remembered what Jacqueline Kennedy Onassis said—if you don't do a good job raising your children it doesn't very much matter what else you do. I look at Liam and I see the heart of a champion and a decent person—a son that I am so very proud of.

From the outset, I wanted to keep Liam out of the spotlight, to protect the privacy of this tiny new being in my life. And I had no intention of ever being separated from him when I decided to go back to work. I was feeling quite energized when I was approached about starring as Evita in a miniseries based on the life of Evita Perón. They offered to pay me a small fortune, so I decided to take the role, which costarred James Farentino as Juan Perón, the infamous South American dictator. Liam was not quite six months old and he was such a good baby. So with Terry, Liam, a crib, diapers, bottles, and a nanny in tow, we set out for Mexico to shoot the miniseries.

The time was split between locations in Guadalajara and Mexico City, and the shooting schedule for the four-hour show was just over a month. By the time we got back to the States, I had lost a lot of weight. Trying to give the character all the passion, energy, and fire of the real Evita, and still spending every spare moment with Liam and Terry, had burned off more calories than I realized. But it worked well for the costumes, some sixty in all. And Harry Winston lent us hundreds of thousands of dollars' worth of jewelry to use, which meant there was a guard who was never far from me to ensure their safekeeping on the set.

WE HAD NOT been back long when the *Mommie Dearest* script was sent to me. I was full of hope at the beginning of the project, having long been a fan of Crawford's work, from *Grand Hotel* and *The Last of Mrs. Cheyney* to *Mildred Pierce*, which I loved both for her performance and for proving to Louis B. Mayer that her career was not over. Though we had never met, she had been kind to me in her autobiography, *My Way of Life*. In looking to those of us who were coming up through the ranks behind her, she said "of all the actresses, to me, only Faye Dunaway has the talent and the class and the courage it takes to make a real star."

I read everything I could about Joan and found a more complex woman than what I saw in the pages of Christina's book. Joan was this little pony on the chorus line, who would stand on the soundstages of Hollywood and hear the lonely sound of the winds that swept across the Texas plains of her childhood. Those winds haunted her, and she would cover her ears with her hands to try to escape the sound. I went and walked through the house in Brentwood she had lived in once she had achieved stardom. I certainly had a sense of the price of her stardom, though I had missed the contract studio era, which seemed even more brutal than the Hollywood I had to deal with.

Crawford had so little growing up and wanted to give everything to this child of hers. Up to this point, Crawford was not unlike most mothers. I think most of us come to be parents wanting more for our children. But after she adopted Christina, something went terribly wrong in Crawford's life. Christina was this cool little girl who didn't love her in the way she thought a child would love her, and she couldn't handle it.

Bill Alfred was working with me on the script and had written some really charming scenes between Crawford and Clark Gable, as the two Franks had promised we could. We were trying to get to the truth of the story, and not let the script dissolve into a tabloid version of Joan Crawford's life. As we worked on the script, Bill said, "Only God will ever know what happened there . . . the inevitable tragedy of a child of plenty and a child of want." The child of want being Crawford—the pony on the chorus line and the very poor girl—and the child of plenty being Christina.

I never once spoke to Christina. Though I had hoped, and had been promised repeatedly, that we would tell the real story of Joan Crawford, believe me, the film was Christina's book. It was a war from the beginning. Christina's husband was the other executive producer, so he was there pushing her point of view, and Terry was there trying to protect mine. And Joan's.

IT TOOK ME a few days to find Crawford once we began filming. I put her picture next to the makeup mirror. Lee Harman was still doing my makeup, and worked at getting the right look. I didn't want anyone to see it until I had it. Finally I realized that it was more than makeup, it was the way that she held herself and her face. It was truly a mask. I finally got it right and opened the trailer door and walked out.

The set fell absolutely silent. Some of the people there had worked with Joan, and they were the first to speak. The place I had gotten to with the look absolutely chilled them. One told me it was like seeing Joan herself come back from the dead. It was as if we moved through our days with the memory of the dead always with us. There were few light moments, none of the pranks and good humor that usually find their way onto the sets where even the darkest stories are being told. At the end even the wrap party was canceled. There was relief that it was finally over, but no one felt much like celebrating.

There were logistical problems that surfaced very early on too. In one case, a key scene designed to show Crawford trying to connect with the young Christina was scheduled for the second day of shooting. They are on the beach, and they've built a campfire. Joan is trying to explain to her daughter who she is and see if they can't get beyond the things that are so painfully dividing them.

I looked at the schedule and asked both Perry and Yablans if they were completely crazy. There was no way any of us could be where we needed to be with the characters to pull off an emotional scene like that on the second day of shooting. But shoot it they did. Ultimately, the scene was cut. It was a crucial scene, one that spoke to the truth of her life. That they cared so little about that scene should have signaled to me the rough waters ahead.

At one point the tone of the talks about the direction the film was taking got extremely nasty. Terry had gone to Yablans' office to discuss it and later told me he was hit with a stream of the most foul, crude, and abusive language imaginable. Nothing but four-letter words. Terry listened for a moment, then decided he had had enough. He stood up and started out the door. "Let's take this out to the gutter," he said, "because that's where this conversation belongs."

WE DIDN'T HAVE too many days on the set before I realized that the nicer, quieter moments that Bill and I had worked on were not likely to make their way to the screen. Though Christina's book was obviously an exploitation book, the first one done of its kind, my task was to portray a woman, a full woman, who she was in all her facets, not just the one.

What forces had created this woman? Christina struck me as being this blond, cool, remote little girl. And I'm sure that could have driven a woman like Joan, who was so needy, and so in need of approval and love, right around the bend. She gave everything to this little girl, wonderful Christmases, wonderful parties, and judging by my research, a great deal of love. And then to be so rebuffed and so coolly treated by this little Scandinavian girl. It was understandable to me that Joan did have areas that could erupt into anger and fury.

Just as I did with Diana Christensen in Network, I tried to illuminate who this woman was. But it was more than just about being angry, it was about trying to examine and explore the forces that undermined her. There were deadly and dangerous rifts in Crawford's mind that ultimately created her violent behavior. She was forever fighting her own demons. That she drank only made it worse. Everything became magnified by the alcohol, and the affronts she felt from Christina bit ever more deeply into her psyche.

A week into production the role really began troubling me. It is difficult to spend the day inside a character that is so dark, and not easy to shed the emotions, like the costumes and makeup, at the end of the day. At night I would go home to the house we had rented in Beverly Hills, and feel Crawford in the room with me, this tragic, haunted soul just hanging around.

Crawford's was a chilly presence, a coming-in-and-sitting-on-the-window-ledge sort of thing, as I would be working at my desk. I had felt my other characters—they became real entities—but it was as if Crawford wouldn't leave me alone. Playwrights say a similar thing. Bill says that the character starts to speak and when it does, it has finally taken life. And they tell you what to say, they tell you what to do, these characters. It becomes a very strange communion between the two of you.

This is what happened with Crawford and me. I remember her being around, but in a very eerie sort of way. It was as if she couldn't rest. Acting becomes centered on the way you and the character meld. I can only be an artist choosing materials, and yet I am the character, because I'm the only one playing it. In a funny way, I am that character's best friend, because I have the body and the mind to protect the character. They become like living people, forces. Crawford was most definitely a palpable force.

The days were always long. It was an elaborate production. I wore fifteen different wigs, and there were more than fifty costume changes. Most mornings I had to be at my trailer by dawn to begin makeup. We did some location shooting at a palatial estate near Sunset Boulevard, but most of our days were spent on two soundstages on the Paramount lot. The huge, marbled front entryway of her estate, the grand staircase and living room, occupied most of Stage 16. The rest of the interiors were carved up in sections on Stage 8.

One of the most difficult scenes for me was a terrible confrontation between Joan and Christina. At the time, Christina is only about five or six and has been caught by her mother playing in front of the makeup mirror. Joan goes into a rage and shears off most of Christina's hair. It was an awful scene, and a very physical one for both me and especially Mara Hobel, who played Christina as a child, and has to struggle against me.

I spoke to Bill the night before we shot the scene. And I thought long and hard, and I worked hard to find a way to understand the extremity of Joan's anger with the child. What I finally realized was that what Christina was doing was mocking Joan—as children do—making fun of her mother, deriding her. By this point in her life, Crawford was emotionally unbalanced and drinking heavily. Seeing herself mocked like that, she snapped in a horrendous way. When we finally shot it, this scene was like too many scenes in the movie, violent and chilling, with no boundaries and no modulation. I felt so bad about Mara even having to do it, I brought her a watch the next day as a present for being such a good sport.

When we were filming the infamous "wire hangers" scene, my voice became so raw from screaming, I couldn't talk. I didn't know whether it was laryngitis or if I had injured my vocal cords. Frank Sinatra was such a love during that time. I called him to get the name of his throat specialist. Not only did he give me that, but he drove in from Palm Springs the next day to spend some time teaching me all the little tricks he used to save his vocal chords. I got my voice back, but never my enthusiasm. I never compromised the acting in playing Joan, but I think the film did ultimately compromise my career.

Frank Sinatra and *Evita Perón* were just about the only things that helped boost my spirits as the production moved on. The miniseries aired in late February and drew a sizable audience. But television is such a transitory medium, it would be Joan, not Evita, that I would be remembered for in 1981.

WITHOUT QUESTION, *Mommie Dearest* was a turning point in my career. The performance I gave as Crawford is one that I'm really proud of. Vincent Canby, writing in *The New York Times*, understood: "*Mommie Dearest* doesn't work very well, but the ferocious intensity of Faye Dunaway's impersonation does," he wrote, "as does the film's point of view, which succeeds in making Joan Crawford into a woman far more complicated, far more self-aware and more profoundly disturbed than the mother remembered in Christina Crawford's book." I was gratified and happy that at least one reviewer saw what I was trying to do. But his voice got lost in the maelstrom.

The studio quickly latched onto the camp side of the movie that audiences were responding to. I picked up the paper one day to find an ad that read: "No wire hangers . . . Ever! *Mommie Dearest*. The biggest mother of them all." That the movie could be reduced to that, stripped of any of the dignity I had tried to give it, was devastating.

Even Frank Yablans was outraged enough to file suit against Paramount, charging "the unauthorized ad is obscene, vulgar, salacious and embodies a racial slur of the poorest taste." The ad was pulled, but the damage was done.

I know you live a life, and you act many roles. But after *Mommie Dearest*, my own personality and the memory of all my other roles got lost along the way in the mind of the public and in the mind of many in Hollywood. Pinter talks in *Old Times* about people being frozen in their smile. I found I was frozen, but in Joan Crawford's smile, not my own. It was a performance. That's all that it was. For better or worse, the roles we play become a part of our persona, and the actress and the woman are identified with that persona. People thought of me as being like her. And that was the unfortunate reality for me about this project.

ABOUT THAT TIME, I was approached about starring in a remake of *The Country Girl* to be aired on the cable channel Showtime, as part of its Broadway series. It was to be staged more like the original Clifford Odets play than a movie. I had loved the 1954 classic starring Grace Kelly and Bing Crosby. It was exactly the kind of part I was looking for, substance without glamour, a woman with strength and softness.

Dick Van Dyke was cast as the alcoholic actor desperate for a comeback, and I would play the long-suffering wife, a part which had won Kelly an Oscar. Ken Howard, big and blond, played the director, the man who holds Van Dyke's comeback in his hands. It was the role Bill Holden had played in the original.

I had long wanted to do *The Country Girl*. I had read the play many, many times. It was one of the books and plays that I would turn to when I would get up in the dead of night not able to sleep. I would read sections into my tape recorder, listen to the playback, and do it until I thought it sounded right, sounded true. I was anxious to get those words to work with, to finally try them out for real.

I came to adore Dick Van Dyke, who is without question one of the sweetest and funniest men in the world. Though it was a valiant effort on all our parts, and there were moments that I thought were good and true, the remake fell short of our hopes and certainly of the original. But doing it helped remind me that I do love this business of acting, something the Crawford movie had come close to making me forget.

I WAS SHOOTING *Country Girl* in November of 1981, when the producers and the director, Gerry Gutierrez, of Bill Alfred's play, *The Curse of an Aching Heart*, asked me about going back to Broadway. Bill wanted me to do it as well, I think, and I was interested in getting back on the stage and doing any work with him. But I wasn't ever sure I was right for this play. Originally it was about lanky teenagers, young kids traveling on the subways to go to work in Manhattan and Brooklyn. After I said I was interested, he then expanded the original core play, adding what happened much later in my character's life. So early on, I had to play her as a young teenaged woman, and then older, as we picked her story up at different stages of her life.

Unlike *Hogan's Goat*, *The Curse of an Aching Heart* was fundamentally a comedy, with a story that had a lightness to it, although it was still one of depth and soul-searching. Like *Hogan's*, it was set in the Irish community in Brooklyn where Bill was raised. The play examined five separate points in the life of Frances Walsh. The story begins when she is a girl of fourteen and follows her into her thirties, when she is a mother finally coming to terms with her past. Set in the forties and fifties, *Curse* was more of a contemporary work than *Hogan*, which was circa 1890.

Through the years, Bill has given me a great gift. There are few actors who have a chance to look into the window of a playwright's mind. But that is what Bill did for me. We would spend hours talking about how one word plays off another, how a moment emerges from that interplay, and then a scene, until, like a jigsaw puzzle, you have something that is whole. More than anyone else in my career, Bill taught me how to work. He taught me how to look at the lines, how to ask the questions.

From Bill, I learned what "seeding" meant. He showed me how foreshadowing prepares you for what ultimately happens. I had been there through draft after draft of *Curse*. I had witnessed its evolution through the years as he sculpted and resculpted its shape and form. I knew what this play meant to him.

The play opened in New York at the Little Theater in late January of 1982, and though I received decent notices for my performance, the play itself was not well reviewed. The production closed after twenty-two days. I always believed that my casting was a problem. It was a little bit too star-heavy with me in it. The play would have been better with just the simplest of women.

For many years now, Bill has been writing a play especially for me called *Nothing Doing*, based on the life of the actress Jeanne Eagels. When it's right, we will bring it to the stage.

AFTER THE PLAY closed, I was ready for some sort of change in direction. I wanted to find a different way to blend work and life. I had a baby that I wanted to spend more time with. Terry missed England terribly and wanted to live there.

I decided that for a while, it would be good for me to leave the States as well. Fame had begun to eat away at my soul. I needed to leave this country that kept grabbing at me. It seemed to me sometimes literally to be taking chunks of me and running off with them. I needed to somehow go to a place and repair, to begin to live life in a calmer, gentler, softer way. I just decided to stop the music, as Jimmy Durante used to say. It had become jangled, out of tune, and I needed to be in a fresh, clean place to find myself again. And these first few years of my son's life, I wanted to be with him.

Terry has always been a real Londoner, so London was our destination. I wanted to keep the Central Park West apartment, so there would always be a place for us to return to in New York. And there would be films to do in England. Several U.S. actors had found an expatriate life in London and surrounds to be a saving grace in their lives. The British director Michael Winner had already met with me in New York to talk over a possible project that would be shot outside London sometime in 1982. A move to Britain seemed promising.

The Connecticut house was sold, and the New York townhouse we had bought when Central Park West proved too small for a toddler, a nanny, a dog, a cat, and two adults was put on the market. We booked a flight for London to have a close look around. As the skyline of New York faded from sight, I looked forward to a softer, gentler time. And I found it. The hot tea, the coal fires, the infinite politeness of the English people.

There were times I would be in a taxicab putt-putting along Piccadilly and I would say to myself, "Why wouldn't I like this place?" There wasn't the edge. And that's what my soul and my heart, and my child and my husband and I, needed at that time.

TWENTY

"**F**AYSIE, WOULD YOU BE SO KIND . . .**"** Michael Winner, who is so very British and absolutely delights in his reputation as the rudest man in London, is just about to launch into what he is looking for in the scene. "Michael," I broke in, sotto voce, "you can't call me that." Michael Caine had called me "Fadun Away," Nicholson had dubbed me "Dread," but "Faysie"? I didn't think so.

"Well, darling, you see, no, you're quite wrong there," Michael went on. "I must call you Faysie, because then people will feel that you are human, and not just a great big American movie star, and that it is going to be easy to deal with you and talk to you. And then the crew will love you. So you have to be Faysie." And Faysie I was.

It was the summer of 1982 when Michael named me Faysie, which I came to love for its soft whimsy. We were shooting a scene on the lawn outside the home of the Marquess of Northhampton, one of the sixty or so locations in beautiful little towns around London that were used for the remake of *The Wicked Lady*. Michael's decision to shoot the film near London was ideal, since Terry and I were toying with the idea of buying a house in the city.

When Michael had first talked to me about the project, it was little more than an idea. There was no script, at least not one that Michael liked, and no funding. As a boy, he had slipped into the theater to see the 1945 version, which starred Margaret Lockwood and James Mason, and had fallen in love with the story. He envisioned the remake as a cross between *Tom Jones* and *Bonnie and Clyde* and wanted me for the lead.

Michael reworked the script and sent it to me with a note that if

I committed, Menahem Golan and Yoram Globas, the producing partners behind Cannon Pictures, would finance the film. Later, Terry and I were in talks with them as well on a project we hoped to develop, *Duet for One*, that would mark Terry's directing debut. I read Michael's take on *The Wicked Lady* and though I was not entirely happy with the script, signed on to do it believing there was enough there that we could make it better. I did regret having to pass on playing Regan, one of Lear's daughters, in a British television production of *King Lear* starring Sir Laurence Olivier, but there was no way to do both.

The part called for either me, or a double, to spend a lot of time on horseback. Much of the film follows the exploits of my character, Lady Barbara Shelton, an outrageous woman who decides she will find a way to compete in a man's world—though she doesn't exactly choose the high ground. Her main pleasures become her nightly forays into the countryside where, disguised as a man, she robs travelers, and her love affair with another rogue, Captain Jerry Jackson, who was played by Alan Bates.

I could ride, but not that well. But I took it on with my usual gusto and began working every day with a riding coach. I rode nonstop in all kinds of weather. On the weekends I sometimes rode all day long. I didn't want to turn any bits over to a stunt double that I didn't have to. As the film was set in the seventeenth century, I had to ride sidesaddle. By the time we began filming, I had become quite good, something of a horsewoman. Once production began, I would pull on my slicker and my Wellingtons—it rained cats and dogs the entire time we were there—and ride for at least an hour each day before we began shooting my scenes, so that I would never stop looking at ease.

Michael told me one of his favorite memories of that film was of looking out in a field one morning about 6 A.M. where we were to begin shooting a scene. Everyone was already drenched by a slow, steady rain. And there I am in the distance, atop my horse, a plastic bag over my head to keep the wig I'm wearing from getting damaged, smiling and waving him a good morning.

My favorite memory of Michael is of his extraordinary desserts. Michael adored lunch—actually I think he just adores life, and lunch happens to come in the midst of it. He had these great feasts when we would break. Our days were quite long and I needed that time to get out of costume for a bit; the clothing was elaborate and often corseted.

It was my long-standing habit to rest quietly during the lunch hour, so I rarely joined Michael and the others. But he would never forget me, and midway through the break there would come a knock at my trailer door, and someone bearing a hearty portion of whatever the dessert of the day happened to be. It was always rich and delicious, and the one indulgence I occasionally allowed myself during the production.

Sir John Gielgud, who had redefined the role of butler in *Arthur*, joined the cast, and was once again playing a butler, this time mine, which turns out to be a perilous assignment for him. He was absolutely delightful, very grand and a bit eccentric. The day we were to have our first scene together, I came to the set with butterflies in my stomach, intimidated at the idea of working with this man who remains one of the finest actors Britain has ever given us.

But I needn't have worried. He exudes such a sense of ease in what he does. There is a fluidity to his acting and the way he is able to move from one emotion to another. Sir John was asked one day how he played speeches that weren't very good. He raised his eyebrows and said, "I say them very quickly, with a slight smile." But more than anything else, he is just lovely and funny and great to be around. I'll never forget listening to Sir John and Denholm Elliott holding forth on the trash cans of London, which are different colors in various sections of town. Their esoteric philosophies on why a certain color did or did not fit the tone and texture of a certain section of the city was hysterical in its mock sobriety. I have to say that one of the first things I would take note of when Terry and I began house-hunting in London was the color of the trash cans.

Though I loved making *The Wicked Lady*, in the end it just didn't have the juice it needed to be a hit. It seemed to never quite decide whether to be a farce or a drama, and so it failed by being neither. There was a short burst of attention directed its way when it was about to be released in the U.K. One scene, in which I horsewhip the woman I discover has also been sleeping with Captain Jack, was substantially cut to deal with the censor's complaints, though Michael didn't change anything without putting up a very public fight. But the ruling that there could be "no blood or lash marks on bare, or near bare breasts" was finally upheld.

BY NOW, both Terry and I had our divorces, Liam was getting older, and we wanted to get married. We had tried very hard to work through annulment proceedings so that we could be married by a priest. When it began to look as if it was simply not going to happen, we decided to go forward with a civil ceremony, nothing elaborate—quiet obscurity was what we were seeking. A magistrate who was on the route from London to Northhampton was retained to handle the ceremony. All the arrangements were made, and on a clear summer day in July, on the way to the set, we stopped in and said our vows.

When we first made the move back to England, we rented a place in Belgravia and began seriously house-hunting. We finally settled on a really wonderful little place in Knightsbridge behind Harrods, the famous London department store. The house in Knightsbridge was a fixer, as we say in the States, and we spent a great deal of time and money in fixing it up. I was very much into eighteenth-century designs. I still am—Louis XV and Louis XVI are my favorites. Those are the kinds of pieces that we chose for this house.

I very much admired this hilariously eccentric southern decorator named Nancy Lancaster, who had lived and worked in London and created the famous design firm Colfax & Fowler there. She had done beautiful private rooms for herself over the firm, in an old, wonderfully proportioned Palladian building. My favorite room was her drawing room. She had painted brilliant "buttah yellow" varnished walls. I copied it in our Knightsbridge drawing room as an homage to her, and because I loved it.

The house really and truly was a fixer and there were various disasters that we lived through. The worst, without question, was when we discovered that many of the pipes were broken, and all of the plumbing had to be replaced. Now, I love fixing up houses, renovating them, taking everything back to the original detail. And I am always willing to accommodate a certain amount of the chaos that goes along with that. But with a toddler and no plumbing, we had to move out at least until the bathrooms were fixed. Every day, though, I went back to the house to supervise all the work. I'd work at my desk, monitor the progress of the workmen, and deal with the hundreds of mini-crises that always come with renovating a house.

Through this, Terry and I were spending much of our time and energy on adapting *Duet for One* for the screen. He would direct. I would act. We began meeting with Tom Kempinski, who had written the play, one that I dearly loved. It is the story of a concert violinist who begins a cycle of self-destruction after learning that she has multiple sclerosis. Terry was a brilliant photographer, visually one of the greatest talents I've ever worked with. We both wanted him to use this very considerable talent toward filmmaking. Hadn't Terry, so long ago, wanted to move from photography to film directing? Didn't it make sense? I was very anxious to work with Terry as a director and to see that expression of his talent.

It is often very difficult to have a creative collaboration with someone you are emotionally close to. When there are no lines between professional and personal, suddenly the professional can become very personal. What was a well-known path for me was still very new to him. Working on the script became a sort of extended agony for us. We would have a good working session, make some progress with the script, and as soon as the writers would leave, we would realize that the problems with the script were still there. It was one step forward, two steps back, day after day.

It was a difficult script that just never quite came together. Ultimately there were rewrites that both Terry and I found outrageous. In the end, we became exhausted with the stalemate we were having with the writers. If we could not make progress, I wanted to begin accepting some of the other roles that were being offered. Cannon finally passed the script along to another director, and it was ultimately made in 1986 with Julie Andrews. Although by then Terry and I had gone on to other projects, I still believe he would make a wonderful film director.

Though this was a difficult period for us, we did have a lot of wonderful moments as well. I remember there was an Easter vacation in Portugal that was wonderful. We took Liam and we rented a house on a golf course for two weeks. Liam loved the pool. He had taken to it like a little duck and was content to spend hours jumping in and letting me catch him there. The strain of working on *Duet for One* faded away, and we had so much fun simply spending time with each other. Terry could be very funny—it's one of the reasons I loved him—and those two weeks were filled with much laughter.

Some of my best memories of our time together are of our Easters. There is an English custom, which Terry always used to do, of putting a clue in one egg that tells where to look for the next one. Terry would never fail to come up with very clever, funny clues. One year, one of the clues led to the doghouse, but Liam didn't guess it. Finally

Terry crawled into the doghouse himself, and I looked on as Liam crawled in behind him. Suddenly two heads popped out, barking. When we were together, Terry was a wonderfully sweet father. And still is.

OVER THE NEXT several years, there were a series of projects I took on mainly because I was living in England and they were being produced either there or in Europe. There were a couple of miniseries, *Christopher Columbus* and *Ellis Island*, for which I won a Golden Globe Award. I did a remake of *Casanova* with Richard Chamberlain, again for television, and two Agatha Christie adaptations, *Thirteen at Dinner* for television and *Ordeal by Innocence*, which was released as a film in 1984.

Though the work was involving, I missed doing movies. The television scripts I was getting were thin. There is no comparison between those and a *Chinatown* script. *Chinatown, Network*—you look at those scripts and they are works of art. At its core, television remains advertising fare; you're selling advertising time. There are talented directors, actors, writers who start in TV. And many of us find our way back there. But the quality of the work too often is not very good, and it remains controlled by far too many people who don't understand how to use the medium to create art. On the other hand, that's what makes it exciting as well; in the right hands, the potential is always there.

One big studio film that did come to London to shoot was *Supergirl*. When I was approached about playing Selena, the evil sorceress, I was very intrigued. It was a chance to play a comedic villain in a superhero movie. I had loved what Gene Hackman had done with Lex Luthor in the movie *Superman*, creating this larger-than-life villain in a way that was very clever and smart. I thought Selena had the same possibilities.

The film was really just a send-up, a spoof, and I had a lot of fun with Selena. Brenda Vaccaro was my sidekick, Bianca, and we had some great moments in our attempt to take over the world from our base in a deserted amusement park. Unfortunately a movie's success depends on more than a few good scenes laced through a film, and *Supergirl* never fulfilled the financial hopes the producers had for it.

•

In England, I began analysis once again. I knew I wasn't as strong and as peaceful and happy as I might be. I had long wanted to do a proper, classic psychoanalysis, on the couch, the five-times-a-week variety, going back over my past. It was a process that intrigued me and I wanted to do it. I had a very troubled early life and had come through many years of the movie-star mill, which had taken great chunks out of me. The life I was living with Terry and Liam was wonderful in many ways, but there were areas I felt I needed to work on myself, to get to the root of some of these things that I was fearful of. Work through them, as they say, and come out in order to be a better artist as well.

I began to see a woman, who was not an M.D. but what is known as a lay analyst. I wanted to work with a woman because I felt many of my problems lay with women.

It was Melanie Klein country, the psychoanalyst who had done much to both expand and challenge Freudian thinking. I had been much impressed with the fact that Klein and her colleagues had successfully treated a schizophrenic without medication. And the roots of her work were tied to the relationships between mothers and their children, particularly mothers and daughters, growing out of her own experience at being raised by a domineering mother and a father who bowed to that will.

But in time, she turned out to be quite fragile. I had formed an alliance with a woman that I had an affinity to and in a way repeated my experience with my mother. Ultimately I came to believe she wasn't skilled enough as an analyst. She simply wasn't strong enough for me. And the analysis fell apart.

But perhaps if she had been stronger, I might not have found Herbert Rosenfeld. Not long after I stopped working with her, I began working with him. A close colleague of Klein's, he was very much an advocate of her school of thought. Rosenfeld was a brilliant analyst, and in many ways he helped put me back together again, after the pain of having the relationship with my previous analyst fall apart. I worked with him for a full year and made enormous progress, I thought, and I grew very fond of him as well.

Rosenfeld was an elegant, bony, Abe Lincoln kind of man who had fled Nazi Germany, as many of the Eastern European Jews had, bringing with them some of the most valuable thought ever to be encountered in the world of music, literature, and more. I remember listening to David Oistrakh and Nathan Milstein when I was working on my role as a violinist in *Duet for One*. When you heard them play Bach's Chaconne, you knew there was real genius at work. Rosenfeld was part of that wave of intellectual emigrés. He was one of the most wonderful, distinguished men I ever met. He was quite old when I began seeing him, and I knew that he was not well, but his death, which was quite sudden, just a few days before I was due to leave London for good deeply affected me.

I went to his house and sat in the room with him. It was so still there. I stayed with him a long, long time. As I sat there, in my own private vigil, his body just got smaller and smaller. The funeral was very sad and I left it feeling that I had lost a good and dear friend. I remember clipping his obituary from *The London Times* and noticing they had mentioned his work with the schizophrenic. I found it so interesting that he had managed that sort of profound change without pills. He was an extraordinary man and I am glad that I was able to know him, if only for a while.

FOR A PERIOD of time I looked to the great god psychoanalysis to give me all the answers on how to change my life. I have worked with some of the top doctors in the world, but I have come to believe in recent years that analysis is limited in what it can do. I've always felt that understanding what happened to you would create the impulse to change. But I've come to believe if you wait for the impulse, you'll be waiting a very long time indeed. Often there *isn't* an impulse to change. You just simply change, you take a contrary action to what you've always done. And in the doing, you change.

I did change with Rosenfeld, though. Something inside me shifted. We would talk about what was true and real and vital in my life right then and how that was linked to my past and my future. And we would discuss the forces that caused me such difficulty, and he would extract and somehow pull out the construct inside me, my psychological life that had been formed. At the end of my year with Rosenfeld, I felt more of a measure of peace in my life, and more in control of my own destiny—but I still wasn't home free.

Two things I came to know clearly—that my marriage with Terry wasn't working well, and that I wanted very much to return to the States. Though I had worked steadily in England, it felt as if I had disappeared completely. I was rapidly becoming invisible. I felt increasingly that my career was being limited to, and limited by, the projects that were being mounted there. Ironically, it would be Terry who would help connect me to a project that would represent my bridge back to the U.S.

He was assigned to take some photos of Mickey Rourke, and I went with him to meet Mickey. We met for dinner at the Chelsea Gardens in London. Over a table filled with great Chinese food, Mickey began telling me about a new film that he had just gotten involved in. There was a meaty role for me, if I was interested. Was I ever.

BUT BEFORE I left England, I wanted to do a play. There the theater is such a vital organ, more so than either film or television, and I couldn't imagine not finding a way to be a part of it. And whatever I give to the theater, it gives more to me. I have come offstage many times absolutely knocked out with what I discovered about my own feelings, because I've had to go into them so deeply to play the role. It is onstage that I feel my most intensely alive. It is in life that I am too fearful to be that alive for a lot of the time.

There is a lot of pain, as well as joy, that comes with the very act of living, especially if you do as I do now and take nothing to numb it. All your emotions and feelings are there under the surface, alive, just awaiting your call.

Harold Pinter, who lived in London's Regent's Park, and I began talking about doing a production of *Circe and Bravo*, a Donald Freed play that Pinter would direct. Ironically, though both of us were living in London, we happened to catch up with each other in Los Angeles, where he had gone to star with Liv Ullman in a production of his play *Old Times*, which I had done in L.A. a decade earlier. When he got back to London, we met again and decided to go forward with it. Pinter wanted to launch it in June of 1986 in a smaller theater, the 175-seat Hampstead, then move it to the West End for the rest of the summer.

Very often, what you do initially in a rehearsal period for a play is you sit around the table and you read the play for a couple, three, four days even. It's wonderful. You don't have to do anything, you just sit there and you read it, and you think, Well, what does that mean? And you'll all ask questions of each other. But when we walked in there was no table with Harold Pinter, no rehearsal hall for *Circe and*

Bravo. Instead there was this taped-out set. Just exactly the size and shape of the set we were going to use on *Circe*.

"Harold, where's the table where we get to sit around and hide and put our feet under . . . ?" I asked. And he just made this kind of wonderful Pinteresque gesture toward the taped-out space. What he said was, "Speak the play." His point was that with him it was all in the words of the play. He didn't want to talk about it. After I, or one of the other actors, would say a line, I can always remember him saying, "I didn't hear that." So it was always about the play. Of course, he's a playwright. But I felt that I learned something from him. It is in the words. Very often in all this endless investigation of why people do things, it can become a barrier to saying the words, doing the action— playing the play.

Though there were flaws in the play, *Circe and Bravo* was one that nevertheless took me to entirely new emotional vistas. For virtually the entire play, I was up there alone. It was basically a soliloquy by a woman who is imprisoned by a Secret Service agent. He is there, but he answers in monosyllables. Freed, who is an American playwright, had loosely based it on the life of Martha Mitchell, the outspoken wife of controversial Nixon attorney general John Mitchell.

My character, code-named Circe, is a former beauty queen who has become the First Lady. She is a bit of a loose cannon and the Administration has essentially exiled her to Camp David. There she is watched twenty-four hours a day by a Secret Service agent, code-named Bravo. She fears him, she seduces him—love and terror get hopelessly mingled.

It was a heavy play, the kind that takes everything from you. Night after night, I was up there for three long hours. The lightest moment of *Circe* came when it was still in its run at the Hampstead Theater, where we were for six weeks before moving to the West End for another ten. We were about halfway into the performance when a man got up from the audience, leaped onto the stage, and said, "I love you, Faye. I've come to take you back with me to Amsterdam." It was such a comically dramatic gesture, but there was enough of a crazed look in this guy's eyes that Stephen Jenn, who was playing Bravo, got me away from the man and off the stage while someone called the police.

While everyone waited for someone to remove this man—we couldn't tell whether he was dangerous or just a little off—he rummaged through the liquor cabinet that was part of the set, grabbed a bottle of whiskey, and poured himself a drink. All he got for his trouble was carbonated water, followed by a hearty round of boos as he was led off the stage. We had the play up and running again in ten minutes, though I admit I was a bit shaken by it all.

THE DYNAMIC driving the action of the play is that underneath it all, Circe is terrified that Bravo is eventually going to kill her. No matter how I tried to establish some human connection with him, he barely talks to me. Circe vacillates between paranoia and rejection. I had to get to places in my mind to make those lines work, to make those moments true. As always, I was looking at my own life for parallel emotions that I could use to fuel this character.

I call it another country. You just go to another country inside you. You walk around. Finally, you go deeply enough into this terrain that you uncover the wellspring, the mother lode. And there you have to mine to get to the deepest part of your own truth. When you get to it, you have to take whatever emotion is there back with you to make the moment onstage or on-screen clear and true. It's an odd profession that causes you to live constantly with things that most people have put to rest. You have to be willing to manipulate your own psyche. What can be said in its favor is that it is something of a catharsis. Many people don't ever deal with that terrain.

At the time, Terry and I had decided that it would be best if we divorced. There were too many things wrong with trying to live our lives together. As someone who had photographed celebrities for years, Terry had very ambivalent feelings about those in my profession—he had made them beautiful, but he had also been at their mercy. I did not have any ambivalence. I loved acting and wanted to return to it. As I looked at the movies I had done in England, there was really nothing of consequence. There had been no Evelyn Mulwrays or Bonnie Parkers for me to take on in England, and there were none in the offing.

The dearth of work in Britain in those years left me feeling very vulnerable. And I knew that though I worked to keep in shape physically, I could not stop time. I didn't feel it or look it, but I was in my forties, and in Hollywood, that's when they begin to start pushing you into the role of aging eccentric. I was not ready for that. And the truth is, I missed my country. I wanted very much to come home.

THAT YEAR, before everything broke apart, a producer came to me wanting help in putting on the British version of *This Is Your Life*, with Terry as the subject. Terry is an important man in England. He was already a distinguished photographer and now photographs the royal family almost exclusively. I wasn't sure whether he'd like doing the show, but we went ahead with it and it turned out to be the most amazing evening.

Terry is a man who connects with people in a very strong way. He has a great storehouse of very good and dear friends. That night, the place was filled with relatives and friends, many who had come over from Cork for the event. All of his children were there, Liam, Keegan, and Sarah. It was such a wonderful tribute to this incredible body of work he had already amassed, and I was so very proud of him.

Both of us were making some attempts at solving our problems, but nothing was working. I didn't want us to become enemies in the way my mother and father had. For all our difficulties, he was very dear to me, and as Liam's father had my fullest respect. And affection.

But the more time I spent sorting my emotions out, finding some sense of direction, which I was beginning to do with Rosenfeld, the further I was from Terry. I began to realize that we were headed down very different paths, looking for different things from life, a divergence that was only going to become more pronounced as I became emotionally stronger. I was beginning to see that this was a journey that I would need to make on my own.

As intent as I was on change, that did not mean our parting was easy. It was painful and difficult. Sometimes everything hurt. The press got wind of our impending divorce and Terry became quite alarmed. We were both so well known in England, it was bound to get picked up by the press. But you're never really prepared for it. It began to look as if our divorce and our difficulties were going to be splashed through the same London newspapers and magazines that so often sought his services.

We were both trying very hard to make this parting as civil as possible. At the center of it there was Liam, and we both cared very much about not hurting him any more than possible. And Terry and I still cared about each other. Above all, I knew that I didn't want my divorce to mean that Terry was lost as a father to Liam, as my father had been lost to me so many years ago.

One night I drove up to the stage door to get ready for that night's performance of *Circe and Bravo* and was unexpectedly faced with a pack of reporters, who were looking for any way to get to either of us about the split. Getting from the cab to the door was like running a gauntlet, with strobe lights flashing, and questions being hurled in my direction. By the time I was able to get inside and slam the door shut behind me, my heart was pounding out of control and I felt very near tears. The stage became a refuge of sorts for me during that time. It was the one place that I felt safe, at least from the photographers and reporters.

Despite that one bad brush with the press, the years in England had helped me recover from the battering I'd felt from the star machine. I was feeling much stronger, less fearful. And at the heart of it, I did want to go home.

I'm not British, nor French. As much time as I've spent in those countries, and as much as I love them, they are not mine. From the early days of my career, I wanted to be a great American actress. That's always been indigenously a part of who I am. I remember being in London and watching Wimbledon, which was lovely. But then I watched the U.S. Open, at night under the lights, and the glamour and edge and excitement of New York was all there. My heart jumped and I knew that I was, as always, in love with my country. In love with New York. In love with my profession. The gentleness and softness of England had healed me and had brought me a ways toward the best of myself. Now I wanted very much to come home to reclaim who I was, to reclaim my country.

Circe and Bravo finished its run and soon afterward, Liam and I headed back to New York. I was filled with hope—that I could reshape my life, that I could rebuild my career. I wanted a shot at another body of work. I knew it wouldn't be easy, but for the first time in a long time, I was looking forward to what tomorrow would bring.

TWENTY-ONE

MY HAIR IS LIMP and matted, the color of wet sand. Shadows hang like dark half-moons under my eyes. My clothes are stained and look slept in. A fine layer of grime leaves my face looking sallow. This stranger that I have become looks back at me from the mirror. If there were any life left in her, the eyes would no doubt mock me. As it is, they are dead, the remnants of a fire extinguished long ago.

When I walk onto the set, the director, Barbet Schroeder, smiles and tells me I look much too good. It takes a few more passes to get to the lower reaches of where I need to be for this character that has become so important to me. Wanda Wilcox, as I see her, is the one who will pull me out of the pit in which I've been trapped. This character in *Barfly*, who has given over her days and nights to a bottle, is my way back to the light. This is a role that I care deeply about. I haven't felt this passion for a character since *Network*. I saw the promise of a comeback for me in the deglamorized face of Wanda, a woman of sweet vulnerability.

It is early 1987, and I have fought like a wildcat to keep this project alive. After I met with Mickey Rourke, then Barbet, the financing began to fall apart. Menahem Golan and Yoram Globas, who are executive-producing *Barfly*, had run into financial difficulties that went far beyond this particular project. By 1987, they were in a desperate fight of their own to keep Cannon Pictures afloat. The sources they usually went to for funding had dried up.

One weekend I stayed on the phone for hours, talking to anyone who would listen, including the head of the French bank Crédit Lyonnais. The producers, Tom Luddy in San Francisco and Fred Roos in Los Angeles, and I conferred hourly. Tom and Fred, whom I adored and have been good friends with ever since, and I mounted a Three Musketeers campaign to get this movie to work. Yoram was in a different European city every time I talked to him that weekend. Menahem was working out of New York. I refused to stop pressing them. I had learned a lot about the business from my association with them during the years in London, and I had a fairly good sense of what they needed to make it happen.

These guys were like buccaneers, swaggering through Europe selling ideas, getting pre-sale commitments so their movies could be made. They were bold and aggressive, but the international movie market had tightened and financing had become tougher to come by. But with *Barfly*, they had a script with a great deal of quality to it, and a wonderful cast and crew attached to it. I knew this was a deal they would not lose money on, and that was my message to anyone I talked to all weekend long.

But by the end of the weekend, Golan and Globas had decided they weren't going to make the movie. Barbet told me they had set an onerous turnaround figure—the amount that would have to be paid to them by another person who would come in wanting to make the movie. What they claimed to have spent on the project, which they wanted to be reimbursed for, was such an impossibly high figure that Barbet became very upset. They would give the film back, but at a very high price, and at a price that we thought was inflated. The details were such that another suitor would be discouraged by this kind of price. It looked as if *Barfly* might be lost to us.

The film was as important to Barbet as it was to me. It was to be his first film made in the U.S., with American actors. And it was his project—he had initiated it, developed it, had been passionate about the work of Charles Bukowski, upon whose life *Barfly* was based, for many many years. So now, to be faced with losing his project without a decent turnaround, without the real possibility of setting it up some-where else, upset him enormously. Finally Barbet went to the office of one of the producers carrying a tiny Black & Decker chainsaw, small but real. "See this finger?" he said, holding up his pinky finger. "I don't need it, really." Then Barbet held up the saw, and flipped it on and off. "Every day I'm going to come here and cut off a piece of this finger," he said. "I will come day after day, until nothing is left or until you give me my deal. I will be here tomorrow."

I made the final offer for a deal that Cannon could not refuse before Barbet's finger suffered the slightest nick. I offered to work for no money up front, to forgo my salary in exchange for a deferment or a percentage of the profits. With that offer, Cannon found the money somewhere and gave Barbet his deal, and we went into production. Usually you celebrate when a movie production wraps; with *Barfly*, we celebrated the first day, a day that almost hadn't come.

By February 1987, when we went into production on the film in Los Angeles, Barbet had been working toward this end for nearly seven years. It had begun when he met Charles Bukowski, an American poet whom Barbet first filmed in a documentary, then convinced to write the semi-autobiographical screenplay for the movie.

Barbet's is a craggy sort of intelligence, like the great French filmmakers, though he is an amalgam of various international cultures from South America to Paris. He is not like Kazan, who understands intimately the actor's process so that if it short-circuits, he can jump in because he knows precisely the point at which it has gone off track. Barbet doesn't get involved in all of those details, very grown-up and French, he just envelopes you in this cloud of love.

There's always a sense of balance and purity to his work, but there is an incredible incisiveness as well. His films bear his personal signature—intelligence and sophistication. When you look at *Reversal of Fortune*, it is a beautiful film, the kind of filmmaking that we generally don't have here unless someone like Barbet imports it. And I knew he would infuse *Barfly* with all of his European sensibilities.

Once production began, everything seemed to be conspiring in our favor. Barbet was an absolute love and I adored Mickey. He prepares for a role for four months, if he can, and then tries to leave room for accidents. In other words, he leaves himself open for the completely unexpected. In one scene, he comes home with money, one of the rare occasions that we have any, and suddenly, without warning, tosses it all over me in bed. I was truly surprised, but it was just as much of a surprise to Mickey. He hadn't known he was going to do that. The freshness in our reaction to each other gave the moment a sense of real life.

My favorite scene is when we happen upon a small plot of corn, planted on a vacant city lot, and steal a few ears. I remember when I bit into the corn, it was still green, and instead of spitting it out, I put the kernels in my hand like a child might. Barbet's mouth fell open, and he said, "Ah! I didn't know you would do it like that." "What did you expect this character to do?" I asked him. "Spit it out and spew it all around the room?" "Yes." He laughed. "I think so." But she wouldn't have. That would have been vulgar and Wanda had such delicate sensibilities. It was a nice moment, because you see in that just how terribly lost she is. It was, I thought, as we wrapped that scene, so nice to come back and do a character so out of control, so real, so vulnerable.

When the reviews began coming out on the film, I was more than heartened. They were the best that had come in years, and Wanda was doing just what I had hoped. Pauline Kael writing in *The New Yorker* said that "Dunaway plays the self-destructive Wanda with a minimum of fuss . . . she wins your admiration by the simplicity of her effects." And Vincent Canby in *The New York Times* said of both my performance and Mickey's that they "rediscover the reserves of talent that, in recent years, have been hidden inside characters who wear designer wardrobes and sleep masks." What I didn't know at the time was that *Barfly* was only the first step down a long path that I would have to go to win back my place in Hollywood.

ON A FLIGHT back from the Montreal Film Festival, where *Barfly* was being shown, I met Warren Lieberfarb, president of Warner Bros. Home Video. He was in the midst of masterminding some deal, and I was enjoying some of the critical attention that *Barfly* was getting. We struck up a conversation when he introduced himself and told me he had loved me since *Network*. Warren was to become the next important man in my life.

For the most part, I have been drawn to men who were artistic by nature. Warren was in the top ranks of what I call the executive elite. I had usually not liked them very much. I remember when Ali Mac-Graw married producer Bob Evans, I secretly thought she was just selling out. How could you possibly have anything in common with these guys who ran studios if you were an artist? I thought at the time. They were the enemy, they took our money and they manipulated us.

But by 1987, I was very much interested in the business of the business. At this point in my life, I had begun to produce my own projects. Where I least expected it, I found in Warren a lot of common ground. He has a brilliant business mind and he was a great companion. We had a lot of fun, Warren and I, and were together for three years. We traveled, spent time in Paris and St.-Tropez, my beloved France. It was an exciting time for me. He was and remains very fond of my son, and though we have not been together for some five years now, he remains a true and valued friend of mine.

Through the years, I had learned much about how movie deals are financed and what a complex maze of transactions are often required to patch a deal together. With Warren I began to gain a deeper insight into all of the various ancillary deals that are possible, like home video. And he was a great sounding board as I waded into the process of producing my own projects, which I was to begin to do not long after we met.

Warren was a very sweet man—while also intense and crazy, like all those high rollers are a bit. He was on a plane more days than not. It seemed there was a major transaction to be put together or closed at every point around the globe that his plane touched down. The scope of what he was dealing with was much broader than what I had witnessed up close in the past. When you're involved in a movie, that becomes a fairly singular focus. But Warren would be juggling dozens of projects all at once. It truly was big business, a high-stakes game. And in his own way, Warren was very creative in the way he did it. He was a visionary in home video and technology, forever breaking new ground. He had single-handedly created Warner Home Video, with seven hundred handpicked men and women all over the world. He's a remarkable, formidable, fascinating man.

THE YEARS since I have been back from London have been among the best and the worst of my life. Though I had relied for so long on analysis as the foundation for self-examination and change, when I returned to the States I began to search for other ways to refashion my life. I knew that I wanted to make some very fundamental changes, from the way I was living my life to the way I was going at my career.

On the personal side, I began to alter everything about how I was living. I stopped smoking. I cut sugar, salt, and most grains from my diet and began eating chicken, fish, fruits, and vegetables. I am a devotee of Paul Newman's "Newman's Own" olive oil and vinegar salad dressing, but before I use it, I pour off most of the oil. The strongest thing I drink anymore is a Diet Coke, or cups of hot, Bill

Alfred Irish tea in the morning. Alcohol is no longer a part of my life. Now, too, instead of spurts of intense physical training, I have a steady regimen of exercise, using a combination of weights and the treadmill.

More profoundly, I began to examine the spiritual side of my life. This has been a longer and more difficult road for me to travel. But I have found friends along the way to walk alongside me, and what I have now is an informal and invaluable network of support, largely among people who are not in the entertainment industry. For years, I looked to the experts to help me with my problems. But within the group of friends that I have now, I have found ordinary people who help me to find ways of solving my problems myself.

Like life itself, the way I attack difficulties now is both simple and complex. I no longer spend so much time agonizing over what went wrong, but focus on my role in it and how I can change to make things right. It is as basic as the platitudes most of us are taught as children, that you must be accountable for your own life and your own actions. History, I am slowly beginning to discover, doesn't always have to repeat itself. People do change. I've changed.

Professionally, I went at reintroducing Hollywood to Faye Dunaway in a very pragmatic way. I came back from London at my softest and most vulnerable. I was determined to find or create, if that is what it took, roles that fed off that juicier, warmer woman that I felt I had become. I began meeting with top directors and studio executives. I talked with other actors. I wrote notes to executives that I hoped to be able to work with. To all of them I said essentially the same thing: *Mommie Dearest* had hurt my career. The hard, brittle persona of Joan Crawford had grafted itself onto me. But that was not who I was then, and certainly not who I was now.

James Brooks told me, "No, it was like a Kabuki performance, brilliant, very stylized." Debra Winger said, "Are you kidding? I watched *Mommie Dearest* eight times, just to study the acting." Ned Tannen, who was then head of Paramount Pictures, bless his soul, was the only person who said, "You're right."

What Jim and Debra and others have said to me about the performance, I'm at peace with too. I now recognize the performance for what it is, a good performance. A performance that, unfortunately, did not have the modulation of a good director. But my job is to go in there and act it to a fare-thee-well, which I did. At the same time I also know that the overall tone of a movie is never really in the hands of the actors; that rests with the director and the producers. On that movie, with the exception of Terry, I had no allies. But these conversations with my colleagues helped, and I was able to slowly begin to undo the damage that film had done.

AFTER BARFLY, which remains one of my favorite films, I tried to be careful about the roles I chose, and within each role, I would always look for the softer side. But I was also faced with the reality that I had to work. I had to support myself and a child, and I wanted to ensure Liam's future as well. It was a slow process. More often than not, I would still get scripts that were variations on the Crawford theme. And I was finding it difficult not to get into the same cycle that had been so hurtful professionally in England, taking on roles that I felt were compromised from the outset, but taking them on nonetheless because they were there. It was at times a terrible double-edged sword. And yet I knew that I had to keep working, to stay out there. That was the only way I could possibly get to the types of characters I wanted to play.

When I came back from England, I realized it was a different Hollywood that I returned to. The Hollywood I came back to had a modus operandi largely initiated by CAA—Creative Artists Agency, a powerful talent agency and the one that I had signed on with. The power structure there was of a very different sort. There was no room for backbiting and petty jealousies. And the same applied to the way the town did business now. Actors could no longer be late, or difficult. You were not forgiven that. People were polite, respectful. There was a real air of everyone working together, of being business people, colleagues. And I liked that.

In the CAA created by Michael Ovitz and Ron Meyer—who both recently left the agency to run entertainment conglomerates—agents were to function as a team. No turf battles were allowed. They didn't compete for clients, they weren't supposed to be envious of each other. In the Hollywood I had left, boy, everyone competed for everybody. There was a military briskness to the way business was being done now. So in that way the CAA achievement was considerable and really positive. Ultimately they handled many big people, and they handled me with a great deal of prestige. While I have great respect for Michael Ovitz and dear Ron Meyer, whom I worked with while I was still in

London, I did ultimately feel as if I answered to their own agenda rather than mine.

But overall, I found the climate in Hollywood in the nineties to be more reasonable. I had become more reasonable too. And there seemed more room for the reasonable, reasoning producer/actress. I started to see my life and my work as pieces of a whole. A friend of mine, Loretta Barrett, once told me the story of an old lady who was making a quilt. She said, "My life is kind of like a quilt. There's some khaki and some rayon, some satin and some silk. But when you sew it all together, it's beautiful."

There will be moments when you think, Oh my God, what a failure that was. Yet you know the failure will lead you to the next success. That's how life is. As I look back at my life, there's a lot of khaki there, but there's a lot of silk and satin too. And I know that my quilt is far from finished.

In late 1988, I struck out on my own to have a go at being a producer/actress. I began production on a movie for Ted Turner. He had only recently started his entertainment network, TNT, and was looking for original programming. The film I did for him was the adaptation of the Olive Ann Burns novel, *Cold Sassy Tree*, the story of a Yankee woman who finds love and a sense of herself in a small southern town just when she thought her life and her prospects were over. My brother, Mac, and sister-in-law, Brenda, had given me the novel to read two years earlier and I had bought the rights to it, determined to develop it on my own.

That in itself was a stroke of luck. Mitch Douglas, at ICM, was the agent handling the book. The day after I bid for it, and Mitch accepted, he got a call from Embassy Films, then later Oprah Winfrey became interested in it. I'm sure Mitch could have gotten more for it, but he stayed with me. And I've always been grateful to him.

The story was set at the turn of the century in Cold Sassy, Georgia, where one of the pillars of the town ups and marries a somewhat younger woman, just three weeks after his wife has passed away. I played the younger woman, Love Simpson, who is old enough that her chances at marriage are rapidly diminishing. Richard Widmark played my new husband, E. Rucker Blakeslee, and Neil Patrick Harris, who would go on to star in *Doogie Howser, M.D.*, played Rucker's grandson and the narrator of this tale.

With Richard Widmark in Cold Sassy Tree, *the first project that I produced and one of my favorite roles still.* Turner Pictures Worldwide and Turner Network Television

Cold Sassy was a perfect vehicle, a story very much in the tradition of *Fried Green Tomatoes.* Love Simpson was a feisty, warm woman with all of the softness and tenderness that I had uncovered in my life and was so anxious to weave into my characters. It was the first time in my career too that I had tried to take on any of the business aspects of putting a project together. I was the executive producer and earned every bit of that title during the two years I worked to get this project up and running, from scouting locations, to working with the writers, to convincing Scott Sassa, president of TNT, who has now gone on to head all of the Turner Entertainment Group, that he should get involved.

We found our Cold Sassy about seventy miles from Atlanta, in the tiny town of Concord. It looks barely changed from the early 1900s. About half the town folk ended up as extras in the movie before it was all over. The demands of producing were so different for me. I was not just responsible for Love Simpson, but for making sure that everything else clicked as well.

Don Ohlmeyer, who is now the president of NBC, was my wonderful co-executive producer. In the two years he's been at the network, he has managed it brilliantly, literally turning NBC around. With Cold Sassy, Don was not only instrumental in getting it made, but quite generous with his time, since I threw myself into this full force and wanted to know absolutely everything. Sassa and his team were great as well. In TNT, they have built a creative haven for so many of us in this business.

One of the things I loved most about doing Cold Sassy was the number of women who were involved. For them it became a labor of love as well. Karen Danaher-Dorr, whom I had worked with on Evita Perón and was now with Don's company, was my producer. She read the book and never looked back. She was tireless in seeing to the details. Joan Tewkesbury, who was ultimately to be both screenwriter and director, has such a gentle and elegant hand in everything she does, and this was no exception. I knew Joan from her days with Robert Altman. For him, she had written Nashville, an extraordinarily complex interweaving of the lives of twenty-four people in the country musical capital. I knew she had exactly the right sensibilities to translate the Olive Ann Burns tale. But it would pass through other hands first and be a while before she had a go at it.

As it seems so often happens in this industry, there were moments when it looked as if the project was going to unravel. I had an unsolicited script for Cold Sassy, but it wasn't very good. But because there was a Writers Guild strike on, the folks at Turner said, "Can't we just do it with this script?" There was only one answer. "No," I said, "we can't." They found a writer who was not in the union and who walked into our script meeting with Scott Sassa and what looked like a Bible in hand. She and Karen and I set out to see what we could do together. We brainstormed through an entire weekend and came away with a little bit more focus on the project, trying to shape the story into a rough script.

It was clear to me that the fate of the project was on the line. We either had to get a shooting script right away or abandon the project. "Leave it to me, Scott. By Monday you're going to have something that you can read," I promised. And so he did. The writer, Karen, and I set out to cut. I acted out scenes. I knew what the script should be—it was all in the book. We brainstormed through an entire weekend and came away with a lot more focus on the project and a script of a more reasonable length.

Finally we met with a director, and we got so much more. I interviewed Joan and knew we could work together. We just connected. She took what we had done and wrote a script that was just what I had wanted. She's really special, I think, someone with as much grace as talent and intellect, and I'd love to see her hit it bigger as a director than she has thus far. But she is very, very special. With Joan we got many of her colleagues, like cinematographer Michael Watkins. We really were like a family. Everybody just pitched in to make it work.

Richard Widmark was great too. Such a pro. He would go and walk the scene the day before we shot it so he knew everything he had to do and what his lines were, and exactly where he would be when he said them. What gave *Cold Sassy* its heart were the people who were involved. It was an incredible collaboration, and I treasure the experience as much as the result, of which I am extremely proud. The film also was a major success in business terms, delivering the highest rating that TNT had ever gotten for any of its movie projects.

NOT LONG AFTER *Cold Sassy* wrapped production, I was approached about taking on the role of the commander's wife in Margaret Atwood's feminist polemic, *The Handmaid's Tale*. The role would reunite me with Robert Duvall, who was to play the commander. And though it was a smaller role, I was intrigued at the idea of being part of this film. It was a remarkable novel, and in it Margaret Atwood had written with much insight about the plight of women and how little it had really changed. Though hers was a harsh view of how the future would define women's roles—and I hoped that it would not be so—I knew if it was done properly, *The Handmaid's Tale* had the potential of making an important social statement. Pinter was doing the screenplay, and I knew that our sensibilities were usually very much in sync.

I agreed to do it, but as I began working through the script, I began to have serious second thoughts. I called the director, Volker

Schlöndorff, who was one of the reasons I had decided to become involved in the film. The 1979 Academy Award–winner in the Best Foreign Film category had been *The Tin Drum*, Schlöndorff's brilliant look at a child's resistance to growing up. He was one of the people I had talked to early on about *Cold Sassy Tree*. While we were working on *The Handmaid's Tale*, he had been incredibly helpful to me on the project and gave me a number of great ideas, including casting Richard Widmark, who had once played a southern sheriff for Volker. I thought if anyone could tread the fine line and keep the extremes that Atwood envisioned from becoming a farce, Volker could. But I was worried.

Particularly troubling was the "sex" scene. In this world Atwood had created, there are wives, who are unable to bear children, and there are young women who are breeders, thus the handmaid reference. A viciously cold method has been devised to ensure that the husband and the handmaid do not enjoy their coupling. Instead, my handmaid, Offred, who was played by Natasha Richardson, is essentially sandwiched between Duvall and me on the bed. I did not see a way to do that scene without looking absolutely foolish.

I decided to drop out of the production. As much as I loved Volker and wanted to work with him, nothing he said changed my mind. Then Margaret Atwood called. This character, Serena Joy, had to be taken seriously or the whole premise of the story would begin to fall apart, she said. Margaret finally convinced me that in my hands, this woman would have the dignity she deserved. The character is someone who is extremely religious, not cold, who believes that all the humiliation she has to endure as a result of having a handmaid will ultimately ensure that there is a child who will fulfill her life.

In the end, Serena Joy, I think, did have a humanity to her. Volker and I added a number of scenes that would allow the audience to better understand that humanity. One I particularly like is set in the garden. I'm there on my knees, trowel in hand, working my flower beds. That scene said a lot about Serena's nurturing side, and the care she would take should she have a child to raise. But the movie was only marginally successful, and the character was still a distance from where I wanted to be.

I had the romantic leads in a number of smaller films, like *Wait Until Spring, Bandini* with Joe Mantegna, who is a really fine actor.

My participation in that film was in part a favor to Tom Luddy, one of the producers on *Barfly*, who had become a good friend. Tom had given me some very good names when I was casting *Cold Sassy*, too. *Bandini* had another attraction for me: it was the creation of writer Joe Fante, who had been a mentor to *Barfly*'s author, Bukowski. Sometimes there are so many concentric circles that bring you to a project.

I did *In a Moonlit Night*, a Lina Wertmuller film, primarily because I thought it would be interesting to work with Lina. The character, though, was just another corporate woman. *The Gamble* was a bit of a romp with Matthew Modine and Jennifer Beals. It was another period piece, one that included a sword-fighting scene for me. I took up fencing and karate, which was fun. But the best thing to come out of that movie was meeting Modine and his wife, Carrie. He is a fine actor, very like a Gary Cooper, and also has what Picasso called *La vrai élégance américain*. Nicholson had it with a twist, but Matthew has exactly what Picasso was talking about.

Scorchers, a story by David Beaird set in the hot Mississippi delta, was another film where the best part of the experience turned out to be the other actors there. We shot in Louisiana during a scorcher of a summer. I was the town whore, James Earl Jones was the bartender, and Denholm Elliott was the town drunk. I knew and loved Denholm from *The Wicked Lady* and it was great to work with him again. James Earl Jones was everything you would expect. He has so much integrity and dignity—an extraordinary talent, with a terrific sense of humor that comes like a bonus. It was such fun performing with him because he was so available as an actor, just turned on emotions full force.

Double Edge offered a role that I wanted to play. The character was an interesting *New York Times* reporter who has been sent to Jerusalem for three weeks to cover the Israeli-Palestinian conflict, just my cup of tea. It was written and directed by, and costarred, Amos Kollek, whose father, Teddy Kollek, was the mayor of Jerusalem for years until his death not long ago. Many of the scenes featured me interviewing the real leaders who were caught in this conflict, access to whom Amos was able to get through his father. I would write up a series of questions and do these largely unscripted interviews. I'm proudest of my work on those interviews, because through my own sources, I got the information, and through research with the English-speaking newspaper men and women in the area, I got the questions.

The New York Times bureau chief in Jerusalem helped me enormously.

I got an idea of the kinds of questions a newspaper person in that area would ask these leaders, and I put it all together, with dossiers on each one. I interviewed Abba Eban, and Rabbi Meir Kahane, who had been shot at a number of times and was assassinated shortly after the film was made. Palestinian spokeswoman Hanan Ashwari was another one I interviewed. And there again I did my homework on her. I wrote up questions that I wanted to ask that I had been advised would be the correct ones to ask for a newspaperman in the area.

I liked Amos. He's an interesting guy with a sort of an Israeli–Woody Allen quality to him, quite clever and funny and very shy. But the film didn't really work as well as I had hoped it would. What I took away were indelible experiences of talking to the people, who were so central to the process of war and peace in the Middle East.

ALL OF THESE were smaller movies, some eight in all, that never managed to draw the attention of a mass audience. I had been working steadily, but still seemed to remain largely invisible, when *The Temp* came along. This was a big studio movie, and with that comes at least the chance at a mainstream hit. What happened during the course of this movie, with its series of broken promises and scarred relationships, is unfortunately all too typical of this industry. We all have our Hollywood war stories; this is one of mine.

Initially, I was very excited about getting the part. Diane Ladd had been in the running for the role that I took on, but she dropped out in a dispute over billing. She wanted her name above the title, as well as more money. I didn't; what I wanted was a chance to begin reconnecting with a larger audience.

The Temp was designed as a thriller, with hopes to cash in on the success of *The Hand That Rocks the Cradle*, though instead of the nanny it was the secretary from hell. Timothy Hutton and Lara Flynn Boyle were the stars of the movie, with Oliver Platt, who is quite a wonderful actor, in a strong supporting role along with me. A murder triangle ultimately surfaces, revolving around my character, a hard-nosed businesswoman; Tim, a fast-track young executive; and Lara, the secretary who will literally kill for her boss. Tom Holland, an actor-turned-director whom I had known during my early years in New York, was directing.

We finished shooting in Portland, Oregon, in the spring of 1992, and I came back home to Beverly Hills, where I had moved in 1990 with Liam, a nanny, and our menagerie of animals. It had been an emotional move, since it had meant I would have to sell 300 Central Park West. But the business is in Hollywood, and I felt I needed to be here. The last day in New York, as I was walking through the totally empty apartment that had been my home for so many years, I was carrying a very large Rolodex that I had kept with me. That's all there was. Me, this Rolodex, and a completely empty space. I went into the bedroom. I turned back and saw something on the floor, a little white card. I picked it up, and out of a thousand cards from that Rolodex only one had fallen—Charles Gwathmey's. It was just like Charles, the architect who had helped me create this wonderful space all those years ago, to still have a grip on that apartment, with a card bearing his name to ensure he would be present at any auspicious moment in that space. And there it was, Charlie and me, as it was in the beginning, making this house, and now it was time to leave it. I thought they would have to take me kicking and screaming from 300 Central Park West. I had loved it for so many years. But it was time to leave. I had lived it up.

I have dreams of going back to New York, and I suppose my environment would be a little bit different—I think it would be more traditional. I always thought the apartment Jackie Onassis created on Fifth Avenue was lovely. When I go back to New York now I have a pied-à-terre, but sometimes I stay at the Carlyle. I think I might do a place more like Mrs. Onassis'. Maybe softer, more traditional.

But those years at Central Park West, it was a space that Gwathmey and I had created together with much passion. We fought over it. I remember once I wanted two speakers that happened to look exactly like brown car seats. And Charles hated them. But I soon talked him into it, and he covered the "car seats" in white raw silk and put a white frame around them and hung them from the wall, and I was happy and he was almost happy. To have created something with such passion—to me it was the ultimate irony that his card was on the floor. I picked it up and put it in my pocket. Loved him, as I always had. He is a great architect. And a great friend.

Months after I returned from Portland, Tom Holland called and wanted to have lunch. We met at the Columbia Bar & Grill in L.A., one of those places where every table is packed with someone making a deal. I should have sensed trouble, but I didn't until I was about halfway through my enormous salad, when he pulled out new script pages for *The Temp*. The movie wasn't working, he said, and they wanted to rework and reshoot another ending. The catch: I was going to be turned into the murderer.

Once again, I could see myself being thrown into playing the extreme—what was initially conceived as a character in the tradition of Diana in *Network* was being turned into a high-gloss female executive/ slasher. I wasn't going to do it. "I'm sorry," I said. "I'm leaving now. Thank you very much for lunch." I was determined to do whatever I could not to play that kind of extreme, angry, destructive woman again. My feelings had not been a secret to Tom or anyone else involved in this project.

For a long while, I refused to take calls, leaving it to my new agent, ICM's Ed Limato, to work things out. Ed is unique among the agents I've known for his brilliant business and script acumen and his genuine love for actors. Scenes were added to make my character more of a red herring, but in the end they agreed I would not be the murderer. I sent a long letter to Stanley Jaffe, then head of Paramount Pictures, the studio making the film, explaining why I had had a problem being a psychotic killer.

If they shot the pages as I had them, it seemed that I couldn't end up guilty, but I had been in the business long enough to know there were ways they could cut it so that I could become the killer after all. Nevertheless, I agreed to do the reshooting later in the year. That Thanksgiving, I seriously injured my back. Nothing seemed to help and the pain was such that it pushed me to the point of considering surgery. The studio was pressuring me to reshoot those scenes, and I was trying to buy some time until I could either find someone who could treat my injury without surgery, or get ready for a back operation. But it soon seemed that surgery was my only option.

The idea of such major surgery terrified me, and I kept looking for alternatives. Two days before I was scheduled to check into the hospital, I was feeling well enough to have dinner at The Ivy, a favorite dining spot of mine not far from my home. Warren Lieberfarb wanted to get me out of the house, knowing what I would be facing if I went through with the operation. We were, by this night, just good friends.

Someone involved in *The Temp* saw me there and began making calls to Tom, Stanley, and Sherry Lansing, now head of Motion Picture Production at Paramount Pictures. Overnight my voice mail was overloaded with messages to the effect that if I was well enough to have dinner, I was well enough to reshoot the movie. It was a truly horrible time. Sometimes Hollywood is just a small town.

I wasn't well enough to go back into production, but once again the phone calls were continuous. I don't like the feeling of being manipulated. It's like swimming with piranhas. On the other hand, I would never do anything to jeopardize this or any other project. I spent the next few days with a series of specialists trying to get my back stabilized enough to finish the shoot. The first day I returned, Stanley Jaffe stopped by my trailer. He was immaculately turned out, with an incredible shirt, an incredible tie, an incredible suit, definitely one of the executive elite. "Thanks for coming," he said.

One of the problems with this additional filming was that I was faced with very physical scenes, including one in which I fall from a catwalk that is high above a warehouse floor. Tom wanted to shoot it without a net underneath. I kept reminding him that I had a child, I didn't want to either die or end up a cripple from this. But he was going for a Hitchcockian effect, and he convinced me that was the only way he could get the shot. I knew that I would absolutely have to do it.

They rigged a harness, and a double pulley system to ensure I wouldn't fall even if one wire broke. I made the stuntman do it a couple of times first so I could watch him. Then I spent the next few hours falling off this catwalk high above the soundstage. I fell, I survived, Tom got the shot he wanted, and over time my back healed without surgery.

The new ending wasn't enough to salvage the film, though. By the final scene, it didn't matter who was the killer, the film had been dead for an hour at least. In the years since *The Temp*, I've talked to most of the key people involved in the project. One of the calls came from Sherry Lansing. We had talked about my character in *The Temp* when I initially took it on. I had modeled this female executive after her—kinder, softer, gentler. So I was glad that we were able to talk as friends once again. I have a great deal of respect for Sherry. Running a studio is an exceptionally difficult job for anyone. For a woman to handle the job with such intelligence and grace, as she has, in what is almost exclusively an all-boys club, is an amazing achievement. She's a formidable woman and very important to the business. But beyond that, I don't like to remain at odds with anyone, and we've mended fences on both sides.

TWENTY-TWO

THE FIRST TIME Jeff Sagansky remembers seeing me in person, I was coming down the staircase in Bill Alfred's home. Jeff was attending Harvard at the time, and he had come there for a tutorial with Bill, who has always opened his home to his students. Jeff is telling me this story over lunch at the Polo Lounge in 1992. He was by then long graduated and the current chief of prime-time programming at CBS. What struck him was that here was Faye Dunaway, standing at the top of Bill Alfred's stairs.

Bill's is a spiritual house and has always been a sanctuary for me from whatever battle has just gone on in my life. It's my refuge from the business. I used to tell him, making movies is like a war. I have no idea which particular war zone I had returned from then, but Jeff's story of our chance encounter did not surprise me.

After I moved to Los Angeles, I had dropped Jeff a note telling him that I liked what he was doing on the network, particularly Monday night with shows like *Murphy Brown*. I was interested in doing a character in the tradition of *I Love Lucy*, *The Mary Tyler Moore Show*, and *Murphy Brown*. These women were smart and the writing on the shows was clever.

The idea of taking on a comedy series was intriguing to me. It was a chance to stretch myself professionally, to shape a character that was both funny and human. Since these shows are generally filmed in front of a live audience, it would have something of the feel of the theater as well. Jeff liked the idea of my doing a show like that for CBS, and we left it that we would try to see what could be found.

The project that finally made its way to my door was a classic fish-out-of-water scenario called *It Had to Be You*. Laura Scofield is a book publisher, an extremely bright woman who is a cut above the rest, one of the best in the business at what she does. Mitch Quinn is a carpenter, a single father with three boys. Mitch and Laura meet, sparks fly, and suddenly she's trying to find her way in very new territory. It could have had a Tracy-Hepburn sort of spice, where opposites attract and the fun is in the friction. That is how I went into the show.

THE IDEA of having a series came at just the right time for me. There is no medium like network television, and no arena like series television—it puts you on stage in front of millions of viewers each week. A lot of this industry's most talented actors have come from TV, Steve McQueen for one. Many of the best writers start there, and directors, like Glenn Gordon Caron. So much talent gets trained and honed on television now. Sometimes, because it is also an advertising medium, compromises are made. But increasingly, that's not true. You not only get the top talent, but they are able to perform at the top of their ability as well. Cable has upped the ante—network TV has been pushed to higher quality.

The work schedule itself, I thought, was absolutely right for me at the time. It allowed me to stay in Los Angeles through the seven months of the year that the episodes would be shot, which meant I wouldn't be traveling when Liam was in school. The hiatus would allow me to pursue movie projects in the off-season. And the character was interesting—this woman loved books. It seemed like the ideal fit personally and professionally.

David Steinberg, who began his career as a stand-up comic and had really done a beautiful job directing many of the *Designing Women* shows, was brought in as an executive producer and director. We got a good pilot script, which let you see dimensions beyond just this upscale businesswoman. One of the scenes which I thought captured the tone of what I wanted the show to be about happens midway through the first show. The leg has broken off one of Laura's tables at home, and she calls Mitch and tells him she needs a carpenter to fix it. "Have you tried the Yellow Pages?" he asks. "I did," she replies, "but it still wobbles."

As I saw her, Laura was the kind of girl who walked around with a book in her pocket all her life and read instead of connecting with people, because she didn't know how. There were some stills where I'm in this very prim robe, looking rather Dickensian, a little bit Charing Cross Road. She was the kind of girl who would choose to say "wobbles" out of all the words in the world. There was something sweet and vulnerable about her. In another scene, both Mitch and I are standing on our heads—it's his cure for the hiccups—which was really a funny, charming scene and something that no one would expect me to do, either in character or out. It brought the house down during the pilot taping.

A search was mounted for the right actor to play Mitch, and finally I saw Bob Urich's work on tape and I liked it. As in any project, when it comes to casting, you are always faced with hard choices. In television it is harder still, because of the number of really fine actors out there who still won't consider doing TV, particularly a series. Bob had a lot of experience in series television, which I thought would work in our favor. And he had the look of a carpenter. So I worked very hard to convince him to do the show.

In the midst of negotiations with him, as well as the myriad other details involved with mounting a new TV series, my mother had a stroke. I flew back to South Carolina to be with her, and left the details to others. Within days, the deal with Urich began to unravel. I got on the phone to anyone connected with the negotiations to try to patch it together again. Finally, when I was set to return to Los Angeles, I stopped off in Salt Lake City, where Bob makes his home, to let him know how strongly I believed that CBS would commit to our show. His wife finally said that if I would fight that hard to work things out with him, surely I would fight equally hard to make the show a good one. And Bob agreed.

We shot the pilot and CBS did pick up the show, which Warner Bros. TV and Highest Common Denominator Productions was producing. But the network gave us literally the worst time on the schedule—Friday night at 8 P.M., which attracts what is called a bipolar audience, essentially young kids and grandparents, with a big hole where my target audience of 24- to 54-year-olds should be. Nevertheless, I went into the season with high hopes, and with my usual grit and determination.

Once we moved into production on the series, there were some changes in the writing team. A key writer on the original pilot, John Steven Owen, was replaced by another set of writers, one of a series of decisions I thought seemed odd. Now instead of drawing my character with some sweetness and vulnerability, the scripts began to revolve around an overly strong, larger-than-life woman, very much the diva. I'm certainly not the only one who has to fight these sorts of battles against perception; we all do in one way or another. But so often you find yourself fighting some perception and you don't know where the heck it came from.

What I did soon realize is that the writer who had given the show a heart and a soul was no longer there, and I could feel it everytime I read a new script. When I broke it down and began to try to figure out why the show was having such a rough go, I realized the scripts were much more joke-driven, and the story line was often the weak link. And increasingly, my character was becoming the butt of all the jokes. There was a scene in one show with Laura and a homosexual salesman in a store in which he was unmitigatedly rude. He kept getting ruder and ruder, but only so that in the end Laura could lay this very vulnerable guy out. Then in the final punch line, as it were, I would get my comeuppance. Build her up, tear her down seemed to be the cycle.

Robin Bartlett, who played my assistant, Eve, was a very good comic actress who has a real facility with funny lines. As they wrote it, Eve is this man-hungry girl, so desperate that if Mitch isn't interested in me, Eve makes it clear that she's willing to take the leftovers. Though I liked Robin very much, Eve I came to dread. By the time we got to the later scripts, the writers had turned me into Eve's straight man. It became a game of "kill the queen," and I didn't want to play.

One of the gravest disappointments to me was how little collaboration there was on the series. I was constantly battling against the image that everyone there seemed to cling to that I was a movie star who should be kept out of the process as much as possible. It was as if there was a sign hanging over my head: Approach with caution. Even my TV agent was wary of me; I could see it in his eyes. I think they were all afraid. Maybe they were worried that my standards were too high that I would try to get TV to measure up to the movies I do, not understanding that TV was faster and more cursory, less detailed than those movies.

They were all buying into a modus operandi that I knew only too well: any time you get the star involved, it will cost you money. But it doesn't cost you any more money to rent a kilim rug for the set than a rag rug. It's about choice. I talked often with Roseanne during that time. She was able to fight with a great measure of success because of the high ratings of her show, *Roseanne*. Having a show that is always in the top ten and often number one gives you a great deal of leverage.

But beyond that, I don't want people to be afraid of me and I don't want to be cut out of the action. To be a part of the process is the way I've always worked. There is a lot of fun to it, this making entertainment. On movie sets, unless I was preparing for the next scene, I did not spend hours isolated in my trailer. I was there watching other actors, the cinematographers, the directors, trying to learn, always trying to learn. When we were a few weeks into this TV show, David Steinberg, the director, said, "You're a student, you want to know everything about this, don't you?" And it's true. I was trying to learn all I could about series television. But on *It Had to Be You*, I had to fight for a voice.

FROM THE MOMENT we began the second episode, I knew we were in trouble. But in television, it is the nature of the beast. There are so many different people; there's the network and three or four people there, the studio and three or four people there, the director, the writers. Research adds yet another layer—audience testing on everything from what the show should be like, to whether or not I was accessible. It was like water running through a cloth in my hands and no Olma to help me wring it dry. I was absolutely powerless to stop it.

With the change in the writing team, something fundamental shifted in the show. Suddenly we weren't likable anymore. The final cut on the second show was a very big disappointment. I was upset. This was a chance, this series, and not just for me. Emotionally, everyone had a lot invested in it, and yet we seemed on a course destined to bring us to failure. I was determined to do whatever it took to help this show survive: even a bus-and-truck tour to get out to the provinces, to talk to people, to sell this show, I suggested. They passed on the idea.

To try to get the problems sorted out, and sooner, not later, I asked for a meeting with Leslie Moonves, the head of Warner Bros. Television, and my agents. Leslie is the reason why Warner is without question the most successful TV producer in the industry. The studio has more television shows on the air than any other production company by far, and Leslie would rewrite television history every season. If anyone could help us out of this muddle on *It Had to Be You*, I thought he could. Now, I feel confident, he will do the same at CBS, where he was only recently wooed to head up the network's entertainment division. Sagansky left CBS in 1994. "Look, we've got to stop this," I said, "because it's not going to work. We got a good rating at first, but the tone's changed." I kept asking them, "How do we fix this?"

I began calling friends to see if I could learn something from their experiences. What I learned is that my troubles were not unique. I talked to Whoopi Goldberg, who had gone through it with her show. She said I should talk to the network if I wanted to, they were the ones who made the final decisions. I called Burt Reynolds, who invited me to come over to the set of *Evening Shade* and watch. He advised having complete control; it is why he also produces. I had a long conversation with Bobby Pastorelli, who was then still playing Eldon, the housepainter on *Murphy Brown*. What I learned from him is that I should be talking to the writers all the time, that I had to fight for the lines that mattered to me. And I called and talked to Jeff Sagansky, where this all began. We talked about what was going wrong and why.

I couldn't have asked for a better director than David Steinberg, he was absolutely lovely. And Leslie, I know, was doing what he could. Nevertheless as we moved toward October, the scripts were only getting worse. The show was becoming a weekly disaster, with the scripts I was getting stripping my character of any whimsy. Laura, the brilliant book publisher, was becoming a slapstick caricature, without a shred of dignity. There was a "Well, let me tell you, honey," speech at the end of each show. It accelerated to the point where I was on a giant, spinning paint wheel at a carnival, with everyone having a shot at splattering me with the color of their choice. I said, "This has gone too far." When I called Bill Alfred to get a second opinion, he said three words: "Are they crazy?"

It was clear to me just being on the set, seeing the scripts, then the staging, and finally the cuts, that the show was sinking fast. For those who had any doubts, the ratings reinforced the story.

During October, I flew back to Boston, where my son was now in prep school, for their annual fall fair. I was staying at Bill's when I got a call from Jeff, who wanted to talk about the show. And I talked honestly with him, tried to outline what I thought the problems were. He said he wanted to try to fix things. As we were on the phone, I realized I was standing on the stairs where Jeff first saw me.

NOT LONG AFTER I returned, we were heading into the November sweeps. It is a critical time for the networks, since the ratings essentially determine how much they can charge for advertising; the more viewers, the higher the price. It is a make or break time for any show on the edge. I got a call from Jeff on a Tuesday night, the first week in November. I remember because my desk was covered with the latest revisions for a show we were supposed to shoot the next day.

Jeff told me he didn't want the show to die on Friday night. He conceded that the time slot was working against us and said the show deserved another chance. He said he had made the decision to pull the show and put it on hiatus to give us time to work out the problems. It was a tough call to take, but I appreciated the fact that Jeff himself made the call. And that he called me first, before he called the Warner executives or anyone else connected with the show. I told him so. "I consider us partners in this, Faye," he told me.

The partnership was not to last for long. Soon, everything started to shake down. We shot that Wednesday, and then began waiting for word to trickle down from the meetings that started taking place. First, there was one in the private dining room at the commissary on the Warner Bros. lot. The CBS people came in smiling. Bob and I were sitting at a table, and we watched them go in, and hung around waiting to see what their faces would be like when they walked back out. It was all very casual. There was a lot of "Oh, everything's fine, nobody's canceling anything," said in our direction. Nobody had come to grips with it yet.

There was a big meeting at CBS two days later. David Steinberg came back and sat Robin and Bob and me down and said, "We're going to do three weeks' hiatus, and two shows, then four weeks' hiatus, and two shows. Everything's fine. No cancellation." Denial.

The cinematographer was the first one who made me feel that though they might be saying "hiatus," they meant "cancellation." Nobody told him, he just had a sense of it. When I told him I was sure it was just a hiatus, he just said "Aaaahhhh." There was a sound of finality in his voice. I swear to God even my bones knew, but I didn't.

I did not want to let this dream of mine perish so quickly.

But perish it did. They tested the last show we did, which had come closer to what I wanted. Joe Voci, who was the third in command over at CBS, worked hand in glove with me on that show. He had a great finger on the pulse of what I should be doing and what the show should be like. That last show went a ways toward that. The show tested well and Jeff called to say he thought it was good. But we were never on the air again.

In the end, we shot six shows, and only four aired. I understand the economics of it, but it didn't seem as if we really had been given time to work out the kinks. I still saw the promise of it, and had a hard time letting that go.

Hearing that the show was being canceled was a deep disappointment. And I was very disappointed that Jeff Sagansky, with whom I'd hatched this series in the Polo Lounge at the Beverly Hills Hotel, did not come out and say something publicly at the end of it. By saying nothing, people were left to wonder where I was in all of this. Jeff never in any way protected me at the end. There was never a press release saying "Look, it didn't work. We tried. We were sorry. The time slot was working against them." Nothing.

I was really left to fend for myself. At one point there were rumors that Bob Urich's character was going to go on alone as a single father in a show, which was a theme Jeff had liked for a while. It wasn't until Army Archerd, the columnist in *Daily Variety*, printed my letter expressing goodwill for the project and the people that the silence was broken. I had to contend with all kinds of murmured rumors that I couldn't play comedy, that it was my fault. I know I can play comedy. Time will tell.

NOT LONG AFTER the show was canceled, I was at the University of North Carolina in Chapel Hill, where I was being given their Playmaker's Award by the drama department. There was a reception later at which I met a wonderful woman, Betty Kenan, and we talked for a bit about the TV show. Though she was married to a very wealthy man, one of the school's benefactors, before they married she had been quite successful in business in her own right, and remains an active businesswoman today. Of all the postmortems done on the show, hers was one of the most insightful.

She believes that professional women are among the most misunderstood people in the universe. "They think we don't have a happy life," she told me. "Well, we do." By applying their logic, since Laura Scofield was very successful, she had to be deprived—emotionally, sexually. "I didn't like that," Betty said, "and frankly, I didn't think the carpenter was all that wonderful, so why would you drop everything for him? And by the way, I'd fire that assistant in a minute." I laughed. She made a lot of sense.

That was one problem. *It Had to Be You* wasn't real. In that moment, when Laura drops everything for the carpenter, we were doomed. That is not to say that a book publisher and a carpenter could not fall in love, but it wouldn't happen that easily, and it wouldn't be based on sheer animal magnetism alone, even in the sometimes surreal world of situation comedy. If you look at the best TV comedies around, they may be slapstick and silly at times but there is an internal logic that is believable. The minute you go against what's real you have lost the bet, especially with a TV audience. You are in their homes, and you are an invited guest, and you'd better be real.

There is a great dignity to the American people. And when TV writers try to cheat the plot and patch up problems with yet another one-line joke, the audience out there just reaches for the remote. We all fought hard to make the show work, but it just didn't.

I did a kind of endless postmortem on the show. I sat with my needlepoint for many long hours over many days in my enormous *duchesse brisée*—the "broken duchess," the name given a two-piece chaise lounge, an apt place for reflection, I thought, for this moment in my life. I was trying to understand my dashed dream.

At one point I asked Voci, "What can I learn from this, Joe?" "Time slot," he said. "You don't belong at eight o'clock on Friday night." He was right. It's either an old, old audience, and that's not my audience, or kids, and that's not my audience either. I wanted the show to be about a woman like all my other pieces have been, some kind of avant-garde woman, who is pushing the envelope and making original choices.

There were two shows that were touted that year based on the idea, the talent involved, and the strength of the pilot: my show and *Dave's World*. Now *Dave's World* was a CBS production. The network had a large financial stake in it. The show got one of the best time slots on the CBS schedule that year—8:30 P.M. Monday night, between

Evening Shade and *Murphy Brown*, both strong shows at the time. It was nurtured along by the network. Art and commerce, commerce and art. It's about making money.

After doing my own soul-searching, I've come to understand that a TV comedy only works when you have one voice that is the show's rudder. That's the first step. Leslie was good, but he was an executive overseeing dozens of shows. David Steinberg was really supposed to be the "show runner," but that didn't work well because typically that slot is filled by the writers, so they assumed that they were the show runners. But they weren't, really. We asked many times, "Leslie, who's the show runner?" And he said, "It's David, it's David." But the writers never accepted that.

Beyond that, to have a hit show, you'd better have come up with something that is very good and very original. Diane English did with *Murphy Brown*, and Jerry Seinfeld did in *Seinfeld*. On my show, nobody was the boss. There was, unfortunately, no Diane English. No single vision.

AT THE SAME TIME, I had another television project in development with NBC. The idea was for a one-hour drama series. It would be about a female sleuth, but more in the tradition of *Columbo*—with the intellect but minus the wrinkled trench coat—than Angela Lansbury's *Murder She Wrote*. I called Peter Falk to find out what I could from him about how you develop that sort of franchise character and keep the intelligence there and the approach fresh week after week. I thought he'd been the most successful person I knew at pulling it off.

As it happened, our conversation reminded him of a script he had written ages ago, and kept on the shelf until he could find the actress he felt would be right for the role. Peter decided to ask me to do it. It was for a two-hour movie version of *Columbo*, one that pits the rumpled detective against a society woman, Lauren. There is, as always, a murder, with Columbo slowly circling his prey. As Columbo and Lauren go at a sort of mental chess game, they begin a flirtation that is really quite sweet. In the end, Columbo gets his woman, but not without a certain sadness that her arrest ends their promise of a romance.

When I read the script I was struck by the real affection between these two, and she was vulnerable and romantic. They had serious

Peter Falk as Columbo. *I was one killer he didn't want to catch.*
Copyright © by Universal City Studios, Inc.
Courtesy of MCA Publishing Rights, A Division of MCA

moments, but a lot of the interaction between Columbo and Lauren was playful, whether they were buying him a tie or eating peanuts together at his favorite bar. It was there in the acting, but it was also there in the writing.

Roy London, too, made playing the role in *Columbo* an experience that would remain indelible. When I signed on to do Peter's movie, I had not worked with an acting coach in some time. Roy was a great, great acting teacher whose students had included an amazing range of stars, from Sharon Stone and Michelle Pfeiffer to Jeff Goldblum and Garry Shandling. He helped me come up with the zaniest and most subterranean choices for this character. With him the invention of it all became such fun again.

I last saw Roy in May of 1994, just as I was beginning production on *Don Juan DeMarco.* When I got back to Los Angeles in August, he was dead. AIDS had just eaten him up. I knew he was not well when I left, but I never realized he was that near the end. Like everyone else in the industry, I read in the trade papers every day how many are losing their battle with AIDS. Roy's death, though, made it all so much more real. The specter suddenly felt very close.

I miss that Roy is not around, and I get angry that we have this monster in our midst that no one seems able to hold at bay. What I'm left with, what all of us are left with, is that at least there was some time. There are moments and memories that no disease, even one as horrific as AIDS, can take away. What I remember most about Roy are his brilliant and innovative ideas for me as an artist striving to re-create myself. He was a talented and incisive man, something of a visionary, and my life is richer for having known him.

PETER'S COLUMBO MOVIE was titled *It's All in the Game*. In every respect, the experience turned out to be the polar opposite of my experience with *It Had to Be You*. Peter was wonderful to work with, another mensch who is so incredibly smart about what he does. With his script, he had given me a character who could be sweet and funny and romantic. Plus there was a solid story underneath it all, complete with dozens of twists and turns so the mystery lingers through it.

Ironically, the first television role I ever had was in a Peter Falk TV series that was produced initially for the Canadian Broadcasting System. I was in a single episode of *The Trials of O'Brien*, in which a rumpled detective solves murders. O'Brien would eventually become Columbo and move to the States. Peter has been working on this character in one form or another for a very long time.

The episode, titled "The Ten Foot, Six Inch Pole," was shot in Toronto in 1965 and aired in this country on CBS in January of 1966, while I was in the midst of doing *Hogan's Goat* off-Broadway. I have to admit that I only vaguely remember the trip to Toronto, and I recall absolutely nothing about the character. But I have never forgotten the experience, that a Peter Falk show gave me my first shot at TV, and that there was a wonderful subtlety to his performance even then.

This role that Peter had given me in *Columbo* must have been a gift of fate. The movie aired Sunday, October 31, 1993, just two days before Jeff told me he was pulling my TV series off CBS. While I was getting nothing but bad news about *It Had to Be You*, cards and notes and really good reviews were streaming in about *Columbo*.

The second time I was to find a champion in a trench coat came some months later. I was in the throes of a very difficult time in the summer of 1994 with a project that had become unraveled in a very public way. In early July, the Academy of Television Arts & Sciences nominated me for an Emmy for my performance in *Columbo.*

That year the Emmy Awards show was held in Pasadena in the fall. Some categories, including mine for Guest Actress in a Drama Series, were to be awarded during a dinner on Saturday night preceding the live broadcast of the major prime-time awards on Sunday, September 11.

I had been trying to survive rough, treacherous seas that were roiled that summer. Most of those attending the Emmy dinner that night were well aware of what I had been going through. It had been such a difficult time, I debated even attending the dinner. But I had not stayed in the shadows during those difficult months, and I was determined not to retreat now.

Nevertheless, I could not quite believe it when I heard my name called. You always hope, and though I felt very good about the role and the way I had played it, I had not expected to win. There were other very strong performances by Stockard Channing, Laura Dern, Bonnie Bedelia, Marlee Matlin, and Penny Fuller that I was competing against. It was no small matter to have been chosen.

As I made my way up to the podium to accept the Emmy, it was as if I was carried along by the applause. People stood, they hugged me, they cheered. I was overwhelmed by the generosity of spirit my colleagues extended me that night. It was like being wrapped up in a warm embrace. Suddenly I didn't feel as if I was waging the battle alone. Though this is more often than not a town of grand illusions and transitory friendships, the moment seemed heartfelt, and touched me deeply. I really felt for the first time since I had returned from England as if I was truly home.

TWENTY-THREE

JANUARY 12, 1995—For Immediate Release: A private settlement was reached today in the dispute between Faye Dunaway and Andrew Lloyd Webber and The Really Useful Company over her dismissal on June 22nd from the starring role in the Los Angeles production of *Sunset Boulevard*. The agreement stipulates that its terms will remain confidential.

Ms. Dunaway said in a settlement: "When strong, artistic personalities are separated by thousands of miles, the process of putting together a production as complex as *Sunset Boulevard* becomes difficult at best, divisive, at worst. I am pleased that we were able to patch up what has been a very painful public rift between us without an extensive courtroom battle."

Lloyd Webber said today, "Faye Dunaway is an extraordinary talent. I hope our paths cross one day in happier circumstances where my regard for her abilities can be shown more fruitfully. I wish her every success in her future endeavors."

"I accepted the role of Norma Desmond, in part, because of my admiration of Lloyd Webber's ability to put his finger on the pulse of the theater-going public," said the Academy Award–winning actress. "He has created memorable musical theater, and I have great respect for his achievements."

The terms of this settlement prevent me from any further comment on this matter.

TWENTY-FOUR

THE FLOWERS WERE INCREDIBLE, a huge arrangement of exotic blooms. The note, penned by hand, read, "This is our trip to the moon." The author of that note and the man behind the flowers was Marlon Brando. After long careers where our paths had almost crossed on any number of movies, we were finally working on a film together. It was the spring of 1994 and the movie was about love.

Don Juan DeMarco also starred Johnny Depp, who had become a friend of mine when we did a film together in 1993. He is an incredible talent, in my mind the heir apparent to Brando. Johnny and I had connected on both an artistic and an emotional level, and had kept in touch since. Francis Ford Coppola, who had been involved in helping to get *Barfly* off the ground, was set to be one of the producers of *Don Juan*. Jeremy Leven, who had written the script he was now going to direct, had the kind of passion for the project that comes with the authorship of an idea. It seemed to be a movie that everyone came to with a great deal of affection.

The idea itself had a cleverness to it that felt fresh. It takes something like that to get Marlon interested. Johnny plays a young man who believes he is Don Juan, and now that he has lost his true love, life is not worth living. Brando is Jack Mickler, a soon-to-retire, burned-out psychiatrist, who after talking Depp's character down from a billboard ledge hundreds of feet off the ground, begins treating him. My role as Marilyn, Brando's wife, is small but the character is smart and sensitive and sweet. We are thirty years married and though we still care about each other, the caring has become a habit and the romance in our lives is at best a dim memory. But as Jack treats his young Don Juan, it is the psychiatrist's own life that begins to change as he gets swept up by the fantasy of the legendary lover. In the process, we fall in love all over again.

Ah, to fall in love with Brando. How could I not want this part? How could I not campaign to get it? It all really began with Johnny, who read the script and said he would do the film if Brando would sign on. He called me and told me about it too, thinking I'd be right for the part of Marilyn. After reading the script, I knew I wanted to be a part of the project, and sent off a note to Marlon, who had a final say in the casting of Marilyn.

Initially, Jeremy didn't see me in the role of Marilyn, this soft and gentle woman. I realized I had to try to get Jeremy to see me in the role. I offered to test. At times in my career I've tested for a role when a director had difficulty seeing me in it. He said, "No, I would like you to read." Okay, so be it. I learned my lines cold. I dressed like Marilyn. I came in with every prop and a CD of *Don Giovanni*. I bought baby aspirin. I bought Metamucil. I looked at it, I tasted it, I knew what it was. I did a complete preparation for this woman. And it worked. All the emotion was there.

I went straight from college to Broadway. That was like going to the moon for a young drama student. In this business, many are called and few serve. I went straight from Broadway to Lincoln Center to *Hogan's Goat*. After *Hogan's*, I got five movies, one after the other. I was a big star. Boom.

Many of my colleagues never get that kind of chance. So maybe it's right that I'm struggling now. I'm redefining myself in many ways. As an artist, as a woman, as a mother. So it's okay.

I was told by Johnny and others that I blew Jeremy away. And he did seem to be pleased in the reading. Still, he stayed on the fence. I didn't hear that I'd got the role and I didn't hear from Marlon right away. Johnny and I talked about it often. In the midst of putting all the pieces together on the film, Jeremy went to England and came back with a British actress he'd suddenly found for the role. When he told Marlon, Marlon hit the roof.

"I have approved Faye Dunaway," Marlon told Jeremy. He had by then. I had gotten word that Marlon wanted to work with me. And as it happens, he had worked with the English actress Jeremy had in mind and was not in favor of working with her again. He wanted me

A *last tango with Marlon Brando on the beach in* Don Juan DeMarco.

in the role of Marilyn. Finally Marlon, Johnny, and I were all set to do *Don Juan*.

It was definitely a high-octane cast, but there is nothing like working on a film where the actors truly enjoy working with each other. That was very much the case on *Don Juan*. Marlon, the god-father, set the tone. The first day we were going to do a table reading, and in comes this big man with a big dog, which put us all immediately at ease, and we start reading the script.

Something happened in that room. He wasn't letting himself be bullied by the demands of the script. He just found a way to swim around in these words, and search and fish and improvise. He never fell into the trap of trying to get a result or to do it "this" way. Or to make the writer happy, or the director happy. He was just immune to those kinds of people-pleasing concerns, where you do something so that somebody else is going to say you're okay. Marlon just never does that. He is who he is. And he's old enough and wise enough to know that's how you do it, though I daresay that's how he's always acted.

Some weeks into the production, we have a scene together—a

romantic, candlelight dinner. We were in the scene when I looked at Marlon and it was just like a bolt of lightning hit me. And suddenly I was in the backseat of the car with him in *On the Waterfront*. He was just as pure and as clean and as vital as he was in that scene with Rod Steiger, and I may as well have been Rod sitting next to him, watching the anguish when he says, "I coudda been a contendah." Talent does not have any age. It was just so beautiful. It made me feel something magical.

Stella Adler, his acting coach in the early years, is credited with saying that she couldn't teach him anything. Marlon was, and is, a natural genius. I've studied and studied, as my Olma would say, about what it is that makes Marlon's magic, what makes him this "genius" that everyone says he is, and everyone knows he is, and I'm still not sure what it is. I just know that when he is "in the moment," when he's acting and when he's there opposite you in a scene, it's deeper and stronger and more intense, and there is never a false moment. There's never a moment where he pretends to act. Marlon seems to have this place inside him where he can go and just exist. He exists rather than trying to do it better, or to make an effect, or pretend to have the feeling when he can't quite make the truth of the feeling—that just never happens with Marlon. He never tries too hard, he just is.

Marlon made it clear to everyone just how approachable he intended to be the very first day we began shooting. Taped to the door of his trailer was a sign that he had made. In black block letters it read: "Don't knock, the door's open, come on in." One day Johnny got there before him, and took the hundreds of scarves that were used in a harem scene and hung them throughout Marlon's trailer. You couldn't move in that trailer without either brushing past a scarf or ending up with one clinging to you, but Marlon was quite taken with the bordello Johnny had created for him.

One of my key scenes was slated to be shot the day my troubles with another project surfaced. The entire cast and crew, as well as the people at New Line Cinema who were making the movie, closed ranks around me. Whatever was necessary to allow me to deal with this, they tried to accommodate. But it was extremely important to me that I not delay the production. I knew what it would mean in terms of money to the film if I asked to postpone shooting that scene. And so I did not. I would find a way to deal with it on my own time.

This was a day where not a single minute was wasted. My scenes were to be shot Friday afternoon. I was to give a press conference that day on a subject that had generated headlines worldwide. The press conference was arranged so that I would be finished before I was to get my call to be on the set. The hairdresser worked on my hair while I went over what I wanted to say to the press. While they were doing my makeup I decided on what I would wear for the press conference. The press conference began. After a last round of questions from reporters, I went across the street to where we were to shoot my scene and walked through it with Jeremy. Though it had been an incredibly intense and emotional morning for me, I told Jeremy I was ready to shoot as soon as he was.

The scene I had to shoot that afternoon was an emotional one. Jack has come home early from work and he sits down beside me on the couch hinting that he would like to go upstairs and make love in the afternoon. I love this man, but what has been happening to him recently has me completely baffled and a little off-balance. I'm not sure if our marriage is going through a rebirth, or if it is going to completely come apart at the seams that have become frayed by the years.

I'll never forget sitting on the couch next to Marlon. He puts my hands in his, very gently. I look at him and say, "I can't take this anymore," and I start to cry. I was prepared for the scene long before problems with the other project arose. I had been worried about the scene because I was coming into it with very little sleep. I was exhausted. But it worked for the scene, as they say. It certainly worked for the scene. Being Marilyn at that moment, and feeling the same things in my life that she was feeling in the scene, it was just like—bang, you're there.

Marlon is one of those actors who truly responds to your performance. In this case, he told me later, "I just ducked behind you." What happened next will always stay with me. Marlon went to Jeremy and told him we had to rework the next scene, because of the emotions that I had brought to this one. We spent a few crazy hours in a grape arbor just outside the kitchen of the house where we were shooting, improvising the changes. There was Marlon, with castanets in hand, doing a very whimsical flamenco. He was wonderful, funny, and brilliant. Ultimately the garden scene was one of the best we had in the movie.

JEREMY ASKED MARLON if he could think of something new and original that we could do in the love scene. "Sure, that's easy," said Marlon. And we proceeded to shoot the most adorble scene. We're having a competition in bed, tossing the popcorn up and trying to catch it in our mouths, keeping score on our arms using one of Marilyn's lipsticks. Everything about the scene is soft and full of humor and affection. This is a woman who is warm and reachable, and playful.

That same vulnerability and openness was there too in the film that Johnny and I worked on together in 1993. *Arizona Dream*, directed by Emir Kusturica, the brilliant Yugoslav filmmaker, was an innovative, quirky film. Emir has woven into the film surrealistic elements that are not unlike the magical realism envisioned by writers like Gabriel García Marquez, where neither the story nor the characters are always what they seem. Emir's cut of the film was released in Paris in 1994, to great critical and financial success. It was a big hit. There were lines around the block for weeks outside the theater where it played.

Warner Bros. held the rights to distribute the film in this country. It is unfortunate that the studio failed to see what a wonderful director Emir is and what a beautiful film *Arizona Dream* was as Emir had cut it. I had high hopes for this film. But ultimately the studio reworked it, reshaped it, and cut it back, simply because this man doesn't make movies in the Hollywood manner. After a year of keeping it on the shelf, they didn't know what to do with it, and after severely editing it back, the studio released it to video only. Now, long after the video release, we have a small art house distributor, Kit Parker Films, that has made a deal with Warner Bros. They have now released the director's cut, and it's quite a hit in the art-house circuit.

I know a lot of people at Warner Bros., and I'm grateful to them always for *Bonnie and Clyde*, and all the others we've done together over the years. It's one of the studios I feel the strongest allegiance to. I believe that had they left the film alone and released it, my performance would have turned my career around. I loved what Emir said when he won his second Palme d'Or at Cannes for his film *Underground* in 1995: " 'My Way,' I wish I could sing 'My Way.' "

ARIZONA DREAM is a tragicomic, very Chekhovian, highly complex story of a woman and her stepdaughter, set in a gorgeous house in the middle of an Arizona desert. And Elaine, my character, goes from quite nutty to adorable, to brave, to adventurous. She wants to fly, and spends her days building crude flying machines. She is so many complicated colors, that's why I really felt lucky when I got the role. It was a complicated role, and the best one I've had since *Network*.

Working with Emir was challenging and so exciting. This is a man cut from another mold. I have compared him many times to Fellini in his use of fantasy. There was one scene where Johnny and I are sitting at a table and I'm talking to him about my desire to fly. And Johnny looks at me and as he looks at me, he falls in love with me. To express that, Emir had the table and the chairs rise into the trees, as if we were all flying. It was just the most beautiful choice, and it was great. I got onto the chair, as if I were a bird about to take off. Emir gave us a chance to really do some inventive, imaginative work. We all felt deeply about the work we were doing.

There were terrible financial setbacks, and the disagreements over how long the movie could run started early on. Five days after we started shooting, we stopped, waiting to resume only when that could get sorted out. And we did resume. We shot for about three months. At that stage the studio was threatening Emir. In the films Emir has done, *When Father Was Away on Business*, which won his first Palme d'Or, and *Time of the Gypsies*, at least half of those films were unscripted. Which means that the director works on a project with his initial thoughts—it's often what I do as well, it's what we'd like to be able to do—and then it evolves, because as Norman Jewison had said, "You make a movie, not a script." And this is how this director works. Halfway through the movie he was still working on it.

Emir disagreed with some script cuts the studio wanted to make. He finally took a stand and left the location. The production manager said, "We have some directors flying in and we'll finish the movie." Johnny and I just looked at him and said, "We don't think so." We had no intention of betraying this man whom we adored. Emir and the rest of us finally returned three months later to finish the film.

WE WERE FILMING in this incredible place, out on the plains of Arizona. The landscape was unyieldingly harsh, dry, and desolate.

The house was huge, with a verandah all the way around it. There was nothing for miles and it was beautiful in its isolation, the perfect stage for my character to play on. These were Wright brothers times, and in the barn behind the house, Elaine builds flying machines. A lot of my scenes look as if they could have been cut from old films of the earliest attempts at flight, with Johnny and me pedaling to power the engine and pulling levers to move the wings.

Near the end of the film, there is a scene that is really mine. I gave myself over to the improvisation of it, and out of a completely spontaneous riff, a very powerful moment emerged. It is a moment in the film I'm proud of. Johnny's character, Axel, has left me for two weeks while he has been dealing with the details and the emotions of his uncle's death. When he finally comes back, I am beyond anger and bordering on dissolving into madness.

He finds me sitting on the porch in one of his old shirts that clearly I've worn for days. My hair is a mess and underneath the shirt I'm wearing an old-fashioned cotton petticoat skirt and little boots that lace up. It's a sad, sexy kind of look. I sat on that porch in Arizona and got ready to play the scene. In an old rocking chair, with the wind whipping the dust in the yard, I thought of my father and all the times I had watched him leave. I went to that place that was really desolate, where the worst that could happen happens. That's what Elaine was feeling. Staring into space, deeply depressed.

Elaine is barely holding on to her sanity when she asked Axel where he's been, what's he doing there, and finally why doesn't he just go. Elaine says, "I want you to go." He says, "You want me to go?" "Yes, I want you stay"—I say "stay" instead of "go," a Freudian slip— this was all improvisation—and he says, "Do you want me to go or stay?" I say, "I want you to go, just go!" But even as I push him away, I take his face in my hands and kiss him. I just devour his face. I knew it was right and Emir loved it.

THERE ARE OTHER PROJECTS that I am working on. As I write this, I am in the midst of filming a kid comedy for Twentieth Century–Fox, *Dunston Checks In*. My costars are Jason Alexander, who has become so popular as George in the hit television series *Seinfeld*, and Sam, a five-year-old orangutan—Dunston—and Eric Lloyd and Graham Sack, as the young boys who are Dunston's best pals. I run an upscale hotel, Jason helps manage it, and Dunston and the boys, like Eloise before them, wreak havoc in my plush hotel. It is an expensive film and designed to appeal to the kid audience in the same way that *Home Alone* did. The studio has high hopes for it as a big comedy in 1996.

The director, Ken Kwapis, is terrific. He had worked with the comedian Garry Shandling to launch his hit series *The Larry Sanders Show* on HBO, a parody of late-night talk shows that has become a critical and cult hit. Ken has a real touch for comedy. He believes in comedy that is rooted in characters and works very hard to let the humor emerge from the natural action of the scene, rather than relying on dropping in a funny line here or there. With that kind of perspective, the movie has a solid chance of being funny and having a believable story line as well.

Dunston is proving to be very unlike my experience on the half-hour comedy on TV, which has really become the domain of the stand-up. And that's not where Ken Kwapis is with this, nor was he with Garry Shandling. It's all rooted in circumstance and character, and that's what's fun. I'm playing a character that's a cross between Ivana Trump and super-agent Mike Ovitz. She's all business. She fires people, because that's her way of keeping the staff sharp. It's funny without being a caricature, and it's not a larger-than-life cartoon in the way that *Supergirl* was directed to be.

There are other scripts that I am considering. Some days are disheartening, when I get the cliché, overly strong female roles. It's not just me, either; that is largely what is being written for any woman over forty. Other days are encouraging, when scripts like *Don Juan De-Marco* land on my doorstep. I still hold out hope for an American *Indochine*, where the title role is a woman who is no longer in her thirties, but is still very sexual and intensely alive. Because these sorts of roles are so rare, it has become incumbent on the actresses of my generation, and those coming up after me, to develop them. And, as I did with *Cold Sassy Tree*, I have a number of projects of my own in the works.

I was talking to Shirley MacLaine once about the shortage of these juicier roles for women over forty and she said to me, "Give in to being old. Once you do, it's terribly liberating." At some point I will do that. But I'm not ready to play those sorts of roles yet.

I have had in my career characters that broke new ground,

women who took control of their own destiny: Bonnie Parker, Evelyn Mulwray, Diana Christensen, and even Joan Crawford. And I have more ground to break still. In the spring of 1995, the National Association of Theater Owners honored me with their lifetime achievement award. New Line Pictures, my studio for *Don Juan De-Marco*, put together a reel of my work for the event. I was stunned to see all those roles put together. When I saw them one after the other, with no time in between, it was really quite moving for me. I'm grateful for the award, but one thing I've learned in Hollywood is to fly in the face of conventional wisdom. Only I know what work is left in me.

I look to the lives of women like Georgia O'Keeffe, and have a growing belief that there can be another flowering and blossoming that comes with age. As a woman, and as an actress, I know I can be just as juicy and rich in emotional intensity at fifty-four as I was at twenty-four, when I first walked onto the set of *The Happening*. It is possible,

I believe, if you are mentally, emotionally, and physically healthy—and I have worked very hard in recent years to become stronger in all of those ways.

I want to go back to the stage as well. It is where it all began for me. I have not been back to the theater since I left London and I know it is time, past time. I have spent my time between film and television projects talking to a number of directors about staging a play either in Los Angeles or New York, and expect to do that in the very near future.

ROBERT COLES, a Pulitzer Prize–winner and the preeminent child psychologist of our day, whose friendship I have long valued, has often talked to me about how our personal history impacts our lives. It is really that we repeat the past because it is what we know. Growing up, I learned the definition of a relationship as what I saw happening between my mother and my father. And it wasn't happy. There was love and anguish, and ultimately, breaking apart. You can tell me there are mothers and daddies in the world who never argue, who love each other dearly. And that is the dream. But I won't believe you, because it's not what I *know* in my bones, my muscles. I will tend to create relationships that fall apart, because that is what I know. Bob and I have talked about this.

Bill Alfred says that artists repeat the patterns of the past because we're trying to make things turn out right this time. As Gatsby believed, "Tomorrow we will run faster, stretch out our arms farther. . . . And one fine morning—" That's what I say too.

Not long ago I went back to Bascom, Florida. I wanted to see the house where I spent so much of my childhood. It is late afternoon on a summer day and the hum of the crickets keeps me company as I walk down the road that runs in front of the house. The dirt road is still a dirt road. The old store where my brother and I bought our Cokes and candy on Saturday mornings is still there, older, the paint chipped and curled, but the Cokes are still ice cold, and jars of hard candy for a nickel a piece line one wall.

The clothesline behind the house, where the sun would bleach and dry the sheets on wash day, is empty, except for a spinster's line of broken clothespins. An old couple is living in the house now, my mother having sold it long ago. They let me walk through it. Room by room, the memories flood in. Olpa, Olma, my cousins, aunts, uncles, Mac, my mother, and me. I search my memory for my father's face, but it eludes me.

The house is smaller than I remembered, but there is a sweet simpleness to it. I stand on the porch and look out at the fields beyond, where cotton and peanuts are still grown. I watch as the sun begins to set, and look on as the fireflies dance around the wisteria, with its ancient, twisted limbs, and gaze beyond to the dusty road. I have come to recognize the beauty and the strength in ordinary things, and I can feel it in this house, and I feel stronger for it.

Though there was much left unresolved with my father, I know now that he loved me. In many ways, he was my Gatsby. It might not have been him, but that's how I see him. It's my love that transforms him. But transformed he is and ever shall be. Whether it was my uncertainty about his love early on in my life that pushed me, or my mother's expectations and dreams, or some other force that drove my ambition, I am glad for it, even though there have been times when it extracted a heavy price. I have come through the crucible stronger, wiser, happier. My life and my art are richer for it.

In the dusk, I fix my gaze on the horizon, and there in the distance is the shadowy shape of a man walking toward me. He has broad shoulders and midnight hair, close-cropped, just like my father. I imagine that he sees me and smiles. They say when Gatsby smiles at you, you feel as if he believes in you just as you would like to believe in yourself.

"If personality is an unbroken series of successful gestures, then there was something gorgeous about him, some heightened sensitivity to the promises of life. . . . it was an extraordinary gift for hope, a romantic readiness. . . . Gatsby turned out all right at the end." I like to think my daddy turned out all right at the end, and that maybe I will too. There were times when I have felt lost. Now I find that like Gatsby, I too have an extraordinary gift for hope. But it is not in the distance, some far off horizon. I have found it within myself. And my green light, full of promise and possibilities, is not at the end of the dock—I hold it in my hands.

Sometimes I think about buying the house in Bascom, fixing it up, using it as a retreat from Hollywood. Other times, when the memories well up, painful and bitter, I think I will never go back. But there are nights, just as I am on the edge of sleep, that I know even if I never go back again, the house, that place, will always be a part of me.

I have traveled a great distance in my life. There were years that I did battle with my past. Years that I never wanted to look back. I was afraid to remember too much, that the memories themselves would crush me. And there were years that I thought I had lost Dorothy Faye altogether. But when I look beyond Faye Dunaway now, I can see a brown-haired, barefoot girl standing in the middle of a dirt road that runs through a small southern town.

STAGE WORK

A *Man for All Seasons* (1962), Broadway production

After the Fall (1964), Lincoln Center

But for Whom Charlie (1964), Lincoln Center

The Changling (1965), Lincoln Center

Tartuffe (1965), Lincoln Center

Hogan's Goat (1965), Off-Broadway

Candida (1971), Summer theater

Old Times (1972), Mark Taper Forum, L.A.

A *Streetcar Named Desire* (1973), Ahmanson Theatre, L.A.

The Curse of an Aching Heart (1982), Little Theater, N.Y.

Circe and Bravo (1986), London's West End

FILM WORK

The Happening (1967)
Hurry Sundown (1967)
Bonnie and Clyde (1967)
The Extraordinary Seaman (1967) (limited release)
The Thomas Crown Affair (1968)
The Arrangement (1969)
A Place for Lovers (Gli Amanti) (1969)
Little Big Man (1970)
Puzzle of a Downfall Child (1970)
Doc (1971)
The Deadly Trap (1971)
Oklahoma Crude (1973)
The Three Musketeers (1974)
Chinatown (1974)
The Towering Inferno (1974)
The Four Musketeers (1975)
Three Days of the Condor (1975)
Voyage of the Damned (1976)
Network (1976)
Eyes of Laura Mars (1978)

The Champ (1979)
The First Deadly Sin (1980)
Mommie Dearest (1981)
The Wicked Lady (1983)
Supergirl (1984)
Barfly (1987)
Burning Secret (1988)
Midnight Crossing (1988)
The Gamble (1988)
In a Moonlit Night (In una notte di chiaro di luna) (1989)
Wait Until Spring, Bandini (1989)
The Handmaid's Tale (1990)
Double Edge (1992)
The Temp (1993)
Arizona Dream (1994)
Don Juan DeMarco (1995)
Drunks (scheduled fall 1995)
Dunston Checks In (scheduled early 1996)
Albino Alligator (scheduled for 1996)

TELEVISION WORK

Trials of O'Brien: "The Ten Foot, Six Inch Pole" (1966), CBS-TV episode

Hogan's Goat (1971), WNET Playhouse

The Woman I Love (Wallis Simpson) (1972), ABC-TV movie

The Disappearance of Aimee (1976), NBC-TV movie

Evita Perón (1981), NBC-TV movie

The Country Girl (1982), Showtime TV movie

Christopher Columbus (1985), CBS-TV movie

Ellis Island (1984), CBS-TV movie

Thirteen at Dinner (1985), CBS-TV movie

Beverly Hills Madam (1986), NBC-TV movie

Casanova (1987), CBS-TV movie

Cold Sassy Tree (1989), TNT TV movie

Silhouette (1990), USA Network TV movie

Scorchers (1992), USA Network TV movie

It Had to Be You (1993), CBS-TV series

Columbo: "It's All in the Game" (1993), ABC-TV movie

A Family Divided (1995), NBC-TV movie

Road to Avonlea: "What a Tangled Web We Weave" (scheduled 11/95), Disney Channel TV movie

Index